Contemporary
Political
Analysis

JAMES C. CHARLESWORTH, *EDITOR*

Contemporary
Political
Analysis

THE FREE PRESS, NEW YORK
COLLIER-MACMILLAN LIMITED, LONDON

First Printing

Preface

THIS BOOK grew out of the recent publication by the American Academy of Political and Social Science of three monographs —*The Limits of Behavioralism in Political Science, Mathematics and the Social Sciences,* and *Functionalism in the Social Sciences.* The articles in this volume written by Easton, Eulau, Sibley, Flanigan and Fogelman, Holt, Benson, and Hacker first appeared in those monographs. Karl von Vorys, who is associated with me in the Academy, suggested that these essays be supplemented by chapters on decision-making, systems, communications, games, and political development theory, and that specially written essays be obtained for those subjects. Accordingly the papers by Kaplan, Spiro, Robinson and Majak, Rosenau, Schelling, Shubik, North, Riggs, and von Vorys were prepared particularly for this volume. The chapter by Deutsch was assembled from his book *Nerves of Government.*

It is hoped that the views of these contributors will be useful to students and teachers who are wondering about the pertinence and adequacy of the discipline of political science.

James C. Charlesworth

Philadelphia

Contents

Contemporary
Political
Analysis

Introduction

Identifiable Approaches to the Study of Politics and Government

JAMES C. CHARLESWORTH

THE SOPHISTICATED READER of this book recognizes that there are distinguishable schools of political science, just as he knows that in the field of history some specialists have emphasized teleology, some anthropogeography, some economics, some the military, some fortuitousness, and so on. In the field of painting he has heard of impressionists, postimpressionists, surrealists, purists. In architecture (which is sometimes an art, sometimes a science, but always a state of controversy) there are such subschools as eclectic, neoclassical, utilitarian, massive, and vertical.

The writer of an essay on identifiable approaches to the study of politics and government might be tempted to look for a chain of evolution in the subject, whether molecular or holistic, but he soon finds that there is no evolution, no continuum. He also finds that there is not even an observable sequence of developments; some are consecutive, some concurrent, and most are apparently fortuitous. The appearances of identifiable schools of thought and purpose have never been secular, hence never predictable. Consequently "approaches" to the study of political science are where you find them, and how you find them.

Also, in distinguishing one approach from another, care must be taken to note the difference between an approach as a *method* and an approach as an *objective*. Thus we have had writers who have purported to adduce extramundane revelation, others who do nothing but weigh, count, and measure the doings of real people, and still others who pretend to see recurring cycles in history. But methods of study need not be related to the purpose sought in making and releasing the study. Thus we have advocates who have little or no interest in method but who are trying to achieve an objective—for example, the denigration

1

of monistic sovereignty and the assertion of pluralistic autonomy for an ancient professional guild—or who are seeking to make society socialistic, or endeavoring to persuade us to adopt the single tax.

Since, therefore, we cannot validly arrange schools of political scientists in chronological order, nor in order of importance, or excellence, or pertinence to the times, they can only be presented in haphazard order—or perhaps in alphabetical order, which many writers believe has some claim to being defensible.

In this book we do not have exhibits representing all of the approaches to the study of political science—that would make too big a book. Hence it is appropriate in this introduction very briefly to identify first all of the more readily recognized methods, and second the more important schools of objectives. In the selections we have concentrated on the later methods, but we do not mean by "later" that any progressive or orderly development of the discipline of political science is discernible.

Earlier Methodological Approaches to the Study of Government

Before we describe these "later" methods of studying government and politics, it is important for the sake of completeness to notice and mention the earlier and hence more familiar ones. To begin with, we have the *allegorical* method, the most famous product of which was Plato's *Republic,* in which he used a sustained metaphor to elucidate the principle of the proper subordination of the elements in the make-up of a man. The *analytical* approach, first exhibited by Aristotle in his *Politics,* is of course the case method, in which known ingredients are associated with known results. The *authoritative-revelational* school, whose votaries presume to know the mind of God and to enunciate an immanent natural law, is exemplified by Thomas Aquinas and James I among many others. The *comparative* school, which has its counterparts in religion, philosophy, and architecture, has provided American students for many decades with the ham-and-eggs of political science. The *cyclical-historical* method is used to purport to show that political history repeats itself, so that wise men are enabled to acquire that very rare faculty—to learn and act from experience. Polybius was the earliest exponent of this key to understanding. The *descriptive* method is closely related to the comparative, but is far less illuminating. Scores of textbook writers on American government use this device to introduce beginning students to a *sui generis* view of our republic. The *empiricist-pragmatic* approach, used, for example, by Montesquieu, de

Tocqueville, and Comte, does not stress normativism or values, but relates political institutions to political ecology. Thus the title of the *Spirit of the Laws* means the relationship between the laws (institutions) and the environment. The *jurisprudentialists* wrestle with the inscrutable question of whether law is anterior to and superior to government. They have a well-developed taxonomy within their own discipline. The *metaphysical* school creates undefinable words like "state" and "sovereignty," then spends centuries trying to define them. The *polemicists*, like Calhoun, the monarchomachs, and the stentors on both sides of the medieval church-state dispute believe that argument is an avenue to the truth. They degrade polarized discussion into courtroom debates. The *presumptive-logical* school starts with a basic assumption of what political man is like, and, with a strong show of adjectival logic, concludes that his political institutions must be thus and so. Adherents have been Hobbes, Locke, Jefferson, Rousseau, and Condorcet, among many others. (The literary economists imitated this device with their "economic man.") Political science has not been without its *realists*, who, beginning with Machiavelli and Bodin in the sixteenth century, have thought it sufficient to portray what is, without moralizing as to what ought to be. Their method was not as drab as this identification would seem to indicate, for what they saw as being real was markedly different from what most contemporaneous people thought was real. A method slightly milder than the realistic was the *skeptical*, exemplified by Hume, which sought to question validity rather than to devise a substitute validity.

In this present volume we do not present a full-length treatment of these older, well-established methods to elucidate the science of government and politics, but have selected the more current and useful of the newer methodologies.

More Recent Methodological Approaches to the Study of Government

One of these, the *behavioral*, is related to psychology, especially animal psychology, and also to sociology. Behavioralists are at once modest and immodest. They do not pretend to know the origin and destiny of man, but conclude that the only way to understand him is to observe him and record what he does in the courtroom, in the legislative hall, in the hustings. If enough records are kept we can predict after a while (on an actuarial basis) what he will do in the presence of recognized stimuli. Thus we can objectively and inductively discover *what* and *where* and *how* and *when*, although not *why*. This is a sober and modest enterprise, but some followers of the school are nevertheless immodest when they declare (not all of them, to be sure) that nothing matters if it cannot be counted, weighed, or measured. These particular enthusiasts are like certain religious zealots who have an excellent therapy for psychosomatic diseases but who extend it to mending broken hips without the aid of orthopedic surgeons. There are some very important elements in human nature, like love in its various manifestations, or rage, courage, and patriotism, which are neither predictable nor measurable. Our ductless glands have a great deal to do with whether we fight or flee, or lie or face the truth with its consequences. These glands have neither eyes nor ears and they are not educable. Behavioral studies are highly desirable to supplement other studies, but like all identifiable methodological approaches they are only part of the whole study of government and politics.

We have clichés which tell us that a sufficient difference in degree becomes a difference in kind, and that a sufficient difference in procedure becomes a difference in substance. The exponents of the *communicational* approach to political science emphasize the importance of distinguishing between what goes out from the source and what is exactly received at the other end. Which shall we examine—what a governmental agency says it says, or what the recipient says he hears? Similarly, must we study carefully what we should write, so that our human targets read and understand exactly what we wish? Many of us remember the parlor game we played as children in which we sat or stood in a large circle, one of us whispering something into his neighbor's ear. The message was passed along, and there was always a lot of merriment when what the last child related turned out to be so different from what the first child had said. This is a trivial matter in a child's game, but the same thing unfortunately happens when an influential journal deliberately or inadvertently misconstrues a governmental statement, and readers and other journals further distort the first distortion. Now if some persons object that these things are theoretical for the psychologist and the epistemologist and practical for the advertising or news copy writer, we must nevertheless remember that the astute government agency must allow for distortion and diffraction of its pronouncements.

In order to correct for distortion we must study the determinants of distortion. Hence, communications is a legitimate methodological segment of political science. This study is unfortunately not well developed, nor is it standardized or unified. If it were, we should have fewer industrial strikes, slum riots, University sit-ins, and crackpot picket lines. The difficulties in communication are of course compounded when messages must be translated. (It is well known, for example, that it is impossible faithfully to translate lyrical poetry and metaphysical philosophy.)

Some writers appear to think that the most important—and interesting—part of political analysis is the study of *decision-making*. Making decisions is most dramatically associated with single leaders, usually executives, but the study also covers decisions by groups, such as Senate committees, regulatory commissions, and city councils. The difference here is more apparent than real, however, for there are few decisions made by executives which are not the product of deliberations by the coterie of ex officio, official, and unofficial advisers that envelop every important political figure. Some writers appear to believe that executives *select* from a limited group of alternative courses and that they do not improvise and formulate entirely new courses of action, but such writers reveal that their horizon has been the library wall and that they have never been close to high executives in action. Among other side-products, the study of decision-making brings in ends-means analysis. This is a complicated consideration, for frequently a desirable end must be abandoned because the pertinent means are unacceptable, and sometimes it seems that the means become the end, or at least transcend it in importance. Decision-making is also mentioned in connection with studies of voting behavior, but these studies are more properly linked with mass response than with courses of action instituted by important executives, which affect the entire pertinent public. The study of decision-making by executives, incidentally, encounters many difficulties. For one thing, every executive knows that it is often unwise to reveal the reasons for a decision or the procedure followed in reaching it. For another, by the time the confidential facts are released via the "memoirs" route, the case is no longer currently or recently important. Nevertheless it is good for men aspiring to be executives to learn how decisions are made, even though the knowledge is not useful for the informed public or to the general confraternity of political scientists.

Two essays in this present volume deal with *political development* theory, for "political development" is a distinguishable method in analyzing government and politics. In some quarters it is associated with observations and conclusions concerning the capacity of what until recently have been called "underdeveloped" countries to develop the will and skill to assume new governmental responsibilities and to earn general acquiescence in the developments. Other writers use the phrase to cover extensions of governmental programs in well-developed societies, as, for example, the industrial nationalization and social-welfare programs of Great Britain.

Another newer school of methodology—*the mathematical-metrical*—

is having a strong vogue at this time. No matter how often and how emphatically it is stated that mathematics has no substance—that it is only a language—and that you cannot get out of a computer something you have not put in it, the zealots-of-glyph become more and more influential, and political analysis tends increasingly to become mere enumeration. Unfortunately, some of this mathematical apparatus reveals a form of scholarly exhibitionism, and mathematics is occasionally used for elegance or window-dressing. In the field of economics, the use of algebra and the calculus (not merely statistics) started earlier and has proceeded much further than in political science; indeed, it is not too much to say that the econometricians are taking economics out of the social sciences. Many "amateurs" wonder if it would not be more helpful to learn the psychological reasons for buying or not buying automobiles, for example, than to fix precisely the trend in their manufacture and sale. Nevertheless political science can benefit greatly from the use of mathematics, provided it is kept in perspective. We must remember that the introduction of mathematics into the study of physics enriched both disciplines.

The *simulational* method of political analysis, also called by some *game theory* and *role-playing*, operates on the theory that the political process is a confrontation, like a chess game, or a contest between two merchants or brokers, or the maneuvers of rival political candidates, or the counteractions of opposed diplomats. Needless to say, institutions and countries can be deployed as individuals. Years ago the game of ticktacktoe was electrified; it was impossible for a human to beat the "machine." Now game situations are commonly computerized, so that the responses to the adversary's moves are not only more numerous but more quickly arrived at. Simulation can elucidate past events, by showing the alternative courses open to a public agency which has made a decision, but it is chiefly useful in prediction. Unfortunately the programmer never knows as much as the actor.

The *structural-functional* approach to the analysis of government and politics is a new name for an old activity. The "structure" part of the approach refers to any human organization that can do things and have an effect on human beings and other human organizations, viz., a family, a public corporation, a court, a bureau, or a legislative body. The "function" part relates to the activity of the agency and its external effects, according to some, are divided into "latent" and "manifest," meaning that the latter are intentional and the former incidental or accidental. In the light of this brief definition or description, must we conclude that there is nothing new about this approach? We may well conclude that up to now in the field of political science proper, as distinguished from sociology (from where the best-known functional treatments have come) there is little that is new (hence the inclusion of the essays in this volume). Perhaps its chief contribution is a shift of emphasis from a physical, legal, and historical description of institutions and agencies to an identification of functions—that is, services—and to regard the whole study of political science as a study of a "system" or "systems." Its shortcoming is that there might be a presumption that functions at the time of the observation are adequate, and hence that the government is adequate if it is performing those functions satisfactorily. Hence the method is not likely to be popular with normativists and progressives.

This brings up for identification the *systems* approach to political science. The protagonists of this school wish for more than do the proponents of any other method. They see all political activity as a manifestation of a grand but as yet unrevealed design, wherein human needs and desires set in motion social and political processes called systems, and these in turn eventually bring about the creation of political laws and institutions. But with or without institutions and laws the all-pervasive, self-generated, parapolitical responses to human demands (whether volitive or not) inexorably appear. But they appear in a kind of intermolecular role with government, and only very careful study can identify them for the regular student. It can easily be seen that this kind of inquiry calls for the most sophisticated and subtle observation of political realities, things much more difficult to descry than the quite obvious institutions and activities of government. Some systems are easy to recognize—the New York Central-Pennsylvania Railroad system, the postal system, gangland discipline, the stock market. But others are hard to delineate—modern nationalism, allocation of the gross national product, the anatomy of war, obtention of a more favorable status by self-conscious racial groups. These latter elements give rise to a great amount of overt governmental activity, but no one has begun to chart their courses adequately, and no one knows what will be needed next.

There are several identifiable methods of approaching the study of government and politics which are not elucidated in separate essays in this volume. One of these, the *eclectic,* can scarcely be called a school, since it utilizes what it needs from a number of schools. Another, which relates to a method of writing rather than to a body of substance, may be referred to as the *esoteric-recondite,* resorted to mainly by younger writers who know more about the thesaurus than about material man and who bandy abstract phrases because everyone nowadays seems to be compelled to write something. These are the pundits who attempt the reification of the unreal, and who defy Ockham's *entia non sunt multiplicanda praeter necessitatem* by continuing to conceptualize concepts. Another distinguishable approach is the *interdisciplinary,* a most sensible way to broaden and enrich the study of international relations, regional development, regional science, city and regional planning, or social-welfare administration. In these pursuits, excellent use is made of linguists, social psychologists, geographers, demographers, and others whose training and knowledge are pertinent. Still another approach may be called the *residence-of-power* method. The subsumption here is that regardless of law or structure, the operation of a political entity can be understood only if the prime movers are identified and measured. Such studies may be made of an urban community, a supreme court, a state legislature, or an entire national political system. It goes without saying that the real power may be discerned by only a few very skillful, patient, and nontraditional observers. A final method or school which may be mentioned here is the *psychiatric*, or more specifically, the psychopathic, which seeks to interpret the actions of some public figures in terms of earlier psychic traumata. This approach more properly may be considered as part of the behavioral.

The approaches labeled in the preceding paragraph are not treated at length in this volume because they are not as well defined as those which are the subjects of our essays, and also because we wished to control the size of this volume.

Schools of Politics Classified by Objectives

We have said earlier that "schools" of political science may be classified according to objectives as well as by method. But purposes sought by political scientists are not part of this volume; our mission here is not why political scientists talk and write but how.

Nevertheless a taxonomy of our field is not complete unless we identify the various classes of objectives pursued by ancient and modern writers in the field.

Among the older groups are the *atomists*, who ring the changes on the perfectibility of man and the brutalizing function of the state. Then there are the *constitutionalists*, who are not interested in the kinetic, or motor, parts of government, but who emphasize restraints and are preoccupied with the protection of the individual. Easily recognized are the *demophilists*, who equate majorities with wisdom and virtue, and hold that since participation in government is itself an ennobling activity, every adult should be included. Less easily recognized are the *instrumentalists*, who see the government as a tool, or at least a vehicle, for a reform such as that put forward by the utilitarians or similarly dedicated groups. Loud and strident are the *nationalists*, each of whom proclaims his people to be God's chosen. They bring together into an indissoluble amalgam language, race, and religion, and regard an attack upon one as an attack upon all. They have managed to evangelize their doctrine so thoroughly that nationalism is now the strongest human force in the world today. Another group, calling themselves appraisers and assessors rather than advocates, assert that monistic sovereignty is a myth, and that government is only one of the associations which shape our lives and direct our movements. These *pluralists* are to be distinguished from pressure groups which try to influence governmental action; they recognize that in a pluralistic society semiautonomous guilds and groups must make decisions rather than recommendations. The *politico-economists,* including a wide range of dogmatists such as physiocrats, so-called scientific socialists, revisionists, Fabians, guild socialists, social democrats, capitalists, agrarians, antimonopolists, progressives, laborists, syndicalists, and Communists, are economic determinists for the most part, and contend that economics is the most important ingredient in the social and political life of man. *State-idealists* accept the Platonic belief in the objective reality of ideas, and postulate the state as one of the ideas (or ideals). According to a German school, a state could exist if there were no people and no land. A British school looks upon the state as an instrument to exercise the necessary guidance and force to cause each individual to reach his highest personal fulfillment.

One of the newer approaches toward political objectives is the *misodemic* (although in politics, strictly speaking, there is nothing new under the sun). Some of the votaries of this school hold that democracy is undesirable and some that it is impossible, and some hold both views. Most of these detractors are of course closely associated with racism and cultural snobbery, but there are also sober scholars who deplore in sadness that *homo homini lupus* (*est*) and that the first law of nature is inequality. Many political scientists are modest and retiring collators of facts and other peoples' ideas, and may be compared to biological epiphytes. But some become *normativists,* and boldly proclaim that no group is better equipped to tell society what is good for it than the scholars who spend their lifetimes studying the many ramifications of politics. Statements on public policy are made freely by ward committees, chambers of commerce, labor unions, houses of bishops, and the like, whose chief lack in the complicated field of government is a lack of modesty—so why should not the vestal virgins change their role and speak out? (Perhaps the best answer to why they do not is that most of them are held in thrall to test-tube handlers and computer programmers.) Another school, the *remedial,* is interested in reform by project, and moves from reshaping Congress to writing a new city charter, to reorganizing the administrative branch, or to improving the civil service. These patchers and menders are not synoptically gifted or disposed, but are the useful male Marthas who make our governmental machine work, while others contemplate. Then, finally, there are the *universalists,* who see no peace and no satisfaction until there is a world government, equipped with sanctions. When this comes to pass, most of what we know as political science will be scrapped, but it will be worth it.

The purpose of the roll call in this chapter is to identify, on a relative basis, the points of view elucidated in the following chapters. Perhaps it may also serve to put certain things in perspective.

1

The Current Meaning of "Behavioralism"

DAVID EASTON

PERIODICALLY, waves of concern pass over American political science as we contemplate the creature, called political behavior, to which we have given birth in the last two decades. The now not-so-young Turks who a decade ago were speaking in loud, strident, and sometimes rude voices about the dire need for scientific method in political research have begun to feel that they have finally acquired the garments of legitimacy. But no sooner do they dare to comfort themselves with this thought than another panel at a professional meeting stirs up new and stormy conflict over the parentage of this latest offspring, its respectability, and its future. No sooner does the profession settle down and seem to accept it, as testified by the growing feeling that no department of political science is complete without at least one representative of this point of view, than a new book or article again challenges its assumptions, meaning, and intent. It may be, as a recent advocate has announced,[1] that the battle for acceptance has really been won, but if so, it is by no means over as yet and not everyone has been willing to give credence to the good news. There are some who would say that we are mistaking a series of continuous preliminary skirmishes for the main engagement.

The truth probably lies somewhere between these two points of view. But, regardless of where the discipline now finds itself with regard to the reception of the behavioral approach, before we can even begin to explore its meaning, there is some sense in outlining in bold relief the nature of the creature about which we shall be talking. Because at least its adversaries are prone to identify this approach as political *behaviorism*, we might well begin by asking whether this is indeed the correct name for the offspring or whether, on the contrary, it is just a sly way

1. R. A. Dahl, "The Behavioral Approach," *American Political Science Review,* Vol. 55 (1961), pp. 763–772.

of calling it a rude name, hoping thereby to keep it out of the front parlor. That there is some genuine doubt about its paternity, however, is attested to by the fact that it is just as often described as behavioristic, not only by its least hospitable critics but by neutral bystanders as well. What validity is there in thus labeling it behavioristic?

I am quite puzzled by the use of this adjective. As far as I know, there is probably no one in political science who would consider himself a behaviorist, however elastic his imagination, or who would wish to be so designated, at least if the term is used in its rigorous and proper sense. In origin, as associated with J. B. Watson, it is a psychological concept which was adopted to help exorcise from scientific research all reference to such subjective data as purposes, intentions, desires, or ideas. Only those observations obtained through the use of the sense organs or mechanical equipment were to be admitted as data. Observable behavior generated by external stimuli rather than inferences about the subjective state of mind of the person being observed was to constitute the subject matter of research.

In the intervening years since behaviorism was first enunciated, most psychologists have come to recognize that, between external stimulus and observable response, subjective experiences occur that influence the interpretation and effect of the stimulus and, thereby, the nature of the response. The original behavioristic paradigm, S-R (stimulus-response), has yielded to the more intelligible one of S-O-R (stimulus-organism-response) in which feelings, motivations, and all the other aspects of the subjective awareness and reaction of the organism are taken into account as potentially useful data. This has, of course, spelled the doom of pristine behaviorism, and as a term, although not necessarily as a point of view, it has just about disappeared from psychology.

Until recently, political science has borrowed little from psychology, so that, even to the extent that behaviorism has been adopted by psychologists, there could have been slight opportunity for it to seep in. It has been even less likely that this would happen in the case of a theoretical position so indefensible to most psychologists themselves. Aside from a rather quaint, not entirely consistent, and, for that matter, not too intelligible formal adoption of Watsonian behaviorism by A. F. Bentley in his *Process of Government,* I know of no one associated with political research who has advocated a position that even begins to approximate so rigid an exclusion of subjective data. Ideas, motives, feelings, attitudes, all appear as important variables. By design at least, students of political behavior have given no indication of intending to adopt a behavioristic posture.

In the eyes of some, it is true, behavorial research may indeed be viewed as behavioristic in its outcome. We must, however, look upon this as problematic, a matter of interpretation. To describe this kind of research as "political behaviorism" is to be guilty either of a very loose usage of words or of prejudging an issue that ought to be a subject for thorough discussion. There is perhaps still another alternative, however, which may help to explain the misuse of the term. In part it may arise out of the polemics surrounding the behavioral movement in political science. As part of a critical counterideology, a behavioristic interpretation is one that those opposed to the assumptions and procedures of the behavioral approach might well seek to keep alive. If this is so, there is even greater reason for abandoning the term in our search for clarity about the correct meaning to attribute to research in political behavior.

To summarize, I shall assume that the term political behavior is not necessarily equivalent to political behaviorism and that the latter description is improperly used except as a conclusion to a relevant argument. The concept of which I am undertaking to discuss the meaning is that of political "behavior," the adjective being "behavioral" as in the phrase "behavioral sciences," not "behavioristic." Support for the clear distinction and difference between the terms is lent by its use in such institutional titles as the Center for Advanced Study in the Behavioral Sciences at Stanford, the section of the Ford Foundation, now liquidated, that was known as the Behavioral Sciences Division, and the Institute of Behavioral Science at the University of Colorado, as well as the journals of *Behavioral Science* and the *American Behavioral Scientist*. Substitution of "behavioristic" in these names would be entirely confusing and misleading about the scope and direction of interest of the institution or publication involved. The generic noun referring to this whole approach in the various social sciences would probably be "behavioralism," but it is such an awkward neologism that most people sensibly avoid it where possible.

Tendency and Movement

Political behavior stands for both an intellectual tendency and a concrete academic movement. As a tendency, it is an intellectual current that may be found among many students of politics, in some minor degree at least; as a movement, it has many fewer outright adherents and advocates. So much is clear and, with respect to it, we could probably obtain agreement from those more or less associated with this point of view. But beyond this the approach is still so new and its limits so poorly defined that it is doubtful whether we could arrive at a consensus on its positive aspects. We would find it extremely difficult to come to terms, first, about who among political scientists ought to be identified as pursuing behavioral research; that is, who are the authentic members of the movement or its valid practitioners. Second, we would also find sharp disagreement on where the emphasis in this research ought to lie—that is, on its nature as an intellectual enterprise.

To consider the first point, aside from the prestige that inclusion in the movement might carry with it for some or the embarrassment it might occasion others, the criteria for membership are as loose and ambiguous as the boundaries are vague and arguable. As in most social movements, membership is not a matter of belonging to a formal organization but of possessing a sense of belonging together, sharing similar assumptions and ideals, respecting one another's interests, seeking reciprocal aid and sustenance, or accepting a common leadership.

In addition, however, there are some physical symbols and behavior patterns that distinguish the movement. Its adherents have tended to publish through a limited number of periodicals such as the *Public Opinion Quarterly, World Politics,* the *American Behavioral Scientist,* and *Behavioral Science,* and, unexpectedly, the movement has even evoked a limited degree of specialization in the choice of book publishers. Although the movement has never crystallized in a formal sense, there are structures such as the Social Science Research Council's Committee on Political Behavior and the Committee on Comparative Politics that provide some institutional focus in at least these two fields. Furthermore, some time ago, the strength or feeling of the adherents was sufficiently strong to stimulate discussion of separatist institutions, such as a special journal.[2] But, unlike the fields of psychology, psychiatry, and other sciences where splinter associations have emerged, in spite of some talk at one time, a special subdivision of the American Political Science Association providing institutional expression for the new approach never did hive off. The Association has proved sufficiently flexible to adapt with the necessary speed to the changing character of the field.[3]

But these material symbols have provided too informal a connection with the behavioral approach, and they have been too fragmented and limited in scope to offer a major or satisfying central focus for the movement. The result is that it has remained quite rudimentary, un-

2. I think that it is fair to say that it was in the atmosphere of these discussions that the *American Behavioral Scientist (formerly PROD)* was founded, on the initiative and responsibility of its present editor, Alfred de Grazia.

3. This in itself has a history which it would be interesting to explore if we are to understand the way in which a discipline successfully copes with changes in its intellectual objectives and methods, an adaptation that cannot by any means be taken for granted. In this history the roles of Evron M. Kirkpatrick, executive director of the American Political Science Association, and of Pendleton Herring, through his leadership as President of the Social Science Research Council, would loom very large.

able to generate a true sense of orthodoxy or of inviolable tenets. The political science profession has thereby been spared the trauma of institutional schisms. But the other side of the coin is that card-carriers in the behavioral movement are not easy to distinguish from fellow-travelers, tolerant sympathizers, occasional supporters, or ambivalent critics. One and the same person may be seen by traditionalists as belonging to opposing camps or may well be disowned by both for diametrically opposite reasons.

Perhaps some of the ambiguity also stems from the nature of the commitment required of a behavioralist. It is such that a devotee is not automatically prohibited or incapacitated from continuing traditional research where it seems necessary and appropriate, as in the study of the relationship among institutions. The behavioral approach has shown its greatest strength in research on individuals, especially in a face-to-face relationship, or with respect to a type of aggregative behavior such as voting. Small groups and organizations in their internal structure and processes and certain aspects of well-defined communities represent the maximal scope for which there have been contrived research techniques entirely harmonious with the assumptions of behavioralism. The techniques become less reliable and their results less valid when applied to the interrelationships of institutions such as party systems and legislatures, or electoral systems and parties, or the effect of alternative types of institutional arrangements on recruitment to positions of leadership and authority.[4]

Criticism to the contrary notwithstanding, it is the rare student of political behavior who overcommits himself to the limits of research as defined by his rigorous techniques. In practice, we find most behavioralists prepared to use the best available technical resources, even if it means that the traditional approach alone is feasible. The behavioralist is, in effect, a product mix of the traditional and the behavioral, weighted on the side of the latter. But it is the particular mixture that frequently leads to difficulty in identifying those who constitute authentic behavioralists.

If our first point is that political behavior has many of the qualities of an inchoate social movement, our second one is that, just because the movement is so ill defined, it is far more easily described by reference to its intellectual content than to its membership. Most students of politics, even those unwilling to accept classification as behavioralists,

4. See M. Sherif and B. L. Koslin, *Theoretical and Research Reports: The "Institutional" vs. "Behavioral" Controversy in Social Science with Special Reference to Political Science* (Norman, Okla.: Institute of Group Relations, University of Oklahoma, 1960). The authors of this work, looking at political research from the perspectives of social psychology, loudly applaud the insistence on an institutional approach that we find in political science.

would probably agree about the general nature of its assumptions and objectives, although strong differences might well arise concerning the precise emphasis to be given to any one of these.

What is the nature of these assumptions and objectives, the intellectual foundation stones on which this movement has been constructed? No single way of characterizing them is satisfactory to everyone, but the following itemized list provides a tolerably accurate and reasonably exhaustive account of them.[5]

1. Regularities: There are discoverable uniformities in political behavior. These can be expressed in generalizations or theories with explanatory and predictive value.

2. Verification: The validity of such generalizations must be testable, in principle, by reference to relevant behavior.

3. Techniques: Means for acquiring and interpreting data cannot be taken for granted. They are problematic and need to be examined self-consciously, refined, and validated so that rigorous means can be found for observing, recording, and analyzing behavior.

4. Quantification: Precision in the recording of data and the statement of findings requires measurement and quantification, not for their own sake, but only where possible, relevant, and meaningful in the light of other objectives.

5. Values: Ethical evaluation and empirical explanation involve two different kinds of propositions that, for the sake of clarity, should be kept analytically distinct. However, a student of political behavior is not prohibited from asserting propositions of either kind separately or in combination as long as he does not mistake one for the other.

6. Systematization: Research ought to be systematic; that is to say, theory and research are to be seen as closely intertwined parts of a coherent and orderly body of knowledge. Research untutored by theory may prove trivial, and theory unsupportable by data, futile.

7. Pure science: The application of knowledge is as much a part of the scientific enterprise as theoretical understanding. But the understanding and explanation of political behavior logically precede and provide the basis for efforts to utilize political knowledge in the solution of urgent practical problems of society.

5. Most of the items can be distilled from what is said about the behavioral approach in the following sources: B. Crick, *The American Science of Politics, Its Origins and Conditions* (London: Routledge, 1959); R. A. Dahl, *op. cit.;* M. Duverger, *Méthodes de la Science Politique* (Paris: Presses Universitaires de France, 1959); D. Easton, *The Political System* (New York: Knopf, 1953); and "Traditional and Behavioral Research in American Political Science" in *Administrative Science Quarterly*, Vol. 2 (1957), pp. 110–115; C. S. Hyneman, *The Study of Politics* (Urbana: U. of Illinois Press, 1959); D. B. Truman, "The Impact on Political Science of the Revolution in the Behavioral Sciences" in *Research Frontiers in Politics and Government* (Washington: Brookings Institution, 1955), pp. 202–232, and "The Implications of Political Behavior Research," *Items*, Vol. 5 (1951), pp. 37–39; V. Van Dyke, *Political Science, A Philosophical Analysis* (Stanford: Stanford U., 1960); D. Waldo, *Political Science in the United States of America* (Paris: Unesco, 1956); *A Report of the Behavioral Sciences at the University of Chicago* (Chicago: Self-Study Committee, 1954); Editorial—"What Is Political Behavior," *PROD*, Vol. 1 (1958), pp. 42–43; and papers presented at the panels on "The Contribution of Studies of Political Behavior" at the Fifth World Congress of the International Political Science Association, Paris, September 26–30, 1961.

8. Integration: Because the social sciences deal with the whole human situation, political research can ignore the findings of other disciplines only at the peril of weakening the validity and undermining the generality of its own results. Recognition of this interrelationship will help to bring political science back to its status of earlier centuries and return it to the main fold of the social sciences.

This list probably includes all the major tenets of the behavioral credo and represents the major differences between the behavioral and traditional modes of research. As such, we have a purely formal statement of the meaning of behavioralism, one that helps us less in understanding its meaning than in appreciating the nature of the kind of questions we must begin to ask. For even if we were to have little difficulty in obtaining formal agreement to this list, there can be no doubt that major differences would immediately well to the surface, not necessarily about the composition of the behavioral credo itself but about the relative prominence of one or another of the articles.

As we review the varied explanations offered by behavioralists themselves, and I include my own writings among them, we find that, within the broad limits set by the credo, the behavioral approach has come to mean about as many things as there are commentators. Every man puts in his own emphasis and thereby becomes his own behavioralist. Is it exclusively the use of scientific method or just a mood favoring that method?[6] Does it represent the use of kinds of data hitherto absent from political research, especially the findings from such "hard core" sciences as psychology, sociology, and anthropology,[7] or does it stand largely for a return to the individual as the focal point for political research?[8] May we interpret behavioralism even more broadly and flexibly and view it as a virtually empty bottle into which one pours any kind of wine, new or old, as long, presumably, as it is aromatic of science?[9] Whatever our point of view, we have authorities to whom we can turn to press out interpretation.

But complete interpretive anomie does not exist. Even though the relative emphases bring different aspects of the landscape into prominence and, momentarily, may even leave the impression that the authorities are geographically far apart, closer inspection does reveal that they are all looking ahead towards the same region in space—a science of politics modeled after the methodological assumptions of the natural sciences, as the well-worn cliché has it.

As I have suggested, this conclusion leaves us with a fundamental question still unanswered. If this is all that the revolt against tradition has really meant, if all that behavioralists are arguing for is the intro-

6. R. A. Dahl, *op. cit.*
7. D. B. Truman, *op. cit.*
8. D. Easton, *op. cit.*
9. *PROD, op. cit.*

duction of scientific method and nothing more, why are we not content with calling a spade a spade? Why has it been necessary or useful to mint and distribute a new conceptual currency, political behavior? After all, science is still an honored and prestigious ideal in the United States. Indeed, during the 1920's and 1930's, the phrase "science of politics" was the preferred way for referring to the newer tendencies of the period out of which the modern revolt has sprung. Need we call the rose by any other name?

If we were satisfied to accept the explanation of political behavior as just the continued application of scientific method to politics begun in the 1920's and 1930's, we could quickly brush aside this change in terminology by attributing it to caprice, to the inexplicable alternations brought about by the fads and fashions of language, or to the need for a distinctive symbol of self-identification in the battles with established orthodoxy. Undoubtedly, such factors as these have played a part in the diffusion of the behavioral label. But, if we stopped here and concluded that this is all that the new name conveys, we would be neglecting some essential substantive implications of the contemporary movement in political science, implications of a kind that show our discipline to be an integral part of a deeper shift taking place in the social sciences as a whole in our age. To appreciate the full and rich meaning of the behavioral trend in political research, we must broaden our horizons momentarily. We must pause to see this development as a reaction to and reflection of the fact that all the social sciences are together advancing to a new stage—one of increased scientific maturity, I am tempted to say.

Caveats

If we are content to accept the behavioral approach as just another way of signifying that we are proposing to use the most advanced methods of social science and nothing more, we saddle ourselves with the following real problem. A number of other social sciences, such as the so-called hard-core sciences we have already mentioned, have for many years, well before World War II, looked upon themselves as devotees of the scientific method. Much of their labor has gone into clarifying and elaborating the methodological premises of the social sciences and developing sophisticated and rigorous techniques for accumulating, interpreting, and analyzing data. The striking point here is that even though these disciplines so conceived of themselves in the interval between the wars, it is only in the last decade that they too have come to describe themselves and to be designated by others as behavioral sciences.

As in the case of political science itself, we might argue that there is really nothing in a name, that the oscillation in nomenclature between social sciences and behavioral sciences today is inconsequential and irrelevant. But if ordinary common sense tells us little else, it does sensitize us to the fact that names reflect and, often in anticipation, reinforce changes already taking place in the objects to which they refer. It is my argument that the name changes have precisely this meaning in the social sciences.

The inclusion of the study of political life as part of the behavioral sciences, if it has indeed got its foot in the door of this privileged club, similarly hints that, regardless for the moment of the nature of the transformation that has taken place, it must involve more than just the importation into political science of the scientific method. It is for this reason that we cannot hope to understand the full connotations of the term "political behavior" unless we see it as part of the evolution of the social disciplines as a whole. It is just too deceptively easy to interpret it either as a synonym for what is virtuous in research or for scientific method; it is only partly correct to see in it an ideological weapon lending color and vigor to the movement of a diffuse and informal group of academic rebels against traditions.

Furthermore, aside from anything else, it sells this new movement quite short. Such simplistic interpretations inadvertently lend credence to the very point that the most impassioned critics of political behavior have advanced. These critics have accused students of political behavior of selecting their problems not in the light of theoretical or ethical relevance but largely on grounds of the accidental availability of technically adequate means for research. If a reliable technique is not at hand, the subject is not considered researchable. As a result of the admittedly early stages in the development of technical means of social research, the argument runs, the behavioral approach is able to deliver reliable knowledge only with regard to political commonplaces or trivia. The really significant problems of political life cannot be challenged by these means, the argument continues; hence insistence upon the priority of technical competence manages to squeeze out the free play of insight and imagination.

This is not the chapter in which the merits of this criticism can be weighed. But, from the point of view of the meaning of political behavior, if we were to concede that it conveys nothing more than the tried-and-true phrase "scientific method," we could not help but leave the impression that its critics were not too far wrong. It would represent basically a change in mood in favor of scientific methodology, methods, and techniques, with the emphasis on the latter.

No one could argue that it does not represent these things, and if it did nothing else it would be significant enough contribution. But we cannot stop at this point if we seek to do full justice to this tendency. It would lead us to neglect or ignore entirely an equally crucial contribution of a substantive kind, one that helps to build a major bridge between ourselves as political scientists and our neighboring disciplines on the one side and the future of political research on the other.

Historical Perspective

To appreciate how far the emergence of a behavioral approach goes beyond a methodological or mere technical reorientation, we have to put recent trends in political research into the context of the whole historical movement of the social sciences. The quickest way of doing this without becoming enmeshed in the intricacies of their history is to trace out lightly the evolution in names used to identify what today we are coming to call the behavioral sciences. These names mirror the essence of the historical transformations relevant to our immediate purposes.

Historically, as we know, all social knowledge was originally one and indivisible; the intellectual specialization of labor appears late upon the scholarly scene in the Western world. For almost two thousand years, from the early classical Greek period to somewhere in the eighteenth century, men basically saw each other not as specialists but as general seekers after wisdom and knowledge, as philosophers in the original sense of the word. It is true as early as the Middle Ages that law, theology, and medicine stood as separate and coordinate fields of learning and teaching in the universities, but philosophy still embraced the bulk of human knowledge about man in society.

With the increasing weight and differential rate and direction of the development of knowledge in the modern historical periods, however, this general corpus gradually began to break up into specialized segments. By the eighteenth century, for example, we can already distinguish what came to be called natural philosophy from moral philosophy, and, as knowledge in both these fields increased remarkably during that century, their names underwent a further subtle modification. Under the heightening prestige of chemistry, physics, and biology, they acquired the names natural and moral sciences. With further elaboration during the nineteenth century, especially under the impetus of Saint-Simon and Auguste Comte with their sharp focus on human relationships in society, the moral sciences finally became known by the contemporary phrase, social sciences. Of course, ethical inquiry and philosophy persisted throughout all of what is a very complicated evolution of social knowledge. But from a repository for almost all knowledge, philosophy has been left as a residual category which until today has continued to shrink in scope and of necessity to redefine its tasks periodically.

If this light survey of names associated with social knowledge at its various stages does nothing else, it alerts us to the fact that the emergence of a new name today is not unique and occurs at a particular point in a history that has been under way for thousands of years and will undoubtedly continue. Each transition—from philosophy to natural and moral philosophy, to moral and natural sciences, then to the social sciences, and now to behavioral sciences—signals a stage in a truly linear movement in the nature and assumptions about our understanding of man in society. We may well suspect that some fundamental transformations have taken place today or are in mid-process.

Recent Development

We are left with the problem, therefore, of seeking to understand why, at this particular moment in its history, a significant part of the social sciences has come to be called the behavioral sciences. In its origins, it may well be that the concept can be laid at the door of accident. At the time a Senate committee was exploring the need for a national science foundation to stimulate and provide funds for scholarly research, representatives of the social sciences worked hard for the inclusion of their disciplines within the scope of the proposed legislation. Whether through genuine error or design, there were some disapproving senators who, from the floor of the Senate, insisted upon talking of social science as socialist science. To abort the growth of further confusion, the phrase "behavioral sciences" is said to have been coined to refer to all living systems of behavior, biological as well as social, an underlying idea being that it would serve to identify those aspects of the social sciences that might come under the aegis of a foundation devoted to the support of hard science.[10] At about the same time, the Ford Foundation was being organized, and, in looking around for an appropriate title for the section devoted to the encouragement of the scientific development of social knowledge, the decision was made to call it the Behavioral Sciences Division. Hence, these two accidental forces converged to popularize the new name.

Whether or not the story about its origin is apocryphal, and however interesting speculation about the source of an idea may be, it is,

10. J. G. Miller, "Toward a General Theory for the Behavioral Sciences," in L. D. White, *The State of the Social Sciences* (Chicago: U. of Chicago Press, 1956) pp. 29–65.

of course, not decisive. Many ideas are born; only a few survive and spread. The task is to try to understand what there is in the nature of the present historical situation in research that has led social scientists to seize upon the new name in place of the much older and more familiar one.

We can see that, in the adoption of this name by the various foundations, institutes, and departmental programs at universities, the idea of behavioral science is applied to any social research concerned with a scientific understanding of man in society, regardless of the disciplinary umbrella under which it may find shelter. We hear talk about the study of religious behavior, economic behavior, political behavior, psychological behavior, and so on. The concept applies well beyond the boundaries of the three so-called hard-core disciplines. But, as we have seen, at least from the point of view of helping to move these disciplines more quickly or surely in a scientific direction, the use of the concept would be superfluous. They were and are well known for their scientific commitments and have given little evidence of changing course. We might ask, therefore, whether, in the broad sweep of the history of social knowledge, the idea of the behavioral sciences does not foreshadow a new turning in the road, the beginning of a fundamentally new direction of development?

The answer is clearly in the affirmative. This new terminology reflects the fact that two new ingredients have been added to contemporary social research that will help to set it apart from all past eras. In the first place, never before has there been so great a demand for self-conscious attention to empirical theory at all levels of generality—middle range as well as general—that, in principle, can be reduced to testable propositions. In the second place, as part of this, the social sciences have been compelled to face up to the problem of locating stable units of analysis which might possibly play the role in social research that the particles of matter do in the physical sciences.[11]

In part, this turn towards empirical theory has been related to a hope that has never been completely lost from sight in the whole history of increasing specialization of knowledge and which appeared again in particularly strong form in the 1930's and 1940's. This was the idea that the understanding of man in society would be immeasurably enriched if some way could be found to draw the social sciences together into a basic unity. For a time, integration of the social sciences became something of an academic will-o'-the-wisp and, although today it has lost its initial momentum, it has left a vital residue behind.

It turned out that scholars could conceive of integration of the dis-

---

11. For the analogy to physics, see T. Parsons, "The Point of View of the Author" in M. Black (ed.), *The Social Theories of Talcott Parsons, A Critical Examination* (Englewood Cliffs, N.J.: Prentice-Hall, 1961).

ciplines as occurring at several different levels.[12] At the applied level, one could bring the data of the social sciences together for the solution of whole social problems. Unification was to take place on the job, as it were. Housing, employment, peace, and the like were not to be seen as sociological or economic or political matters exclusively; adequate consideration of these would include the use of knowledge from a whole range of disciplines. Teams of specialists working together for practical purposes might thereby provide one kind of disciplinary integration.

A second kind might emerge through programs of research training. Students would be expected to address themselves not to a discipline but to social problems in the hope that they would learn to bring to bear on them the modes of analysis and data from any area of knowledge and research that seemed relevant and appropriate. The student was supposed to ignore the walls between the disciplines and to consider himself simply a social scientist. In such programs, reference to the formal name of a discipline might be strictly taboo.

Related to but nonetheless different from this approach was a third kind in which it was felt that thorough training of a person in two or three disciplines might bring about a limited integration in the mind of a single individual, or at least encourage it within the limits of the capacity of a single person to absorb and independently to synthesize a number of social fields. Here training was to be disciplinary in its orientation, but in the outcome two or more disciplines would be fused.

Each of these three levels had something to commend it, each has left its mark on curricula for the training of social scientists today, and each has helped create a new self-image of the social sciences, at least with respect to their intrinsic interconnections. But none of these paths led towards any integral unification of the disciplines; at most, what was proposed was some kind of cross-fertilization or exchange of knowledge. They left the way open to search for a means of genuinely synthesizing the disciplines, and this has come to form a possible fourth level of integration.

The key idea behind this approach has been the conviction that there are certain fundamental units of analysis relating to human behavior out of which generalizations can be formed, and that these generalizations might provide a common base on which the specialized

---

12. For some suggestions along these lines: L. Wirth (ed.), *Eleven Twenty-Six, A Decade of Social Science Research* (Chicago: U. of Chicago Press, 1940); C. Dollard, "A Middleman Looks at Social Science," in *American Sociological Review*, Vol. 15 (1950), pp. 16–20; B. F. Hoselitz, "The Social Sciences in the Last Two Hundred Years," in *Journal of General Education*, Vol. 4 (1950), pp. 85–103; E. R. A. Seligman, "What Are the Social Sciences," in *Encyclopaedia of the Social Sciences* (New York: Macmillan, 1930), Vol. 1, pp. 3–8; W. Gee (ed.), *Research in the Social Sciences* (New York: Macmillan, 1929).

sciences of man in society could be built. In place of some mechanical combination of the social sciences, this substituted an underlying basic science of behavior. Although, in reductionist vein, some have argued for psychology as the already existing basic science and others have put in a plea for sociology or anthropology or even political science, the main effort has gone towards the search for an entirely new foundation.

The expectation and hope that it will be possible to develop a common underlying social theory impel research in certain inescapable directions.[13] The most significant of these for our purposes is that it has led to the search for a common unit of analysis that could easily feed into the special subject matters of each of the disciplines. Ideally, the units would be repetitious, ubiquitous, and uniform, molecular rather than molar. In this way they would constitute the particles, as it were, out of which all social behavior is formed and which manifest themselves through different institutions, structures, and processes.

We can concretize the meaning of this conviction if we glance at the way it has worked itself out to this point. As an example, in the case of Talcott Parsons, the Weberian derived notion of *action* seemed to provide the most fruitful unit out of which a common macrotheory might be constructed, one that would be serviceable to all of the social disciplines. Although the action frame of reference can thus be easily associated with the name of one scholar, there are other units of analysis that have been proposed but of which the paternity is multiple, diffuse, and converging. For some who have been strongly influenced by social psychology, the *decision*, or choice, among alternatives has seemed to be the most promising unit. It even infected economics, which is the one social science that seemed invulnerable to change in this direction, so tightly knit and self-contained a theory did it already have. For others deriving from anthropology, *functions* of varying kinds supplied a rather broad and different kind of unit, somewhat slippery to handle, to be sure, but nevertheless a unit that could be discovered and utilized in all of the disciplines.[14]

Most recently, *systems* have made their appearance as a possible focus, beginning with the smallest cell in the human body as a system and working up through ever more inclusive systems such as the human being as an organism, the human personality, small groups, broader institutions, societies, and collections of societies, such as the international system. The assumption is that behavior in these systems may be gov-

---

13. Some of these directions are indicated in R. R. Grinker (ed.), *Toward a Unified Theory of Human Behavior* (New York: Basic Books, 1956).

14. R. K. Merton, *Social Theory and Social Structure* (New York: Free Press, 1949); M. J. Levy, *Structure of Society* (Princeton: Princeton U. P., 1952); K. Davis, "The Myth of Functional Analysis as a Special Method in Sociology and Anthropology," *American Sociological Review*, Vol. 24 (1959), 757–773

erned by homologous processes. General systems analysis is perhaps an even more ambitious effort than action theory to draw disciplines into a common framework, for it spreads its net over all of the sciences, physical and biological as well as social, and views them all as behaving systems.[15]

Let us disregard for the moment the particular answers designed to form the bridgework of a general theory. In its broadest sweep, adoption of the label "behavioral sciences" symbolizes the hope that, ultimately, some common variables may be discovered, variables of a kind that will stand at the core of a theory useful for the better understanding of human behavior in all fields. In some vague way there has been added to this the feeling that psychology, sociology, and anthropology are the core sciences out of which such a theory may well spring.

This approach, it is clear, reaffirms a commitment to the assumptions and methods of empirical science, especially for those disciplines such as political science that have hitherto been reluctant to adopt them. But it goes further. It enriches this method by stressing the hitherto quite neglected theoretical component. Out of the whole scientific credo presented earlier, it is the theoretical tenet which is becoming magnified in our present historical period and which gives the scientific enterprise in the social disciplines the special character implied in the idea of behavioral sciences.

Relevance to Political Science

At this point, we may ask: This is all very well for the current historical position of the social sciences as a whole, but what relevance for the meaning of the behavioral approach in political science can we attach to these trends? Bearing in mind the broader context in which we have been placing our discussion, we can now begin to draw together the threads so that we may more clearly see the source of some of the ambiguity about the meaning of behavioralism in political science.

As I have already pointed out, the literature on the subject insists upon interpreting the behavioral approach in politics as the symbol of scientific method, the introduction of new kinds of data from the hardcore social sciences, and the like, each interpreter providing his own favorite emphasis. At the risk of laying myself open to the accusation of adding still another special plea and emphasis, I am now going to argue the following. What all of these points of view fail to take into

15. A. R. Radcliffe-Brown, *A Natural Science of Society* (New York: Free Press, 1957); various articles in *General Systems*, Yearbook of the Society for General Systems Research, especially those by L. von Bertalanffy and K. Boulding in Vol. 1, 1956; R. R. Grinker, *op. cit.*

account in any serious way is the connection between the behavioral
approach in political science and the current trends towards theory in
the general body of the social sciences, sparked as this new theoretical
tendency has been by a strong interest in the integration of the disciplines. The behavioral aspect of the new movement in political research
involves more than method; it reflects the inception in our discipline of
a theoretical search for stable units for understanding human behavior
in its political aspects.

How does it come about that current interpretations of the behavioral movement in our discipline have failed to appreciate this theoretical aspect? Our neglect is understandable; it flows from the peculiar
historical conditions under which political science finds itself today.

If we look again for a moment at the so-called hard-core sciences,
especially psychology and sociology, we can see that, in them, the techniques of empirical research had been slowly maturing long before
World War II. In fact these disciplines had even had plenty of time
to become overcommitted to the bare technical skills associated with a
scientific approach. They had fallen into the bad habits of crude empiricism—that is, the accumulation of data for the sake of the data
themselves with relatively little consideration to matters of relevance
and broader significance of the findings. It was only late in the interval
between the two world wars that they began to respond seriously to
the idea that crude empiricism is not enough and to rediscover what
some few had been long insisting upon, that relevance and understanding could be achieved only through the development of broad theory.
But the reception of scientific method took place long before the term
behavioral science was ever heard of. Commitment to and engagement
in scientific research were therefore antecedent to the relatively recent
reawakening to the need for general theory relevant to human behavior.
These disciplines, therefore, had experienced a two-stage effect: first
came scientific method and considerably later, through behavioralism,
theoretical concerns.

But, in political science, there has been no such orderly sequence
of exposure to the different aspects of scientific method. From the
point of view of the experiences of other social sciences, our discipline
has been undergoing two revolutions simultaneously. We have come
to scientific method at about the same time as the social sciences as
a whole have been shifting their emphasis from the methods of research
alone to theory as well. In effect, we have jumped a stage experienced
by the so-called core disciplines, or, alternately, we can say that we
have combined two stages in one. We are in the process of absorbing
the basic assumptions of scientific method at the same time that we
proceed to the equally trying task of giving meaning to the behavior we
study by relating it to some empirical theoretical context.

At the risk of adding to the complexity of an already sufficiently involved analysis, I would suggest what has been happening in political science is as follows. We have been adopting the assumptions and technical means associated with a science of society and at the same time we have been moving toward a behavioral approach. There is a danger to this formulation. It implies that behavioralism is different from scientific method, whereas it is only this method with a shift in emphasis to the substantive problems of concept formation and theory construction. But because the behavioral emphasis is extremely visible in other social sciences today, we have adopted this label to apply to both kinds of changes that happen to be taking place simultaneously in political science. If we temporarily keep the technical imperatives of scientific method separate from the behavioral approach, we shall have a much better opportunity to understand the true character of the dual revolution currently under way in political science. By any logical criteria, of course, both these aspects, the technical and theoretical, are part and parcel of scientific method.

With regard to the reception of the technical aspect, surely little has to be said. Its origin lies in the early part of this century with the development by the 1920's of a series of conferences devoted to the new science of politics. But the full invasion did not occur until after World War II. The increasing prevalence in political research of the use of carefully devised interviews, survey research, technical methods for measurement, and the formalization of analysis in logical and mathematical symbols testifies to the growing inroads that rigorous techniques are making. These have been fortified by the widespread introduction of instruction on the scope and method of political science and training in the use of mechanized procedures for recording and analyzing data. It is becoming increasingly difficult to keep up with political research unless one has at least a reading familiarity with the techniques being used. There can be little doubt about the nature and prevalence of this segment of the dual revolution.

Although, as I have indicated, we may include this technical change as part of the behavioral movement, it seems to me sensible to do so only if, at the same time, we are equally conscious of the second revolution that has been concurrently under way and which much more faithfully reflects pressures that have transformed other social sciences into behavioral disciplines. As we saw, this revolution has involved the sharp consciousness in recent years that, without far more concentrated effort on empirical theory, our technical resources would be squandered.

In political science, we may not always be conscious of the progress we have slowly been making with respect to the search for useful theoretical orientations under the very broad and poorly outlined behavioral umbrella. Perhaps this is due to the fact that we have been concentrating on the difficult and time-consuming task of refashioning our tools of research, learning new languages of analysis, and familiarizing ourselves with the methods, data, and findings of related disciplines. But, the long traditional preoccupation of political science with theory has left us peculiarly sensitive to the theoretical implications of the behavioral tendencies and, without being overly conscious about it, we have been responding to these tendencies. In fact, when we pause to look at our inventory of empirically oriented theoretical ideas, it is slight, as we might expect. But, given the very short time that the behavioral approach has been persuasive in political research, it may come as a pleasant surprise to discover that we have a respectable number of alternative conceptual approaches for the study of political life or some of its major segments. Not that these conceptual structures are fully developed or close to any ideal form. But they do constitute a beginning and a promise for the future.

As in the case of the purely technical revolution, not all theoretical innovations have been confined to the postwar period. In a few instances, during the interval between the wars, empirical frameworks of analysis were proposed and elaborated. Catlin, for example, had turned to the "will" as his basic unit of analysis,[16] Merriam and others in the Chicago School had focused on power, and the group had been elevated to a central position. But in recent decades many important additions have been offered, and these have helped to broaden our range of choice, to link us to the main currents of research in other disciplines, and to enrich our theoretical insights. Undoubtedly this search for adequate units of analysis—whatever the degree of awareness present—is preparing the ground out of which, in the none too distant future, may well emerge some minimal consensus.

We can get a better sense of the theoretical ferment that is accompanying the behavioral tendency and which forms a central part of it if we look somewhat more closely at the kinds of units that have emerged. Until the 1940's Lasswell, virtually alone, had carried the burden of seeking to weave together theory and empirical research. But at the end of the war he was joined by Herbert Simon. Although little recognition has been given to the fact, in retrospect there can be little doubt that to Simon is due major credit for awakening postwar political scholarship to the role of empirical theory. The very title of his ground-breaking volume, *Administrative Behavior,* showed how closely the new behavioral movement was linked with theory—in this case, in administration. At the same time it introduced the profession to the theoretical and empirical potency of his main unit of analysis, the decision.

16. G. Catlin, *A Study of the Principles of Politics* (New York: Macmillan, 1930).

The use of this variable as a central unit quickly spread to other areas of political science, aided as it was by its prevalence in other fields of social research as well. Today, decision-making has become the most generalized new concept in political research. It has been seriously and systematically adopted for research in community political structure and processes, in the empirical understanding of international relations,[17] and, at the formal level, in the logic of choice as expressed in game theories.[18] Simultaneously, research on voting, under the stimulus of social psychology, discovered a theoretical matrix for itself in the decisional concept.[19] The vote now came to be interpreted not just as a rather unique kind of act in a democratic system but as one that brought to a head a special kind of decision that persons are expected to make in any number of contexts, such as committees and the economic market place as well as elections. The integrative quality of the decisional approach is most apparent at this level.

Furthermore, in a vague and general way, it has been adopted by large numbers of political scientists in their research on general political processes; these tend to be described as the processes through which political decisions or public policies are made. The result is that at the present time it may be that the decisional orientation has begun to lose its original impetus, not because it has proved unequal to its tasks but rather because its points of major value may now be largely absorbed into the mainstream of political research.

Units of analysis other than the decision have been proposed or elaborated for the study of political behavior. For example, although the concept of the group had been prominent in the interval between the wars, Truman elevated it to a new level of refinement and thereby made it eminently more usable for theoretical purposes.[20] In the last few years Almond has sought to weave together the ideas of system, culture, function, structure, and action into a conceptual scheme designed particularly for comparative analysis and research.[21] Deutsch

17. Particularly in the works of Richard Snyder.

18. See the writings of M. Kaplan, Arthur L. Burns, and R. E. Quandt and the symposium in *World Politics*, Vol. 14, 1961.

19. See the prevalence of this orientation in B. R. Berelson, P. F. Lazarsfeld, and W. N. McPhee, *Voting* (Chicago: U. of Chicago Press, 1954); there is a brief comment on this in D. Easton and R. D. Hess, "Youth and the Political System," in S. M. Lipset and L. Lowenthal (eds.), *Culture and Social Character* (New York: Free Press, 1961), pp. 226–251, esp. at p. 232.

20. D. B. Truman, *The Governmental Process* (New York: Knopf, 1951). In this respect the brief remarks by A. de Grazia should be examined in "Research on Voters and Elections," *Research Frontiers in Politics and Government*, pp. 104–134, esp. at p. 121.

21. G. A. Almond, "Introduction: A Functional Approach to Comparative Politics," in G. A. Almond and J. S. Coleman (eds.), *The Politics of Developing Areas* (Princeton: Princeton U. P., 1960). For a greater structural emphasis, see the writings of David Apter.

has organized a conceptual structure around the message and its networks as the major unit for a kind of analysis that leads towards a theory of political communications.[22] In my own work I have been exploring the utility of the system as the major unit, focusing on political life as a system of behavior operating within and responding to its social environment as it makes binding allocations of values.[23] And for many others associated with the behavioral movement, the major unit has been at least some undefined but nonetheless real "behaving individual" in relationship with other behaving individuals, all of whom have determinable attitudes, motivations, knowledge, and values and who thereby constitute the universal "particles" of political life.

Although this list may not be exhaustive, it does illustrate the increasing attention to empirically or behaviorally oriented concepts in political research. Entirely aside from the merits of any one conceptual perspective, we cannot easily separate from a behavioral approach the fact that we now have a considerable variety of alternative units from which to select and that we are sharply aware of the need to articulate and to question critically the theoretical premises of empirical work.

Hence, too, we can better understand the efforts to redefine or describe the limits of political science as a field of relatively self-contained phenomena. What some have felt to be fruitless and wasteful inquiries into the theoretical boundaries of our discipline have simply represented a groping toward at least the gross units in terms of which political life can be identified, observed, and analyzed; power, policy- or decision-making, groups, systems, political communications, functions are all such units. Slay the dragon of disciplinary redefinition as we may, it insists upon rearing its head in a new form each time and to higher levels of conceptual sophistication.

Summary

Behavioral research thus stands for a new departure in social research as a whole; it is the most recent development in a long line of changing approaches to the understanding of society. It means more than scientific techniques, more than rigor. This alone would indeed mean *rigor mortis* as its critics from the traditional points of view, both classical and institutional, have been so quick and correct to point out.

22. K. W. Deutsch, *National and Social Communication* (New York: Wiley, 1953).

23. D. Easton, "An Approach to the Analysis of Political Systems" in *World Politics* (1957), pp. 383–400, and *A Framework for Political Analysis* (Englewood Cliffs, N.J.: Prentice-Hall, 1965), and *A Systems Analysis of Political Life* (New York: Wiley, 1965).

The behavioral approach testifies to the coming of age of theory in the social sciences as a whole, wedded, however, to a commitment to the assumptions and methods of empirical science. Unlike the great traditional theories of past political thought, new theory tends to be analytic, not substantive, general rather than particular, and explanatory rather than ethical. That portion of political research which shares these commitments to both the new theory and the technical means of analysis and verification thereby links political science to broader behavioral tendencies in the social sciences and, hence, its description as political behavior. This is the full meaning and significance of the behavioral approach in political science today.

2

Segments of Political Science
Most Susceptible to
Behavioristic Treatment

HEINZ EULAU

MY ASSIGNMENT, if I understand it correctly, is to assess the promises of behavioral research in different substantive areas of political science. It is not my task, then, to be programmatic—to prescribe what behavioral research in political science should or might do, or to be codificatory—to review or systematize past and current research. Rather, my assignment involves specification of criteria of relevance in terms of which appraisal of the question posed by the title of this chapter can be made. This, immediately, creates a predicament.

Practitioners of behavioral approaches in political science are by no means agreed on the standards by which to judge the strong points and the weak points of their enterprise. What in one perspective appears to be an element of strength may, in another perspective, appear to be an element of weakness. For instance, many agendas for future research notwithstanding,[1] the fact that behavioral research in politics has not been committed to a single strategy may represent a point of weakness.[2] Were it possible to follow a definite strategy, criteria of relevance and significance not now available would facilitate appraisal. Yet, this very absence of a master strategy and clear directions also

---

1. For an early agenda of the behavioral persuasion, see Charles E. Merriam, *New Aspects of Politics* (Chicago: U. of Chicago Press, 1924); for more recent statements, see some of the articles in Heinz Eulau, Samuel J. Eldersveld, and Morris Janowitz, *Political Behavior: A Reader in Theory and Research* (New York: Free Press, 1956).

2. The argument for a strategy of inquiry has recently been made by James A. Robinson, "The Major Problems of Political Science," in L. K. Caldwell (ed.), *New Viewpoints on Politics and Public Affairs* (Bloomington: Indiana U. P., 1962).

represents a point of strength. It protects the behavioral enterprise from premature closure, from being cut off from alternatives which may be dictated by future contingencies. This being so, it is admittedly difficult to say just what "segments of political science" are or are not—more or less, or not at all—"susceptible to behavioristic treatment."

Having stated a predicament and made a reservation, I shall nevertheless throw caution to the winds and assert rather categorically that, potentially at least, *all* segments of political science can be treated behaviorally—depending, of course, on a clarification of the terms used in this chapter's title. But, whatever such clarification may entail, it seems to me that human creativity, and especially scientific creativity, knows of no predetermined limitations. Of course, limitations there are. But they are conditional: limitations of time, opportunity, and resources; limitations arising out of bias, fear, and shortsightedness; limitations inherent in the scientific enterprise itself—false starts, wrong moves, errors of omission and commission; and limitations in the armory of available research tools and methods. But if inquiry remains open, these limitations are surmountable. We may not as yet know how to overcome them, but this is precisely the challenge that the behavioral sciences in the study of politics present. Man has smashed the atom and defied the gravity of the earth—whether for better or for worse we may disagree on. And, perhaps, as Albert Einstein once said, politics is actually much more difficult than physics. But only the assumption that politics is not immune to scientific inquiry into human relations and behavioral patterns can justify the entire venture called "political science."

To state an assumption, however, is one thing; to appraise future possibilities, another. The future is always contingent, and contingencies are difficult to foresee. Needed for appraisal, then, are not only criteria of relevance but also conceptions of future conditions. These conceptions may differ. Political science, despite its roots in the great tradition of classical political theory, is a very young discipline as an empirical study. As a behavioral science, it is even younger. The time perspective of youth is short range. The future always looks brighter than it is likely to be. Not long ago, a distinguished political scientist, Peter H. Odegard, took "a new look at Leviathan":[3]

There is a new look in the study of politics; an increasing awareness of the baffling complexity of what since Aristotle has been called the queen of the sciences—the science of politics. No longer a hostage to history, and freed at last from its bondage to the lawyers as well as from the arid schematism of the political taxonomists, political science is in the process of becoming one of the central unifying forces for understanding why we behave like human beings. As the dominant mood of the interwar period was one of specialization

3. Peter H. Odegard, "A New Look at Leviathan," in Lynn White, Jr. (ed), *Frontiers of Knowledge in the Study of Man* (New York: Harper, 1956), p. 94.

and isolation among the major disciplines, so the mood of this postwar generation is one of specialization and integration.

Such is the short view. As I commented on Professor Odegard's statement elsewhere, it seems to me an unduly hopeful view:[4]

Certainly, those laboring in the vineyards of political behavior research can take heart from such acclaim. Certainly, too, it is true that much progress has been made in political science in recent years. But a sober, second look also suggests that Professor Odegard's picture is still more in the nature of a snapshot of a possible future than of a richly painted current canvas. In fact, there is no surer way to kill the newer trends than to "co-opt" the label "political behavior" without reservations. As one considers the requisites of behavioral research, one must recognize a continuing need for intellectual humility. For few are those who can say that they have fully mastered these requisites.

In retrospect, this rejoinder sounds almost prophetic. Only a few years after Professor Odegard's hopeful appraisal, another distinguished political scientist, Professor Robert A. Dahl, announced the demise of what he called the "behavioral mood":[5]

Where will the behavioral mood, considered as a movement of protest, go from here? I think it will gradually disappear. By this I mean only that it will slowly decay as a distinctive mood and outlook. For it will become, and in fact already is becoming, incorporated into the main body of the discipline. The behavioral mood will not disappear, then, because it has failed. It will disappear rather because it has succeeded. As a separate, somewhat sectarian, slightly factional outlook it will be the first victim of its own triumph.

This may be the long view, but I do not think it is the correct view of the immediate future. Professor Dahl overestimates what he calls the "triumph" of the behavioral persuasion and underestimates the resilience of "the main body of the discipline"—whatever that is. His prognostication is sufficiently ambiguous to permit varying interpretations. But if he means, as I have reason to assume, that the historical, legal, or doctrinal approaches to the study of politics will succumb under the onslaught of the behavioral movement, his view must be very long indeed. On the contrary, I believe that these approaches will persist. And it is for just this reason that I believe the behavioral approaches in politics will continue as separate and distinct—unless, of course, there is an unpredictable failure of nerve.

In stating conditions, then, I shall try to avoid both the short view and the long. If one takes a closer look at particular developments in the behavioral study of politics, what is most evident is the very uneven-

---

4. Heinz Eulau, "Political Science," in Bert F. Hoselitz (ed.), *A Reader's Guide to the Social Sciences* (New York: Free Press, 1959), p. 126.
5. Robert A. Dahl, "The Behavioral Approach in Political Science: Epitaph for a Monument to a Successful Protest," *American Political Science Review*, Vol. 55 (December 1961), p. 770.

ness of the rate of growth, output, and quality of behavioral research in different subfields of the discipline. In public administration, for instance, following Herbert A. Simon's trenchant criticism of the field, one might have expected a flowering of behavioral research.[6] But none occurred.[7] On the other hand, in the field of judicial decision-making where one might least have expected such development even a few years ago, a growing number of venturesome scholars are producing a sophisticated list of behavioral studies.[8] These are extremes. I can only guess why this is so. But it suggests that between past and future there is an intervening, conditional present. What present conditions of behavioral research in political science, then, are likely to fashion future conditions in different segments of the discipline?

Before tackling this question, it is necessary to come to definitional grip with the terms used in my assignment. I must confess to some hesitation in accepting the assignment in terms which were not of my own choosing. But some conceptual clarification may contribute to enlightenment about assumptions which may be implicit in the assignment.

Meaning of Terms

First of all, what is meant by "behavioristic"? The term is unfortunate in this connection because it was used in the 1920's to denote a particular school of psychology known as "behaviorism." Modern behavioral inquiry has little in common with the physiological stimulus-response psychology of behaviorism which, in some departments, sought to exorcise from social science what were considered "merely mental" phenomena—drives, motivations, attitudes, defenses, and so on. On the contrary, modern behavioral science is eminently concerned not only with the acts of man but also with his cognitive, affective, and evaluative processes. "Behavior" in political behavior, then, refers not simply to directly or indirectly observable political action but also to those perceptual, motivational, and attitudinal components of behavior which make for man's political identifications, demands and expectations, and his systems of political beliefs, values, and goals. "Behavioral"

6. Herbert A. Simon, *Administrative Behavior* (New York: Macmillan, 1947).

7. Of course there has been vigorous development in organizational theory, decision-making theory, and empirical research on bureaucracy—but by sociologists and social psychologists, not by political scientists specializing in public administration. For instance, only a handful of political scientists is listed in the comprehensive bibliography in James G. March and Herbert A. Simon, *Organizations* (New York: Wiley, 1958), pp. 213–248.

8. See Glendon A. Schubert, *Quantitative Analysis of Judicial Behavior* (New York: Free Press, 1959) and Glendon A. Schubert (ed.), *Judicial Decision-Making* (New York: Free Press, 1963).

is, therefore, preferable to "behavioristic," and I shall use it in this dynamic sense.[9]

Moreover, it is a particular characteristic of modern behavioral science, including political behavior research, that it is concerned with man's behavior not simply in psychological terms at the level of the individual personality but also at the levels of the social system and culture.[10] Its orientation is multicausal or multidimensional and, therefore, necessarily interdisciplinary. In being interdisciplinary, political behavior research makes use not only of the theories and findings of the behavioral sciences but also of those of their methods and techniques which may be appropriate. It is necessary therefore to distinguish between the study of political behavior and the behavioral study of politics. The distinction is not simply a play on words. It is possible to do research on political behavior without making use of the concepts and methods of the behavioral sciences. The only requirement for the study of political behavior is that the individual actor be the empirical unit of analysis whose behavior is described—though probably not explained. Much of the work in the fields of voting and legislative behavior during the 1920's and early 1930's was of this kind.[11] In the behavioral study of politics, on the other hand, the individual remains the empirical unit of inquiry, but the theoretical units of analysis may be role, group, institution, organization, culture, or system, and so on, whatever conceptual tools may be most adequate for the purpose of a particular investigation. Though I cannot pursue this distinction further here, it is critical in appraising the promises of behavioral research in political science.[12]

Second, how are we to interpret the term "treatment"? I have partly answered it already. Treatment, presumably, refers to the application of the methods and techniques of the behavioral sciences to political data. But what is to be treated? The title of the chapter suggests that segments of political science are to be investigated by these methods. This, again, is a somewhat circuitous formulation. On embarking on a piece of research, one does not first ask whether it falls within this or that segment of political science and whether the segment is or is not susceptible to behavioral analysis. Rather, one asks: "What is the prob-

9. The most useful inventory of behavioral definitions is still Harold D. Lasswell and Abraham Kaplan, *Power and Society: A Framework for Political Inquiry* (New Haven: Yale U. P., 1950).

10. See Talcott Parsons and Edward A. Shils (eds.), *Toward a General Theory of Action* (Cambridge, Mass.: Harvard U. P., 1951). For an application of the Parsons-Shils schema in political science, see Gabriel A. Almond, "Comparative Political Systems," *Journal of Politics*, Vol. 18 (August 1956), pp. 391–409.

11. See, for instance, Stuart A. Rice, *Farmers and Workers in American Politics* (New York: Columbia U. P., 1924).

12. For fuller and more explicit discussion of this matter, see my essay, *The Behavioral Persuasion in Politics* (New York: Random House, 1963).

lem?" And, in trying to define the problem to make it amenable to research on the level of the individual as the empirical datum, one tries to mobilize all the resources that might be helpful in doing so: personal experience, common sense, existing information, normative doctrine, available theory, preliminary observation, inventories of techniques, and so on—regardless of whether this involves invasion of one or another academic territory. At this stage of behavioral research, nothing is rejected out of hand—either because it may be doctrinally obnoxious or counter to common sense, or because it might be difficult to handle conceptually or impossible to pursue operationally, and certainly not because it may "belong" in someone else's bailiwick. In other words, "treatment" must mean attacking a problem in the most intuitive, speculative, and imaginative ways possible—proceeding from studied openness to cultivated closure. The choice of behavioral methods of analysis and the specification of empirical data requirements are the last steps, not the first, in the design of political behavior research.

Third, as follows from what I have just said, "segments" is best translated into "problematic areas" or simply "problems." The notion of segment implies that it is possible and necessary to define the boundaries of an area of inquiry. Indeed, the fine art of boundary-setting is both exhilarating and troublesome. It is exhilarating because skillful classification and codification make for intellectual order in and control over the huge array of theoretical propositions, approaches, and empirical findings which constitute an arena of scholarship. If done creatively and imaginatively, boundary-setting is very useful in locating a problem and orienting the scholar toward it. But, boundary-setting is also troublesome, because boundaries may rigidify an intellectual enterprise and impede both the finding and the solving of problems.[13]

In contemporary political science, the problems of empirical research defy the necessarily arbitrary limits of scholarly occupations and preoccupations. How to ask questions and how to define a problem has always been at the core of inquiry, regardless of whether the answer was sought in supernatural magic, speculative philosophy, or empirical science. It is only a matter of habit, convenience, or ignorance that we initially tend to pose our questions in terms of those boundaries in which we feel most at home. Each subfield, with its own traditional subject matters, propositions, and methods, becomes a principality of specialists, fearful and jealous of encroachments.

There is, of course, much functional advantage to be derived from this division of labor. Even within a single major discipline, the range of problems, theories, and methods is so great that expertise is ever

13. See Robert K. Merton, "Notes on Problem-Finding in Sociology," in Robert K. Merton, Leonard Broom, and Leonard S. Cottrell, Jr., *Sociology Today: Problems and Prospects* (New York: Basic Books, 1959), pp. ix–xxxiv.

more difficult to come by. How much more the contemporary student of government and politics must master to earn his sheepskin than his predecessor of only twenty-five years ago! I do not believe that specialization means, as some contend, that we know more and more about less and less. This easy metaphor ignores the fact that, along with specialization on particular problems, we also expand the frontiers of investigation. But as the frontiers expand in depth, contact is also made with subfields and neighboring disciplines, and boundaries are difficult to respect. Those working at the frontiers are, therefore, less inclined to draw exact boundaries than those who travel in the hinterland. They come to see things as their neighbors do. Indeed, they may come to have more in common with the neighbors than the old core. This is, of course, a matter of more or less, varying from researcher to researcher. Specialization makes for cross-fertilization.

All of this suggests, perhaps, why behavioral researchers in political science seem to be rather disrespectful of intra- and interdisciplinary boundaries yet refuse to allow themselves to be pigeonholed as a subfield, some pressure in this direction notwithstanding.[14] The traditional boundaries between the subfields of political science are not particularly viable avenues in terms of which to explore the promises of behavioral research, though they may represent contingencies. The latter may be illustrated: a subfield which can state its *problems* specifically is more likely to expose itself to behavioral research than a subfield that remains unproblematic in its formulations. This, perhaps, accounts for the difference I noted earlier between behavioral development in public administration and in public law. Public administration likes to state programs; public law likes to state problems. If my speculation is at all plausible, the difference may well lie in the different intellectual styles taken by these two fields. Nevertheless, it seems to make more sense to ask what problems are susceptible to behavioral research than to ask in what subfields it is more likely to advance.

Finally, a few comments on the meaning of "most susceptible" in the title. Implicit in this formulation seems to be the assumption that there must also be "segments least susceptible" to behavioral investigation. It is more fruitful to ask, therefore, which problems are more likely to be solved under certain conditions than others. This at least avoids the polarization implicit in the title. But even this reformulation leaves me somewhat uncomfortable. For it still seems to assume that susceptibility is a function of the problem alone and not a function of the kind of analysis that may be made, as if a problem had certain intrinsic or essential qualities which do not lend themselves to behavioral

---

14. See Heinz Eulau, *The Behavioral Persuasion in Politics* (New York: Random House, 1963).

investigation. But this assumption, it seems to me, precludes by fiat what is to be concluded upon investigation.

The medical analogy seems relevant. Success in a patient's treatment is both a function of the patient's relative state of health and the physician's relative therapeutic skills which, in turn, depend on the state of medical knowledge. Admittedly, some patients and their problems react to treatment better than others, and some may not react at all. But it must also be admitted that recuperation may have something to do with the kind of treatment administered. For most medical problems there are alternate solutions. There are alternate theories and methods of medical research. In any case, medical science does not proceed on the assumption that some problem is per se more susceptible to solution than another. It assumes that, given time, resources, and inventive skills, all problems of disease are soluble—more or less satisfactorily at any one time, to be sure, but soluble nevertheless. Finally, as my medical friends tell me, almost every problem solved is, more often than not, the take-off point for discovering new problems. In other words, problems are not given but found, if not created. How one finds or even creates problems in research is likely to have a great deal to do with how one solves them. A political problem stated in terms of theoretical propositions amenable to translation into empirical indicators is necessarily susceptible to behavioral research. Whether the traditional problems of politics—the great issues of politics, so-called—can be stated in behavioral terms is for the future to decide. The possibility of doing so, though it depends on many conditions and contingencies, cannot be ruled out by prejudgment.

Limitations on Development

Even if a complete inventory were possible, no attempt can be made here to attend to all of the conditions and contingencies which, in one way or another, are likely to circumscribe developments in the behavioral study of politics. I shall, therefore, deal with only three conditions which, it seems to me, are particularly relevant because they are most likely to change: the state of theory, the state of research technology, and the state of professional skills.

Of these, the state of theory is the most critical because our ability to formulate problems in behaviorally feasible yet politically significant terms depends on it. Here the traditional boundaries between the subfields of political science have been especially impedimental in extending the range of behavioral analysis. The segmentalization of political theory very early in the development of political science as an autonomous academic discipline has had unfortunate consequences in a dual sense: on the one hand, for decades political theory failed to fertilize the other subfields of the discipline with more empirical-institutional or policy concerns; on the other hand, political theory, as history of political doctrines, became a rather scholastic enterprise unrelated to experiences in the real world of politics. As an even more immediate result, especially germane in this connection, those trained in political theory were altogether incapacitated for having what I can only describe as a feel for the methodological needs and empirical dilemmas of political science. There were, of course, exceptions, such as Charles E. Merriam, who "came out of" political theory, and a few others. But, as a group, political theorists, if not concerned with the history of political thought, busied themselves with values in the speculative tradition of philosophy.

When, at long last, books like David B. Truman's *The Governmental Process*, David Easton's *The Political System*, or Robert A. Dahl and Charles E. Lindblom's *Politics, Economics and Welfare* appeared, their impact was impressive, not because they were just good books or even excellent, but because they were directly oriented in a behavioral perspective.[15] Yet, relevant behavioral research was still largely laggard, and these works could be debated as if they were statements of knowledge rather than suggestive theoretical leads useful in the process of creating knowledge. Yet, it seems to me, the virtue of these theoretical efforts was not to be found primarily in either the logic or validity of their arguments—which could be and were challenged, as is to be expected—but in the fact that they were cast in a theoretical frame of reference which could, and did, stimulate empirical research along behavioral lines. The next step—theoretical work which could build on or at least rely on empirical research of a behavioral sort—has been altogether slow in coming, though books like Dahl's *A Preface to Democratic Theory* or Seymour M. Lipset's *Political Man* are suggestive of new theoretical departures from behavioral research as a base.[16] But, even today, those specializing in political theory do not expend enough effort on theoretical work that could advance the frontiers of behavioral knowledge of politics.

It seems appropriate here to point to a very interesting and understandable paradox in theory construction. There seems to be an inverse relationship between theorizing as an independently creative activity and the empirical accessibility of the phenomena theorized about. I find that the most exciting theoretical work of potential behavioral research relevance now being done falls into the range of problems tradi-

15. David B. Truman, *The Governmental Process* (New York: Knopf, 1951); David Easton, *The Political System* (New York: Knopf, 1953); Robert A. Dahl and Charles E. Lindblom, *Politics, Economics, and Welfare* (New York: Harper, 1953).

16. Robert A. Dahl, *A Preface to Democratic Theory* (Chicago: U. of Chicago Press, 1956); Seymour M. Lipset, *Political Man* (New York: Doubleday, 1960).

tionally of interest to the student of international relations—precisely the area where access to behavioral data is perhaps most difficult to come by.[17] On the other hand, theorizing has been sluggish in problem areas where empirical research is relatively easy—for instance, the study of elections and voting behavior. Here we are now facing an enormously rich mine of empirical research for which there does not exist even a comprehensive conceptual schema within which to organize and order the data.[18] What theory there is is largely of a middle-range, post-factum variety.[19] These two extremes underline the need for research in which behaviorally relevant political theory and theory-relevant behavioral analysis go hand in hand.[20] There is a range of problems where self-conscious theoretical formulation and empirical behavioral research can fruitfully meet to extend the margins of political knowledge. I might mention Dahl's recent study of urban-community decision-making, *Who Governs?*,[21] and the work of John C. Wahlke and colleagues on legislative behavior reported in *The Legislative System*.[22]

The important point to be made here is not that there is legitimate room for theoretical disagreement but that efforts are being made to resolve such disagreements by demonstrating the validity of theoretical propositions, or at least their utility, by subjecting them to empirical tests in the crucible of research rather than by debating them in the fashion of dialectics where it is usually convenient to set up one's intellectual adversary in his weakest posture and then strike him down with one's strongest arguments.[23] Whatever entertainment value it may have,

17. For an excellent collection of this genre, see James N. Rosenau (ed.), *International Politics and Foreign Policy: A Reader in Research and Theory* (New York: Free Press, 1961) and Klaus Knorr and Sidney Verba (eds.), *The International System: Theoretical Essays* (Princeton: Princeton U. P., 1961).

18. But, for an attempt to organize the data in a "funnel of causality," see Angus Campbell, Philip E. Converse, Warren E. Miller, and Donald E. Stokes, *The American Voter* (New York: Wiley, 1960), pp. 18–37.

19. See, for instance, Bernard Berelson, Paul F. Lazarsfeld, and William N. McPhee, *Voting* (Chicago: U. of Chicago Press, 1954), pp. 305–323; or Morris Janowitz and Dwaine Marvick, *Competitive Pressure and Democratic Consent* (Ann Arbor: Bureau of Government, University of Michigan, 1956).

20. See Robert K. Merton, *Social Theory and Social Structure*, rev. ed. (New York: Free Press, 1957), pp. 85–117.

21. Robert A. Dahl, *Who Governs? Democracy and Power in an American City* (New Haven: Yale U. P., 1961). The lively debate in this range of problems is likely to extend the range of empirical concerns covered. See, for instance, Raymond E. Wolfinger, "Reputation and Reality in the Study of 'Community Power,'" *American Sociological Review*, Vol. 25 (October 1960), pp. 636–644, and Lawrence J. R. Herson, "In the Footsteps of Community Power," *American Political Science Review*, Vol. 55 (December 1961), pp. 817–830.

22. John C. Wahlke, Heinz Eulau, William Buchanan, and LeRoy C. Ferguson, *The Legislative System: Explorations in Legislative Behavior* (New York: Wiley, 1962).

23. See, for instance, Bernard Crick, *The American Science of Politics* (Berkeley: U. of California Press, 1959).

I have always found this bit of "theoretical"polemics rather incongruous
with the aspirations of a discipline which presumably does not sub-
scribe to the comfortable assumption that theory is the same thing as
knowledge. In any case, increasing remarriage of political theory and
empirical research is one of the most important conditions likely to
facilitate the development of behavioral analysis in politics.

The earlier observation on the inverse relationship between theoretical development and access to data should not be interpreted to mean
that I believe accessibility to be somehow an absolute limitation on
extending the range of behavioral research. On the contrary. It seems
to me that accessibility is itself a variable, subject to the progressive development of instruments and techniques of inquiry. A second condition
likely to influence the future of behavioral inquiry in different problem
areas is, therefore, the state of technical know-how and methodological
sophistication at a given time. Indeed, what has been called the revolution in the behavioral sciences is, to no small extent, a technological
revolution—though I would not say that its impact on political science
is only a technological breakthrough.[24] The range of problems susceptible to behavioral treatment is, therefore, always also a function of
advances in research methodology and technology.

It is true, of course, that behavioral researches have been initially
successful in problem areas where data could be most easily harvested,
processed, packaged, and, if not sold, at least freely distributed. For a
time, political behavior was more identified with voting behavior than
anything else. Stores of data were readily available in the aggregated
election statistics of many jurisdictions, large and small, and cutting
across international frontiers.[25] But it was the development of the random sample survey in the last twenty years and the use of panels, first
introduced in the memorable Erie County study of 1940,[26] which made
possible the analysis of problems in the area of mass political behavior
not even dreamed about when I went to college. The success of the systematic interview in the study of voting and public opinion is gradually
encouraging researchers to use these techniques in the study of institutionalized populations like legislatures or bureauracies.[27] The use of the

24. See David B. Truman, "The Impact on Political Science of the Revolution
in the Behavioral Sciences," in Brooking Lectures, 1955, *Research Frontiers in
Politics and Government* (Washington, D.C.: Brookings Institution, 1955), pp.
202–231.
25. This identification of "political behavior" and "voting behavior" was probably due, in part, to the use of "political behavior" in Herbert Tingsten's *Political
Behavior: Studies in Election Statistics* (P. S. King: London, 1937).
26. See Paul F. Lazarsfeld, Bernard Berelson, and Hazel Gaudet, *The People's
Choice* (New York: Columbia U. P., 1948).
27. When the data were collected for V. O. Key's *Southern Politics in State
and Nation* (New York: Knopf, 1949), there was still much hesitation about the
systematic interview. While the interviewers had been sensitized to the kind of

interview in institutionalized groups, in turn, makes possible much more carefully controlled comparative analysis, at least of relatively small political systems like local administrative bodies or city councils.[28] In any case, much can still be done in perfecting the interview as an instrument of behavioral-institutional research.

The bias long held against systematic interview research was characteristic of a state of mind in the discipline which even today is still widely shared. Similar biases exist against other techniques which are simply denied out of existence because they are new and strange. Yet once these techniques are applied to political problems, the range of phenomena accessible to behavioral research increases enormously. For instance, the use of roll calls in the study of legislative policy, introduced into the discipline by A. Lawrence Lowell as long ago as 1901, did not seem to yield remarkable new findings as long as the technology involved in their use remained relatively rudimentary.[29] Stuart A. Rice extended their use in the 1920's with his indexes of "cohesion" and "likeness,"[30] and subsequently Julius Turner applied chi-square analysis.[31] But only very recently have roll calls again yielded fresh results. These results had to await technological developments which escaped our vision not so long ago. The application of Guttman scaling[32] and factor analysis[33] once more increased the range of problems which can be fruitfully investigated.

It is not my purpose to review technological developments systematically, but to suggest, by way of some illustrations, that the susceptibility of problems in political science, as in other disciplines, is always

information that was sought, they had to assume considerable responsibility for the kind of interview they were conducting and the kind of data they tried to elicit. Yet, Key's project represented a noteworthy breakthrough in interviewing in political science. As Key's associate Alexander Heard later reported, the project accepted "the conviction that much significant information could be obtained only from politicians themselves or from their close associates." See "Interviewing Southern Politicians," *American Political Science Review*, Vol. 44 (December 1950), p. 886.

28. See Robert L. Peabody, *Organizational Authority* (New York: Atherton Press, 1964), who systematically interviewed and compared responses concerning authority and responsibility in three formally differently structured small agencies—a school system, a police department, and a welfare agency.

29. A. Lawrence Lowell, "The Influence of Party upon Legislation in England and America," *Annual Report of the American Historical Association,* Vol. 1 (1901), pp. 321–542.

30. Stuart A. Rice, "The Behavior of Legislative Groups," *Political Science Quarterly,* Vol. 40 (1925), pp. 60–72.

31. Julius Turner, *Party and Constituency: Pressures on Congress* (Baltimore: Johns Hopkins U. P., 1951).

32. See Duncan MacRae, Jr., *Dimensions of Congressional Voting* (Berkeley: U. of California Press, 1958).

33. For this and other techniques of legislative study, see the section on "Research Orientations and Techniques" in John C. Wahlke and Heinz Eulau (eds.), *Legislative Behavior: A Reader in Theory and Research* (New York: Free Press, 1959), pp. 355–413.

conditioned by the state and development of research technology. What this technology will be in the future is difficult to say, because developments are rapid and radical. For instance, the use of electronic computers is likely to have important consequences for the kind of behavioral analyses of politics that may be possible in the near future. But the application of new techniques depends, of course, on the availability of skilled personnel to handle them. For, as Harold D. Lasswell has put it succinctly, "discretion is here to stay."[34] The extent to which behavioral research is possible depends, therefore—a third condition—on the training given at this time to students interested in research. This training, I daresay, if compared with the training given in neighboring disciplines, is at present generally deficient in view of the technological opportunities which are on the horizon of behavioral political science.

I do not want to labor it, but I find a peculiar line of reasoning in a rather unreasonable resistance to the kind of research training which, I think, a political science deserving of its name requires. If we have to learn calculus and probability theory, content analysis, factor analysis and what not, questionnaire construction and computer work, so the reasoning goes, we might as well drop politics and take up physics. Few would admit to being too stupid to study mathematics or statistics as a requisite for theoretical and empirical work in political science.[35] Instead, shelter is sought and found in the image of a political science which protects the student from having to involve himself in what appears to be such dismal and difficult preparation. Instead, the student will dutifully learn two foreign languages which he may never use! And, because he has not acquired the newer research skills, our student, once he becomes a teacher, will protest that the problems of political science are not amenable to behavioral investigation. The circle is full: *quod erat demonstrandum!* What this line of reasoning really says is this: "I don't want to do what I don't want to do"—a case of scientific infantilism. As long as this attitude prevails, many potential problems of political science will, in fact, escape behavioral treatment.

Not that I would require every political scientist to acquire all the skills now available! In the first place, as I said earlier, historical, legal, and normative approaches are here to stay. And, second, not all skills are needed in every piece of behavioral research, though one might

34. Harold D. Lasswell, "Current Studies of the Decision Process: Automation versus Creativity," *Western Political Quarterly*, Vol. 8 (1955), p. 399. For a report on computer handling of voting data, see Ithiel de Sola Pool and Robert Abelson, "The Simulmatics Project," *Public Opinion Quarterly*, Vol. 25 (Summer 1961), pp. 167–183.

35. How a political scientist might go about studying the relevant mathematical literature in a year's time is suggested by Richard R. Fagen, "Some Contributions of Mathematical Reasoning to the Study of Politics," *American Political Science Review*, Vol. 55 (December 1961), pp. 888–900.

expect at least a speaking acquaintance, if for no other reason than communication, if needed, with skilled technicians. Yet, the curious thing is that, sooner or later, at least those with an open mind in the matter who are oriented toward research confront or pose problems which seem to force them into technological ventures. When this point is reached by a particular group facing particular problems I cannot say. That it is reached is quite clear. Those of my generation who came to behavioral analysis are largely self-taught. The important point I wish to make is that what stimulated this retooling was not simply some more or less vaguely felt dissatisfaction with the state of political science as a whole but that we confronted some particular research problem which could not be handled satisfactorily by legal or historical treatment. This point, it seems to me, has been missed by those who in very general terms have written about the behavioral approach or behavioral mood. Though there may have been general protest, it is dissatisfaction with theory, research, or method in a particular problem area which stimulates interest in the new technology. It stands to reason that, if theory, research, and method were not useful in solving a new problem one encounters, there would be little incentive to involve oneself in the expensive and time-consuming business of retooling and fresh study. Yet, there are those who are generally dissatisfied with their discipline but who do very little about it except argue their conviction at professional meetings or write a manifesto. They rarely take a year out to study statistics or spend endless hours learning how to do a reliable content analysis.

The discovery and susceptibility of problems to behavioral treatment depend, then, on the quality and quantity of trained personnel that may be available in the future. How lack of proper training—even of training that is eminently qualitative—retards disciplinary growth is perhaps best illustrated by the inability of younger political scientists to follow the pioneering leads of Harold D. Lasswell's *Psychopathology and Politics*.[36] One need not accept Lasswell's particular formulations, but all political scientists, whether they know it or not, make assumptions about "human nature" in their varying approaches to political problems. I think this is particularly true of those who take pride in their concern with political values and political ethics. It would seem, therefore, that the intensive study of personality in politics would rank high on the agenda of political science as a whole. Yet perhaps less has been done here than in any other problem area of political science, though a few exceptions are noteworthy.[37] Little has been done not

36. First published in 1930. But see the most recent edition "With Afterthoughts by the Author" (New York: Viking, 1960).

37. Especially the work in progress by Robert E. Lane. See his "The Fear of Equality," *American Political Science Review*, Vol. 53 (March 1959), pp. 36–51,

because the study of political personality is not susceptible to one or another kind of intensive behavioral inquiry, but because the skills needed to do an adequate job are difficult to come by. But possibly even more important is resistance to personality analysis as a mode of inquiry. Again, as in the case of objections to quantitative treatment, I have heard it said that, if personality were what politics is "all about," we might as well be psychologists! This is, of course, a very feeble argument, for no one, Lasswell least of all, has ever asserted that politics is "all about" personality. In this range of political inquiry, I suspect, resistance to training stems less from cultivated ignorance than from irrational fear.

New Dilemmas

The susceptibility of particular problem areas of political science to behavioral treatment, I have argued, varies and will continue to vary with the state and development of relevant theories, appropriate techniques, and available skills. But if, as I have also asserted, the behavioral approaches are complementary and supplementary to the more traditional methods of the discipline, there arise a number of methodological questions about the relationship between the older and the newer approaches which present certain dilemmas on whose solution the behavioral persuasion is in turn contingent. Needless to say, perhaps, I can only indicate very superficially here what some of these dilemmas are, but even a few comments might be suggestive for an elaboration of the theme assigned to me.

In the first place, taking it for granted that political science is interested not only in the behavior of individuals but, above all, in the actions and policies of groups, institutions, and "states," the problem arises as to how meaningful statements about large systems can be made on the basis of inquiry into the behavior of individual political actors. This is the problem of the relationship between macro- and microanalysis. For, clearly, only if the relationship between macro- and microanalysis is satisfactorily settled can it be legitimate to say that, as I have said, all problems of interest to political science are potentially susceptible to behavioral treatment. In trying to solve this methodological problem, it is easy to fall into various errors. For instance, there is the fallacy of extrapolation from micro- to macrophenomena. Small

and "Fathers and Sons: Foundations of Political Belief," *American Sociological Review,* Vol. 24 (1959), pp. 502–511. Dynamic depth analyses based on documentary materials are Alexander L. and Juliette L. George, *Woodrow Wilson and Colonel House* (New York: Day, 1956) and Alex Gottfried, *Boss Cermak of Chicago* (Seattle: U. of Washington Press, 1961).

systems are treated as analogues of large systems, and the findings on the microlevel are extended to the macrolevel.[38] There is, secondly, the fallacy of personification: large-scale phenomena are "reduced" to the individual level, as in the more grotesque descriptions of "national character."[39]

This is not the place to suggest solutions. One solution, I believe, will involve the recognition that the distinction between macro- and microunits as the empirical objects of inquiry is relative to the observer's standpoint, and that units like individual, primary group, organization, community, or even state are not polar but continuous variables of political analysis. If this is so, it should be possible to order these units on a macro-micro continuum, and the task of research will be to link these units in terms of vertical and horizontal patterns of relationship as parts of a continuous chain.[40]

The issue is not, as it is sometimes posed in normative political theory, one of individual versus group or group versus state. Rather, from whatever point on the continuum one proceeds, the task of research is to build, by patiently linking one unit with another, the total chain of interrelations which link individual to individual, individual to primary group, primary group to primary group, primary group to secondary group, secondary group to secondary group, secondary group to organization, organization to organization, and so on, until the total vertical system of interpersonal and intergroup relations has been given a continuous order. In this order, what is to be considered macro or micro will always depend on the observational standpoint occupied by the investigator. Behavioral analysis of units larger than the individual depends, it seems obvious, on some construction of the total system in which the individual is a necessary link. Let me emphasize that I am not thinking here of theoretical linkage alone but of empirical linkage also. Clearly, the susceptibility of a broad range of "large" problems, like war or peace, or freedom and responsibility, and so on, to behavioral analysis is contingent on the solution of this methodological dilemma.

Second, and not unrelated to the macro-micro problem, is the problem of using both discrete and aggregate data in behavioral analysis. The difficulty arises out of the fact that what may be true of aggregates need not be true of the individuals who compose them. The reason for this is simple enough: moving from statements about the behavior of aggregates, such as electoral districts, to the behavior of any one indi-

---

38. For an example of the fallacy, see Ralph K. White and Ronald O. Lippitt, *Autocracy and Democracy* (New York: Harper, 1960).

39. But, for an imaginative use of the concept, see David M. Potter, *People of Plenty* (Chicago: U. of Chicago Press, 1954).

40. See Oliver Garceau, "Research in the Political Process," *American Political Science Review*, Vol. 45 (March 1951), pp. 69–85.

vidual within the aggregate involves an inference which may be wrong. The dubious procedure involved was pointed out sixteen years ago in a widely read article by the sociologist W. S. Robinson.[41] Indeed, in the case of voting behavior, for instance, the sample survey has made this procedure unnecessary. As Warren E. Miller has shown, generalizations from aggregate data about the "presidential coattail" are untenable if tested against information about the behavior and attitudes of individuals.[42] Similarly, Wilder Crane, Jr., found, though on legislative roll calls members of both parties vote alike, that party may yet be a salient variable influencing individual behavior and that the occurrence of party conflict in legislative divisions need not mean that the party is, in fact, the crucial factor in bringing about a party-line division.[43]

The use of aggregate data, therefore, is likely to conceal a good deal of the variance in the behavior of individual political actors which the use of discrete data reveals. This does not mean that statements based on aggregate data can be abandoned. Aggregate data are often the only kind of behavioral data available for the purpose of making statements about groups or larger collectivities. But this necessity should not be made into a virtue. For the problem remains that, if behavioral statements are to be made about large systems, aggregate data are evidently not sufficient. On the other hand, even if individual data are available and are aggregated to permit statements about superindividual units to be made, such aggregation may still do violence to findings about individual behavior. It has the advantage of showing how great the variance may be which aggregate or broad institutional language conceals. But, what we empirically mean when we speak of a group's loyalty, a party's cohesion, or an organization's morale remains unanswered. Do we speak about a "group property" which is independent of the behavior of the individuals composing a group, party, or organization, or are we really speaking only about the aggregated characteristics of individuals? It seems that the extent to which certain problems of politics are susceptible to behavioral treatment depends on an answer to these questions.[44]

Finally, as a third example among many other dilemmas that could be cited, I want to mention only briefly the methodological problems involved in closing the gap between case analysis and systematic analysis. I am not concerned here with the use of cases as pedagogic de-

41. W. S. Robinson, "Ecological Correlations and the Behavior of Individuals," *American Sociological Review*, Vol. 15 (June 1950), pp. 351–357.

42. Warren E. Miller, "Presidential Coattails: A Study in Political Myth and Methodology," *Public Opinion Quarterly*, Vol. 19 (Winter 1955–1956), pp. 353–368.

43. Wilder Crane, Jr., "A Caveat on Roll-Call Studies of Party Voting," *Midwest Journal of Political Science*, Vol. 4 (August 1960), pp. 237–249.

44. See Hanan C. Selvin, *The Effects of Leadership* (New York: Free Press, 1960).

vices but as instruments of research. In this connection, a number of questions arise. Though a great many cases have been accumulated with respect to various problematic areas of politics—from the administrative process to legislative decision-making to party and pressure-group politics—the grounds on which these cases were selected are somewhat obscure. In general, the substantive interests of the researcher and his convenience, such as accessibility of documents and persons, seem to be the guiding criteria—hardly scientific criteria. Moreover, most of the cases now available deal with the exciting, spectacular, and perhaps critical situations rather than with more modal situations. As a result, the degree to which the cases are typical or not, and of what they might be typical, is always open to doubt. I have also always wondered about the reliability of case studies: would a second researcher, working with the same materials and having access to the same respondents, come up with findings—leaving aside the matter of interpretation—reasonably similar to those of the first researcher, so that findings cannot be attributed to chance? Finally, few cases are cast in a theoretical framework that controls the cases, making inferences from a variety of cases extremely hazardous.

Although cases are said to be rich sources of hypotheses about politics for future systematic research, few follow-up studies of that character have ever been made. One of the few exceptions is James A. Robinson's *Congress and Foreign Policy-Making* which also deals rather ingenuously with the difficulties involved in trying to cope systematically with several dozen other cases, presumably covering similar policy processes, yet prepared by as many researchers.[45] Perhaps the most successful and certainly the most sophisticated use of cases has recently been made by Edward C. Banfield in *Political Influence*, a behavioral-institutional study of the politics of decision-making in a metropolitan area.[46] Not only were the cases shaped by an identical theoretical framework, but inferences and generalizations were made on both middle-range pragmatic and high-level systematic bases. Both Robinson's and Banfield's works are important steps in broadening the range of problems susceptible to systematic behavioral analysis through the use of relatively few but intensively studied cases.

Conclusion

I have argued in this paper that, potentially at least, all problematic areas of political science are amenable to political behavior research, provided certain conditions are met and dilemmas resolved. The future

---

45. James A. Robinson, *Congress and Foreign Policy-Making* (Homewood, Ill.: Dorsey Press, 1962).

46. Edward C. Banfield, *Political Influence* (New York: Free Press, 1961).

success of behavioral research depends first on the construction of empirical theory which is behaviorally relevant; second, on the continuing progress in research technology; third, on the recruitment into behavioral research of properly trained and skilled personnel; fourth, on the closing of the gap between macro- and microanalysis; fifth, on the reciprocal uses of discrete and aggregated behavioral data; and sixth, on the reconciliation of case and systematic analysis. The discussion was intended to be suggestive rather than exhaustive, to illuminate the road which the behavioral persuasion in politics is traveling rather than to guide along it.

3

The Limitations of Behavioralism

MULFORD Q. SIBLEY

ANY ESSAY purporting to suggest the limitations of behavioralism is likely in these times to take on a sharply polemical character and will often generate more heat than light. The literature about and for and against the behavioralist approach to the study of politics has become so enormous,[1] its devotees and critics frequently so committed, and its defenders and attackers so aggressive that calm discussion is not infrequently very difficult. Yet not all those who participate in the debate take extreme positions, and there are many on both sides—if, indeed, there are only two sides—who are searching for positions and analyses which will enable investigators to decrease the proportion of time and energy given to merely "methodological" discussions.

In part, our difficulties stem from the varied definitions and interpretations of the term "behavioralism." As David Easton correctly points out, it is sometimes confused with "behaviorism" and, in such cases, the

---

1. To refer to most of it in a brief note would be impossible. During the past decade or so, however, it has included such books as L. Festinger and D. Katz, *Research Methods in the Behavioral Sciences* (New York: Holt, 1953); Charles S. Hyneman, *The Study of Politics: the Present State of American Political Science* (Urbana: U. of Illinois Press, 1959); M. Shubik, *Readings in Game Theory and Political Behavior* (New York: Doubleday, 1954); Helmut Schoeck and James W. Wiggins (eds.), *Scientism and Values* (Princeton: Van Nostrand, 1960); Leo Strauss, *What Is Political Philosophy? and other Studies* (New York: Free Press, 1959); and Bernard Crick, *The American Science of Politics, Its Origins and Conditions* (Berkeley: U. of California Press, 1959). Among articles we might mention Interuniversity Summer Seminar on Political Behavior, Social Science Research Council, "Research in Political Behavior," *American Political Science Review*, Vol. 44 (1952), pp. 1003–1045; Robert A. Dahl, "The Behavioral Approach in Political Science: Epitaph for a Monument to a Successful Protest," *American Political Science Review*, Vol. 55 (December 1961); Walter Berns, "The Behavioral Sciences and the Study of Political Things," *American Political Science Review*, Vol. 55 (September 1961), p. 550; and Harry V. Jaffa, "the Case Against Political Theory," *Journal of Politics*, Vol. 22 (1960), pp. 259–275.

debate becomes unusually muddled. Then, too, we must agree with
Easton's statement casting doubt on whether "we could arrive at a consensus on its positive aspects." Who are the true behavioralists and who
are false claimants to its mantle of authority? We are not vouchsafed
any definite answer to questions of this kind.

In using the term here, we must certainly agree that it should not
be employed as a synonym for "behaviorism." Beyond that, David
Easton's statement that it is both an "intellectual tendency" and a
"concrete academic movement" can be accepted. More positively, we
can perhaps identify it with a whole complex of current American
political-science thought which appears to be searching for a more
sophisticated and rigorous empiricism—an empiricism that stresses both
"scientific" theory and a verification process testable by reference to
"behavior." If all this still appears rather vague, we can only plead that
behavioralists themselves are often astonishingly imprecise in their
statements.

The present essay endeavors to get beyond the sharply polemical.
Hopefully, it can be irenic, while yet not trying to hide differences.
Many "behavioralists," we believe, will assent to the limitations which
are suggested here. For them, this statement may simply recapitulate
what they already understand. Others may question the ways in which
the limitations are stated but may be in fundamental accord with the
substance of the argument. A few may, of course, maintain that the
writer does not understand what behavioralism is all about.

We are not questioning the proposition that behavioralism in its
several forms has an important contribution to make in the study of
political things. We do question, however, whether the behavioral
approach is adequate in itself for an understanding of politics. The
politicist, we are maintaining, must be much more than a behavioralist—
he must be a historian, a lawyer, and an ethicist as well. Much will turn,
of course, on what one means by "understanding" the political sphere.
Here it will be suggested that to understand politics implies the kind
of insight characteristic of the artist as well as the precision which we
usually associate with science—the comprehension of interrelations of
parts to wholes in addition to the analysis of parts themselves.

Essentially, we shall examine the major elements which are involved
in an understanding of the political world and, in the process, endeavor
to show what part behavioralism can and cannot play. The main propositions assert that (1) the very selection of subjects for investigation is
shaped by values which are not derivable from the investigation; (2) in
the end, the concepts and values which do determine what and how
one studies are related to one's judgments of the goals which one
identifies with political life and to one's general "life experience"; (3)
once the investigation is launched, there are definite limits to what one

can expect from behavioral studies; (4) behaviorally oriented study will remove one from the stuff of everyday politics and cannot be related to that stuff except by means which would usually be regarded as non-behavioral; and (5) if clarification about policy-making is one objective of the politicist, behavioralism, although destined to play a significant role, is restricted in what it can be expected to do.

Primary Value Judgments

By now there is surely little need to comment at length on the proposition that values are prior to any investigation, whether in politics or in any other area. Research arises when there are "problems" to solve: peculiarities or puzzles about phenomena or the question of giving meaning to them. But puzzles exist in many realms, and the issue of how one ranks them in terms of priorities is always with us. The political investigator, no less than others, must have some notion of his own order of priorities before he proceeds to use the behavioral or any other approach. He presumably holds, to take only an elementary illustration, that the "political" sphere is more important for him to investigate than any other area, and, whatever the reason for his judgment (he may, for example, think that he is better equipped in terms of ability), imputations of value are always present. Thus if he states that the "political" is important, he must ask himself "important in terms of what?"—which involves a judgment of value that is beyond "science" (at least as the term is understood in the United States).[2] Although some things may be valued because they are instrumental to others, always there comes a point at which the judgment must suggest that the thing valued (whether in the aesthetic, ethical, or scientific realms) is valued as an end in itself.[3]

To emphasize what is perhaps the obvious, the behavioral, as well as every other, student presumably places great value on "truth" and the characteristics of "logic." He also assumes that an examination of "facts" is valuable and, if he is sophisticated, that all "facts," for purposes of scientific inquiry, are not born free and equal.

2. A position, it might be noted, with which both David Truman and Robert Dahl, two exponents of behavioralism, appear to agree thoroughly. See Robert A. Dahl, "The Behavioral Approach in Political Science: Epitaph for a Monument to a Successful Protest," *American Political Science Review*, Vol. 55 (December 1961), especially pp. 767–768.

3. Or, as Professor R. C. Pratt puts it: "Primary values are first order values, the core beliefs of one's ethical and political value system for which we feel no justification is required, and for which none can be offered. Secondary values are these for which reasons can be offered, reasons which refer back to the more fundamental primary values held by the individual." *Canadian Journal of Economics and Political Science*, Vol. 20 (1954), p. 373.

Now, however one accounts for our value experiences, it would seem clear that value statements in the ultimate or primary sense cannot be validated or verified by what are ordinarily thought of as empirical and behavioral methods. Behavioralism will inevitably be used within a framework of value judgments which cannot be supported through behavioral techniques alone. The behavioral investigator is confined by an unbehaviorally derived set of primary value judgments just as he is restricted by a whole framework of ultimate assumptions about the nature of the thing he is investigating.

Areas and Objects of Study

Pushing this first proposition further, we must note that the values and concepts which do determine what and how one studies in politics are related to one's general life experience and to the goals which one associates with the purposes of political society. Let us note what this means.

The first problem for the behavioralist is presumably to define the area and object of his study. If he is to study political behavior, and not sociology or psychology, precisely what is the "political"? Various ways of looking at this issue have been suggested, but none of them would seem to be based on anything distinctive of behavioralism. It appears to be impossible to define political things without answering the question of what constitutes a peculiarly "political" society, and a society cannot be defined without reference to its purpose. Ultimately, as Professor Strauss emphasizes, the problem of the nature of the "political" can be solved only dialectically.[4] And dialectical terms take their meaning from the world of general (perhaps we could say "prescientific") ideas and action. Their meaning is reached through the logical processes of definition, inclusion, exclusion, and implication. The user of dialectic locates the meaning of his categories in logical relationships of his system and his discoveries can therefore not be empirical.[5]

The political object might be one thing in a "liberal" culture and another in an anarchist or a Marxist society. If the investigator declines to accept conventional meanings of politics, whatever they may be, he must formulate his own. But his own will inevitably entail some kind of over-all view of "society" and of the precise meaning of "political" in relation to it. It will, moreover, entail some conception of function that

4. See Leo Strauss, *What Is Political Philosophy? and Other Studies* (New York: Free Press, 1959).

5. Cf. Richard Weaver, "Concealed Rhetoric in Scientific Sociology," in Helmut Schoeck and James W. Wiggins (eds.), *Scientism and Values* (Princeton: Van Nostrand, 1960), particularly pp. 88–90.

will ineluctably involve purposes or goals, either as conventionally formulated or as stated by the investigator before he initiates his researches.

In a recent article, Professor Berns has rightly emphasized that one of the dangers of some versions of behavioralism is that the study of political phenomena tends more and more to be turned over to professional students of sociology, psychology, or psychiatry. When this happens, there is implicit a kind of reductionism which assumes, for example, that men vote in ways which will gratify their repressed wishes or express individual "needs." The political, that is to say, tends to be analyzed away into the subpolitical, the result being that the student who claims to be a political behavioralist becomes primarily a sociological or a psychological behavioralist. And Berns goes on to argue, correctly in the judgment of this writer, that the political, generally speaking, is not visible to any of our senses or even a combination of them. Racial segregation in the United States

is seen by the observer because he can see the injustice of the practice. . . . Through the "eye of the mind" we are enabled to see the injustice and hence the political; with the eye alone we would see only men of dark skin sitting in the balconies of theaters marked "colored," or *not* sitting at Woolworth lunch counters. Out of the millions of so-called factual events that pass within the range of our vision, we could not single out these events except as they are seen by the eye of a mind that is not blinded by prejudice or a fallacious theoretical commitment. It is this commitment that accounts for political science books devoid of political content.[6]

But identification of the political is only the beginning. The particular questions for behavioral research must now be put. Here again, a rational choice of problems necessitates some conception of relative importance, and relative importance, in turn, is related not merely to judgments of scientific import but also to those of political significance—to the value choices, that is to say, which are involved in the political process.

The whole issue of concept formation is raised—a complicated series of questions with which sophisticated behavioralists are no doubt thoroughly familiar. Here we do not intend to pursue this theme in any detail. It is important to suggest, however, that both the motivations and the basic conceptual frameworks which the student brings to his study arise out of the total life experience of the investigator: before he breaks apart "reality" for "scientific" analysis and experiment, he must have some vague notion or hunch of what that "reality" is in terms of its wholes and some impression of the relation of its parts to its wholes and to one another.

But how account for notions of this kind? It would appear that,

6. Walter Berns, "The Behavioral Sciences and the Study of Political Things, the Case of Christian Bay's *The Structure of Freedom*," *American Political Science Review*, Vol. 55 (September 1961), p. 550.

whatever the value we impute to behavioral studies as such—and here
we include under the term both the scientific theory and the process of
verification—the ideas with which we begin and the conceptions which
lead us to scientific investigation must rest ultimately on over-all insights and what Leo Strauss has called prescientific knowledge as well
as on something very akin to aesthetic experience. Direct experience of
certain "facts"—for example, the distinction of human beings from one
another—is presupposed by all scientific investigation; and such fundamental knowledge, as Strauss emphasizes,[7] is not derivable from class-
rooms. As for the aestheticlike experiences which lie at the root of our
desire to know and to understand, they seem to arise out of general
life-experience and not from scientific and behavioral analysis.

At this point, it is perhaps relevant to refer to the analysis of Michael
Polanyi. In two significant recent books,[8] he develops the thesis of what
he calls "personal knowledge." In general, he argues that the sharp
distinction between "objective" and "subjective" fails to understand the
apparent fact that all investigation takes its point of departure from
what Polanyi calls "intellectual passion." Thus, all knowledge is "tainted"
by personal participation at all levels. We cannot even begin to know
and to understand without shaping that which is known. But this does
not, Polanyi maintains, "invalidate knowledge," although it does impair
"its objectivity."[9]

He distinguishes between two types of "knowledge": tacit and
explicit. The former is both prescientific and postscientific. It is prescientific in the sense that it arises out of direct experience which has
not yet been made explicit through maps, books, formulas, and scientific
experimentation. It is, in a sense, postscientific in that it furnishes us with
clues to an understanding of the experience which we have tried to
analyze explicitly.

Tacit knowledge is involved in the process both of communicating
and of receiving communications. Because the symbols which we are
compelled to use in explicit knowledge cannot be said to communicate
an understanding of themselves, we must rely on tacit knowledge to
achieve this result. And, Polanyi adds,

though such statements will be made in a form which best induces an understanding of their message, the sender of the message will always have to rely
for the comprehension of his message on the intelligence of the person addressed. Only by virtue of this act of comprehension, of this tacit contribution
of his own, can the receiving person be said to acquire knowledge when he is
presented with a statement.[10]

    7. *Ibid.*
    8. *Personal Knowledge* (London: Routledge, 1958) and *The Study of Man*
(London: Routledge, 1959).
    9. *The Study of Man,* p. 13.
    10. *Ibid.,* pp. 21–22.

Basically, tacit knowing is a process of comprehending whereby we grasp parts and fit them into a whole. When we engage in this act, our attention is shifted from the parts conceived "focally" to the parts seen "subsidiarily." And Polanyi maintains that we can often comprehend wholes without ever being aware of their parts "focally": the parts in such instances are related or grasped only in relation to the whole. This is particularly true in the area of practical skills and practical experience, he adds. Particulars that are not known "focally" are "unspecifiable," and there are vast domains of knowledge, relating to living things, the particulars of which are largely "unspecifiable." As an example, he instances the human physiognomy and suggests that "we know a face without being able to tell, except quite vaguely, by what particulars we recognize it." And he argues that what is true of the face is also true of our knowledge of the human mind: "A man's mind can be known only comprehensively, by dwelling within the unspecifiable particulars of its external manifestations."[11]

Throughout his analysis, Polanyi suggests that our ways of knowing are the same, whether in the studies which deal with nature or in those having to do with man. Whether in physics or in politics, we are concerned with both tacit and explicit knowledge, the latter being roughly the equivalent of scientific theory and verification, the former having to do with prescientific and postscientific understanding. In explicit knowledge, we are critical and endeavor to advance knowledge through symbolization; in tacit knowledge, we see parts in relation to wholes, develop creative over-all new ways of grasping "reality," and accept or reject the results obtained through explicit knowledge.

In connection with the role of tacit understanding in accepting or rejecting pictures of reality derivable from scientific and explicit investigation, Polanyi cites the case of Copernicus. Ultimately, Copernicus accepted the heliocentric conception of the universe and rejected the geocentric because of the "greater intellectual satisfaction he derived from the celestial panorama as seen from the sun instead of the earth." And he goes on:

Copernicus gave preference to man's delight in abstract theory, at the price of rejecting the evidence of our senses, which present us with the irresistible fact of the sun, the moon, the stars rising daily in the east to travel across the sky towards their setting in the west. In a literal sense, therefore, the new Copernican system was as anthropocentric as the Ptolemaic view, the difference being merely that it preferred to satisfy a different human affection.[12]

But Polanyi suggests that this preference is not wholly a matter of

11. *Ibid.*, p. 33.
12. *Personal Knowledge*, pp. 3–4.

"personal taste" on our part "but an inherent quality deserving universal acceptance by rational creatures. We abandon

the cruder anthropocentrism of our senses—but only in favour of a more ambitious anthropocentrism of our reason. In doing so, we claim the capacity to formulate ideas which command respect in their own right, by their very rationality, and which have in this sense an objective standing.[13]

If this has a Platonic ring, if it does not conform to certain versions of even sophisticated empiricism, it still, nevertheless, would seem to conform to what in fact goes on before any actual scientific theorizing and empirical investigation take place. As Polanyi again points out:

Our vision of the general nature of things is our guide for the interpretation of all future experience. . . . Our vision of reality, to which our sense of scientific beauty responds, must suggest to us the kind of question that it should be reasonable and interesting to explore. . . . Without a scale of interest and plausibility based on a vision of reality, nothing can be discovered that is of value to science; and only our grasp of scientific beauty, responding to the evidence of our senses, can evoke this vision.[14]

But the vision spoken of here, while it may rely in part on results of previous scientific investigations, always goes beyond them. It embraces as well transscientific insight into rationality and aesthetic value and, in moral and political study, notions of ends or purposes. This is the kind of foundation indispensable to scientific discovery, whether in the natural or social studies. Upon this ground the structure of empirical observations and controlled experiment is built; and the criteria of relevance, so indispensable for the development of any behavioral inquiry, are established out of the "vision"—criteria which enable the student to distinguish between "facts" which must be considered and those, on the other hand, which can be disregarded. And, if we are to adopt the contentions developed by Polanyi, even the acceptance of "new" scientific and explicit "knowledge" turns on a tacit understanding akin to aesthetic appreciation. Thus, both the grasp of wholes which initiates the quest for explicit knowledge and the judgment of wholes which comes after it are rooted in an understanding which lies beyond scientific propositions. Putting it in another way, we proceed from nonbehaviorally derived wholes to the development of explicit knowledge, and we return ultimately to a knowledge which transcends scientifically verifiable propositions.

If this seems to make the foundations and evaluations of scientific work somewhat like those of the poet, artist, and religious mystic, one can only reply that this would indeed appear to be so.[15] Because be-

---

13. *Ibid.*, pp. 4–5.
14. *Ibid.*, p. 135.
15. Cf. Rosamund E. M. Harding, *An Anatomy of Inspiration*, 3rd ed. (Cambridge, England: Heffer, 1948).

havioral scientific investigation is dependent in its very inception on a vision and a body of conceptualizations which arise in part out of direct personal experiences and knowledge gained nonbehaviorally, behavioral investigations themselves are limited by the kinds and quality of these nonbehaviorally derived experiences and knowledge.

Capacity and Deficiency

But, once the investigation is launched and however much the behavioral student may discover by his carefully formulated scientific conceptualizations and verifications, there are questions which seemingly cannot be answered by a strictly scientific behavioralism or at least can be answered only in part.

First, however, let us note what behavioral methods *can* accomplish.

Fundamentally, it appears, the behavioralist, once he has settled on his problem and decided what is relevant and important, seeks to (a) explain the conduct of men in politics under specific assumptions and within controlled situations and (b) predict how men will probably behave under like circumstances. The first achievement we may designate scientific explanation and the second scientific prediction.

Now, there is no good reason to believe that both of these objectives cannot be accomplished with an increasing degree of precision. True, there are many difficulties to be overcome. For example, it has frequently been charged that the behavioralist is not fully aware that classifications of political behavior must be in terms of concepts which are meaningful to the agent as well as to the observer. Thus, one critic points out:

> The world of nature, as explored by the natural scientist, does not "mean" anything to the molecules, atoms, and electrons therein. The observational field of the social scientist, however, namely the social reality, has a specific meaning and relevance structure for the human beings living, acting, and thinking therein.[16]

This is, of course, true. But the behavioralist does and can overcome this difficulty by techniques which discover concepts that are meaningful to both the observed and the observer.[17] Although there are, perhaps, limits to the exactitude with which this can be done, there would seem to be room for considerable development. The more sophisticated be-

16. Alfred Schuetz, "Concept and Theory Formation in the Social Sciences," *Journal of Philosophy*, Vol. 51 (1954), p. 266.

17. One might instance, for example, the study reported by Herbert McClosky in "Conservatism and Personality," *American Political Science Review*, Vol. 52 (1958), pp. 27–45.

havioralists are aware of this difficulty and are far more knowledgeable about it than, for example, such an early exponent of behavioral research as A. F. Bentley.

Once concepts meaningful to both student and studied have been discovered, the behavior of human beings in politics can then be examined within the framework of understanding thus demarcated. The investigation does, of course, involve a more complicated process than that connected with the study of purely natural phenomena, but the fact that common meanings must be identified before behavioral studies can proceed does not mean that the procedure of verification and empirical validation cannot take place by methods not unlike those utilized in the natural sciences.

When all the difficulties have been recognized, it does seem that there is no reason to deny that behavioral and scientific explanations of politics can indeed increasingly add to our sum of knowledge.

As for the possibility of scientific predictions, they would appear to be as feasible in politics as in physics. In both realms, we bring to the study of phenomena concepts and insights which are not behaviorally derived, and in both we seek the objective of scientific prediction; that is to say, we endeavor to state the several possibilities of future experience and the limits within which such alternatives must lie. Science in this sense of the term tells us what *cannot* be under specified conditions; or, as Karl Popper puts it succinctly, the "lawfulness" of phenomena "can be expressed by asserting that *such and such a thing cannot happen;* that is to say, by a sentence in the form of the proverb: 'You cannot carry water in a sieve.' "[18] Negations of this kind, which involve statements of limits, can certainly be validated by behavioral methods, and we can expect the techniques of study to become more refined as serious students proceed with their work.

Nor need we deny that, in the actual process of verification, the values of the observer can be separated in considerable degree from the facts to be observed. Among the critics of behavioralism, there has been a tendency in recent years to maintain that the modern dichotomy between fact and value has been overdrawn and that, in fact, values either cannot or ought not be separated from facts.[19] As we have argued,

18. Karl Popper, *The Poverty of Historicism* (Boston: Beacon Press, 1957), p. 49.

19. Thus Thomas I. Cook appears to argue that the behavioralist holds that it is his task to "observe, analyze and organize the facts, including man's professions and practices of values, with a supreme and cold aloofness." And he goes on to aver that the behavioralist deduces from this that he must "reject convictions either of direction in actual history or of other than relative purposes in human existence." "The Prospects of Political Science," *Journal of Politics,* Vol. 17 (1955), pp. 268–269. See also John Hallowell, "Politics and Ethics," *American Political Science Review,* Vol. 38 (1944), p. 643, where Hallowell argues that what he calls "positivism" undermined "all belief in transcendental truth and value." It is obvious that Hallowell thinks that, because the behavioralist tries to separate facts from values in scientific investigation, he therefore must deny any objective moral order.

of course, valuations enter into the choice of field and the subject for investigation. Science itself presupposes certain values and the moral values of the observer in politics do in fact help determine what he thinks significant for study. Moreover, one can maintain that one's over-all view of life experience constitutes both an evaluation or aesthetic insight and a judgment of fact, and certainly this would appear to be Polanyi's position.

But once we descend to the formulation of scientific hypotheses, the process of verification, it would appear, can in principle proceed without the value judgments coloring the observation. This is not to deny, of course, that the bias of the observer may affect the verification procedure. It is, however, to assert that methods exist in political as well as in natural science investigation to minimize the danger of such bias. Within the wholes, that is to say, whose comprehension in part transcends the scientific process, the parts can be investigated with relative objectivity.

Within his nonbehaviorally derived framework, then, the behavioral scientist can be expected to provide us with an increasing body of scientific explanations and predictions. He will explain *how*, under carefully given and controlled circumstances and conditions, men have in fact acted. He will also be able to suggest how, under precisely formulated conditions and circumstances, they *would* probably behave in the future, and he will provide us with statements of limits beyond which, under specified controlled environments, they would probably *not* act. These are the regularities which, as David Easton has told us, it is the purpose of the behavioral scientist to discover.

We must now ask, however, whether *scientific* understandings, explanations, and predictions are the only understandings, explanations, and predictions involved in a discussion of behavioralism and its limits. Are there, in other words, things which the behavioralist approach cannot tell us about the world which the politicist endeavors to understand?

It would appear that there are indeed several questions for which behavioralism cannot supply answers. Among them we might consider the following.

Behavior of the Behavioralist

It would seem that, although the observer can provide scientific accounts of those he observes, he cannot explain—by behavioral methods as usually understood—his own behavior as an observer.[20] He might, indeed, provide an interesting hypothesis to explain his conduct, but

20. See Alfred Schuetz, "Concept and Theory Formation in the Social Sciences," *Journal of Philosophy*, Vol. 51 (1954), p. 262.

this could hardly be verified by the statistical and other methods which he uses to study the behavior of groups.

What Ought We to Value in Political Life?

Behavioralism can cast light on the circumstances under which professed value schemes are likely to be held or are held. It can also, in principle, help tell us that, if we value certain things, specific types of action under given specified circumstances are likely to frustrate the implementation of those values—that is, it might conceivably show that, if we value "truth-telling," certain crisis situations under carefully defined conditions are likely to work against the probability of this value being realized.

Behavioralism can also show that, if we have a given value hierarchy under precisely defined conditions, the possibilities of its implementation are or are not great. It might also tell us that, under certain hypothetical conditions, if we value X and Y, the possibilities of our attaining both are or are not remote. Or it might conceivably provide us with a statement that, if we value X, we cannot, under such and such circumstances, expect to attain Y also.

All this is to say that behavioralism is not irrelevant in the making of value judgments. Under hypothetical value schemes and hypothetical empirical conditions, it can help us see the possibilities within which we would have to work. It can, following Popper's illustration, relate the size of empirical sieve holes to the length of time in which given quantities of water-value can be carried in alternative types of vessels.

But always, it will be noted, behavioralism must state both the value and the fact conditions hypothetically. Admittedly, it cannot tell us what we ought to value but can only assume a given set or hierarchy of values as the basis for its statements. It must likewise carefully prescribe the fact conditions under which given values can or cannot in all probability be attained.

Behavioralism may cast considerable light on "ought" questions insofar as value judgments at the secondary or tertiary levels are concerned. That is to say, it can tell us that we ought to do so and so, under given circumstances, if we value such and such as ends in themselves. Insofar as the hypothetical statements which it makes illuminate possible consequences of given acts, in other words, it can assist us to make the political choices which presumably would bring us closer to a realization of our primary or first-order ends.

But it is incapable of telling us what those first-order values ought to be. However we account for our first-order moral experience, it is clear that all the behavioral research in the world, however refined it might be, cannot tell us what goals we ought to seek as ends in themselves. Whatever it may contribute to our political choices at the secondary and tertiary levels, it is powerless to provide us the values upon which those choices must depend.

All this has been summed up nicely by Arnold Brecht in his statement on what he identifies as "scientific values relativism." Brecht enunciates two propositions:

1. The question whether something is "valuable" can be answered *scientifically* only in relation to
   a) some goal or purpose for the pursuit of which it is or is not useful (valuable), or to
   b) the ideas held by some person or group of persons regarding what is or is not valuable; and that, consequently:
2. It is impossible to establish scientifically what goals or purposes are valuable *irrespective* of
   a) the value they have in the pursuit of other goals or purposes, or
   b) of someone's ideas about ulterior or ultimate goals or purposes.[21]

But the fact that the behavioral method cannot determine what we *ought* to value in an ultimate sense does not imply anything about whether ultimate values exist "objectively" and apart from our particular perceptions of them. Occasionally critics seem to suggest that, because behavioralists obviously cannot tell us what to value, they are therefore affirming that values are purely "subjective." But this does not follow at all. Some behavioralists may, indeed, believe that there are no ultimate values in a Platonic sense; others may affirm them. But both must agree that their existence can neither be proved nor disproved by the methods characteristic of behavioral investigation.[22] Whether it can or cannot be proved by other methods is not the purpose of our present inquiry. It is sufficient to emphasize that behavioral study as such can neither affirm nor deny the being of an independent realm of values.

Forecasting the Future

Unfortunately, some who have been enamored of the word "science," and who look to the natural sciences for models in the study of politics, fail to see that, at best, one can only expect *scientific* predictions from behavioral methods. A scientific prediction, as we have emphasized earlier, is always a hypothetical if-then kind of statement. It is *not* a general forecast or a prophecy. There are those among the behavioralists,

---

21. Arnold Brecht, *Political Theory: The Foundations of Twentieth Century Political Thought* (Princeton: Princeton U. P., 1959), pp. 117–118.
22. A point very much stressed by Brecht at pp. 6–9.

however, who have apparently confused scientific prediction with what is alleged to be a scientific forecasting or fortune-telling.

In its most egregious form, this fallacy may be said to have been characteristic of Marx and Engels, who claimed scientifically not only to be able to formulate and verify if-then propositions but also to foretell the future of the world. And Marxists not infrequently have followed their example. If one pushes Marx and Engels aside as outside the pale of modern behavioral method, one can cite Charles E. Merriam and Harold Lasswell as moderns who often appear to confuse scientific prediction with over-all forecasting.[23] And, during the 1950's, several others associated with the behavioralist mood appeared to follow in their train.[24] Hypothetical propositions, given this viewpoint, are somehow transformed into unhypothetical statements; and the scientist asserts that by virtue of his science he can, in principle (whatever the practical difficulties), see into the future.

Obviously, not all behavioralists either state or imply that this can be done. But the confusion of forecasting with prediction is common enough to warrant a careful restatement of the distinction between scientific prediction, as the term was used earlier in this paper, and the forecasting of events. The former, we argued, is clearly within the scope of the behavioral approach and we can probably expect development in the future. The latter, however, is beyond the capacity of behavioral science as such—whatever we may think of the possibilities inherent in other approaches and however much or little we value the possibility of forecasting.

The behavioral if-then proposition is hypothetical; the forecast, insofar as it exists, must be unhypothetical or unconditioned, else it ceases to be a forecast. Thus, one can perhaps predict what Congress will do about a proposed piece of legislation under carefully assumed conditions and contingencies. But one cannot—at least scientifically—purport to forecast what it will do. One can conceivably predict what the population of the world is likely to be twenty years hence if trends ycx continue under conditions zoa and bbm. But one cannot—behaviorally—forecast what the population of the world will be twenty years hence,

23. Evidences of this may be found in Merriam's *New Aspects of Politics* (Chicago: University of Chicago Press, 1925) and in Lasswell and A. Kaplan, *Power and Society* (New Haven: Yale U. P., 1950). It will also be reflected in various other works of both men.

24. Note, for example, Louis H. Bean, *How to Predict Elections* (New York: Knopf, 1948). Stuart Dodd, "Predictive Principles from Polls—Scientific Method in Public Opinion Research," *Public Opinion Quarterly*, Vol. 15 (1951–1952), pp. 23–24; R. A. Dahl, "The Science of Politics: New and Old," *World Politics*, Vol. 7 (1955); and David Apter, "Theory and the Study of Politics," *American Political Science Review*, Vol. 51 (1957) also seem to give hostages to this point of view.

period. Any forecast of this kind would be guesswork based on over-all "hunches" and could never be classified as "scientific."

It has often been pointed out that we cannot foretell what new knowledge will be discovered in the future, for if we could do so we ourselves would be the discoverers. Thus, the very proposition that we could forecast such discoveries would be belied: the discovery would not lie in the future but, rather, with us in the present. And Karl Popper, echoing this observation, maintains that, if we hold that human history is in part shaped by the growth of knowledge and we cannot foretell exactly what knowledge will be gained, we cannot predict in any scientific sense the future of human events. "There can," he asseverates, be no "scientific theory of historical development serving as a basis for historical prediction."[25]

The contrast between scientific prediction and an alleged capacity to foretell political events is pointed up nicely by Clarence Lewis when he tells us:

> The prediction of future reality is prediction of future experience if—; but that *if* is an *if* of action which it is in our power to make true or make false. The *if-then* statement which expresses the objective reality in question remains true whether the antecedent *if* of action be true or false; the statement of reality is categorically asserted. But this categorical assertion of objective fact is only the hypothetical assertion of a verifying experience dependent on the hypothesis that a certain mode of verifying activity be adopted. The future experience still depends upon our choosing to actualize this *if* of action. . . .[26]

Essentially, the if-then kind of statement is an isolated and fragmented particle of the whole. We may, indeed, become more and more exact about these if-then isolates, and this is presumably to the good. But the forecasts of what is likely to be in the macrocosm that is "practical politics" must somehow put the fragments together, and, in this task, behavioralism as such would seem to have little to offer. Its concern is neither to reconstruct imaginatively what *has happened* in human history nor to forecast *what is likely* to take place in future history. Instead, it seeks to discover regularities and limits.

How, for example, can it tell us the weight to be attached to religious factors in explaining macrocosmic historical events? How, moreover, can it provide us with behaviorally derived forecasts as to the role which economic factors will play in future history—as contrasted, let us say, with subrational passions? How can one assess behaviorally the relative importance of the many tangled skeins which are the stuff of human history, whether in the past or in the years to come?

25. *The Poverty of Historicism*, pp. ix–x.
26. Clarence I. Lewis, *An Analysis of Knowledge and Valuation* (LaSalle, Ill.: Open Court, 1946), p. 3.

Questions of this kind cannot be answered scientifically. Instead, the answers are to be sought in a combination of imaginative (and unscientific) reconstruction of the past; practical experience in the world of politics; and over-all insights to be drawn from science, experience, and what one might call intuition.

Understanding politics, to state the matter somewhat differently, includes trying to comprehend not only how the parts are related to one another in hypothetical situations but also how the parts interact in actual history and how the whole helps shape the parts. While behavioralism has an important role to play in understanding the political universe, its kind of understanding is not the only one required for comprehension.

The Place of Behavioral Science

The distinction between hypothetical if-then explanatory and predictive statements, on the one hand, and observations and forecasts about the complex and interacting world of historical politics, on the other, is basically that between "theoretical" (in the strictly "scientific" sense) and "practical" science and philosophy. In politics, the purpose of theoretical science is not only to develop and verify hypothetical statements but also to serve the needs of practical science; and practical science, in turn, will be built on the foundations not only of theoretical scientific propositions but also of judgments about over-all historical trends, identification of value hierarchies, understandings of specific cultures, and speculations about the relation of physical and geographical to cultural and political factors.

This does not mean that we reject behavioral science. On the contrary, to suggest its limited role in practical science and philosophy is to prevent disillusionment about what it can accomplish. Writing from the viewpoint of a psychologist, Joseph R. Royce makes the same point when he observes that we should wish to apply the "scientific method" to "any and all problems." However, he goes on,

> My point is that the final putting together of the segements of life will always be a highly subjective and individual task . . . which cannot be scientized.[27]

Stating the matter in yet another way, if-then behavioral science takes us far out of the world of macrocosmic political "reality" into the universe of pure scientific speculation, and it is indeed an important universe to which we are invited by behavioral scientists. But, if the

27. *American Scientist,* Vol. 47 (1959), p. 534.

understanding of politics includes comprehension not only of conduct as it could be under specified conditions but also of what it is, has been, possibly will be, and ought to be, the pure vision of the behavioral scientist must be corrected by unscientific judgments about history and primary values.

Thus—somewhat surprisingly to those who think that behavioral science deals with political "reality"—we are asserting that, in itself, it takes us away from the world in which men must make political judgments.[28] True, it may return with its verified conditional statements that add to our store of scientific knowledge, but it cannot in itself and alone build a practical philosophy and science of politics. For that, we must turn not only to the behavioralist but also to the historian of political ideas, the moral philosopher, the cultural historian, the speculative political philosopher of the classical tradition, the descriptive politicist, and the man of direct political experience.[29]

That the scientific theorist can assist us greatly should by now be apparent—for, in his quest for precision, scientific verification, and the refinement of propositions, he is endeavoring to find the limits of what can be in politics. Yet, because politics is historical, we are also concerned to know not only what *can* be but also what *has been* and possibly *might be* in the total context of a given culture.[30] We cannot proceed by a single leap, and without the introduction of other approaches, from scientific theory to the world studied by practical science and philosophy. The best behavioral scientists would not, one assumes, assert that the descent from pure scientific theory to conceptions of historical reality can be made without the assistance of understandings other than those derived from pure science.

It is here that the distinction between two kinds of "theorizing" must be stressed. In the recent and current discussion of behavioralism, some of its extreme exponents appear to maintain that all "theory" can and ought to be reduced to scientific theory. Any other type, one learns —at least in private conversations, for the extreme position is not as frequently stated in print—fails to contribute to knowledge. But "knowledge" in this context appears to mean scientific or, as Aristotle might have put it, "theoretical" knowledge. Meanwhile, one can legitimately ask the "advanced" behavioralist what he would do about knowledge

28. A point stressed by Harry V. Jaffa, "The Case Against Political Theory," *Journal of Politics*, Vol. 22 (1960), pp. 259–275.

29. As Polanyi points out, "practical skills and practical experience" embrace much more information than scientific "experts" are sometimes willing to acknowledge. *The Study of Man*, p. 33.

30. There is not a little justification for the arguments of Glenn Tinder, in "The Necessity of Historicism," *American Political Science Review*, Vol. 55 (1961), pp. 560–565. He maintains, for example, that the social scientist needs a framework of meaning which involves a theory of history that is essentially a scientifically undemonstrable intellectual construction.

at the "practical" level—that which is frequently identified with the "merely armchair" speculations of the traditional theorist—speculations which attempt to embrace within their confines scientific, historical, practical, and normative statements. In response to questions of this kind, the answer is not infrequently that such tasks are for the layman or, perhaps, for the "philosopher."

But responses of this kind would appear to be unsatisfactory. To be sure, the layman as citizen must indubitably engage in the function of practical speculation if he is to make rational decisions in the political realm. But in a highly complex world, where the interrelation of parts to parts and of wholes to segments is exceedingly involved, there is an urgent need for what we might call the professional politicist—a student who, because of both his scientific involvement and his knowledge of history, can offer alternative syntheses for consideration by the citizen. This is the function of the "political scientist" as "practical philosopher," and the behavioralist as such cannot, in view of the limitations we have noted, perform it.

As for asking the "philosopher" to carry out this function, much would depend on the school of thought to which he belongs. But, if the trend to "analytical philosophy" continues, ethics, for example, tends to become increasingly a matter of linguistic discussion and the questions of practical philosophy (in its traditional sense) are often never examined. Moreover, the philosopher is usually not involved in the scientific, descriptive, or historical study of politics and, from this point of view, is perhaps less well equipped than the traditional political "theorist" to carry out the synthesizing and normative tasks.

Policy-Making

Finally, most of the limitations of behavioralism are summarized when we turn to the relation between the study of politics and the making of policy. The central issue has already been suggested in the preceding section. Here we simply draw out a few of the implications.

Practical philosophy, public policy, and politics are intimately related to one another. Because politics involves the shaping of policies and policies in turn necessitate choices among contesting value systems, the ethical dimension is always ubiquitous. The professional student of politics has traditionally been called upon to lay down guidelines for action, as Arnold Kaufman has pointed out. "The political philosopher," he rightly maintains, "should provide those who make policy with principles which will aid them in the attempt to cope with specific sociopolitical problems."[31] And Gabriel Almond also emphasizes this policy role: "Practical judgment of 'good and evil' in the area of public policy is the special responsibility of the social scientist."[32]

The whole problem of policy-making illustrates both the potentialities of behavioralism and the ways in which its contributions are circumscribed by the nature of the policy-making process. If in what follows there is some repetition, therefore, it is because an analysis of what goes into the formulation of policies draws together both the strengths and limitations of behavioral approaches.

Policy-making would seem to involve three elements: the moral; what might be called the empirical; and the legislative. They are closely interrelated aspects, to be sure, and are tied together by reason and understanding, but they can be separated for purposes of comment.

The moral phase involves awareness and formulation of the value hierarchies which are to be used. Ultimately, that is to say, such traditional problems as those of righteousness, justice, obligation, and legitimacy cannot be avoided. Even though in the formulation of a particular policy we may assume much without question, a full inquiry would have to lay bare the normative framework. Why, for example, is it better for the "many" to be consulted than the "few"? Or, to illustrate again, which is more valuable—to use scarce resources for exploring space or for clearing slums?

What role can behavioralism play in this aspect of policy-formation? Given its own framework, it cannot, as we have pointed out, tell us what we ought to value in any ultimate sense. It can, of course, cast light on what men do in fact value under given circumstances and conditions, and it can predict, within narrow confines, what they are likely to value assuming given temperaments, upbringing, culture, religious faith, and other factors. It can also help us understand whether given acts are likely under specified circumstances to lead or not to lead to an implementation of particular values. But first-order "oughts" are beyond behavioralism.

The formulation of value hierarchies would seem to be the task not of behavioral science but rather of a combined utilization of linguistic analysis, rationality, and intuition. At any rate, the characteristic behavioral techniques cannot assist us.

What, then, can we say of the relevance of empirical study for policy-

31. Arnold S. Kaufman, "The Nature and Function of Political Theory," *Journal of Philosophy*, Vol. 51 (1954), p. 9.

32. "Politics, Science and Ethics," in "Politics and Ethics—A Symposium," *American Political Science Review*, Vol. 40 (1946), p. 292. See also the writer's paper "The Place of Classical Political Theory in the Study of Politics: the Legitimate Spell of Plato," in Roland Young (ed.) *Approaches to the Study of Politics* (Evanston: Northwestern U. P., 1958), pp. 125–148.

making? By empirical study we mean something more than behavioral science. We include also such elements as the investigation of historical politics, the analysis of culture, and personal experience.

It is in the area of empirical study that the behavioralist can presumably make his greatest contribution. He can cast light on how men are likely to behave under given value systems, and, negatively, he can suggest the ways in which they are unlikely to act under carefully defined and isolated conditions. He can formulate and test if-then statements of an explanatory and predictive character. And we have argued that he can become more and more precise in statements of this kind.

But his precision is purchased at the price of isolating fragments from the whole, and it is still not clear how the behavioralist can, using methods usually thought of as hallmarks of his technique, characterize the whole in which his own circumstances and conditions either may not exist or may flourish only under highly complex systems of distortion and with many impurities introduced. In selecting his subjects for investigation, moreover, and in formulating his concepts, he proceeds within frameworks and insights which cannot be derived through behavioral methods. The element of "personal knowledge" is always present throughout his investigations.

Finally, the legislative aspect of policy-making, which is built upon the foundations of what we have called practical science and philosophy, involves such elements as relating abstract, primary values to secondary or instrumental ones, making judgments about possible consequences of alternative policy schemes, and formulating policies which seem most likely to implement primary and secondary values. Obviously we have here a task which calls, to be sure, for far more precise information as to how men are likely to act under given circumstances, but it calls also for much more than that. In forecasting likely consequences of proposed alternative policies, for example, one usually has to speculate about conditions which will probably be considerably different from those laid down by pure behavioral scientific theory. Both the form and the substance of policy involve an interweaving of impurities at every level. And the interrelationship of the many factors which have to be taken into account is not merely a mechanical one; it is also, in a sense, organic. Factors of uniqueness in this organically related world of impure, uncontrolled (in a scientific sense) conditions make even more difficult the task of relating scientifically derived behavioral statements to the problems of policy-making.

The limitations of behavioral science are not merely those of youth[33] —for it can be argued that, given enough time, the restrictions might

33. On the problem of the "youth" of the behavioral approach, Eliso Vivas has certain interesting comments. See "Science and Studies of Man" in Helmut Schoeck and James W. Wiggins, *Scientism and Values* (Princeton: Van Nostrand 1960).

be overcome—but inhere in if-then or hypothetical knowledge itself. The policy-maker must make over-all judgments about possible consequences of given lines of action under probable circumstances of the historical world of politics rather than in the hypothetical universe of science. It is difficult to see how these synthesizing judgments can be derived from behavioral science, however much its methods may be perfected. How can one possibly combine—behaviorally—an elaborate complex of hypothetical propositions into that over-all assessment of wholes which is the essence of a practical judgment?

It requires more than behaviorally derived statements to "understand" politics. And to answer questions posed by the problem of consciously and deliberately ordering human affairs, one must necessarily resort to "dialectic," as many classical thinkers would have put it; to over-all judgments about possible historical tendencies (admittedly a shaky venture at best and one which can never be scientific); and to the kind of reasoning characteristic of the judge and the lawyer. We have become so enamored of the term "science"—in its narrower connotations—that we have tended to be imprisoned by it. We have often forgotten that there are other methods of understanding than those of science and that, indeed, in the making of policy, these modes are just as important as the technique and substance of science.[34]

But, if there are severe limitations to behavioralism, we ought not for this reason to ignore the restrictions characteristic as well of nonbehavioral approaches. No one perspective on the problems of political ordering is without its difficulties, and, even if we assume that all are used, the limits remain. To achieve political order in human affairs is, as the ancients were often pointing out, a labor requiring divine gifts. Yet we are called upon to carry out this superhuman work with the equipment merely of men.

34. For many of the references in this paper, I am indebted to Dr. Arthur Kalleberg's unpublished doctoral dissertation, *An Analysis of the Nature and Validity of the Idea of a Science of Politics in Recent Political Theory* (Minneapolis 1960). I am also greatly indebted for research assistance to Dr. Ernest Katin, formerly a graduate student at the University of Minnesota.

4

Functional Analysis

WILLIAM FLANIGAN and
EDWIN FOGELMAN

As IT APPLIES to contemporary political science, "functionalism" can refer to several rather disparate types of political analysis; there is no broad, distinctive functional approach to analysis which can be contrasted, say, to an institutional, or legal approach. At no time has functionalism been a prevalent mode of analysis in political science, and political scientists have never borrowed extensively from the functionalists in anthropology and sociology. Functional analysis has come to political science only recently, and relatively few major works in the discipline have explicitly developed a functional analytic scheme. In order to appraise the contributions of functionalism to contemporary political science we must first clarify the variety of types of analysis that are included within this ambiguous term.

Eclectic Functionalism

In its widest usage functionalism means simply that in analyzing some phenomena the political scientist will be concerned with, among other things, their functions in the sense of the purposes served by the phenomena. Here function is treated as one—and not necessarily a more significant one—among many relevant considerations that together comprise a comprehensive political analysis. In addition to function, the analyst may be equally concerned with the structure, history, ideology, and other aspects of the phenomena. We can call this type of analysis "eclectic functionalism," and in this sense it is not too much to say that we are all functionalists now, although the implications of the commitment differ greatly from scholar to scholar. Eclectic functionalists are found in all branches of contemporary political science; they can be identified by their tendency to ask the question: "What functions does *X* perform?" There may be reference to the functions of individuals— the functions of the president; groups—the functions of political parties; institutions—the functions of the International Court of Justice; or ideas —the functions of Communist ideology. Depending on the analyst, this simple form of functionalism may only provide a list of activities in which *X* is engaged, or it may provide answers to more or less explicit questions with respect to how *X* contributes to the performance of certain purposes or activities.

Eclectic functionalism involves no commitment to a distinctive functional approach, and the theoretical implications of including the concept of "function" among the categories of analysis are quite limited. Function is not the focus for analysis, but only one aspect of the analysis; nor is the functional aspect considered in any way primary or exceptionally significant. But by making these limited claims eclectic functionalism is not exempt from criticism for failing to face the problem of specifying the basis upon which functions are identified.

Eclectic functionalism is by far the most widespread and at the same time the least developed theoretically of current types of functional analysis.

Empirical Functionalism

The attempt to analyze politics from a more consistently functional standpoint without, however, basing the analysis on a general functional theory has produced a second type of functional analysis which we can call "empirical functionalism." Empirical functionalism was given its greatest impetus and its most convincing justification in Robert K. Merton's well-known study of the political machine, contained in his "Latent and Manifest Functions."[1] Unlike the eclectic functionalists, Merton does not merely consider function as one among a number of equally significant aspects of a political machine, but rather he concentrates upon function as the "most promising orientation." Moreover, for Merton, function is not the commonsensical concept that it is for eclectic functionalists. Within every social system individuals make varied demands which are satisfied to some extent. For empirical functionalists, functions are performed insofar as activities satisfy these demands. For empirical functionalists the purposes or consequences of

1. Robert K. Merton, *Social Theory and Social Structure* (New York: Free Press, 1957), Chap. 1, esp. pp. 72–82.

activities are the satisfaction of these demands. Functional analysis requires an elucidation not only of manifest functions, the obvious and intended purposes and consequences, but also of latent functions, the more covert and unintended consequences that are equally important and enlightening as subjects for analysis.

In making the functions of any phenomena the primary focus for his analysis and in enlarging the concept of function to include a variety of significant relationships, Merton gives to functional analysis considerable range and subtlety. For example, Merton argues that the political machine serves several social functions including the provision of welfare assistance in a personal manner. While comparable aid is available through governmental channels, the machine provides assistance without loss of self-respect. This is a thoroughly plausible and typical form of argument in what we are calling "empirical functionalism."

It is important to notice what Merton does and does not do in his functional analysis. First, he does not make reference to functions which must somehow be served in this or all social systems. He simply notes that there is a demand for welfare assistance, and meeting this demand —serving this purpose—is what Merton calls fulfilling a social function. He does not in any sense treat the political machine as a social subsystem with functional requisites of its own fulfilled in various ways. There is so little concern with the functions as such that he does not attempt to assess the extent to which political machines engage in welfare activities. The main aspects of the analysis are straightforward empirical statements of relationship.

With and without explicit acknowledgement to Merton, a number of political scientists have followed the path of empirical functionalism. For example, analyzing the Mexican Revolutionary Party (PRI) Vincent Padgett[2] goes beyond the overt structural and ideological aspects of the party to an examination primarily of the party's various sociopolitical functions. Although other aspects of the party are considered, these functions provide the focus in terms of which the party can be understood; moreover, functions include not simply the obvious political purposes of the party but also its less apparent though highly significant social effects. The analysis departs markedly from eclectic functionalism in its consistent reliance on a functional perspective and in its refinement of the concept of function.

A similar example of political analysis employing functionalism is Alan Fiellin's "The Functions of Informal Groups—A State Delegation"[3]

2. L. Vincent Padgett, "Mexico's One Party System," in Roy C. Macridis and Bernard E. Brown (eds.), *Comparative Politics: Notes and Readings* (Homewood, Ill.: Dorsey Press, 1961).

3. Alan Fiellin, "The Functions of Informal Groups: A State Delegation," in Robert L. Peabody and Nelson W. Polsby (eds.), *New Perspectives on the House of Representatives* (Chicago: Rand McNally, 1963).

which in part deals with the functions of an informal group within the Democratic party delegation to the House of Representatives from New York in several larger systems. The informal group performs functions for the House of Representatives, for the party, for the state delegation, and—somewhat out of the spirit of more recent functionalism—for the individuals in the group.

Theodore Lowi's article "Toward Functionalism in Political Science: The Case of Innovation in Party Systems"[4] also falls in this category, although it does have more ambitious intentions. Lowi treats innovation as a function which parties perform, but the place of innovation in a functional theory of the political system remains ambiguous. In our terms, he argues against the theoretical deficiency of eclectic functionalism and in favor of the central significance of function as the orienting concept in political analysis. He attempts to interpret party systems with his hypothesis that "in a party system, innovation is a function of the minority party."[5]

Empirical functionalists remain limited in their use of a functional perspective. For one thing they show no concern with functional requisites at the level of the system as a whole. For another they isolate particular elements within the total system and treat them as discrete units without any presumptions about the significance of these units for the system as a whole. Moreover, empirical functionalists find in functionalism a framework for analysis with limited theoretical implications. It is upon the validity of their empirical findings rather than the analytic power of a possible functional theory that they rest the case for functional analysis. Justification for the restricted perspective adopted by empirical functionalists is provided by Merton in his argument for "middle range" theory. He asserts that whether or not a general functional theory to explain the social system as a whole is ultimately possible, the most advisable course is to deal with more limited units in terms of reasonably precise concepts.

Structural-Functional Analysis

The most ambitious attempts to introduce a functional approach into contemporary political science have come from those scholars who have applied in political analysis the structural-functional framework developed by Parsons[6] and Levy.[7] Here functionalism assumes a theoreti-

4. Theodore Lowi, "Toward Functionalism in Political Science: The Case of Innovation in Party Systems," *The American Political Science Review*, Vol. LVII (September 1963), pp. 570–583.

5. *Ibid.*, p. 570.

6. Talcott Parsons, *The Social System* (New York: Free Press, 1951), and with Edward Shils (eds.), *Toward a General Theory of Action* (Cambridge: Harvard

cal significance potentially far greater than in either eclectic functionalism or empirical functionalism. The promise of structural functionalism is nothing less than to provide a consistent and integrated theory from which can be derived explanatory hypotheses relevant to all aspects of a political system. As William Mitchell explains in his structural-functional analysis of *The American Polity:* "I have chosen to use the 'structural functional' approach largely because it seems to offer the best possibilities for eventually developing a general theory . . . of political systems."[8]

Actually, structural-functionalists do not all use the same terminology and formulations, and the divergencies among such structural functionalists as Almond,[9] Apter,[10] and Mitchell are by no means superficial.

Analytic Framework

Mitchell, like other structural functionalists, concedes that the present stage of development falls short of scientific social theory. Despite variations in terminology and some confusion within the approach itself, structural-functional analysis does embody certain characteristic features: first, an emphasis on the whole system as the unit of analysis; second, postulation of particular functions as requisite to the maintenance of the whole system; third, concern to demonstrate the functional interdependence of diverse structures within the whole system.

Although all the structural-functional frameworks in political analysis are more or less related to Parsons' work, some analysts like Almond have restated the scheme so drastically that they have an influence independent of Parsons. For political analysis Almond proposes two categories of functions, the political and the governmental, and in the major

U. P., 1951), and with Robert F. Bales and Edward A. Shils, *Working Papers in the Theory of Action* (New York: Free Press, 1953) are the main theoretical works on Parsons' structural functionalism. Political scientists will find his " 'Voting' and the Equilibrium of the American Political System," in Eugene Burdick and Arthur Brodbeck (eds.), *American Voting Behavior* (New York: Free Press, 1959) more readable and more concerned with familiar subject matter. His more recent study of one of the four subsystems, the economy—with Neil Smelser, *Economy and Society* (New York: Free Press, 1959)—suggests how he might go about studying other subsystems like the polity, and also touches on more matters of traditional interest to political scientists.

7. Marion Levy, *The Structure of Society* (Princeton: Princeton U. P., 1951).
8. William C. Mitchell, *The American Polity* (New York: Free Press, 1962), p. vii.
9. Gabriel A. Almond, "A Functional Approach to Comparative Politics," in Gabriel A. Almond and James S. Coleman (eds.), *The Politics of the Developing Areas* (Princeton: Princeton U. P., 1960).
10. David E. Apter, *The Gold Coast in Transition* (Princeton: Princeton U. P., 1955).

study employing this framework, *The Politics of Developing Areas*,[11] he emphasizes the political functions. Almond's five political functions are: political socialization, political recruitment, interest articulation, interest aggregation, and political communication. The governmental functions with their obvious parallel to the three branches of government are: rule-making, rule application, and rule adjudication. Rather than offer an elaborate rationale for these functions, Almond simply observes that all political systems appear to perform these functions in some way or another, and while this may be true enough, it is not a firm theoretical footing. It seems that Almond is merely making a recommendation that political scientists ought to concern themselves with these activities if they hope to understand politics, and particularly politics under conditions where governments are not highly developed or stable.

The paucity of theoretical structure around these concepts leaves us without detailed hypotheses of the reciprocal relationships among functions, the relationships of groups and institutions to the functions, or the relative significance of the functions. Almond's attempt to present the main analytic interests of political analysis in a system-wide framework leads him to introduce some incongruent elements. The political communication function—an opinion leader proposition basically—is unlike the other functions in that it is more of a mechanism or process, a means of performing functions, but Almond is unwilling to omit an area of investigation which he believes important simply because it does not fit neatly into a structural-functional framework. The initial elaboration of Almond's scheme did not suggest many reciprocal interrelationships between structures and functions, nor is there a theoretical concern with mechanisms by which structures perform functions. The area specialists who contributed the chapters on the developing areas were left with a collection of apparently unrelated categories which served as little more than a basis for organizing the material in each chapter. This level of analysis may be a necessary first step, but the remaining tasks of reformulation and theoretical specification are enormous.

Also in contrast to Parson's formulation, Almond's framework is not strictly a requisite analysis. Requisite analysis specifies a set of functions as necessary and sufficient for the persistence of a system. Almond merely identifies his set of functions as recurring in all political systems, but the theoretical significance of these functions is obscure. In this respect Almond is closer to empirical functionalism, since he does not justify the selection of his set of functions in terms of requirements for the persistence of social systems.

Mitchell's structural-functional analytic scheme is much closer to

11. Almond and Coleman, *op. cit.*

Parsons'. He offers four requisite functions which are performed by the polity: the authoritative specification of system goals, the authoritative mobilization of resources to implement goals, the integration of the system, and the allocation of values and costs. The polity is defined as the subsystem primarily concerned with the mobilization of resources to meet system goals, one of the four basic functions postulated by Parsons. Mitchell does not limit himself to a consideration of mobilization of resources to meet system goals, but, rather, ranges over all of the functional requisites of the social system, pointing ways in which political processes contribute to the performance of all the functions.

Mitchell employs secondary analysis of major works on the American political system, works which without exception were not written within a structural-functional framework, and he grapples with the difficult problems of noncomparable studies unevenly distributed over his analytic scheme. This is bound to be the role of anyone who would impose theoretical analysis on a large unit of study like the United States political system, and while Mitchell's work may be a ruthless departure from the studies on which he draws, for the benefits of structural-functional analysis to accrue, he must impose even more on his material. He is too often content with illustrations of the many particular ways in which structures of all kinds contribute to the fulfillment of functions. Perhaps better than any other work in political science, *The American Polity* demonstrates the capacity of structural-functional analysis to provide the foundation for unlimited insights, and at the same time demonstrates the need for reduction of the insights into more orderly, interrelated statements of relationship. In the sections of the book where Mitchell is able to draw on more prior research and become more systematic in the presentation of his main propositions, the discussion is least relevant to the structural-functional framework.[12]

One concern of structural-functionalism in political science has been simply to advocate the approach. Karl Deutsch persuasively argues that Parsons' scheme is widely applicable in political science and an improvement on most of the conceptualizing in political science as a step toward general systems theory.[13] Deutsch emphasizes the conceptual advantages of viewing Parsons' four fundamental functions as competitive with one another and observing the interchanges among the structures which perform the four functions. Deutsch concedes that there are bound to be difficulties in implementing Parsons' scheme for empirical research, especially in the attribution of observable reality to

---

12. Mitchell, *op. cit.*, esp. Chaps. 13 and 14.
13. Karl W. Deutsch, "Integration and the Social System: Implications of Functional Analysis," in Philip E. Jacob and James V. Toscano (eds.), *The Integration of Political Communities* (Philadelphia: Lippincott, 1964).

the categories. He manages to create the impression of considerable dynamism within the structural-functional framework, a dynamism lacking in other schemes. To some extent Parsons and Deutsch are coming to discuss structural-functionalism in terms of capabilities. The study of the subsystem polity is the study of the capacity of the society to attain its system goals. The analytic framework can be narrowed to a study of the varying capabilities of the structures in the system to perform different functions with available resources. It is too soon to guess what analysis oriented in this way would produce, and while it would omit much of interest to political scientists, it might provide a limited but sophisticated method for studying the survival and disintegration of political systems.

Critical Evaluation

Before indicating our own reservations about the structural-functional approach we may notice an ideological criticism of structural-functionalism which seems to us unwarranted. The ideological criticism holds that structural-functionalism is implicitly conservative and biased against social change. Although it is true that in the works of Parsons and Levy analysis of the conditions for the stability and survival of a society appears at the very center of the structural-functional approach, it is also significant that most political scientists who have found a use for structural-functional analysis have been explicitly concerned with the study of political change, and political change of a profound sort. Almond, Apter, and Binder[14] have all drawn upon structural-functionalism for the light it could throw on the process of political modernization, and none of these scholars was led to a repudiation of modernization in the name of conservatism. Despite its emphasis upon the conditions for stability, structural-functionalism does not lead necessarily to a defense of the status quo or to a disregard for processes of change.

An argument against the logic of structural-functionism has been offered by Carl Hempel,[15] and we must differ somewhat from his interpretation. In our view the central limitations of structural-functionalism for political analysis are related mainly to its tautological character. Hempel has construed the logic of functional analysis in such a way that the main conclusions prove the existence of a given trait or a given

---

14. Leonard Binder, *Iran* (Berkeley and Los Angeles: U. of California Press, 1962).

15. Carl G. Hempel, "The Logic of Functional Analysis," in Llewellyn Gross (ed.), *Symposium on Sociological Theory* (New York: Harper, 1959).

activity. Actually, in political science explanation of a structure in functional analysis does not refer to predicting the existence of the structure, but rather refers with inappropriate terminology to the existence of a particular activity performed by the structure.[16] Although some functionalists may have argued more or less teleologically that structure X exists because it—and perhaps it alone—performs function F, to reject functionalism in this form is to knock down a straw man. The most interesting statements in functional analysis at the present time, it seems to us, are about structures performing functions, and Hempel treats these statements as suspect premises. What is explained—predicted—by functionalism ideally is the performance of functions and inferentially the maintenance of the system.

The basic form of the structural-functional argument can be presented in two syllogisms:

I. (1) If system s is to be maintained adequately under conditions c, then requisite functions $fl, f2 \ldots fn$ must be performed.
   (2) System s is being maintained adequately.
   —— Requisite functions $fl, f2 \ldots fn$ are being performed.

II. (1) If requisite functions $fl, f2 \ldots fn$ are being performed this will be accomplished by existing structures.
   (2) Requisite functions $f1, f2 \ldots fn$ are being performed.
   —— Requisite functions are being performed by existing structures.

Armed with this argument, the structural-functionalism sets out in search of the particular structures which perform the requisite functions. As Robert Holt points out in his article in this volume, "The major descriptive task is to indicate what structures contribute to the satisfaction of what functionality requisites."[17] In the argument itself, however, there is no guidance concerning where to look in this quest and no basis for asserting the extent to which any particular structure does in fact perform a specified function. Nor are there any grounds for supposing that one set and only one set of functions is requisite. In short, the analyst can define his "requisite functions" as he pleases, and he can be equally imaginative in locating which structures perform what functions. There is nothing illogical about his discrete observations which do no more than illustrate again and again that structures perform functions.

As a basis for analysis, the structural-functional argument leaves important problems unresolved. First of all, it is difficult to say when

16. Our reconstruction of the logic of structural-functional analysis is roughly equivalent to Hempel's scheme 5.1 (*ibid.*, p. 289) which he concedes does not have the severe limitations of scheme 4.1 (*ibid.*, p. 283).

17. Robert Holt, "A Proposed Structural-Functional Framework," p. 86 this volume.

a system is being "adequately maintained." We must have some objective criteria for determining when a system is adequately maintained. But these criteria have not been provided, and as a result the analyst cannot tell whether the system he is observing is flourishing or declining. Thus he can never be sure when the minor premise in syllogism I is fulfilled, and the same is true of the minor premise in syllogism II, since it actually depends on the former syllogism.

Another difficulty is the failure to elaborate and specify the nature of the interdependence of particular structures. Changes in any structure—which must involve changes in how a function is being performed —must have repercussions throughout the system, but the nature of these effects cannot be determined from the argument. What happens when a structure changes? With its emphasis on structural alternatives in different societies, functional political analysis gives few leads concerning what to expect within a single system over time. This difficulty is related to the failure to classify the conditions of the system. A scheme which indicates when a system is adequately maintained and when it is not would almost necessarily deal with structural continuity and change. Such a taxonomy of systems would introduce new demands for theoretical clarification. This might well entail a categorization of social systems based on the various conditions in which we find them, such as the various schemes suggested for categorization of stages of modernization.

Finally, when we attempt to spell out the functional requisites mentioned in the first major premise, upon which the entire argument rests, we encounter such amorphous concepts that the connection with reality becomes dangerously strained. From the diversity of requisite functions employed in political analysis to date—very nearly a unique set for each study—it is clear that a major weakness of political functional analysis will persist until precise criteria are established for the identification of functions and a theoretically sophisticated argument is made for a particular set of functions. Eventually a set of functions will be selected on the basis of performance in empirical research in comparison with other sets of functions, but for the time being the rationale for a given set of functions cannot be ignored. We need some discussion in political analysis for the rationale of particular functional requisites in order tentatively to arbitrate the differences between incongruent analytic frameworks.

Political scientists have been attracted to functionalism for a number of reasons. Eclectic functionalists find in functionalism an important additional dimension for their analysis, a dimension which brings the analysis into closer touch with the actual consequences of political activity. Empirical functionalists find in functionalism not simply an additional dimension for their analysis but a central organizing concept which serves to illuminate unexpected aspects of important though limited political phenomena. Structural-functionalists find in functionalism the promise of a scientific theory of politics, and this is certainly the most ambitious claim that has been made for functionalism by political scientists.

We have already indicated that the promise of structural-functionalism has not yet been fulfilled. But the claim of structural-functionalists must be taken seriously, and we will attempt to specify some of the qualifications which functionalism must meet in order to justify this claim.

A broad, systematic functional political theory must aspire to a set of statements from which refutable hypotheses may be deduced. The set of statements must have this capacity, although any given analyst may arrive at the hypotheses he tests by induction, deduction, retroduction, or inspiration. The tight, logical qualities of this set of statements, the "theory," may have been exaggerated in the epistemological analysis of scientific knowledge, but nevertheless the requirement persists for a summary of accumulated knowledge and a broad guide to "theoretically" critical investigations. Beyond this, useful theory must inspire imaginative hypothesizing—"retroduction" as some social theorists would now call it—and like much of political and social theory functionalism appears richly suggestive of a wide range of relationships. The crucial criterion then becomes the capacity of functionalism to generate imaginative hypotheses which can be tested empirically and refuted. The endless proliferation of "interesting and suggestive hypotheses" must be disciplined by empirical tests.

If it is true, as we have suggested, that structural-functionalists have usually operated on a level of analysis which did not permit empirical testing of interesting hypotheses, we must inquire whether or not there are elements in structural-functional analysis which make it unsuited for empirical hypothesizing. In order to generate refutable hypotheses, functional theory must have the capacity to operationalize its terms. "Integration" or "pattern maintenance," for example, must have precise definitions, definitions which relate them appropriately to social reality. Furthermore, the operational definitions of basic terms must retain the richness and complexity of the referents in the theoretical discussion. (One of the purposes served by Mitchell and Almond for political science is to generate a body of ideas with sophisticated insights and observations which will serve as a guide to the more precise defining and restating of political relationships.) To operationalize without retaining at least most of the meaning of the concepts would lead to unfair testing of the generated hypotheses, although tentatively we might have to accept some quite arbitrary definitions to get on with investigations.

Structural-functionalists have not taken the enormously difficult step of refining, operationalizing, and testing hypotheses. At the same time they have been well aware of the problems involved in doing so. As yet, however, no convincing solutions have been proposed. It remains for the critic to ask why the remedies have been lacking. Why has no scholar succeeded in presenting a structural-functional formulation which meets the requirements of empirical analysis? Although it may be both reckless and presumptuous to pose this question so soon after the introduction of functionalism into political science, nevertheless we can recognize at least three possible explanations for the failings of structural-functional analysis: first, limitations of the scholars; second, unavoidable stages in the development of any scientific theory; and third, deficiencies of functionalism itself.

Insofar as the deficiencies of functionalism derive from the limitations of present-day scholars, there is always the chance that tomorrow may see the appearance of a work of genius which will in fact solve the problems of functionalism and vindicate the hopes of its advocates. It is obvious, however, that structural-functionalism has attracted some of the ablest political scientists; it would be unreasonable to attribute the defects of the analysis to the limitations of these scholars.

A second explanation for the present inadequacies of functional analysis lies in the possible requirements of an historical pattern through which systems of ideas develop. It may be that the contributions being made now provide a necessary part of the foundation for subsequent achievements. In time the weaknesses of contemporary analysis may be remedied through subsequent theoretical developments. There is, of course, no way for us to be sure whether this will be the case, but the contemporary critic must hazard an evaluation before the verdict of history has been rendered.

This brings us then to a third explanation for the deficiencies of functional analysis: the defects of the intellectual framework itself. During any active period in the development of an intellectual discipline we find a variety of interesting formulations being proposed and explored as a basis for progress. From among these various proposals some will prove fruitful within the discipline and others will be remembered only as abortive bypaths. Although there is no certain test for determining at the time which formulations hold the greatest promise, one of the most significant characteristics of any proposed framework for social analysis is the nature of the phenomena which are selected as the focus for examination. No framework can encompass all of reality; it is, indeed, a major purpose of any framework to exclude as much of irrelevant reality as possible and to emphasize only selected features. With regard to structural-functionalism, we raise the question whether the emphasis upon "functions" as the focus of analysis is likely to prove fruitful.

The contention that an emphasis upon functions may prove abortive as the focus for analysis at the level of the political system as a whole is based on the difficulties encountered first in defining functional requisites operationally, and second in specifying the indefinite range of activities which fulfills these functions. In attempting to define functional requisites operationally, the scholar is likely either to impoverish his concepts with arbitrarily narrow definitions which deprive the analysis of its characteristic advantages or to complicate his concepts to the point that they are unresearchable. In attempting to specify in advance the range of activities which fulfills functions, the scholar is faced with the impossibility of anticipating which activities will prove to be relevant to his analysis, so that each study becomes an exploration of particular relationships of structures to functions. To study the few critical factors which determine the survival or disintegration of the political system is undeniably compelling, but it may be that the discovery of these factors is only the culmination of extensive, more sophisticated empirical investigations. To attempt to speculate what these factors may be involves one at this stage in highly abstracted formulations far removed from the realities of political activity which must, after all, comprise the material of political analysis. While these difficulties may not be in principle insurmountable, they bode ill for structural-functionalism.

Conclusion

The contributions of functionalism to political science have taken three main forms: eclectic functionalism, empirical functionalism, and structural-functionalism. In eclectic functionalism the concept of functions remains merely one of several equally significant categories; in empirical functionalism functions become the focus for the analysis of a limited range of phenomena; structural-functionalism aims to provide a scientific theory of the political system.

The difficulties encountered in applying structural-functionalism to the analysis of political systems—such as defining terms operationally and specifying which activities perform functions—suggest that this type of analysis is unlikely to achieve its objectives. Nonetheless even if structural-functionalism will not provide a scientific theory of politics, it has enriched the discipline of political science. First, there are several heuristic contributions to political analysis: (1) sensitizing analysis to the complexity of interrelationships among social and political phenomena; (2) drawing attention to a whole social system as a setting for political phenomena; (3) forcing consideration of functions served—particularly latent functions—by political actors or groups as something of an antidote for moralizing and "rational" analysis. In addition, structural-functionalists have employed a number of frameworks for political analysis which have provided some opportunity to assess the applicability of these frameworks to one's own interests.

In comparison to structural-functionalism, the promise of empirical functionalism is more modest. Yet, in departing from analysis of the system as a whole and in restricting the focus of attention to more manageable problems, empirical functionalism suggests opportunities for functional research which have not been fully explored in political science.

The functionalists have not as yet offered more than a loose analytic approach to the study of political systems. At this early stage of functional analysis in political science most functionalists are reinterpreting other studies through secondary analysis, so there is little to point to as the benefits of original research conducted with a functional scheme. Although it is not insignificant to restate the findings of others in a different way, this is not enough to qualify functionalism for a major role in political analysis.

5

A Proposed Structural-Functional Framework

ROBERT T. HOLT

IN HIS PRESIDENTIAL ADDRESS to the American Sociological Association in 1959, Kingsley Davis argued that there is no "special method or body of theory called functional analysis which can be distinguished from other methods or theories *within* sociology and social anthropology."[1] Although it would be difficult for any contributor to this special issue to accept Davis' central proposition, it does force one to be explicit about the ways in which the various "approaches" in the behavioral sciences can be distinguished.

Often the characteristic traits of a given approach are most clearly identified by the critic, and critics and commentators have had little difficulty in identifying functionalism as a special breed.[2] Hempel and Brown distinguish functionalism from other approaches by identifying a particular kind of "functional explanation." For Hempel, this is simply a particularly inconsequential type of nomological explanation,[3] but for Brown, a functional explanation is something different from an explanation on the basis of laws.[4]

In this article we take the position that structural-functional analysis[5] is a distinguishable approach primarily because of the selective aspects

1. Kingsley Davis, "The Myth of Functional Analysis as a Special Method in Sociology and Anthropology," *American Sociological Review,* Vol. 24 (December 1959), p. 757.

2. Carl G. Hempel, "The Logic of Functional Analysis," in Llewellyn Gross (ed.), *Symposium on Sociological Theory* (New York: Harper, 1959), pp. 271–310; Robert R. Brown, *Explanation in Social Science* (Chicago: Aldine, 1963), pp. 109–132; and Don Martindale, *The Nature and Types of Sociological Theory* (Boston: Houghton, 1960), pp. 441–524.

3. Hempel, *op. cit.,* pp. 282–284; 296.

4. Brown, *op. cit.,* pp. 110–123.

5. Following Levy, we use the term structural-functional to refer to the kind of framework presented in this paper. The term functionalism will be used as a shorthand substitute in some places.

of social reality that it seeks to describe, explain, and predict. It describes social reality largely in terms of structures, processes, mechanisms, and functions, and these four concepts are of particular importance in the laws and theories that are developed. There is no reason to develop some unique type of explanation to accommodate a functional analysis, nor is there any reason why nomological explanations whose basic propositions take a functional form should be inherently weaker than any other kind of nomological explanation in the behavioral sciences.

It is not merely the use of the terms *structure* and *function* in descriptions of social reality that differentiates functionalism from other approaches, but the special way in which these terms are employed. The unique characteristics of functionalist description may be illustrated by looking at what is one of the most frequently cited examples of a functional analysis, namely, Robert Merton's treatment of the functions of the political machine in a large city. The machine "fulfills the important social *function of humanizing and personalizing all manner of assistance* to those in need."[6] The machine "serves the function of providing those political privileges [to business] which entail immediate economic gains."[7] The machine fulfills the function of "providing alternative channels of social mobility for those otherwise excluded from the more conventional avenues for personal 'advancement.' "[8] One could describe the same concrete behavior which Merton observes by reporting, for example, the actual giving of a food basket, the actual providing of legal advice, the actual granting of a political scholarship. On a more analytical level, one could focus on the attitudes of the various participants in the crucial relationships and present descriptive statements in which attitudes are correlated with role, status, and certain kinds of behavior. But this would not be a functionalist analysis. It is the particular way that Merton describes reality in terms of structures and the "needs" (functions) of the system[9] and the manner in which these concepts are used to explain the phenomenon of the political machine that mark his as a functionalist description.

There are, however, a number of pitfalls into which the functionalist can fall which make this description devoid of empirical content and his explanations trivial. If the structural-functional framework is to provide the basis for useful description, explanation, and prediction,

6. Robert K. Merton, "Manifest and Latent Functions," *Social Theory and Social Structure* (New York: Free Press, 1957), p. 75.

7. *Ibid.*, p. 75.

8. *Ibid.*, p. 76.

9. Although Merton's is a typical structural-functional description, we have considerable objection to treating functions as essentially identical to needs of subgroups in the system rather than as system requirements.

care must be taken to define crucial concepts and to establish the limits of applicability of the approach.

System, Structure, Function

It is typical for those who have made important contributions to functionalism to ·define function more or less explicitly as an *effect*. Merton speaks of functions as "observed consequences";[10] Radcliffe-Brown refers to "functions of any recurrent activity";[11] Levy, more explicit than most, defines function as "a condition, or state of affairs, resultant from the operation of a structure through time."[12] Hempel points out with devastating simplicity, however, that the term *function* cannot be used synonymously with the term *effect*. He presents the following statement for consideration: "The heartbeat has the function of producing heart sounds; for the heartbeat has that effect."[13] No functionalist would, of course, accept this proposition. Function is not a synonym for effect; it is a subtype of effect. Functions are *system relevant* effects of structures. The term has meaning, therefore, only if the terms *structure* and *system relevant* are explicitly defined and if the system under study is explicitly identified.

The system with which the functional analysis proposed in this paper is concerned is the *social system at the societal level*. This rather cumbersome phrase is used in order to differentiate the approach presented here from a more typical formulation. To explain its use certain other concepts must be introduced. A society—a type of organization—is a system of action that is: (1) composed of a plurality of interacting individuals who are primarily oriented to this system and who are recruited primarily from the sexual reproduction of the individuals, (2) is theoretically self-sufficient for the actions of the plurality, and (3) is capable of existing longer than the life span of the individuals.[14] From any society there can be abstracted two societal-wide systems—a social system and a cultural system. The social system is the system of interdependent roles and corporate structures of the society and the cultural system is the pattern of interrelated beliefs and values. In this conceptualization, for reasons to be discussed later, it is important to keep the social system and the cultural system logically independent of one another. Therefore, the basic units of each must be defined

10. Merton, *op. cit.*, p. 51.
11. A. R. Radcliffe-Brown, *Structure and Function in Primitive Society* (New York: Free Press, 1952), p. 180.
12. Marion J. Levy, Jr., *The Structure of Society* (Princeton: Princeton U. P., 1950), p. 56.
13. Hempel, *op. cit.*, p. 279.
14. This definition is adopted from Levy, *op. cit.*, pp. 112–113.

independently. Although all of the details of the definition are not relevant here, it should be pointed out that the role is defined solely in terms of actual behavior; there is no "belief-value" component and thus by definition there is no "role expectation" aspect of a role. In other words, we use the term role to refer to what is commonly identified as "real role" as opposed to "ideal role." Beliefs and values, by contrast, are defined independently of the behavior that is included in the definition of role.

A structure is a pattern of interrelated roles, and a corporate structure is a structure that can be identified in terms of its membership and which has a central decision-making apparatus that enables it to act purposively as a collective. It is, along with the role, the basic unit of the social system.

Some of the reasons for this unique formulation will be discussed below. At this point we simply want to identify the social system at the societal level—not a society, which is *not* a social system by these definitions—as the system with which we shall be concerned and move on to the problem of how one can establish the system relevance of an effect.

There is a major problem of differentiating between the system relevant and the nonrelevant effects of a structure. We propose to make this distinction by equating *system relevance* with *system requiredness.* For any social system there is a set of *functional requisites*[15]—operational conditions that must be satisfied if the system is to continue to exist. These functional requisites consist of analytically related aspects of the activities of corporate structure and roles which are not included in the definition of the system. A distinction is being made here between an *activity* as the effect of a corporate structure or a role, and a *function* as the effect of a corporate structure or a role. The distinction can best be made clear by the use of an illustration: some of the effects of a government may be to arrest, try, convict, and execute an individual who commits homicide. These are activities of government—not functions— because their system relevance has not been established and, given the restricted definition of system relevance used in this paper, probably could not be established.

It is possible, however, for one to postulate a set of functional requisites and to view various activities as contributing to the satisfaction of one—or more—of these requisites. For example, if the maintenance of the basic values of the society—pattern maintenance—is postulated as a functional requisite, and if a theory of social control is developed in which capital punishment for the violation of certain basic norms is one of the techniques aiding in the control of deviant behavior, then

15. For the best discussion of functional requisites and the way in which they are developed, see *ibid.*, pp. 34–55.

the activity of a government in executing the individual who commits homicide can be treated as the government making a contribution to the satisfaction of the function of pattern maintenance.

An activity is not distinguishable from a function on the basis of the concrete behavior involved, but only in relationship to a conceptual framework and the chain of referents which that framework provides. The activities of any role or corporate structure are the raw data of a functional analysis. The major descriptive task is to indicate what structures contribute to the satisfaction of what functional requisites. In order to provide this description, it is necessary to do two things: (1) to specify the system under consideration, and (2) to postulate a set of functional requisites for that system. It is essential to specify the system under consideration, because an activity that may contribute to the satisfaction of a functional requisite at one system level may be nonfunctional at another system level. It is necessary to postulate a set of functional requisites, because in our formulation system relevance can be established most efficaciously in terms of system requiredness. There are, however, a number of characteristics of the kind of structural-functional framework presented here that should be discussed before formulating the functional requisites.

1. The definition of structure and function presented above involves a differentiation similar to that made by some psychologists between stimulus variables and response variables. We conceive of structures as being independent variables and functions as being dependent variables.[16] The purpose of this distinction is not to provide a basis for the formulation of empirical generalizations which link structures and functions and which have explanatory import. Its purpose, rather, is to create a framework for description. A structural-functional description of a system, then, is a description of a certain order of determinate relationships.

2. The classification of structures as independent variables and of functions as dependent variables should, in the context of stimulus and response, raise some red flags. It gives to structural-functional analysis the flavor of the $S \rightarrow R$ psychology of the 1920's, which proved to be simplistic and woefully inadequate. Intervening variables had to be introduced to provide for those factors that mediate between stimulus and response and which account for some of the variation in the dependent variable. In our formulation of a structural-functional framework, social processes and social mechanisms are intervening variables. Any complete description of a social system would include, therefore, a treatment of the social structures, of the various functions of these structures, and of the social processes and mechanisms that must be in operation if struc-

tures are to satisfy certain functions. Space limitations make it impossible to present any systematic theoretical treatment of the place of mechanisms and processes. It may be useful, however, to provide some illustrations.

There is a biological analogy that is instructive in indicating the way in which processes and mechanisms may be incorporated into a functional analysis of a social system. Goodman, for example, points out that the configuration—structure—of a globular protein molecule is "responsible for the primary functional activity of a protein, for example an enzymatic, hormonal or antibody [functional] activity."[17] For purposes of elucidation, let us assume that the structure of a specific globular protein gives it a hormonal function and that to contribute to the satisfaction of this function it must enter into certain organs. There is a membrane barrier through which the protein must pass, and others through which it must not pass. A process of osmosis, with which certain mechanisms are associated—or some process of active transport—is involved. The example of the government contributing to the satisfaction of the pattern maintenance functional requisite can be treated in analogous terms. There is a social control process involved in the satisfaction of the pattern maintenance requisite. The relevant mechanisms are the social sanctions. When a government arrests, tries, convicts, and punishes a person who has violated the basic norms of the society, it activates the legal sanction, which in turn is involved in the social control process. In the social system of a society of another type a different structure—for example, a kinship structure—may contribute to the satisfaction of the pattern maintenance requisite by activating the retaliation-compensation sanction.

Variation in the dependent variable—function—may be the result of variation in either the structure—independent variable—or in the intervening variable—process or mechanism. To give an extreme example, a globular protein molecule may fail to make its contribution to a hormonic function either because of a change in the structure of the molecule or because of a failure of a mechanism necessary to the process that enables the protein to pass through certain membranes if it is to operate.

3. The phenomenon of structural alternatives—that different structures in different types of systems may contribute to the satisfaction of the same functional requisites—is fundamental to this whole framework. It is this phenomenon that is of explanatory and predictive interest. The problem is to explain why a certain structure rather than another contributes to the satisfaction of a given requisite or requisites in a given social system at a given time and to predict what specific structure or

17. Morris Goodman, "Man's Place in the Phylogeny of the Primates as Reflected in Serum Proteins," in Sherwood L. Washburn (ed.), *Classification and Human Evolution* (Chicago: Aldine Press, 1963), p. 206.

structures will contribute to the satisfaction of a given function at some specific time. It is interesting to note that, according to Hempel, an explanation of this phenomenon would, in contrast to other functional explanations, be both meaningful and significant. His objection to this approach is on empirical, not on logical, grounds.

This course is hardly promising, for in most, if not all, concrete cases it would be impossible to specify with any precision the range of alternative behavior patterns, institutions, customs, or the like that would suffice to meet a given functional prerequisite or need. And even if that range could be characterized, there is no satisfactory method in sight for dividing it into some finite number of cases and assigning a probability to each of these.[18]

Part of the reason for his pessimism derives from the wide range of items—behavior patterns, institutions, customs, and the like—which may be substitutes for one another. This is, of course, a proper inference from all functional formulations except Levy's. Merton, for example, imputes functions to "social roles, institutional patterns, social processes, cultural pattern, culturally patterned emotions, social norms, group organization, social structure, devices for social control, etc."[19] Part of the empirical difficulty that Hempel anticipates is avoided in our conceptualization by the fact that social structures alone satisfy functions and hence only social structures are substitutes for social structures.

An analysis of structural alternatives that would be of explanatory and predictive importance would be based on the fundamental proposition that the state of the system at any time t_1 is determined by its state at some other time t_0 and by all the events which occur on the boundary during the time interval t_0-t_1 The state of the system is described in terms of the determinate sequence of structure—process and mechanism—function. Changes in the system occur as responses to changes in the environment on the boundary of the system, but the state of the system places limits upon the kind of responses which can be made. If the kind of analysis suggested by this formulation is to be fruitful, it is necessary to be precise about the dimensions of the environment in which a social system operates and about the kinds of events that occur on the boundary of the system. These problems, however, can be treated more easily after a discussion of the functional requisites of any social system at the societal level.

Functional Requisites

Fundamental to this whole approach is the postulation of the functional requisites of the system under consideration, because, by defini-

---

18. Hempel, *op. cit.*, p. 286.
19. Merton, *op. cit.*, p. 50.

tion, there are no functions that are not functional requisites. In this work we have adopted with fundamental modifications the conceptualization developed by Parsons. He and his associates have postulated that any social system has four functional requisites: (1) pattern maintenance and tension management, (2) goal attainment, (3) adaptation, and (4) integration.[20]

Pattern Maintenance

Every social system exists in an environment that has a non-human component, a cultural component, and a social component. The cultural environment is the cultural system at the societal level. This cultural (belief-value) system specifies the goals both for the social system as a whole and for the roles and corporate structures within it, as well as the acceptable means for attaining goals. One of the functional requisites of the social system is the maintenance of conformity to the prescriptions of the cultural system. Three major processes are involved in the pattern maintenance functional requisite. First, major values must be passed on from one generation to the next. This might be called an enculturation process. Second, a social control process is concerned with the application of sanctions for violations of the prescriptions of the value system. Third, a tension management process attempts to prevent the development of situations that increase the probability that large numbers of actors will violate basic norms. Prolonged mass unemployment and galloping inflation in a modern industrial society are examples of these kinds of situations.

Goal Attainment

The cultural system specifies a set of goals for the social system as a whole. These goals are sets of desired relationships between the system and its environment. As the environment is continually changing—at least potentially—goals are not terminal states of being that can be finally achieved; goal attainment involves a cluster of ongoing activities. The environment that is relevant for goal attainment is complex, including an aspect of the cultural system and the nonhuman environment, and other societies.

One of the most important goals of the social system at the societal level is the preservation of the society itself. Thus, the *defense of the realm* involves a set of activities that contribute to the satisfaction of

---

20. Talcott Parsons and Neil Smelser, *Economy and Society* (New York: Free Press, 1956), pp. 16–19.

the goal-attainment functional requisite. The relevant environment in this case consists of other societies. The achievement of societal goals also often involves the preservation of certain relationships with important deities. Many activities that can be classified as religious, such as ritual observances, contribute to the meeting of the goal-attainment requisite. The relevant environment in this case is the cultural system.

In order to maintain desired relationships with the environment it is necessary to have resources and thus the most significant process related to goal attainment is the process of mobilizing societal resources for a societal effort.

Adaptation

Resources must be mobilized before they can be used in support of system goals. If they are to be mobilized, they must be available. The adaptive functional requisite involves the activities that provide these mobilizable resources. It is concerned with the relationships between the social system and its nonhuman environment—relationships that lead to the supplying of disposable resources which can be used as means to realize the goals of the system as a whole or the goals of any of its subunits.

The processes that are relevant to the satisfaction of the adaptive functional requisite are those typically associated with economics—processes of production, resource allocation, and resource management.

Integration

All of the activities that are necessary if the functional requisites are to be satisfied cannot be carried on by each individual in the society.[21] Even in the most simple of human societies there must be some differences in the roles that various individuals occupy. Since some differentiated roles are interdependent, provision must be made for their integration. Hence, one of the functional requisites of the social system is to provide for the integration of the interdependent units—roles and structures—in the social system.

Of the several processes that are relevant to the integrative functional requisite, three will be discussed briefly. The activities that are necessary for the achievement of an acceptable degree of integration are partially specified by norms, and the integration problem is partially

---

21. This is tantamount to holding that role differentiation is an analytical structural requisite of any social system at the societal level. Space limitations prevent a presentation of the role of analytical structures in this framework.

solved by maintaining conformity to these norms. Thus, the integration functional requisite involves an aspect of the social-control process.[22] But all of the behavior that is required if basic units are to be sufficiently integrated cannot be achieved simply by manipulating the mechanism of social control successfully. In every social system there is some behavior that is not prohibited by norms but is nevertheless malintegrative. Furthermore, there is some behavior that is integrative even though it is in violation of norms.

If the activities of various roles and corporate structures are to be properly integrated, information concerning such matters as reciprocal role expectations and demands must be communicated to the role occupants. Thus a communication process is involved in the satisfaction of the integration requisite. Since the interests of the various role occupants are likely to be divergent to some degree, however, a coercive process—but one that, by definition, does not involve the use of legitimate violence—is also involved.

The paradigm in Figure 5.1 is an aid to understanding this particular statement of functional requisites. It draws attention to the fact that three of the four requisites are specifically concerned with interaction between the social system and its complex environment. The adaptive requisite is concerned with the relations between the social system and its nonhuman environment; the pattern maintenance requisite involves relationships with the cultural environment—relevant aspects of the cultural system; the goal attainment requisite is concerned with relations with specific aspects of these two environments plus relations with other societies. The integration requisite is primarily concerned with the internal problem of coordination of differentiated but interdependent roles.

This conceptualization specifically identifies the different environments in which the social system operates, and indicates the functional requisite that is primarily concerned with changes occurring in one or another of the environments. Some examples will be given below to indicate the way in which the social system may adjust to changes in the environment and the way in which the state of the system before the change in the environment limits the adjustments that can be made. But before we turn to the problem of adjustment, another line of projected conceptual development should be introduced.

If this kind of conceptual framework is to be useful, particularly for the analysis of social change, it is necessary to develop a taxonomy of social systems. The crucial criterion of classification is the pattern of

22. The distinction between the social control process relevant to pattern maintenance and that relevant to integration follows Durkheim's distinction between repressive sanctions and restitutive sanctions. See Emile Durkheim, *Division of Labor in Society,* tr. George Simpson (New York: Macmillan, 1933), p. 69.

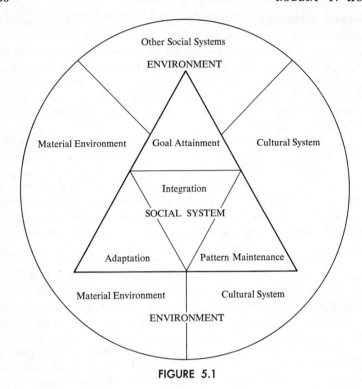

FIGURE 5.1

Note (1) the complex environment, components of which relate to three of the four functional requisites, and (2) the central position of the integrative requisite. Compare with Talcott Parsons and Neil J. Smelser, *Economy and Society* (New York: Free Press, 1956), p. 19.

structures that contribute to the satisfaction of a given requisite. This pattern is called the *social structuring* of the system. Social systems in which there are significant differences in the corporate structures and roles that contribute to the satisfaction of a given requisite will be classified as different major types. Two points should be made concerning this proposed taxonomy.

1. It should be clear that the phenomenon of structural alternatives is basically related to this proposed classification. The major types are differentiated by the fact that different structures contribute to the satisfaction of a given requisite or requisites. In Hempel's critique of functional analysis, one of the examples used in the discussion of structural alternatives is that of the circulatory functions of a dog's heart.[23] This is not a particularly useful analogue for the conceptualization proposed in this paper. A dog without a heart is a dead dog, and though it might be

23. Hempel, *op. cit.*, p. 287.

interesting to study a dead dog—for example, its decomposition and putrification—it is not studied as a living organism—that class of systems to which biological functionalism is relevant. The insightful analogy is suggested by the fact that dogs have hearts and hydras do not, yet in each case the functional requisite of circulation is satisfied.

2. Each of the major types in the proposed taxonomy would be associated with certain kinds of environment. Characteristics of the environment, however, would not be included in the definition of the type, but would be left open for empirical investigation. Secondary subtypes would be developed on the basis of less significant differences in social structuring, while tertiary subtypes would include different social structurings that exist in similar environments.

A hypothesis of self-regulation is directly related to this taxonomy. Hempel points out how important such a hypothesis is if a functional analysis is to have any empirical meaning, and he indicates the form which an acceptable hypothesis of self-regulation would take:

Such a hypothesis would be to the effect that within a specified range C of circumstances, a given system s (or: any system of a certain kind S, of which s is an instance) is self-regulating relative to a specified range R of states; i.e., after a disturbance which moves s into a state outside R, but which does not shift the internal and external circumstances of s out of the specified range C, the system s will return to a state in R.[24]

One order of subtype of the taxonomy—either secondary or tertiary —should be established in such a way that the range of environmental variation associated with the subtype would be the same as the range within which a given social system is self-regulating, that is, a social system confronted with changes within these limits would respond— for example, by attempting to modify the environment—so that the social system could return to its initial state. If there were changes in the environment beyond this range, the social system would either cease to exist—the society would disappear—or the social system would evolve into a new type. Hempel does not provide for a treatment of the latter alternative. His biological analogy is to a single organism: he uses the example of the regenerative properties of the hydra. A more appropriate analogy would be to the "accommodating" characteristics of the species.

When a species—more technically, an interbreeding population—is confronted with a change in the environment, there are three alternatives. If the change is minor, a slight change in some minor characteristic might suffice. For example, if the climate becomes cooler, individual bears with heavier fur might have an increased survival and reproductive rate contributing to an interbreeding population with more fur. If the change in the environment is major, the species might

24. *Ibid.*, pp. 296–297.

either fail to survive or evolve through the Sewall Wright effect—genetic drift—or through the selective survival of mutants into a new species.[25] All of these alternatives have a social parallel. The last alternative is in many ways the most interesting, and this is the one which is not revealed by the biological analogy to the individual organism.

Brief reference to some social parallels might be helpful. It would seem reasonable to treat the collapse and disappearance of Tasmanian society as a case in which the requisites of the social system were not satisfied when there was a radical change in the environment, and to view this as analogous to the disappearance of the passenger pigeon. Changes in the material environment, along with the hunting expeditions of the white hunter, eradicated both. The social structure of the Tasmanian social system made impossible the kind of changes that would have been necessary to cope with the change in the environment. But the reasons for the disappearance of Tasmanian society are so obvious that it would seem a bit pedantic to bring in the entire apparatus of this functional approach to explain it. In any event, this is certainly the uninteresting case.

The interesting case is that of, for example, Tokugawa, Japan, or *ancien France*.[26] The social system of these societies failed to satisfy the functional requisite in a rapidly changing environment. These societies "disappeared," but not in the same way as the Tasmanian society did. They evolved through "developmental accommodation" into something else. The biological analogy would be with a species which was not eradicated leaving no trace, but with one which evolved into another species.

In addition, therefore, to a hypothesis of self-regulation, a hypothesis of "developmental accommodation" must be developed. This hypothesis would apply to the major or secondary subtypes in the proposed taxonomy and would indicate the range and kind of environmental changes to which a social system of a given type would accommodate by developing a new type of social structuring. A typical way in which changes in the environment are met is by increased role specialization in regard to the satisfaction of the requisite most directly affected. For example, an increase in the hostile contacts with other societies might well lead to greater specialization of roles relating to the military and to tax collecting.

Limits would be placed on the range of environmental changes to

25. Theodosius Dobzhansky, *Evolution, Genetics, and Man* (New York: Wiley, 1963), pp. 41–133.

26. For a treatment of Tokugawa, Japan, and *ancien France*, partially from a structural functional point of view, see Robert T. Holt and John E. Turner, *The Political Basis of Economic Development* (Princeton: Van Nostrand, 1966). In this work the authors treat the relationships between politics and economic growth within the general framework of a requisite analysis.

which the system could accommodate itself by the degree to which (1) existing structures primarily responsible for satisfying the requisites related to the aspect of the environment that was changing inhibited increased differentiation and specialization; and (2) the structuring related to the satisfactions of the integrative requisite inhibited modifications that would enable the system to cope with increased differentiations. Again, a biological analogy is instructive. Goodman states:

As a result of the superior metabolic efficiency of its members, the advanced species is supplanting competitors and colonizing the largest range of exogenous habitats. Hence the new conditions of the external environment select for new gene mutations and genetic heterozygosity since only this state can give the species a variety of new "outward-directed" adaptations. However such a state tends to disorganize the established network of highly specific protein interactions. Indeed the probability of interference with physiological processes by any mutated protein specificity is in direct proportion to the number of "inward-directed" molecular adaptations of an organism. Thus two opposing selective pressures (one favoring genetic heterozygosity, the other favoring genetic homozygosity) operate with special force on the anagenetically advancing species.[27]

The "outward-directed" adaptations are roughly comparable to the structural changes that occur in regard to pattern maintenance, goal attainment, and adaptation, where pressure is generated for greater role differentiation, while "inward-directed" adaptations are roughly comparable to the changes in integration where the pressure is to limit increased differentiation.

An Example of a Structural-Functional Analysis

The discussion thus far has been somewhat abstract, and it may be useful, in the interests of clarity, to offer a few examples of how functional formulations presented in this paper might be applied. For the past few years the author has been working on a study of the determinants of the functions of government in primitive societies.[28] In that study government has been defined in a relatively restricted manner. All of the technicalities of the definition are not relevant here; suffice it to say that government has been defined generally as a corporate structure that has access to legitimate violence in enforcing its decisions on roles outside as well as inside the corporate structure itself. By this definition some primitive societies, for example, the Nuer and the Great

27. Goodman, *op. cit.*, p. 210.
28. This work, entitled *The Functions of Government in Primitive Societies*, will be forthcoming.

Basin Shoshone, have no government—kinship structures and religious roles are structural alternatives—while in other primitive societies, for example, Dahomey or Hausa, there is a government that makes a contribution to the satisfaction of all four functional requisites. A number of hypotheses have been developed for testing, and several of them will be presented here. We shall not attempt to provide tests of the hypotheses here. Although these hypotheses will be illustrated by a few examples, the major purpose of including them is to provide a substantive context for a discussion of some of the concepts introduced above.

1. *The contributions of government to the pattern maintenance functional requisite will increase as dissensus—lack of agreement on values—in the cultural system increases.*

Degrees of consensus and dissensus are structural characteristics of the cultural system. Changes in this structure are changes in the environment of the social system which are relevant to the pattern maintenance functional requisite. A high degree of consensus, we would argue, is a necessary but not sufficient condition for the structural alternatives to government to satisfy the pattern maintenance functional requisite. Hoebel describes very clearly a society where these alternatives are operating. He says of the Eskimo:

A people more tabu-ridden would be difficult to find. The multitude of tabus are mostly directed to spirits of animals or their controlling deities in order to guard against conduct offensive or disrespectful to them. So comprehensive is the tabu system that the paucity of legal rules in Eskimo culture is in large part caused by the encompassing supernatural sanctions which dominate Eskimo social and economic life. Magic and religion rather than law direct most of their actions.[29]

The literature in anthropology presents a number of cases which suggest that an increase in the activities of government that contribute to the satisfaction of the pattern maintenance functional requisite is apparently related to an increasing dissensus.

Gutmann, for example, observed an interesting development among the Chagga. It had been customary in Chagga society for young girls to marry shortly after their initiation. Occasionally, a young girl would try to postpone her marriage in order to retain the greater freedom of a maiden for a longer time. At one time, however, Gutmann noticed the members of a whole age set—*Maedchenaltersklasse*—who refused to join their betrothed. And theirs was not a quiet refusal; they roamed through village streets singing songs, making fun of marital life, and openly defying the authority of the elders. This was not simply an adolescent prank; single girls in the past who had unreasonably delayed marriage had been sold into slavery. However, the revolt of a whole

29. E. Adamson Hoebel, *The Law of Primitive Man* (Cambridge: Harvard U. P., 1954), p. 70.

age-set was something new, and probably represented a developing lack of consensus. The result is consistent with our hypothesis. The chiefs went to the British Administration and secured approval for a law which provided that under certain circumstances young girls would be compelled by law to marry.[20] This kind of regulation of marriage was a new activity of government. A norm previously supported in small groups came to be supported by government.

Nadel also has some interesting and relevant observations about changes among the Nupe after the Fulani conquest. The Fulani conquest introduced elements of a new value system into Nupe society. We can assume that the value system was less integrated after the conquest than before. Nadel reports:

I was told in Mokwa that during the Fulani regime fathers of headstrong sons sometimes appealed to their feudal lord, and that the latter would lend his authority to the more severe forms of domestic punishment (i.e., flogging). This official cognizance of what is essentially a "family affair" clearly represents an incipient stage of state jurisdiction. It is only one step from this appeal for moral support of the official organ of the state to a full acceptance of political jurisdiction in the sphere of kinship offences or litigations, for example, litigation over inheritance or divorce, which has become reality today.[31]

This statement is a clear report of the expansion of the functions of government—problems that formerly were "family" or "kinship" affairs become subject to government jurisdiction. And this was not because the conqueror had forced the adoption of a particular structure, but because in the presence of conflicting moral codes there were real pressures from the subject people which led to the expansion of the pattern maintenance function of government.

These examples facilitate the statement of the basic problem in a manner that introduces the more general theoretical and methodological problems we are interested in. The process that is involved in these illustrations of change in the structures contributing to the satisfaction of the pattern maintenance functional requisite is the social control process and the mechanisms are the social sanctions. We identify four major sanctions of the social control process that can operate on a macrosocial level: retaliation compensation, withdrawal of reciprocity, supernatural sanctions, and legal sanctions.[32] A sanction is a legal sanction if its application is decreed by an agent of government. The other sanctions are not defined in terms of any given social structure. Studies have suggested, however, that relatively specific kinds of social struc-

---

30. Bruno Gutmann, *Das Recht der Dschagga* (Munich: Beck, 1926), pp. 70–72.
31. S. F. Nadel, *A Black Byzantium* (New York: Oxford U. P., 1942), p. 168.
32. The definition and analysis of these four sanctions are contained in Holt, *The Functions of Government in Primitive Societies*, Chapt. 4 (forthcoming).

tures are necessary if they are to be effectively employed. In addition to these sanctions that operate on a macrolevel, we recognize that the social control process in small groups may make a major contribution to the maintenance of conformity to societal values, but we argue that any difference among societies in the amount of the pattern maintenance requisite handled by small groups is explainable in terms of the macrostructure of the social system, or of its environment, or both. The rationale behind the hypothesis that the functions of government will increase as dissensus increases is twofold: (1) When there is lack of agreement on basic values, the processes of social control operating on a macrolevel will make less contribution to pattern maintenance at the societal level. Thus greater reliance must be placed on the mechanisms operating at a macrolevel. (2) A necessary—but not sufficient—condition for the successful operation of retaliation compensation, withdrawal of reciprocity, and supernatural sanctions is a high degree of consensus. In the absence of a high degree of consensus, legal sanctions—whose employment by definition involves function of government—will replace nonlegal sanctions. In other words, certain mechanisms become ineffective as the environment assumes a certain characteristic, and another mechanism of the same general type but requiring a different social structure must be activated.

This hypothesis has been presented in its most crude form. It must be refined, keeping two factors in mind. (1) There is a certain minimal level of consensus that is required by any society. If the increase in dissensus exceeds this limit, the society will cease to function. (2) Changes in the contribution of government to the satisfaction of the pattern maintenance requisite are partially dependent upon the state of the system at the time of the change in the environment. The most restrictive limits would be imposed by the existing state of a system in which there is no government and in which a government must develop if the pattern maintenance functions of government are to increase. Certain types of social structuring make the development of government very difficult.

In its most refined form, the hypothesis must include a statement of the range of variation of dissensus within which given types of systems are self-regulating—and would respond to changes within this range by attempting to return the environment to its original state—and a statement of the range of variation of dissensus within which given types of systems can accommodate developmentally. For changes between the maximum range of self-regulation and the maximum range of developmental accommodations, increasing dissensus would be met by an increasing pattern maintenance function of government.

2. *As there occurs an increase in the use of inanimate sources of*

energy and in the use of tools, there will be an increase in the contributions of the government to the integrative functional requisite.

For reasons which we have no space to discuss here, an increase in the use of inanimate energy sources and in the use of tools—a change in the nonhuman environment—probably will lead to increased differentiation and specialization in those structures involved in the satisfaction of the adaptive requisite. Thus new integrative problems are created.

We have already pointed out that there are three major processes involved in the integrative functional requisite—a social control process to support norms that relate interdependent roles, an information process by which knowledge of reciprocal needs is communicated, and a coercive process. We conceive of four different integrating mechanisms that may be involved: a market mechanism, a reciprocal mechanism, a clientage mechanism, and an organizational mechanism.[33] The argument we advance in support of this hypothesis is briefly as follows: the clientage mechanism cannot operate effectively if there is much division of labor. The market mechanism and the organization mechanism can handle the integrative problems that accompany a great division of labor, but only with the support of government. Only the reciprocal mechanism can handle a sizable division of labor—for a primitive society —without any government involvement. Let us look briefly at the case of the market mechanism and the reciprocal mechanism.

The argument that the market mechanism cannot operate effectively in the absence of government is well known. The forces that bind the various roles linked by contract are not only those created by the complementarity of interests of the contracting parties. The laws, practices, and customs that govern various aspects of the contractual relationship but which are not a part of the terms of contract are necessary if the market is to operate effectively. These laws, customs, and practices are what Durkheim regarded as the most significant binding force among roles that are integrated through a market mechanism. We go one step farther, and argue that a body of laws—norms that can be enforced by a government—is necessary if the market is to have a significant integrating role. In other words, the norms that govern contracts cannot be effectively enforced by nonlegal sanctions—retaliation compensation, withdrawal of reciprocity, or supernatural sanctions. If the market is to operate, there must be a government to deal with breaches of contract and violation of the other norms that make up the "noncontractual elements of contract."

The case of the reciprocal mechanism is not so well known. A recip-

33. Compare with Karl Polanyi, Conrad Arensberg, and Harry W. Pearson (eds.), *Trade and Market in the Early Empires* (New York: Free Press, 1957), pp. 250–254.

rocal mechanism exists when all full-time occupational roles of a given kind are incorporated into a given corporate structure. Exchange between interdependent specialized roles takes place on the basis of a "contract in perpetuity" between the corporate structures—a contract that specifies the goods and services to be exchanged, creates monopolistic rights for each group of specialists, and specifies the terms of trade. There is no price making market, because prices are set in perpetuity. Under specific conditions the reciprocal mechanism can accommodate a high degree of division of labor—for a primitive society—with no government enforcement of the norms governing exchange. Withdrawal of reciprocity can be an effective sanction.

The society in the Nilgiri Hills in South India before 1900 is an excellent example.[34] There were specialists in dairy farming, grain farming, and blacksmithing and handicrafts. Specialists of each of these kinds were dependent on specialists of each of the other kinds. Each type of specialist was incorporated into a corporate structure, and exchange between the specialists was treated for some purposes as exchange between the corporate groups. If one of the norms of exchange was violated—for example, if a grain farmer refused to supply the traditional amount of grain to the blacksmith who supplied him with tools —no government or court of law would step in, because there was none. All of the blacksmiths would refuse to supply tools to all of the grain farmers. The reciprocal exchanges of goods were supported by the exchange of ritual services. For example, the artisan group provided a necessary part of the funeral ceremony for the grain farmers. All of these ritual services would also be withheld until the situation which gave rise to the boycott had been rectified. Under these very special conditions, withdrawal of reciprocity can be an effective alternative to legal sanctions.

The second hypothesis would have to be refined in the same way as was suggested for the first one. The ranges over which the hypotheses of self-regulation and developmental accommodation operate would have to be established. In addition there would have to be a specification of the kind of structuring that would permit the development of the structures necessary for the reciprocal mechanism as an alternative to the market or organizational mechanism as a response to an increasing division of labor.

A third hypothesis—that the contributions of government to the satisfaction of the goal-attainment requisite will increase as the content with other societies increases—will simply be mentioned. Examples of how increases in hostile relations increase the functions of government

---

34. See David Mandelbaum, "The Kotas in Their Social Setting," *Introduction to the Civilization of India,* ed. by Maureen Patterson and Ronald Inden (Chicago: U. of Chicago Press, 1956), pp. 1–45.

are well known in the literature since the time of Gumplowitz and Oppenheim. This hypothesis, however, can be used to suggest a case where the state of the system at the time of the change in the environment placed a limit on the accommodation that could have been made. When the Nuer began moving into the territory occupied by the Dinka, the hostile contacts between the Dinka and another society increased. Our hypothesis would predict that this would lead to an increase in the goal-attainment functions of government which, for the Dinka, would involve the establishment of government. This has not happened nor has there been the kind of modification in kinship and territorial structures which other hypotheses would predict.[35] The existing social structuring of the Dinka social system blocked the development of these new social structures that one would predict would emerge as a result of changes in the environment, because their development would undercut other structures that make crucial contributions to the satisfaction of other requisites. The inability to accommodate could, if some outside factor does not intervene, lead to the destruction of the Dinka.[36]

Concluding Comments

One major objection that may be leveled at the conceptualizations presented in this paper concerns the concept of corporate structures and the activities that are attributed to them. It may appear that we are attributing supraindividual characteristics to these collective entities. Some might see in the explicit biological analogue which has been employed an attempt to reintroduce a discredited organicism into social theory.

In no sense, however, do we attribute supraindividual characteristics to corporate structures or to any other collective entity. There are no attributes of corporate structures that are not definable either in terms of individuals or of the relations among individuals or both. In other words, we reject any emergent description or metaphysical holism.

The use of group concepts to explain group phenomena, however, raises an entirely different issue. Brodbeck states the difference with great clarity:

The belief that there are no emergent *properties* rests on our criterion of the meaningful. It is thus, broadly speaking, a matter of logic. The assumption

35. See Marshall D. Sahlins, "The Segmentary Lineage: An Organization of Predatory Expansion," *American Anthropologist*, Vol. 63 (April 1961), pp. 322–345.

36. For a discussion of the ways in which various kinds of kinship structure affect environmental adaptation, see Robert T. Holt, "Modernization and Political Stability: A Theoretical Framework." Paper presented to the International Congress on French-Speaking Africa, Washington, D.C., 1964.

that the *laws* of group behavior are or are not, as the case may be, emergent
with respect to laws about individuals is a matter of fact, a matter for empirical determination.[37]

We have severe doubts that there is any reasonable probability that
the kinds of macrophenomena we try to account for can be explained
in terms of either individual or small group behavior, because the composition laws necessary for such a reductive explanation are not known
and perhaps may never be known. (There may not even be any such
laws to discover.) Therefore, all of the theoretical propositions—hypotheses, laws, and the like—stated in terms of this framework will concern
the relations between corporate structures—or roles. The explanations
that these propositions will provide will be emergent explanations.[38]

It is obvious that the kind of functional framework proposed in this
paper is not a framework that is inclusive enough to encompass all of
the sciences of man. It has been designed specifically for the analysis
of macrosocial phenomena—excluding all microphenomena and all cultural considerations. The latter exclusion is so crucial that a few words
are in order about the kind of science of society that is compatible with
this explicitly limited approach.

This explanation can best be made by reference to the diagram in
Figure 5.2 adapted from Margenau. The heavy line with the hash marks
represents the phenomena in the empirical world—nature with a capital
N. The portion of the diagram to the left of the line contains the concepts, laws, and theories of a science. It can be called theoretical space.
The first task of any science is to delineate that aspect of the empirical
world it seeks to describe, explain, and predict. The horizontal lines
through the heavy vertical line extending into theoretical space represents the identification of *society*.

We propose to analyze societies in terms of the analysis of a social
system and a cultural system. These two systems are represented by
the dotted circles. The small circles represent concepts which may be
defined operationally—as indicated by the double lines linking certain
small circles to empirical reality—or they may be defined in terms of
other concepts that in turn have been defined operationally. This latter
kind of relationship is symbolized by the single solid lines. The laws
of science are sets of empirically validated propositions that interrelate
concepts that have not been defined in terms of one another.

We suggest that a science of society could well consist of two subsets
of laws that apply to a social system and a cultural system, respectively,
and a set of laws that apply to the relationship between the two. Only
if the two have been defined independently of one another can one

---

37. Brodbeck, *op. cit.*, p. 6.
38. *Ibid.*, pp. 19–20.

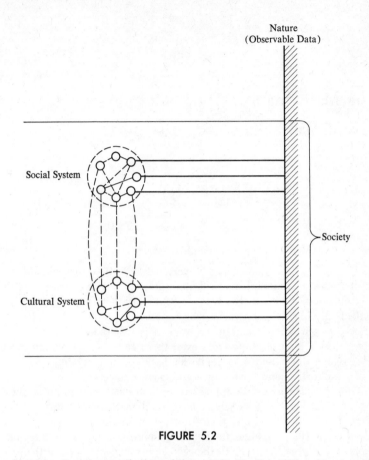

FIGURE 5.2

Adapted from Henry Margenau, *The Nature of Physical Reality* (New York, 1950), p. 85.

keep a significant tautological element out of such laws. The structural-functional conceptualization presented here applies only to the social system, but it has been designed to be compatible with a theory of the cultural system so that a science of society can emerge from a linkage of the two—by empirically testable propositions. If this vision of a mature science of society has any potential, a structural-functional analysis of the social system would have a future as a distinct approach within the behavioral sciences.

6

The Mathematical Approach
to Political Science

OLIVER BENSON

BECAUSE POLITICS is everybody's business, it is not surprising that most of the mathematical literature relevant to political science is by outsiders—by those who would not identify themselves as primarily students of political phenomena. On the other hand, because mathematicians are particularly careful to keep their discipline "pure"—that is, separate as a field of study from even those scientific and engineering fields which have used it most—its methods are immediately available to any political scientist who takes the trouble to learn them.

Political science as a discipline has its traditional roots in philosophy, history, and law—subjects which have used mathematics little or not at all. It is understandable, then, that use of mathematics by political scientists is still peripheral to the main interests of the average practitioner. The great stimulus to the development of mathematical methods has been the relatively recent emphasis known as "behavioralism" and its tendency to concentrate attention on discrete actions of individual actors—the reader will find no better introduction to this focus than in J. C. Charlesworth (ed.), *The Limits of Behavioralism in Political Science.** As the unit of empirical research becomes thus atomistic, the need for quantification of data and at least elementary mathematical manipulation of it becomes clear. In increasing numbers, then, some political scientists are now struggling to acquire the rudiments of some mathematical techniques, enough perhaps to permit them to discuss intelligently with the professional mathematician more sophisticated methods for use in their research. Though this development is limited in scope—no subdiscipline of "politico-metrics" has emerged (nor is it

---

* Published by the American Academy of Political and Social Science, Oct., 1962.

likely in the foreseeable future!)—there is already an impressive literature at hand for the beginner to study, much of it contained in his own professional journals.

An important reason for the association of mathematical method in political science with the recent behavioralism focus is that the behavioralists, concerned as they are with the actual world of people, repeatedly find themselves involved in interdisciplinary research, particularly with the other social scientists. In coping with many new problems which have become the concern of government in contemporary society, they have been forced to draw on the work of economists, sociologists, psychologists, and anthropologists, many of whom have long since become familiar with quantification, statistical treatment, and mathematical approaches. In using their contributions on topics now of central concern to him, the political scientist finds methodological patterns which he must understand in order to deal adequately with his own work.

In this process, it is good to report, a laudable caution has been maintained on all sides. There has been no easy assumption of relevance nor any indication of a view that the more traditional methods of political science should be abandoned for all but untried techniques. With few exceptions, also, there has been restraint from outsiders: few have rushed in with sweeping promises of great enrichment of the discipline by grafting new methods on the old. Nor, on the other hand, has there been any stubborn "traditionalist" rejection of mathematized treatment of political problems: the journals have been open to the scholarly products of these methods, indeed have welcomed those which seem to suggest valuable approaches or which report on research undertaken with the new tools.

Parallel to this process, and contributing strongly to it, is the general revision of traditional mathematics instruction, from the public schools through college curriculums. Topics formerly studied only at advanced levels are often now included in elementary form at an early stage, so that their relevance to social research is possible to comprehend without the prerequisite of advanced mathematical equipment which the social scientist rarely possesses. A centralizing concept in making topics simpler has been that of "finite mathematics," used by the Dartmouth mathematics department in developing an introductory course for students in the behavioral sciences. By eliminating the rigor of infinite sets, continuity, and so on, they found it possible to include such topics as symbolic logic, set theory, probability theory, vectors and matrices, linear programing, and game theory, with a rich content of behavioral-science applications.[1] In the traditional mathematics program,

1. John G. Kemeny, J. L. Snell, and G. L. Thompson, *Introduction to Finite Mathematics* (Englewood Cliffs, N.J.: Prentice-Hall, 1956). A second and more

these subjects come late if at all, and some of them are of little interest to the professional mathematician, who tends, as most contemporary scholars, to specialize. The social scientist, however, if so introduced to certain mathematical specialties which have opened up promising paths of investigation in his own field, will be more likely to understand their potential value and to undertake the hard work needed to learn them.

It is true that there is still an ambivalence in the discipline regarding quantification. For some, the use of mathematics is anathema; for others, a coveted arcanum. Some idealists identify aesthetically with the individual digit, seeing it as a symbol of human individuality, vested with an eternal right not to be averaged, have its square root taken, or to be namelessly merged into a sum of squared deviations. Others are overly enthusiastic and see in mathematics the answer to all social problems. A point not always fully grasped is that mathematical models can never incorporate all factors in the real world, nor can they ever supply precise or definite answers to nonmathematical questions. They can merely simulate what are thought to be the salient concepts of reality —physical or behavioral—and their usefulness must be judged by the adequacy of their results. If the results do not agree with further observation, the model must be modified or discarded for another—a process which has been repeated over and over again in every field of mathematical applications.

Another source of suspicion is on the point of prediction, an aspect of the old argument between social mechanics and intuition. It should be clear that the most complicated and rigorous mathematical model will probably not generate any very certain predictions as to major political events in detail. On the other hand, such a model may very well aid in a better understanding of the processes involved, and such understanding may often differ essentially from the "common sense" intuitive understanding—though more often it will probably confirm intuition.[2]

---

advanced course is based on John G. Kemeny and J. L. Snell, *Mathematical Models in the Social Sciences* (Boston: Ginn, 1962).

2. It is sometimes argued that any political truth which can be discovered by mathematical rigor is equally susceptible of intuitive or subjective analysis. The following example, from permutation theory, will show that intuition is not always enough. Let us assume a group of newly elected congressmen are given their committee assignments at random. We further assume an equal number of congressmen and committees, and that each of the group would prefer a different committee. What is the probability that none will receive the assignment of his choice? The intuitive reaction is that the information given is insufficient, and that the answer will depend on the size of the group involved. Actually the probability is (for more than a very small number) essentially independent of the number: the problem involves a *complete permutation* (one leaving no item fixed) and turns out as $1/2! - 1/3! + 1/4! - \cdots \pm 1/n!$, approaching $1/e$, e being the number 2.7182 . . . , the base of natural logarithms. The probability is slightly less than two-thirds that at least one congressman will get the committee of his preference, regardless of the number.

Reception of Mathematics
by the Traditional Fields

Of the traditional subdivisions of the discipline, public law and political theory have been least subjected to mathematical methods. It is true that a series of cluster-bloc analyses, content and opinion scaling methods, and even game-theory formulations have been applied to court decisions, but these have not so much influenced the main body of public-law research as they have defined the beginning of a new study of judicial behavior. Political theory is usually divided into two distinct areas—the history of political thought and systematic theory. The latter has felt strongly the influence of behavioralism and is presently concerned with the development of theoretical concepts related to the findings of empirical behavioral research. Value theory is involved with such mathematical formulations as those of Kenneth Arrow and Duncan Black, but few political scientists have tackled seriously the challenges they present.[3]

Specialists in international relations have been peculiarly alert to interdisciplinary approaches and have used some mathematical formulations almost from the beginning. Quincy Wright's interdisciplinary seminar in international relations at the University of Chicago set a pattern in the United States, and most graduate centers of this specialty have followed that lead. In Europe, the Graduate Institute of International Studies at the University of Geneva was founded after World War I to bring together the disciplines chiefly concerned with international affairs. Economists, with their standard mathematical equipment, have always been involved in such unified programs, and their political-science colleagues have thus been regularly exposed to a mathematical approach. The problems of conflict and war, in particular, have usually been handled with some statistical and other mathematical treatment, even by political scientists—from Wright's *A Study of War* (Chicago: U. of Chicago Press, 1942) to Morton Kaplan's *System and Process in International Politics* (New York: Wiley, 1957).

Comparative government has traditionally dealt chiefly with institutions but is moving rapidly to more behavioral methods. The impact of interdisciplinary research is felt here, particularly in the study of the

---

3. Cf. Kenneth J. Arrow, *Social Choice and Individual Values* (New York: Wiley, 1951); Duncan Black, *The Theory of Committees and Elections* (Cambridge: Cambridge U. P., 1958); and the excellent summary and discussion by William H. Riker, "Voting and the Summation of Preferences," *American Political Science Review*, Vol. 55 (1961), pp. 900–911. A more general formulation, with a critique of Arrow's impossibility theorem, is James M. Buchanan and Gordon Tullock, *The Calculus of Consent: Logical Foundations of Constitutional Democracy* (Ann Arbor: U. of Michigan Press, 1962).

newly emerging nations. Many of these new states—sixty-four at present count in Africa and Asia—fit poorly the traditional categories of the comparative-government specialist, who increasingly finds use for some of the mathematical techniques of his associates from other fields. Karl Deutsch's work is particularly promising of patterns for typing states on the basis of quantitative factors indicative of political characteristics.[4]

Public administration is an area which might seem ready-made for mathematical techniques but, with the exception of Herbert Simon and a few others, has made relatively little use of them. General management theory, as developed by economists and business-administration specialists, has gone much further in the mathematical handling of such topics as the theory of large organizations, decision processes, and communication theory.

It is the field once known as "popular government"—concerned with political parties, voting, elections, pressure groups, and public opinion —which has made most extensive use of statistical methods and which has welcomed most heartily the new behavioral approach. Forced to deal with the actual world of varied social forces and endowed with an abundance of quantitative data, students in this area have developed more mathematical sophistication than other political scientists.

In making a selection of political topics which have been treated mathematically, it has proved difficult to arrange them under the traditional segments of the discipline. This is understandable because, for the political scientist, mathematics is a tool which may be found useful at almost any point in his work. It has seemed best, in the presentation which follows, to identify several centralizing themes which cut across the traditional subdivisions. These themes—voting, conflict, and group relations—by no means exhaust the list of political material which has been handled with mathematics. They are illustrative, not comprehensive. The reader interested in a more complete account should consult the fine bibliographical article by Richard Fagen ("Some Contributions of Mathematical Reasoning to the Study of Politics," *American Political Science Review*, Vol. 55 (1961), pp. 888–899), which will also serve as a good reading guide for those interested in improving their own math-

4. Cf. his "Toward an Inventory of Basic Trends and Patterns in Comparative and International Politics," *American Political Science Review*, Vol. 54 (1960), pp. 34–57, and "Social Mobilization and Political Development," *ibid.*, Vol. 55 (1961), pp. 493–514. In *The Nerves of Government* (New York: Free Press, 1963), Deutsch supplies several provocative models, especially in the field of communication. His leadership at Yale has been a seminal influence in the development of quantitative methods in the study of comparative politics, stimulating such contributions as B. M. Russett, H. R. Alker, Jr., K. W. Deutsch, H. D. Lasswell, et al., *World Handbook of Political and Social Indicators* (New Haven: Yale U. Press, 1964), and R. Merritt and S. Rokkan, *Comparing Nations* (New Haven: Yale U. Press, 1966).

ematical equipment. A more comprehensive "intellectual stimulant" is Hayward R. Alker, Jr., *Mathematics and Politics* (New York: Macmillan, 1965); several specialized political models are presented in the two monographs based on conferences at Southern Methodist University under the direction of Joseph L. Bernd: *Mathematical Applications in Political Science* (Dallas: Arnold Foundation, Southern Methodist U., 2 vols., 1965 and 1966).

Voting

Quantitative data being abundant on voting at all levels, it is natural that political scientists should have confronted the task of interpreting them. Methods employed run the gamut from simple arithmetic to Guttman scaling, statistical inference, game theory, and symbolic logic. Voting situations subjected to analysis include elections, roll calls in city councils, state legislatures, courts, Congress, and the United Nations, as well as purely hypothetical votes. The examples mentioned below could be expanded almost indefinitely.

Elections

A pioneer in the analysis of voting data in elections was Cortez A. M. Ewing, who used simple tabular arrangements with little mathematical treatment beyond the derivation of percentages. Breaking new ground, he was able to assemble most of the available information on presidential and congressional elections and discovered ways to acquire records of southern primaries.[5] V. O. Key, in his *Southern Politics in State and Nation* (New York: Knopf, 1949), pioneered the use of interviewing in political science and employed more sophisticated statistical methods in portraying his findings. The classic Erie County study of 1940, using random sampling and panel interviewing, added a new dimension to the investigation of voting behavior (which has proved of considerable value to the professional pollsters).[6]

5. See his *Presidential Elections* (Norman: U. of Oklahoma Press, 1940), *Congressional Elections* (Norman, 1947), and *Primary Elections in the South* (Norman: U. of Oklahoma Press, 1953). Ewing also used a variety of personal data to supply useful profiles of political elites in his *Judges of the Supreme Court* (Minneapolis: U. of Minnesota Press, 1938) and *The Presidential Cabinet* (unpublished manuscript).

6. Paul F. Lazarsfeld, Bernard Berelson, and Hazel Gaudet, *The People's Choice* (New York: Columbia U. P., 1948).

The Cube Law

A mathematical oddity of "psephology" (as election studies are sometimes critically labeled) is the apparent equality between the ratio of votes in a two-party election and its cube as the ratio of contested seats won by the two parties. James G. March has examined this principle closely ("Party Legislative Representation as a Function of Election Results," *Public Opinion Quarterly*, Vol. 21 (1957–1958), pp. 521–542) and has recast the equation into one which expresses the proportion of votes for a given party as x and the proportion of seats won by the same party as y: $y = x^3/(3x^2 - 3x + 1)$. Close approximations to the cube-law predictions have been established for the United States House of Representatives and for elections in Britain and New Zealand. Robert Dahl derived a linear regression ($y = 2.5x - .7$) for congressional elections from 1928 to 1954, and March points out that the cube-law curve does indeed approximate a linear function for values of x from .40 to .60. The actual fit of the cubic equation to American elections is skewed somewhat by the one-party constituencies of the South.

Roll Calls

Use of the statistician's tools has sharpened research methods in the study of elections, legislative behavior, and judicial decision. Indeed, an encouraging aspect of this development is that it has already evoked protests (such as that of Wilder Crane, "A Caveat on Roll Call Studies of Party Voting," *Midwest Journal of Political Science*, Vol. 4 (1960), p. 237).

Among the more valuable techniques employed to study legislative behavior are scaling, whereby a legislator's votes on a series of roll calls are rated to locate his approximate position in a predetermined array, and various indices of cohesion and conflict which serve to measure association or opposition.[7]

7. Cf. Stuart Rice, *Quantitative Method in Politics* (New York: Knopf, 1928); Julius Turner, *Party and Constituency: Pressures on Congress* (Baltimore: Johns Hopkins Press, 1951); John C. Wahlke and Heinz Eulau (eds.), *Legislative Behavior: A Reader in Theory and Research* (New York: Free Press, 1959); David B. Truman, *The Congressional Party: A Case Study* (New York: Wiley, 1959); John G. Grumm, *Quantitative Methods in Legislative Behavior: Probability Models, Cluster Analysis and Factor Analysis* (mimeo, Lawrence, Kansas, n.d.). An excellent introduction to the rapidly growing field of roll-call analysis is Lee F. Anderson, Meredith W. Watts, Jr., and Allen R. Wilcox, *Legislative Roll-Call Analysis* (Evanston: Northwestern U. Press, 1966), one of Northwestern's useful methodology handbooks appearing under the editorship of James A. Robinson.

Among applications to international organizations are the ground-breaking works of L. N. Rieselbach, "Quantitative Techniques for the Study of Voting Behavior in

Rice's index of cohesion, for example, takes the arithmetic difference between the percentages of a group voting for and against a measure. It ranges from zero when votes are evenly split to 100 when unanimous. Beyle's use of the same index, adapted to an index of cohesion of pairs, is used to find the degree of agreement among pairs of legislators on a number of bills, as a means of discovering "attribute-cluster-blocs." Beyle established zero cohesion at .25 and perfect cohesion at 1.00. Use of the chi-square test permits determination of the statistical significance of differences, as developed by Turner and others.

Grumm's "coefficient of conflict" and "index of colligation" are proposed as refinements: the coefficient of conflict is defined as the square root of χ^2/n and the index of colligation as an average of these coefficients when each member is matched with each other. In a neat example, Grumm points out that the older index of cohesion will show a positive association of .33 in a case where each member voted differently from each other in four cases out of six (his index develops a negative result):

	Vote	1	2	3	4	5	6
Member	A	+	+	+	+	−	−
	B	−	−	+	+	+	+
	C	+	+	−	−	+	+

In an intensive analysis of the Eighty-first Congress, Duncan MacRae applied scaling techniques to establish patterns of voting groups in such broad areas as civil rights, Fair Deal, welfare-state, foreign-aid, and rural-urban questions.[8] His principal data consisted of roll calls, but he also projected research plans for analysis of the differences in constituencies of members and supplied a sophisticated "mathematical framework for the analysis of legislative choices." Charles Adrian has studied bloc voting on city councils in four Michigan council-manager cities, using methods which permit identification of an antimanager group, a city employee's group, and a chamber of commerce group.[9]

Practical use of roll-call analysis methods is made routinely by the *Congressional Quarterly* staff, particularly in identification of an underlying or "latent" factor which may be considered to explain the voting on a group of bills otherwise not substantively similar. An example is

the United Nations General Assembly," *International Organization,* Vol. 14, No. 2 (Spring 1960), pp. 297–304, and Thomas Hovet, Jr., *Bloc Politics in the United Nations* (Cambridge: Harvard U. Press, 1960). More recently, Hayward R. Alker, Jr., has applied the powerful technique of factor analysis in his "Dimensions of Conflict in the General Assembly," *American Political Science Review,* Vol. 58 (September 1964), pp. 642–657.

8. *Dimensions of Congressional Voting* (Berkeley: U. of California Press, 1958).

9. "The Role of the City Council in Community Policy-Making," paper read at the American Political Science Association convention, Washington, September 1959 (mimeo).

the concept of the "Federal role," used in a series of annual studies. For the 1962 sessions, all roll calls were examined and eight each from the House and Senate were selected as likely to reveal members' basic support of a larger role for the Federal government. The technique makes possible comparison of the two houses on a common factor, independently of whether the same legislation came to a vote in both. Not surprisingly, the 1962 study found Democrats and Republicans in opposition on most of the votes (10 of the 16), though in six cases majorities of both parties voted together—four times to expand the Federal role and twice to limit it. The average Democrat supported a larger Federal role 74 per cent of the time; the average Republican 35 per cent of the time. In the Senate, only Mansfield and Goldwater stood at the two extremes, with clean slates. In the House, ninety-six Democrats and seventeen Republicans plus seven southern Democrats had perfect scores.

Studies of this kind, by adding item after item to our information, gradually build up a foundation of empirically based generalization from which broader theory may grow. The discipline has become adjusted to the routine incorporation of such information, hardly considered to represent extreme methodology.

Voting Power

The Shapley-Shubik index of voting power is based on the number of times a given member's vote is pivotal: mathematically, the percentage of all permutations in which the member's vote falls at the point crucial to passage or failure of the measure. In a committee of three, for example, each with one vote, obviously each has voting power of $1/3$. If one of the three, as chairman, has a veto, he is pivotal in 4 of the 6 permutations and so has voting power of $2/3$, each of the other members dropping to $1/6$. Shapley and Shubik carried out an analysis of the unusual combination of voting rules involved in the United Nations Security Council and determined that each of the five permanent members has $76/385$, or .197, voting power and the six elected members share a total of $5/385$, or about .002 each. So precise a method may be questioned, yet the result shows a reasonable relationship to the intuitive concept that the nonpermanent members, though not entirely without influence, are essentially overwhelmed in Security Council voting by the Big Five.[10]

Glendon Schubert has used scaling and cluster methods to identify blocs on the Supreme Court and has developed indices of cohesion,

10. L. S. Shapley and Martin Shubik, "A Method for Evaluating the Distribution of Power in a Committee System," *American Political Science Review*, Vol. 48 (1954), pp. 791 ff.

interagreement, and adhesion, based on matrices of paired agreements in both assent and dissent in Court decisions, originally suggested by Herman Pritchett.[11] In an ingenious adaptation of game theory, he postulates the 1936 Court term as a three-person zero-sum game, involving the three liberal justices (Brandeis, Cardozo, and Stone) as one player, the four conservative justices (Van Devanter, Sutherland, Butler, and McReynolds) as a second, and "Hughberts" (Hughes and Roberts) as a third. Using the Shapley-Shubik power index to supply pay-off quantities, he conjectures a "pure" strategy for "Hughberts"—to form a coalition with the liberal bloc when it would win, to form a coalition with the conservative bloc when the liberal bloc could not win, and to join the two when they voted together. On this basis, he establishes that the actual results in 195 decisions of the 1936 term (the court-packing controversy of that year makes this concept especially apt) indicate a pay-off for the three "players" almost exactly equal to the theoretical results of a three-person game.

The Voting Paradox

Of great theoretical importance to the very foundations of democratic theory is the "voting paradox," discovered originally by Condorcet and developed for general cases by Arrow, Black, and Riker.[12] The paradox is shown in an example of three voters' ordered preferences among three choices—for example, of candidates or policy alternatives. If we let A, B, and C represent the voters and X, Y, Z the choices, then the possible orderings are XYZ, XZY, YXZ, YZX, ZXY, and ZYX. There are 216 different ways in which the three voters may select their orderings: (1) all three may prefer the same ordering—there being six ways in which they may do so; (2) any pair of voters may choose the same ordering, the third selecting one of the five remaining—a total of $3 \cdot 6 \cdot 5$, or 90 ways; (3) each of the three may select a different ordering—which may occur in $6!/3!$ or 120 different ways. In the 96 cases under (1) and (2), there is no problem of majority choice. However, one fourth, or 30, of the 120 possible outcomes under (3) involve the paradox. These are the outcomes of the nature indicated in the sequence:

$$A \quad XYZ$$
$$B \quad ZXY$$
$$C \quad YZX$$

11. Glendon A. Schubert, "The Study of Judicial Decision-Making as an Aspect of Political Behavior," *American Political Science Review*, Vol. 52 (1958), pp. 1007–1025.

12. *Op. cit.* Riker suggests that legislative strategy "which most writers have treated as a mystical art . . . may turn out to be a science with quite coherent rules."

Notice that X is preferred to Y by two voters and Y to Z by two voters, leading to the initial conjecture that the majority ordering is XYZ. However, Z is preferred to X by two voters, so that the conjecture fails. Similarly, Z is preferred to X by a majority, and X to Y by a majority, but the sequence ZXY is illogical as a majority ordering, for Y is preferred to Z by a majority. The process is circular. Kenneth Arrow has shown that discrepancies of this sort are inevitable in a large number of cases when people choose among more than two alternatives. William Riker has calculated the probabilities of a majority ordering up to ten alternatives and finds the chance to be quite small—for $n = 10$, only $5/256$—that simple majority voting will produce a consistent ordering.

Conflict

Though the study of conflict has been of primary interest in international relations, it is involved as well in intergroup relations at all levels of magnitude. Much of the current work is interdisciplinary, focused in *The Journal of Conflict Resolution*. The field has found mathematical models most fruitful, inspired in large part by the theory of games, though other approaches have been employed as well. For that reason, we preface the illustrations below with an elementary account of simple game theory.

Game Theory

Rigorous analysis of problems involving three persons seems to present difficulties in mathematics comparable to those of the three-body problem in mechanics (or those of the Trinity in theology). The Condorcet voting paradox just described is an example.

Similar difficulties arise in game theory where more than two players are involved, each attempting to optimize his pay-off in accordance with the basic assumption of the theory. In the voting paradox, let us ignore for a moment the problem of ordering and assume that the three choices confronting the three voters are: $X =$ appropriating a given sum of money to one of the three voters (or to interests he represents); $Y =$ dividing the same sum between the two members of any given pair; $Z =$ dividing the sum equally among all three. Consistent with game theory, some pair should form to force alternative Y, because the pay-off will be greater for each member of the winning coalition than under alternative Z. Game theory, however, offers no single solution to the problem; we must be content with the set of three winning coalitions for Y, that is AB or AC or BC. Common sense might conclude that, in a practical political situation, one of these outcomes might indeed turn up, that alternative X is certainly ruled out, but that, given the psychological intricacies of forming a two-member winning coalition (unless already pre-existing on other issues—not an assumption of the model), alternative Z might in fact be the most likely.

No such difficulties occur for the simpler two-person zero-sum games, with which most beginners are acquainted. These fall into two main groups: the strictly determined and the non-strictly determined games. A strictly determined game is one with a minimax entry, or saddlepoint, in the pay-off matrix (an entry which is the lowest in its row and the highest in its column: like the seat of a saddle with respect to its longitudinal and lateral axes). Rationally each of the two players must choose the strategy which selects this pay-off, as in the illustration.

Column

	Row	1	2
		2	3

In this simple pay-off listing, positive entries show Row's pay-off, and, in a zero-sum game, Column's pay-off is, of course, the negative of Row's. The saddlepoint is Row 2, Column 1. Row might prefer pay-off 3 but realizes that Column, with complete information, would never play so he could obtain it.

The nonstrictly determined game, one with no saddlepoint, must be optimized by a mixed strategy on the part of both players.

Column

	Row	1	0
		−1	2

Each has a mixed strategy which will yield a minimax value for his play over a series, based on probability theory: Row should play his first strategy ¾ of the time, his second ¼ of the time; Column should play his first strategy ½ of the time and his second strategy ½ of the time. Because the game is "unfair" (that is, biased against Column), we are also interested in its value, which works out as ½ unit to Row per game (and, of course, −½ unit to Column).[13]

---

13. For the reader interested in pursuing this example, the canons for determining strategies and value in this simple game may be briefly described. Each is expressed as a probability fraction of which the denominator is $a + d - b - c$, the variables referring to the type matrix $\begin{pmatrix} ab \\ cd \end{pmatrix}$. Then the numerators are, respectively, for:

Row to play Row 1	$d - c$
Row to play Row 2	$a - b$
Column to play Column 1	$d - b$
Column to play Column 2	$a - c$
Value of the game (to Row)	$ad - bc$

Such simple equalities are not possible for more complicated games.

Adaptations of game theory to the study of international conflict include both analogical theory (well represented by Morton Kaplan's *System and Process in International Politics, op. cit.*) and mathematical treatment. The well-known model of Lewis Richardson, an English Quaker with obvious preconceived values, is based on a calculus of arms races, but Rapoport has shown that many of Richardson's concepts are capable of game-theory analysis.[14] Richardson begins with what he calls "simple-minded assumptions" regarding the defense politics of two hypothetical states, Jedesland and Andersland, each interested in increasing its armaments to keep pace with the other. These conflicting aims he expresses in a set of paired equations: $dx/dt = ky$, $dy/dt = kx$, where x and y are the armaments, respectively, of Jedesland and Andersland, t represents time, and k the ratio of desired increase. Richardson shows this system to be normally unstable, armaments increasing indefinitely and exponentially except in unusual cases of relative equilibrium.

Maurice Ash has developed a model of "constant power curves" of maximal security for two states, rising ever more steeply as reserves are mobilized.[15] At a certain point, as reserves and coalition possibilities are exhausted, the probability of war arises as the only means left to redress equilibrium. The concept, like Richardson's, is not strict game theory, but the underlying principle is closely related. Arthur Burns has used a more subjective but still graphic treatment, with "multiplier diagrams," to examine the special situations of secret armament and radically new weapons of destruction.[16] He logically finds the "rectangle of greatest danger" to lie in the region which represents the combination of secrecy, new weapons of unknown power, and conflict between two states.

Thomas Schelling and Kenneth Boulding, both economists, have examined the relevance of game theory to international conflict in book-length studies.[17] Schelling calls for additional work by mathematicians,

14. See Lewis F. Richardson, "Generalized Foreign Politics," *British Journal of Psychology* (Monograph 23, 1939); A. Rapoport, "Lewis F. Richardson's Mathematical Theory of War," *Journal of Conflict Resolution*, Vol. 1 (1957), pp. 249–299, and *Fights, Games, and Debates* (Ann Arbor: U. of Michigan Press, 1960). In *Game Theory and Related Approaches to Social Behavior* (New York: Wiley, 1964), Martin Shubik has assembled a collection of highly readable articles on game-theory applications, as well as supplying an extended introductory essay for the general reader. William H. Riker's *The Theory of Political Coalitions* (New Haven: Yale U. Press, 1963) develops the provocative theory that a coalition of the whole will tend to diminish to a minimal majority, based on the game-theoretic principle of maximization of pay-offs.

15. M. A. Ash, "An Analysis of Power, with Special Reference to International Politics," *World Politics*, Vol. 3 (1951), pp. 218–237.

16. A. Burns, "A Graphical Approach to Some Problems of the Arms Race," *Journal of Conflict Resolution*, Vol. 3 (1959), pp. 327–342.

17. T. C. Schelling, *The Strategy of Conflict* (Cambridge: Harvard U. P., 1960); Kenneth Boulding, *Conflict and Defense* (New York: Harper, 1962).

to include analysis of situations where goals are mixed and bargaining, threats, and partial mutuality of objectives are involved. Boulding develops a more far-ranging model of conflict, starting with concepts from Richardson and game theory, drawing on studies of economic and industrial conflict, and suggesting approaches to the examination of ethical and ideological conflict. Rapoport, whose *Fights, Games, and Debates* is a good introduction both to Richardson's calculus and to game theory, written in nontechnical language, feels with Schelling that eventually new mathematical ground will need to be broken for the investigation of the interaction of large human groups, perhaps a development between the two extremes of Richardson's deterministic model and game theory's probabilistic allowance for human choice.

Internal Forces

Assumptions that external conflict may be related to internal tensions underlie several models which attempt to express relationships among factors thought to account for a broad variety of societal characteristics. Quincy Wright, whose *A Study of War* represents the first major interdisciplinary attack on this problem by a political scientist, suggests in his later *The Study of International Relations* that a centralizing quantitative core of the discipline, using more or less rigorous analysis, should be developed and empirical studies made with relation to it.[18] His own algebraic models are hardly more than idealized generalizations but represent an approach which might permit a researcher to move from one empirical study to another, as the simple manipulation of variables suggests. An example (from *A Study of War*) follows.

$s = o/n$ — Severity of opposition varies proportionately to the total amount of opposition in the community and inversely to the number of groups in opposition.

$o^2 = fs = k$ — Assuming a law of the conservation of opposition, then the product of the components of opposition, the average severity of each opposition, and the frequency of opposition will be constant.

$f = on$ — Combining, the frequency of oppositions should be equal to the product of the amount of opposition and the number of groups in opposition.

In *The Study of International Relations*, Wright designs a complete theoretical "field" model, consisting of coordinate systems with six "capability" dimensions and six "value" dimensions, within each pair of which states may be located by such indices as are available. As an

18. Quincy Wright, *A Study of War*, 2 vols. (Chicago: U. of Chicago Press, 1942) and *The Study of International Relations* (New York: Appleton-Century-Crofts, 1955), pp. 531–603.

example, he assumes that resource abundance and technological advancement are related to defensiveness and satisfaction. For the various combinations of signs for these values as vectors, $(+r, +t)$ points toward satisfaction, $(-r, -t)$ toward unsatisfaction, $(+r, -t)$ toward defensiveness, and $(-r +t)$ toward expansiveness. Similar designs are included for the combinations of flexibility-energy, cooperation-strength, objectivity-abstractness, liberality-situation orientation, and affirmation-manipulation.

Karl Deutsch, who has worked extensively with quantitative methods and argues for a continuing interplay of qualitative and quantitative thinking, suggests a model of governmental stability, to be approximated by the expression:

$$St = (g/L \, pol) \cdot (y/y_{10})$$

where St indicates stability; g, the ratio of the government income to total national income; L, the percentage of literacy; pol, the percentage of political participation; y, total national income; and y_{10}, the percentage of total income received by the top 10 per cent (an indicator of inequality in income distribution). Deutsch reasons that stability may be considered to reflect a relationship between the rising burdens on a government and popular habits of loyalty, together with resources available to government for dealing with these burdens.[19]

Rummell and Tanter use factor analysis (for the first time in the examination of comparative political data) to identify types and frequency of both internal and external conflict, and they are continuing an investigation into the dimensions of internal cultural structures which promises to be useful not only in conflict study but in comparative politics generally (Rudolph J. Rummel, "Dimensions of Conflict Behavior Within and Between Nations," *General Systems Yearbook*, Vol. 8, 1963, and Raymond Tanter, "Dimensions of Conflict Within Nations, 1955–60: Turmoil and Internal War," *Proceedings of the Peace Research Society*, Vol. 3, 1964).

Fred Kort applies Pareto's income-distribution theorem, as expanded by Harold Davis in a concentration ratio, to Aristotle's theory that the cause of revolution is to be found in inequality— by which he means, Kort assumes, a separation of political and economic power.[20] The formula for this ratio is $r = 1/(2a - 1)$, where a is the exponent in Pareto's hypothesis that $N = A/x^a$, N being the number of people with income greater than x in an economy of size A. Davis hypothesized that an income distribution of .5 represented a stable level of concentration

19. Karl Deutsch, "Toward an Inventory of Basic Trends and Patterns in Comparative and International Politics," *American Political Science Review*, Vol. 54 (1960), pp. 34–57.

20. Fred Kort, "The Quantification of Aristotle's Theory of Revolution," *American Political Science Review*, Vol. 46 (1952), pp. 486–493.

of income; that, when this ratio fell substantially below .5 (meaning relatively wide dispersion of income), a civil war was likely to occur; that, when it rose substantially above .5 (meaning relatively high concentration of income), a revolution was likely to occur. Kort supplies the additional refinement that, in the first case, economic power has shifted to the masses, though political power is retained by the few—who will resort to civil war to restore their economic power; in the second case, with economic power concentrated in the few and political power in the many, a revolution is likely. Kort does not make extravagant claims for the model but suggests it as one whereby a qualitatively expressed principle of classical political theory may be given a quantitative form which would permit empirical verification or refutation.

Group Relations

The concept of the group as the significant unit for research investigation in political science has exercised a powerful influence, particularly on the behavioralists. Inasmuch as the original publication of Arthur F. Bentley's *The Process of Government, a Study of Social Pressures* (Chicago: U. of Chicago Press, 1908) came early in the discipline's history, the concept can hardly be considered novel. The book remains a seminal classic, still controversial, postulating the group and intergroup relations as prime focal points of empirical study. Bentley was strongly influenced by Newtonian mechanics as a source of hypotheses on aspects of intergroup action, parallel to the forces exerted by and on physical bodies, but without putting his ideas in a completely formalized mechanistic framework.[21] The influence of Bentley's work on contemporary group analysis is more indirect than direct; it is an example of a theory built by analogy with natural science, with all the pitfalls of such formulations. Nevertheless, it has served as a source of many particularized research projects.

Formal mathematical treatment of group relations has not been a conspicuous feature of political science, though many quantitative studies have been conducted on identification of group characteristics. Karl Deutsch's work on community and social mobility, mentioned above, is an example of a combination of theoretical and empirical work. Herbert Simon's work, particularly his *Models of Man* (New York: Wiley, 1957), supplies a variety of mathematical models, many of which are relevant to group relations. Herbert McClosky and associates conducted an extensive survey of party leaders and, in co-operation with

21. Cf. R. E. Dowling, "Pressure Group Theory: Its Methodological Range," *American Political Science Review*, Vol. 54 (1960), pp. 944–954.

Gallup, of party members, testing on a scale of 390 items, including opinions on twenty-four major national issues deemed of primary importance at the time.[22] They found party leadership to be significantly at odds on most subjects, but their findings confirmed the Elmira study of 1948 which showed members of the two parties to be largely in agreement on issues. Whether such an investigation confirms intuition or suggests a need for re-evaluation of lore, it affords a more solid basis for both future empirical research and future theoretical constructs.

In the illustrations which follow, there are presented several suggestive models from other social sciences, which seem to offer possibilities for development of the study of groups. The examples may seem trivial, but each represents an elementary aspect of a major field of mathematics which may in the future be exploited by those concerned with the structure of groups and intergroup relations.

Dominance

Dominance of individuals over others in given groups can be expressed by the sociologist's device of the square matrix, with zero entries on the main diagonal and elsewhere when Row does not dominate Column and a 1 when Row does dominate Column. Thus, the matrix

$$M = \begin{array}{c} \\ A \\ B \\ C \end{array} \begin{array}{ccc} A & B & C \\ \left[\begin{array}{ccc} 0 & 1 & 1 \\ 0 & 0 & 1 \\ 0 & 0 & 0 \end{array} \right] \end{array} \qquad M^2 = \left[\begin{array}{ccc} 0 & 0 & 1 \\ 0 & 0 & 0 \\ 0 & 0 & 0 \end{array} \right]$$

means that A dominates B and C, B dominates C. By squaring the matrix, we obtain the number of "two-stage" dominances (in this case only one: A over C).

The Spread of Rumor

Assume that a given item of information is passed to A and that he in turn passes it to B, B to C, and so on, each time to a new individual, and with probability p of inaccuracy, implying $1 - p$ of accuracy. With what probability does the nth individual receive the information accurately? It is not immediately obvious that the answer is independent of p. The model of this problem is a transition probability matrix:

22. Herbert McClosky and Others, "Issue Conflict and Consensus among Party Leaders and Followers," *American Political Science Review*, Vol. 54 (1960), pp. 406–427.

$$M = \begin{bmatrix} 1-p & p \\ p & 1-p \end{bmatrix}$$

where $1-p$ represents probability of accurate information, p of inaccurate information. Then the probability that the nth person will receive the information in one state or the other is given by successive powers of the matrix M, that is, by the matrix M^n. In fact, the answer in this case rapidly approaches ($p = \frac{1}{2}$, $1-p = \frac{1}{2}$), after any considerable number of people are involved. If we switch the situation to successive voting situations in Congress and substitute the probability of a member changing his mind for that of changing the rumor, we arrive at a possible model for explanation of the standard parliamentary device of minority delaying actions.

Communication Nets

A matrix similar to the dominance matrix may be used to show communication links among persons in a given group. Like the dominance matrix, the communications matrix has zero entries on the main diagonal, to indicate omission of the case of one person communicating with himself. Unlike the dominance matrix, however, two-way links are shown. The matrix below is an example of a society of perfect communication among three persons (two-way communication between the members of each pair).

$$M^1 = \begin{matrix} & \begin{matrix} A & B & C \end{matrix} \\ \begin{matrix} A \\ B \\ C \end{matrix} & \begin{bmatrix} 0 & 1 & 1 \\ 1 & 0 & 1 \\ 1 & 1 & 0 \end{bmatrix} \end{matrix} \qquad M^2 = \begin{matrix} & \begin{matrix} A & B & C \end{matrix} \\ \begin{matrix} A \\ B \\ C \end{matrix} & \begin{bmatrix} 2 & 1 & 1 \\ 1 & 2 & 1 \\ 1 & 1 & 2 \end{bmatrix} \end{matrix}$$

As with the dominance matrix, the square of the matrix shows the number of two-stage communication links between any two members. The 2's on the main diagonal in M^2 show the number of two-step feedback communication links for each member; that is, in this case, each member has such a reciprocal relationship with each of the other two members of the group. The 1's show two-step communication links (for example, A to B not only directly, as in M^1, but also indirectly through C). In a group of n members having perfect two-way communication between both members of all pairs, each member has $n-1$ two-step feedbacks. Similarly, M^3 will show the number of three-step linkages. The summation of matrices from M^1 to M^n will show the total number of one-step, two-step, . . . , n-step linkages between members of each pair and will display on the main diagonal the number of basic feedback communications for each member:

$$M^n = \begin{array}{c} \\ A \\ B \\ C \end{array} \begin{array}{ccc} A & B & C \\ \left[\begin{array}{ccc} 2 & 3 & 3 \\ 3 & 2 & 3 \\ 3 & 3 & 2 \end{array}\right] \end{array} \qquad \Sigma M^i = \begin{array}{c} \\ A \\ B \\ C \end{array} \begin{array}{ccc} A & B & C \\ \left[\begin{array}{ccc} 4 & 5 & 5 \\ 5 & 4 & 5 \\ 5 & 5 & 4 \end{array}\right] \end{array}$$

A, for example, has feedback links as follows: A-B-A, A-C-A, A-B-C-A, A-C-B-A.

Set Theory

Not much used in political science, set theory is helpful in clarifying complicated combinations of overlapping groups or factors. As an illustration, let us take a hypothetical voting constituency consisting of 10,000 voters of Irish descent, 10,000 suburbanites, and 10,000 white-collar workers. The following overlaps are given: Irish-suburbia, 2,000; Irish-white collar, 2,000; suburbia-white collar, 8,000; all three, 1,000. Previous experience indicates the party will normally obtain 70 per cent of the Irish vote, 50 per cent of the white-collar vote, and 30 per cent of the suburban vote, with the expected vote in overlapping groups proportional to these percentages. What are the party's prospects in this district? As a preliminary, we may use the set-theory formula for three overlapping groups to determine the number of voters in the district:

$$\begin{aligned} N &= I + S + W - IS - IW - SW + ISW \\ &= 10,000 + 10,000 + 10,000 - 2,000 - 2,000 - 8,000 + 1,000 \\ &= 19,000. \end{aligned}$$

We may compute the total favorable vote by using the indicated percentages together with ones derived for the overlaps:

$$\begin{aligned} P &= 7.(10,000) + .5(10,000) + .3(10,000) - .5(2,000) \\ &\qquad - .6(2,000) - .4(8,000) + .5(1,000) \\ &= 10,100. \end{aligned}$$

This result comes out as 53 per cent of 19,000, which we may take as the margin indicated by the information.

Statistical and Computer Applications

Although an ever increasing amount of statistical work is being done by political scientists (we can now point to a text on the subject by a former president of the American Political Science Association[23]), most active practitioners do not have the statistical equipment needed for the problems which concern them. This is partly because the complexities of political research demand at least some of the methods for handling multivariates and the common tests used in statistical inference. If the political scientist does not go this far in statistics, he will probably abandon the whole thing as a bad job. His work with data has already convinced him that few of his problems can be approached with bivariate methods or with descriptive statistics only. On the other hand, the usual treatment of multivariates and of inferential tests is so formidable as to suggest an extraordinary retooling effort, and, even once the retooling were accomplished, there is the likewise forbidding prospect of laborious calculations at every hand.[24]

For the average political scientist, the obvious solution of resort to the nearest computer laboratory does not occur. An unnecessary air of mystery overhangs many of these installations, and some require expensive rental fees. In reality, these obstacles often dissolve. Many academic computer installations are "open," that is, available for bona fide research work, at least by local faculty; often they welcome a research project which may result in publication. More than one hundred educational and research computer centers are now established on campuses, and frequently their personnel are energetic in efforts to promote their use. Where charges are necessary, there is often help available to make out the grant application. As for the mystery, two major considerations are relevant: with a little effort, at least the intuitive meaning of the principal statistical routines and tests can be learned, and, with an elementary command of computer programing, the novice can make use of expertly developed subroutines for machine

23. V. O. Key, *A Primer of Statistics for Political Scientists* (New York: Crowell, 1954).

24. Besides Key, who deals chiefly with descriptive statistics, there is the excellent introduction to statistical inference by Solomon Diamond, *Information and Error* (New York: Basic Books, 1959). Diamond leads the reader entertainingly step by step through the more important inferential tests. A psychologist, he is more alert to the social scientist's problems than most statistics text writers.

For the interested beginner, the author notes here one statistical measure which is readily grasped and computed—Spearman's coefficient of rank correlation. In cookbook fashion, the formula is: $r = 1 - [6\Sigma d^2/(n^3 - n)]$, where n is the number of paired rankings and d^2 the squared deviations from one ranking to another. As an illustration, if two judges have ranked four congressmen (say from liberal to conservative) as follows: Judge 1—1, 2, 3, 4; Judge 2—4, 3, 2, 1, obviously we cannot depend on the reliability of the judging. The rank deviations from Judge 1 to Judge 2 are $+ 3, + 1, - 1,$ and $- 3$; the sum of squared deviations is $9 + 1 + 1 + 9 = 20$. Applying the formula, we obtain $r = 1 - (6 \cdot 20/(64 - 4)) = - 1$. Because the coefficient varies from $- 1$ for a perfect negative correlation to $+ 1$ for a perfect positive correlation, the answer is intuitively recognized as correct. Though of limited use, the statistic is quickly and easily applied to many imprecisely defined political orderings and, nevertheless, contains a minor element of an inferential test.

manipulation of his data. Such subroutines are a part of the program library of any center and include all of the standard statistical procedures and tests. Program compilers, moreover, permit one to prepare programs without the need of learning the details of computer operation. A compiler is a machine-oriented "language," with fixed rules governing statements, which permits the use of expressions and symbols already familiar to the uninitiated. With a few hours of study and practice, one can master the compiler's rules and write programs which will be translated into machine codes without further human intervention.

FORTRAN

The powerful FORTRAN language developed by IBM, for example, is adaptable with variations to some dozen different computers and permits the beginner to formulate his program in statements and symbols already familiar.[25] The DO $nI = J$, K, or loop statement, the IF (E) N_1, N_2, N_3 branching statement, and the arithmetic statement, together with miscellaneous "housekeeping" statements, enable one to develop quite complicated patterns of computation with relative ease. Omitting details of no concern except for actual use of the computer, a FORTRAN program fragment to compute variance and standard deviation might be (for 1,000 values):

```
      SIGX   = 0.0
      SIGXX  = 0.0
      DO 1 I = 1, 1000
      SIGX   = SIGX + X(I)
    1 SIGXX  = SIGXX + X(I) ** 2
      AVGX   = SIGX/1000.
      VARX   = (1000. * SIGXX - SIGX ** 2)/(1000. ** 2)
      STDEV  = SQRTF (VARX).
```

The DO statement instructs the program to iterate the sequence following to and including statement 1, beginning with value $I = 1$ and continuing until $I = 1000$. SQRTF brings into play the square root subroutine incorporated in the compiler. In the arithmetic statements, addition is indicated by $+$, subtraction by $-$, division by $/$, multiplication by $*$, exponentiation by $**$, grouping and subscription by $(\ )$, and replacement (of a variable by a new one) by $=$. With the single ex-

25. The nontechnical beginner will find helpful lessons in programing in Richard V. Andree, *Programming the IBM 650* (New York: Holt, 1958) and in Daniel D. McCracken, *A Guide to FORTRAN Programming* (New York: Wiley, 1961). Both volumes are prepared by experienced teachers, unlike most of the technical manuals produced by computer manufacturers.

ception of =, these operation symbols are identical or similar to those of ordinary notation. The codelike words used for variables are arbitrary; within few limits, the programer may use any convenient mnemonic.

Political Computer Programs

The brief listing below will give an idea of the scope and range of projects currently underway, with some suggestion of the formidable power of this new research tool. For the first time, the political scientist may be able to make use of the vast quantities of data available to him for the study of political man.[26]

John Grumm[27] has developed an IBM 650 program for cluster analysis of legislative bodies, capable of handling 115 variables (that is, an initial matrix composed of 13,225 cells). The process involves intercorrelation of cluster members in such a way that successive units added are those which cause the least reduction in the average of previous members, using the Spearman sum of variables method. Not only does the program make practical a research project impossible without the computer (even with electronic speeds the running time for the forty member Kansas Senate is from fifteen to twenty minutes), but it is at once adaptable to use for any legislative body within its range. Such a program, moreover, once constructed, becomes a potential research tool for others, who may put it to work with no more than an intuitive grasp of the complexities of statistical theory or intricacies of computer skills involved.

Ithiel de Sola Pool, with others, developed the Simulmatics program[28] for the computation of a great variety of factors thought to influence voting, for specific use in the 1960 presidential election. A multitude of influences can be introduced into the program, together with modi-

26. One useful handbook on the organization of census data and similar compilations is E. E. Schattschneider and Victor Jones, *Local Political Surveys* (New York: Holt, 1962). The authors suggest methods for quantitative research on organization and functions of local government, local politics, election statistics, demographic and social data, political geography and economic data, and a variety of projects based on census tract breakdowns for metropolitan areas.

Particularly valuable are the matrix computation methods supplied by Paul Horst, *Matrix Algebra for Social Scientists* (New York: Holt, 1963). Written especially for the social-science research worker without mathematical training, the book is oriented to the use of matrices for the three analytical methods most commonly used in behavioral research: multiple regression analysis, factor analysis, and analysis of variance.

27. John G. Grumm, *op. cit.,* p. 38.

28. Ithiel de Sola Pool and Robert Abelson, "The Simulmatics Project," in Harold Guetzkow (ed.), *Simulation in Social Science: Readings* (Englewood Cliffs, N.J.: Prentice-Hall, 1962).

fications of a strategic nature, and the results bear on both prediction and choice of strategy, much in the manner that elaborate market research influences business decision on manufacture and sale of a new product. The Simulmatics project assembled a basic matrix of voter types and "issue clusters" (480 of the former and 52 of the latter, making a total of 24,960 cells), consolidating as values the accumulated archives of polling on all kinds of questions. The records of the Roper Public Opinion Research Center at Williamstown were used as source material. With no data later than 1958, the simulation achieved a correlation by states of .82 with the actual Kennedy vote.

James Coleman has programed community political conflicts after the development of his theoretical model.[29] Karl Deutsch has used computer programs for the analysis of international trade statistics entailing comparisons of data on trade among 100 international units at three stages in time, that is, of three 100×100 matrices (10,000 cells each)— again, a project inconceivably involved without the aid of the machine.[30]

This author has programed a simulation of international political conflict which develops indices of strength and propensity to violence for each of nine major states and an index of "interest" of each of the nine major states in nine minor states.[31] The simulation deduces logical counteractions to redress loss when any of the nine actor states makes any of nine moves (scaled in order of increasing aggressiveness) against any of the nine minor states. It provides different rules to govern different power distributions (tight bipolar, loose bipolar, and balance-of-power universes).

The Systems Development Corporation is developing the Leviathan project, a simulation of large organizations intended to reproduce key aspects of large social groups engaged in the production of goods or services. Sydney and Beatrice Rome, who have worked intensively on the project, report separate sets of programs to simulate the productive processes, an inventory of productive agents, the communications nets, the technological system, the governing system, and the decision-making processes. They conceive of the complete simulation as an instrument for investigation of a great variety of social relationships in large productive social groups, "an elaborate engine for determining

29. James S. Coleman, "Analysis of Social Structures and Simulation of Social Processes with Electronic Computers," Guetzkow, *op. cit.*, pp. 61–69.

30. Karl W. Deutsch, "Toward an Inventory of Basic Trends and Patterns in Comparative and International Politics," *American Political Science Review*, Vol. 54 (1960), pp. 34–57.

31. O. Benson, "A Simple Diplomatic Game," in James N. Rosenau (ed.), *International Politics and Foreign Policy, a Reader in Research and Theory* (New York: Free Press, 1961) and "Simulation of International Relations and Diplomacy," in Harold Borko (ed.), *Computer Applications in the Behavioral Sciences* (Englewood Cliffs, N.J.: Prentice-Hall, 1962).

the consequences of theories of an intermediate level between real life and the most general theory of social process."[32]

Factor Analysis

Although the statistical technique of factor analysis is not dependent on computers, its application to extensive political data is impossible without the computer's aid. Schubert and Rummel pioneered the use of this method in political science, and Alker applied it to his intensive study of United Nations voting patterns. Especially valuable for a discipline in which data are extensive but theory weak, factor analysis is used to identify clusters of variables by successive isolation of sources of their variance. From an initial correlation matrix, the process first identifies a factor which accounts for the greatest amount of variance, continuing until no further significant explanatory factors can be found. The statistical work completed, the analyst often finds it possible to attach meaningful sociopolitical labels to the factors which the procedure has identified.

Using the data of *A Cross-Polity Survey*,[33] Gregg and Banks conducted a factor analysis of sixty-eight variables, leading to a tentative listing of seven major sources of variation among political systems.[34] In order of "importance"—that is, in order of the amount of variance accounted for, these factors were: (1) access to political channels, (2) differentiation of political institutions in former colonies, (3) degree of consensus on political rules, (4) sectional differentiation of political institutions, (5) variation in means of legitimizing authority, (6) interest circulation, and (7) strength of executive leadership in domestic and foreign affairs. Relevance of their typology to the scientific study of comparative politics is suggestive of the results to be anticipated in future from continued use of this powerful analytic tool.

Agenda

In political science, mathematics has already proved a useful tool for the ordering and analysis of information, for the development of

32. Sydney C. Rome and Beatrice K. Rome, "Computer Simulation toward a Theory of Large Organizations," in Borko, *op. cit.*, pp. 522–555.
33. Arthur S. Banks and Robert B. Textor, *A Cross-Polity Survey* (Cambridge: M.I.T. Press, 1963).
34. Phillip M. Gregg and Arthur S. Banks, "Dimensions of Political Systems: Factor Analysis of *A Cross-Polity Survey*," *American Political Science Review*, Vol. 59 (September 1965), pp. 602–613.

theory, and for suggesting patterns of theory development by analogy. It has also supplied leads which need following up: an example is Riker's suggestion that usual democratic practices of dichotomous decision in voting may be due to an inherent characteristic of the voting process as indicated by the Condorcet paradox; another is the curious similarity to reality of the cube law of representation; several theoretical concepts of game theory have worked out in empirical situations. The use of mathematical graph theory to the study of balance, communication, and hierarchical relations in social organizations, as illustrated by Kemeny,[35] is essentially in its infancy.

Could mathematical group theory, or some application of it, fit the forthcoming challenge of measuring and fitting together the variety of social groups of interest to political scientists? One of the serious questions now confronting behavioralism is the relevance of small-group studies to the actions of large social groups like nations, or of nonpolitical groups to political processes. Mathematics may furnish a happy meeting ground for traditional theory and behavioralism; its precise patterns afford a healthy safeguard against either traditional or behavioral dogmatism and discourage muddled argument.

A word of caution is in order, however, particularly with respect to prospects of prediction. Even the Simulmatics project, with its high correlation of .82, could never have predicted the actual outcome of the 1960 election except with the standard hedge for (in this case fatal) error. It may be pointed out that prediction is by no means a completely identified concept. Problems of prediction are often divisible into two or more parts, ranging from the known to the unknown. That is, they may include components parallel to those of "predicting" the population of 1990, a population which will include (from this viewpoint) two groups: those already born and whose age in 1990 will be 23 years or more, and those yet to be born. (Technically one could add to the first group the borderline group now in gestation.) "Prediction" is quite different for the two groups. With the former, we "predict" merely that, if normal patterns of population erosion continue, a certain number of people now living, now countable, will survive. Conscript armies plan their annual intake on this basis. For the second group, we are speculating completely, even if on reasonable assumptions: The "if" of our "if-then" is now a 100 per cent ingredient, where with the first group our "if" is closer to the "if" of "if the sun rises tomorrow." Similar clarification of other prediction situations may aid in reducing the range of the unknowable.

We may think of mathematics and political science up to now as engaging in a sporadic conversation. Once in a while, a mathematician

35. John G. Kemeny and J. L. Snell, *Mathematical Models in the Social Sciences* (Boston: Ginn, 1962), pp. 95–108.

asks a question which the political scientist might be able to answer or to reshape. Essentially, what he says is that an idea has struck him from his own work which he thinks may be relevant to ours. To engage in this dialogue, we must be able to understand him. The discipline will profit if, in turn, we can ask questions of mathematicians.

Rapoport[36] tells a story about a man enamored of his new screwdriver. He went about the house tightening every screw and, when he could find no more screws, took a file and filed grooves in the nailheads so he could screw the nails. The man was not so stupid as the story means to suggest, unless he kept doing this indefinitely. The method is a familiar handy man's trick for loosening old rusted nails. A sharper barb would conclude that, finding nails easier to turn than screws, he devoted his entire effort thereafter to slotted nails. There is nothing inherently wrong with trying one's equipment on new problems—sometimes an imaginative combination leads to discovery.

36. In *Fights, Games, and Debates; op. cit.*

7

The Utility of Quantitative Methods
in Political Science

ANDREW HACKER

SEVERAL YEARS AGO there appeared an article entitled "Measurement Concepts in the Theory of Influence."[1] The author's intention was to construct a mathematical model capable of measuring the relative influence of two actors in a political setting. Terms were defined and delimited with care and precision: in place of ambiguous prose, rigorous symbols were used throughout. The basic model was a four-cell table (Figure 7.1), but, as the article proceeded, it was

		R_1	
		B_1	B_2
R_2	B_1	O_{11}	O_{12}
	B_2	O_{21}	O_{22}

FIGURE 7.1

shown that many variations could be played on the fundamental theme. Quite clearly, the author felt that only if such techniques of analysis were used would discourse on a subject like political influence become meaningful.

1. James G. March, "Measurement Concepts in the Theory of Influence," *The Journal of Politics*, Vol. 19 (May 1957), pp. 202–226. This article and the ones to be cited subsequently are simply used as illustrations and are not intended to be a systematic review of the literature. For such a review, see Richard P. Fagen, "Some Contributions of Mathematical Reasoning to the Study of Politics," *American Political Science Review*, Vol. 55 (December 1961), pp. 888–900. This bibliographical essay cites 18 books and 66 articles and papers by 64 authors.

The President and the Speaker

Those who are preoccupied with model-building are usually quick to acknowledge that formalized constructs must ultimately be put to an operational test. In other words, the empty boxes must sooner or later be filled with empirical contents. Therefore, readers were told that the influence model could easily be applied to a real and important aspect of political life. It could measure "the influence relationship between the President of the United States and the Speaker of the House of Representatives, with respect to outcomes defined in terms of a bill passing the House."[2] This is an excellent example, one allowing full scope for comparing the legislative influence of two key individuals. Thoughts come to mind of such Speakers as Henry Clay, "Uncle Joe" Cannon, and Sam Rayburn—congressional titans prepared to do battle with successive occupants of the White House. The reader's appetite was further whetted as the author proceeded to fill in his original matrix. For he was not unwilling to provide numerical indices signifying the outcomes when the President and the Speaker alternatively announce that they support or oppose a particular piece of legislation (Figure 7.2).

		President	
		For	Against
Speaker	For	0.9	0.4
	Against	0.6	0.1

FIGURE 7.2

Which President, which Speaker, and what bill are involved here? The answer, one learns, is none at all. This is, we are told, a "hypothetical matrix." It is not a description of anything that has ever happened in real political life. The numerical indices—.9, .4, .6, .1—do look as precise as one might hope for. But they are a Potemkin's Village covering the fact that the framework has yet to be used to study legislative influence.

The author, however, persists in his desire to be helpful. He is willing to tell us just what kind of data are needed if the boxes are to be filled properly. We have to know:

1. The political party of the President.
2. The political party of the Speaker.
3. The substantive area of the bill considered.

2. March, *op. cit.,* p. 217.

4. The President's position on the bill.
5. The Speaker's position on the bill.
6. The outcome of the bill in the House.[3]

The comment that follows is, beyond a doubt, the most illuminating of all: "There is no need to go into the details of securing information on these values. The techniques are the standard ones of historical and field research."[4] "No need"? There may be no need to tell us how to obtain these six straightforward facts. We all know where to find the *New York Times* and the *Congressional Quarterly*. And it is not impossible to corner the Speaker and find out his position on a bill. But what we do need to be told is how these pieces of information are to be transformed into numerical "values." Here the need for enlightenment is overpowering.

The year is 1947. The President is a Democrat. The Speaker is a Republican. The bill, sponsored by Robert A. Taft and Fred Hartley, is in the area of labor relations. The President has announced that he opposes passage of the bill. The Speaker has said he favors passage. The Taft-Hartley bill passes the House by a large majority. There is the information in a nutshell. But it defies comprehension to see how these data can be translated into "values" such as .9, .4, .6, and .1 so as to fit the cells of the matrix. What, it may be asked, are the "standard" techniques of "historical and field research" that will permit us to quantify the comparative influences of Harry Truman and Joe Martin over the fortunes of the Taft-Hartley bill? The author does not go into this question at all. "There is no need to," he has said. The suspicion arises that those who build models have little knowledge of or interest in empirical research. Perhaps they feel that their mathematical contributions are the truly creative work, that the drudgery of fact-grubbing can be relegated to lesser scribes.

Senatorial Power

Yet such an accusation may be unwarranted, or at least premature. An attempt to link model-building and empirical research is to be found in a study entitled "The Concept of Power."[5] The article opens with a straightforward attempt to define power and to express that definition symbolically. Power is viewed as a relationship between individuals,

---

3. *Ibid.*, p. 223.
4. *Ibid.*
5. Robert A. Dahl, "The Concept of Power," *Behavioral Science*, Vol. 2 (July 1957), pp. 201–215. In the opening footnote, the author acknowledges "a particularly heavy debt to March."

not as a substance or a property that a person may happen to have. The strength or weakness of a power relation can, for example, be stated in terms of relative probabilities.[6]

The probability that the Senate will vote to increase taxes if the President makes a nationwide television appeal for a tax increase is .4. The probability that the Senate will vote to increase taxes if the President does not make such an appeal is .1.

Such probabilities, it is suggested, might be worked out if the following formulas were employed:

$$P(a, x|A, w) = p_1 = .4,$$
$$P(a, \bar{x}|A, \bar{w}) = p_2 = .1,$$

where

(A, w) = A does w. For example, the President makes a nationwide television appeal for tax increases.

$(A, \bar{w})$ = A does not do w.

(a, x) = a, the respondent, does x. For example, the Senate votes to increase taxes.

$(a, \bar{x})$ = a does not do x.

$P(u|v)$ = Probability that u happens when v happens.

Of course, the indices .4 and .1 are again hypothetical. For no specific President, Senate, tax bill, or television appeal has been studied here. Nor is it suggested how data for a problem such as this might be secured or translated into quantitative terms. The figures .4 and .1 are apparently introduced to imply that it is possible to transform power relations into numerical indices.

If this were the end of the exercise, it would be of small interest. What is significant is that the author proceeds from his symbolic rendering of power to rank not hypothetical actors or role-players but actual members of the United States Senate. He takes thirty-four senators, sitting between 1946 and 1954, and ranks them in order of the power each has been shown to possess when it comes to determining the course of foreign policy and tax legislation. Put very briefly, a senator's power is measured by how frequently a majority of his colleagues line up with him on a side of an issue.[7] Using sixty-five foreign-policy roll-call votes in this nine-year period, for example, it is possible to rank the senators on their relative power. Thus, Carl Hayden of Arizona and Warren

6. *Ibid.*, p. 204.
7. There are, of course, all sorts of common-sense objections to such a definition of senatorial power, and they are anticipated by Dahl. See also Duncan MacRae, Jr., and Hugh D. Price, "Scale Positions and 'Power' in the Senate," *Behavioral Science*, Vol. 4 (July 1959), pp. 212–218.

Magnuson of Washington are tied for first place, Wayne Morse of Oregon ranks sixteenth, and Harry Byrd of Virginia is twenty-ninth.

This is an interesting and informative exercise. There is one troublesome question that tends to arise, however, whenever a transition from model-building to empirical research is attempted. In this case, it is not at all clear just how far the symbolic rendering of power at the outset of the study in any way aided the ranking exercise that came later. By all appearances, it seems quite possible to have analyzed the roll-call votes of the thirty-four senators without first formulating mathematical equations on probability. Doubtless the author would reply that his mathematical model helped him to introduce a rigor into his thinking that he would not otherwise have had. He might even say that his formal conceptualization of power opened his eyes to new insights concerning legislative behavior and that, aided by these new perceptions, he was stimulated to rank the power of senators in the way that he did. It is, of course, impossible to explore either motives or motivations in instances like these. Mathematical reasoning, like all efforts at clear thinking, can sharpen the mind. But whether such exercises lead to a heightened sensitivity to the realities of political behavior cannot be either proved or disproved.

What will be raised at this point is a seemingly simple-minded query but one with important ramifications. If sixty-five foreign-policy roll calls are used as a basis for ascertaining the relative power of senators, can it be said that all sixty-five of these votes are of equal significance? In the method that was employed, each of the roll-call votes was given identical weight. That is, no effort was made to distinguish "significant" bills from those which might be considered comparatively inconsequential. Presumably, it takes more power to rally the majority over to your side on an important foreign-aid appropriation than it does to recruit votes for an uncontroversial amendment. If power is to be scaled in a meaningful way, then weights must be assigned to the items comprising the scale. The problem, treated rather casually up to now, is how to devise weights that reflect the actual emphases which operate in political life.

Judicial Opinions

At least one attempt has been made at a solution. In an article on "Predicting Supreme Court Decisions Mathematically," an effort was made to analyze the factors that led the judges to decide cases one way or another.[8] In studying a group of right-to counsel cases, the

---

8. Fred Kort, "Predicting Supreme Court Decisions Mathematically," *American Political Science Review*, Vol. 51 (March 1957), pp. 1–12.

author concluded that there were twenty-four "pivotal factors," any one or combination of which might guide the Court in making up its mind. These factors are apparently quite standard ones in right-to-counsel cases, and the record will show which ones were present in any given case. Thus, a plaintiff may have had his request for an assigned counsel denied or he may have had no assistance of counsel at time of sentencing or he may have been especially young or immature. It is possible to categorize these factors because the Supreme Court, unlike the Congress, hands down official opinions giving the reasons why it acted as it did. Close reading of these opinions should show which factors guided the judges and to which they assigned greatest weight.

The assumption of the study was that the weighting was actually in the data themselves. In some cases, many factors will be cited in the opinion as leading to the Court's determination. In other cases, one or only a few factors will be mentioned. The presumption is thus drawn that the more important a factor is the less it will have to be supported by additional factors. Conversely, the presence of few supporting factors in a decision indicates that the one or two that are cited carry significant weight. This is an imaginative approach, and the author has created a formula that assigns a numerical weight to each of the twenty-six factors noted in right-to-counsel cases. The formula is a technical one, involving square roots, and there is no need to reproduce it here. Thus, for example, "request for assigned counsel denied" receives a weight of 43.7; "no assistance of counsel at time of sentencing" is weighted at 38.0; and "youth and concomitant immaturity of defendant" has 33.7. The twenty-six weights range from a low of 5.2 to a high of 68.3. Thus, the weights assigned to the factors mentioned in any case can be summed, and this gives an indication of the strength of a plaintiff's plea in the eyes of the Court. The author shows that, if the weights total 389.1 or more, the petitioner will win; if they are less than 370.4, he will lose.

But can it be said that the weights are "in" the opinions and need only be extracted and inserted in the formula? Unfortunately for the readers of this study, the author did not make public which of the twenty-six factors he found in the cases he read. This is a serious omission, for it is not at all clear that his reading of the cases is the last word in interpretation. A Supreme Court opinion is not presented in tabular form. It is a work of prose, often quite disorganized prose. Content analysis of an opinion is far from being a simple or unambiguous matter. Because this is so, one colleague took it upon himself to obtain privately from the author a list of the factors presumed to be present in each of the right-to-counsel cases. This colleague then read the cases for himself and, not surprisingly, discovered that his assessment of which factors were present in a given opinion differed from the one originally made.[9] The point, of course, is that, in political science as in medicine, diagnosticians can differ. And here, it should be noted, the difference of opinion between scholars was not on an issue like which of two foreign-policy bills is "more important." On the contrary, the weights given to the factors were supposed to have been derived from the judges' own behavior, from what they said in their written opinions. One would think at least that scholars could agree on the content of a Supreme Court opinion, but apparently even this is impossible. Yet if this cannot be done, it is hard to visualize a scholarly consensus on systems of weighing for the far more complex behavior to be found among legislatures and electorates. All in all, it is necessary to conclude that weights cannot be thought of as lying dormant in the data.[10] For weighting is ultimately a question of interpretation, and it requires the scholar to impose his personal judgment on the facts he has before him.

Computers and Campaigns

No review of the use of mathematics in political science is complete without reference to computer simulation. It is quite clear that these electronic machines are invaluable for their speed and their ability to store information. So far, the chief use of computers has been to simulate the behavior of the real world. In other words, an artificial environment is created: an election campaign, an episode in international diplomacy, a decision-making process in a large organization. Those drawing up the computer program decide which factors are to be operative in the model. They will decide who are to be the participating actors, what resources and dispositions they are to have, and what are the goals to be sought and the means acceptable to securing those ends. Simulation is model-building in that the number of variables is controlled and their behavior is restricted. Needless to say, "all" the variables can never be included in a program. Nevertheless, the idea is to see how far reality

9. Franklin M. Fisher, "The Mathematical Analysis of Supreme Court Decisions," *American Political Science Review,* Vol. 52 (June 1958), p. 334 and footnote 24.

10. Guttman Scaling is frequently used to measure intensity, but the operation it performs should not be regarded as weighting. A Scale will contain a number of items, e.g., eight roll-call votes on foreign aid or six survey questions on civil rights. But the "distances" between all of the items on the Scale are equidistant. In consequence, the Scale itself is unweighted even though the persons whose behavior is analyzed by it will be shown to act or feel with varying intensities. There is, of course, nothing to prevent anyone from setting up the Scale items any way he wishes. Thus instead of 100-80-60-40-20, he might take note of the differences in importance of the "space" separating items and have the Scale read 100-70-60-35-15. However, such an adjustment is usually frowned upon for fear of introducing a subjective evaluation of the data into the Scale.

can be reproduced or even predicted through simulation. There is also the expectation, common in all model-building, that new insights will emerge as the computers permute variables in new and unanticipated combinations.

An impressive example of computer research was an attempt to simulate the 1960 primary election in Wisconsin.[11] There were three contestants in this "open" primary. Put more conventionally, the Democratic primary was contested, and there was only one name entered in the Republican primary. This meant that Republicans would and could cross over to vote in the Democratic contest. The computer was asked whether John Kennedy or Hubert Humphrey would benefit most from the intervention of Richard Nixon's supporters in what was ostensibly a Democratic race. Two sets of data were fed into the computer. The first was a group of "voters." This simulated electorate consisted of the coded interview responses of a sample of Wisconsin residents who had been selected and questioned by the Elmo Roper organization. Each voter, upon being interviewed, was revealed as having opinions and dispositions on various campaign issues. The individuals in the sample had been asked to rate issues and arguments as being strong or weak, and all of these opinions were stored on the computer's memory drum. Thus the sentiments of the Wisconsin electorate were in the computer and the voters' reactions to campaign stimuli could be observed.

The second set of data was derived from the actual primary campaigns as conducted by Kennedy and Humphrey. Unfortunately, no details are given on the data used for this phase of the programing. Presumably, the author observed the campaign and concluded that Kennedy was stressing certain issues whereas Humphrey was emphasizing others. Or he may have noted that the two candidates embodied different personal characteristics. At all events, a group of issues and characteristics was compiled to simulate the campaign, and these, too, were fed into the computer. These data were regarded as stimuli that reached the voters, made an initial impression, became objects of discussion, and ultimately had a greater or lesser impact depending on the strength of the original disposition of the citizens in the sample. The entire operation was planned mathematically, stimuli and responses being expressed in symbols. The formula emphasized the sequential pattern of the campaign, assuming that candidates and voters were engaging in a dialectic that was both cyclical and cumulative.

There is no indication that the data were weighted before being

11. William N. McPhee, "Note on a Campaign Simulator," *Public Opinion Quarterly*, Vol. 25 (Summer 1961), pp. 184–194. For a summary of this article and a general review of the field, see Rufus P. Browning, "Computer Programs as Theories of Political Process," *Journal of Politics*, Vol. 24 (August 1962), pp. 562–582.

programed for the computer. If the voters were interviewed to ascertain their political attitudes, it seems that the responses they gave were taken at face value. In other words, if a respondent said he felt that a particular issue was important, it was assumed that he would tend to support the candidate stressing that issue. But can it be taken for granted that an individual has such insight into his own motives? Experience has surely shown that voters are all too often unaware of why they vote as they do. Indeed, one of the canons of social research has always been that the "outsider" doing the research has a better understanding of a person's behavior than that individual does himself. The scholar must have this much confidence in his powers of perception and analysis. He must be prepared to analyze what the voters say about themselves, on the one hand discounting what are clearly rationalizations and on the other reading between the lines for unexpressed sentiments. There is little to be gained in taking as given what people say about themselves. Nor can one assume, in computer simulation as elsewhere, that the appropriate emphases are contained "in" the data. The weights must come from the outside and be imposed on the data that have been secured through surveys and other techniques.

What data are used to simulate a campaign? There are the candidates themselves—handsome or homely, loquacious or taciturn, Catholic or Protestant. There are television and personal appearances. There are newspaper stories and magazine articles. There are posters on telephone poles and billboards on highways and bumper stickers on automobiles. There are campaign workers in the precincts and personal influences at work everywhere. If these stimuli can be reproduced on a computer program, it must be confessed that available research reports have yet to show how it can be done. The point, to repeat, is that a campaign must be analyzed by someone with the ability—the experience and the sophistication—to detect what are the critical elements when it comes to swaying voters. The folkways of campaigning require that the candidate go through all of the customary motions. He must kiss babies, attend coffee parties, and answer questionnaires from the League of Women Voters. No one, not even the candidate, knows which of these are a waste of time and which are not. But no one dares omit an ingredient for fear that it may be the one making for a successful cake. In their after-the-fact analyses, the newspapers tell us that this man won because of his charming personality or that man lost because the tide was going against his party. These may be valid explanations, but no one has shown how data on these questions suitable for computer simulation can be obtained.

Computers, it goes without saying, have no judgment. The sad thing is that those who are running the machines are themselves reluctant to exercise that quality which the computer lacks. One reason is that most such projects are team operations. No single scholar secures and programs the data; rather, it is done by a committee. Each member of the team will have, individually, his own perception of political reality. But, taken collectively, the members of the group will inevitably disagree on the significance of the role played by various factors. The enterprise will not get off the ground if such dissension is allowed to persist. So models are created with the controversial variables stripped away, leaving only those on which there is a consensus. Such a procedure, one that is more common than might be thought, may make for more equable social relations among those participating in a project. But playing it safe seldom leads to advances in political knowledge or understanding.

The Unbridged Chasm

We have arrived at a great divide, a yawning chasm than can only be crossed if someone undertakes to build a bridge. But the bridge is not being built, and there is some reason to suspect that it never will be. Therefore, the explorers who have reached the canyon's rim have pitched their tents and are apparently settling in for good. They occupy their time designing models that will be useful once the chasm is spanned. But they make no serious effort to build the bridge, even though they know it is needed. For one thing, it is a dangerous operation and there may be heavy casualties. Anyway, bridge-building is for engineers, and these explorers pride themselves on being scientists and mathematicians.

The problem has two parts to it. The first is securing the facts, and the second is evaluating the facts once they have been obtained. Game theory, for example, is currently one of the more fashionable mathematical approaches. Much has been said and written about its potentialities for increasing our political understanding. Yet one of its most enthusiastic proponents admits that "as matters now stand, the application of game theory is limited by the absence of needed data."[12] What is perhaps most interesting is that the kind of information needed if game theory is to be made operational is called "data" at all. For facts are only transformed into data if they are obtained and ordered in a systematic way. The problem for political research, it hardly needs saying, is that there are too many of the wrong kind of facts and too

12. Richard C. Snyder, "Game Theory and the Analysis of Political Behavior," in *Research Frontiers in Politics and Government* (Washington, D.C.: Brookings Institution, 1955), p. 73.

few of the right kind. Most of the facts we have are either not facts at all, being rather opinions, or they refuse to fit into a systematic order. The facts we do not have are unavailable not for lack of digging but because the human mind is simply not capable of understanding some aspects of individual and social behavior. It is, for instance, impossible to "synthesize" the psychological and sociological aspects of a problem. The question remains unresolved not because work is not being done but because there are limits to man's comprehension of himself and his environment. The "data" needed to apply game theory to the Supreme Court or the Cold War are of such an order that they will never be secured. Whether it is worth refining the mathematics of the model, given the futility of the whole enterprise, is a serious question.

But suppose that the "data" could be obtained. We have, to use another illustration, all sorts of information on the social influences that form political attitudes. Survey research, for the most part unassisted and unhampered by mathematical models, has been able to turn up all manner of facts about the ways in which environment shapes the outlook of individuals. However, almost everyone has had parents, has a job or is supported by someone with a job, has gone to school, and has aspirations concerning his role in society. We may be able to secure data on a wide range of social influences working on a person, but these facts must be assessed for their significance compared with the other facts we have. What, say, is the role played by formal education?

While it is plain that education significantly shapes politically relevant attitudes, it must be conceded that isolation of the effects of the school system from other influences forming political man is not readily accomplished. Intensive studies in life histories of individuals would permit more confident assignment of weights to the factors of family, education, occupational interests, social status, and other such influences.[13]

We might, indeed, study the life histories of a sample of adult citizens. In each case, we would doubtless come up with some kind of factual information on the influence of family, education, occupation, and social status on the formation of politically relevant attitudes. But, if past experience is any guide, the information in these biographies will be so difficult to interpret that assigning weights to the several influential factors will never be realized.[14] Nor is there much likelihood that a "general theory" of attitude formation will emerge from such a research exercise.

13. V. O. Key, Jr., *Public Opinion and American Democracy* (New York: Knopf, 1961), pp. 341–342.
14. David Riesman's *Faces in the Crowd* (New Haven: Yale U. P., 1952) is a collection of twenty-one such life histories. It would be a challenging exercise for someone to go through these biographies and try to assign weights to the factors that influenced the political outlooks of the individuals who were studied.

Measuring "Goodness"

Does this mean that the weighting of variables is entirely futile? The answer, on the contrary, is that it is a necessary enterprise which has been done in the past and which should be continued in the future. Over twenty years ago, when research was conducted in a far more simple-minded way, there was a scholar who thought it would be a good idea to rate various American cities on the "goodness of life" enjoyed by their inhabitants.[15] There is no point in claiming that life in Dallas is preferable to life in Seattle unless one has a way of measuring the quality of existence in those two cities. So a "G-Score" was constructed. The "goodness" of a city was determined by summing its ratings on twenty-four statistical items. The scale contained items like the infant death rate, the average salary paid to teachers, the per capita number of automobiles, and so forth. If an item was negative—that is, signified a diminution of the quality of life—then the reverse ratio of that factor was used in the scale. The decision that there would be only twenty-four items on the G-Score and the selection of the particular items to be included were made, unilaterally and unblushingly, by the scholar who conceived of the project in the first place.

To be sure, some factors contribute more to the "goodness of life" of a city than do others. Modern agnosticism might protest that there is no objective way of knowing if one factor is more significant than another. In contemporary research, all factors would be weighted equally, for this would at least avoid controversy. Alternatively, residents of cities might be asked what they felt were the most significant factors making for civic virtue, and, in this way, the judgments of the citizens themselves would be accepted as an index. But the man who invented the G-Score was neither an agnostic nor a democrat. He assigned a weight to each of the twenty-four items on the scale. And, moreover, they were his, presumably more competent, evaluations and not those of the man in the street. Thus, the frequency of home ownership was weighted at four points, standing higher than the literacy rate (which got 2.5) and lower than the per capita expenditure on textbooks and school supplies (which got 5.0).

The selection of items and the distribution of weights, then, was the reasoned judgment of a single scholar. Although doubtless he could have given justifications for the choices he made, he did not bother to do so, probably knowing in advance that his explanations would be unsatisfactory to anyone inclined to be critical of the project. Put another way, some decisions simply cannot be justified—although that is

15. E. L. Thorndike, *Your City* (New York: Harcourt, 1939) and *144 Smaller Cities* (New York: Harcourt, 1940).

TABLE 7.1—G-Score Weights

High Per Capita or Percentage	ELT	HS	DA	DR	JS	RS
Expenditure on teachers' salaries	4.0	4.0	5.0	7.0	3.0	7.5
Expenditure on textbooks and supplies	5.0	5.0	5.0	7.0	5.0	3.0
Persons 16 to 17 attending school	3.0	6.0	4.0	5.0	5.0	6.0
Persons 18 to 20 attending college	5.0	6.0	4.0	5.0	5.0	6.0
Average high school teacher's salary	3.0	5.0	6.0	7.0	5.0	7.5
Average grade school teacher's salary	2.5	4.0	6.0	7.0	3.0	7.5
Average factory worker's wage	3.0	5.0	4.0	5.0	5.0	4.5
Home ownership	4.0	4.0	2.0	1.0	3.0	4.5
Electricity installations	3.5	4.0	3.0	2.0	7.0	4.5
Gas installations	5.0	4.0	1.0	2.0	1.0	1.5
Automobile ownership	3.0	2.0	1.0	2.0	7.0	—
Telephone installations	7.5	0.5	1.0	2.0	3.0	3.0
Television sets	4.5	2.0	1.0	2.0	3.0	—
Literacy	2.5	6.5	7.0	5.0	7.0	6.0
"Quality" magazine circulation	3.5	4.5	1.0	5.0	3.0	3.0
Reversed Indices						
Infant death rate	8.5	4.0	6.0	5.0	7.0	4.5
General death rate	6.5	6.0	4.0	1.0	7.0	1.5
Typhoid death rate	3.5	4.0	5.0	3.0	3.0	3.0
Appendicitis death rate	3.0	4.0	4.0	1.0	1.0	3.0
Mothers' childbirth death rate	3.0	4.0	6.0	5.0	5.0	6.0
Syphilis death rate	3.0	4.0	5.0	5.0	1.0	3.0
Homicide death rate	2.5	4.0	7.0	10.0	3.0	4.5
Automobile accident death rate	3.0	0.5	5.0	1.0	1.0	4.5
Incidence of poverty	8.5	7.0	7.0	5.0	7.0	6.0

not the same as saying that the making of such decisions is unjustifiable. Table 7.1 lists the twenty-four items in the G-Score, and the first column gives the weights assigned to these items. The next five columns contain the weights that five other persons, working independently and without knowing the original weights, gave to the items.[16]

The result is a series of comparative judgments on G-Score weights, all made by individuals who may be presumed to be competent in the field under consideration. It is not surprising that their weights differ from those originally assigned, and this is not simply because the criteria of "goodness" have changed since 1939. Nor is it any less surprising that they do not agree with each other, for quite clearly there cannot be a consensus on what makes for the quality of life in 1963. It would be silly to ask these five persons to confer around a table, compromise their differences, and concur on a weighting system. The judgment of a committee is hardly what is wanted on a question like this. It may

16. The original G-Score summed to 144 points, but for present purposes it has been adjusted to 100 points. Only one change was made in the items in asking for new assignments of weights: the original items on radios were changed to television sets. The following graduate students in the Department of Government at Cornell University were kind enough to participate in this exercise: Harvey Simmons, Dean Alfange, Donald Robinson, John Stanley, and Roger Smith.

be suggested that the G-Score is in fact a "moral" evaluation, providing more area for disagreement than might a "factual" problem. But is this so? A twenty-four-item scale might be drawn up listing factors influencing the passage of the Taft-Hartley bill. A group of scholars might similarly be asked to weight each item as was done for the G-Score. All indications are that they would fail to agree no less on this than on a "moral" question. Perceptions of reality vary as between observers, and, so long as they do, "objectivity" will remain not only a fiction but a harmful one. For the vain pursuit of "objective" knowledge deflects attention and energy from more worthwhile avenues of approach to political understanding.

In Praise of Subjectivity

Scholars always have differed and always will differ in their descriptions and explanations of the political world they see. If it has been reiterated here that there is a need for weighting—for determining the significance of operative factors—the conclusion must be that this is a highly subjective endeavor. The G-Score is not a mathematical model, but it can serve as a fine model for contemporary model-builders. What must be abandoned is the hope that political analysis can be either objective or scientific. The underlying method of the natural and physical sciences is inapplicable to political study: "Objectivity is closely bound up with the social aspect of scientific method, with the fact that science and scientific objectivity do not and cannot result from the attempts of an individual scientist to be 'objective,' but from the cooperation of many scientists."[17] There may be cooperation among political scientists in the sense that they share and criticize each other's research. However, this communication does not produce an agreed-upon body of knowledge. Indeed, controversy rather than consensus is the rule on all questions of method and content transcending the commonplace. At this time, it is hard to point to any "findings" that have been accepted by the scholarly community. As matters now stand, there are cliques, coteries, and lone wolves talking past one another or to themselves.

"At this time. . . ." "As matters now stand. . . ." Phrases such as these have become all too familiar in recent years. The pleas for more *time* assume that mathematical methods are but babes in arms, creatures with unlimited potentialities if only they may be nurtured to adulthood. The assumption is that the passage of time will somehow bring not only more refined techniques but ultimately an enhanced understanding

17. Karl Popper, *The Open Society and Its Enemies* (London: Routledge, 1945), Vol. 2, p. 205.

of the political process. Yet those who ask for time never really examine just what it is their request implies. Will there be a greater consensus among scholars on perceived realities in 1977 than there is now? The evidence, if such it can be called, is that, so long as scholars are affected by differing interests and spring from differing backgrounds, disagreements over political facts will persist. There is little reason to believe that mathematical approaches will lead to changed perceptions within a discipline or produce a consensus among its members. The demand for more time carries with it a theory concerning the progress of human knowledge that is highly tenuous. It assumes that, somehow, contrary to all past experience, students of politics will begin to agree on some major propositions about the world they are studying. Just what breed of men these scholars of the future will be, devoid of opinions and obstinacy, is difficult to imagine.

We must make do with and make the best of the materials at hand. What is wanted is more subjective analysis, more individual scholarship, and more research that is highly personal in conclusion and design. Each student of politics must describe the world as he sees it, holding onto the faith that his perceptions and evaluations are valid. There must be a certain display of arrogance here, a sense that everyone is out of step except one's self. There is also involved the courage to weather the scorn of more conventional colleagues. For their agreement will only be obtained if controversial elements are stripped away, leaving ideas and approaches that are unexceptionable. If the great theorists of the past—from Plato through Freud—made some contribution to our understanding of politics, it is not simply because they were men of surpassing intellect. It is also because they had the audacity to select those factors they felt were important and to emphasize them to the neglect or even exclusion of others. This is what Thomas Hobbes and Edmund Burke did. It was also the method of Karl Marx and Sigmund Freud. It is easy enough to say that any of these theories overweights a single factor, but what emerges is a caricature rather than a rounded depiction. These men knew they were drawing caricatures, but they had the courage to omit the qualifications and reservations that would detract from the major points they sought to make. If the traditional writers were wrong—and all of them were—their errors were brilliant in conception and imaginative in design. Their wrongheadedness, in short, has aided our political understanding more than all the level-headed models of those who manage to avoid criticism by confining their generalizations to the unobjectionable.

At the same time, there is little profit in exhorting scholars to surpass their native talents. The man who is now sitting in a cubicle at some university drawing up a computer program is not an unborn Rousseau or a stifled John Stuart Mill. It may seem unkind to say so, but the typical mathematical political scientist is no more an extraordinary person than the rest of us. His perception of reality is as conventional or as distorted as those of others, and his powers of analysis are apt to be as muddled as the next person's. Access to an electronic computer or knowledge of the calculus does not transform a mediocre mind into a superior intellect. For this reason, then, it is idle to tell the model-builder that he should turn to old-fashioned political philosophy in the hope that his redirected efforts will take us farther toward attaining the good life or the just polity. Even if he abandoned mathematics for moral philosophy, it is doubtful if his contribution to political knowledge would be much more memorable.

If these comments have been critical of so much of the pretentiousness that surrounds the mathematical approaches, it is only because most of us are rather unpretentious individuals. At the risk of sounding patronizing, it may be noted that the expansion of higher education will require more professors of political science, and the quality of the persons entering this expanded profession will not be very high. Yet the customs of academe require that all do research, at least to obtain the doctorate. If the researcher is a rather ordinary individual, and most will be, then it does not really matter whether he spends his time building models or if he mulls over the minor works of Montesquieu. Unlike medicine, where there is the problem of allocating scarce resources, political science can permit each scholar to labor in whatever vineyard he thinks is important. Although the suggestion may have been made here that model-building is a waste of time, it should also be noted that no alternative activity is being proposed for those lured by the siren call of mathematics. Political knowledge will only grow as each of us does the kind of research he wants to do. Throughout history, most of what has passed as scholarship has been profitless and is soon forgotten. But the atmosphere in which most of us are allowed to engage in fads and fantasies is also the atmosphere that will nourish a serious thinker who, probably unappreciated by his contemporaries, will eventually be acknowledged as someone who made a significant contribution to our understanding of political life.

8

Systems Theory

MORTON A. KAPLAN

THE CLASSIC STATEMENT of systems theory occurs in W. Ross Ashby's, *Design For A Brain*.[1] A brief and nontechnical description of the objectives of systems analysis would include: the study of a set of interrelated variables, as distinguished from the environment of the set, and of the ways in which this set is maintained under the impact of environmental disturbances. This definition emphasizes the articulation of the system and of its components and the behaviors by means of which it maintains itself over time.

This orientation does not imply the actual or potential existence of a general theory of systems. We will later explain how and why systems theory implies the probability of comparative rather than general theory. Neither does systems theory imply the desirability or the actuality of system stability. It is true that the systems that do persist usually have the greatest importance for us; this reason would no doubt justify a concern with systems in equilibrium. There are, however, prior and theoretically more interesting reasons for concern with the problems of equilibrium. Differences in types of equilibrium are important in distinguishing differences in types of systems. This important problem will also be explored below. In addition, there is an important reason stemming from the principle of economy. Many more systems fail to persist through time than those that do persist. Although the parameter values that produce instability are large in number and differ in multifarious ways from case to case, the conditions producing stability are much more limited in number. Thus concern with stability, at least in the initial stages of inquiry, focuses attention on a relatively small number of systems, a limited number of variables, and a limited range of variation. Although the problem of inquiry may still be most

1. New York: Wiley, 1952.

difficult, it is much more focused and manageable than is a concern with problems of instability. Moreover, to the extent that we can understand systems in equilibrium, we have a fulcrum for the study of systems in disequilibrium. If we can construct a theory for a system or type of system, as a system in equilibrium, we can then inquire how individual variations in the parameters will produce deviant or unstable behavior. To know why a system changes, develops, or breaks down it is surely helpful to know why the conditions of change are inconsistent with the prior states of the system. If we cannot answer this latter question, it is doubtful whether we have correctly assigned the reasons for instability or change.

The systems theoretical approach is also chosen for the following additional reasons: for explicitness of categories so that the framework of reference will not shift as new "facts" are brought in; for the integration of variables that do not fall within a single discipline; for a degree of explicitness that helps to reveal incompleteness; and for the generation of hypotheses by indicating structural similarities to other subject matters.

The Concept of Equilibrium

The distinctions between equilibria are in some ways more important than their similarities. Systems analysis is concerned with two basic problems with respect to equilibrium. The first concerns the stability of the equilibrium. It is important to recognize that the concept of stability has meaning only in relation to the questions the investigator puts to his data. The same system may be stable or unstable from two different standpoints. The second question concerns the value of the concept of equilibrium from the standpoint of explanation. Whereas the concept of mechanical equilibrium provides an explanation of observed behavior, the concept of homeostatic equilibrium has a different role.

Stability

Equilibria may be regarded as unstable, static, or stable. Illustrations of the three types respectively would be a ball on a ridge, on a flat surface, and in a valley. Alternatively we can regard equilibria as locally stable or as generally stable. Locally stable equilibria are stable only in a favorable environment. A stable equilibrium, on the other hand, is capable of persisting through many large and unexpected environmental disturbances. The biological system of man, which persists unchanged through many different political and social systems, is an example of a system in stable equilibrium.

It is also important to distinguish between those cases where a system behaves differently because of an environmental disturbance but returns to its old behavior when the disturbance is removed and cases where the changed behavior persists even after the disturbance is removed. The disturbance that produces the latter form of change is called a *step function* and the system result is called *system change*. For instance, during wartime in England normal liberties were suspended and political suspects incarcerated without recourse to the courts. With the return of peace, normal liberties were restored. Thus only the state of the system but not the system itself had changed. In other cases, however, the removal of the disturbance that led to the new behavior does not lead to the restoration of the old pattern of behavior. The inflation and subsequent depression in Germany were among the factors making for the Nazi takeover. However, the restoration of the economy did not lead to the removal of the Nazi regime. If one is habituated to opiates, then the pupil will not contract when a flashlight is shined into it. These latter cases are called *system change*. Carthage was destroyed by the Romans. This is called *system destruction* or *dissolution*.

System Reference

In keeping with the explicitness of systems theory, we must be careful not to shift systems reference. Thus, for instance, one system may change while another system remains constant. Kennedy replaces Eisenhower and the Democrats the Republicans in the presidency, but the American constitutional system continues. Hitler replaces Hindenburg. The German political system changes but the social system continues. The Chinese Communists break up the extended family system and the Chinese social system has changed. The Chinese cultural system continues. Immigrants enter the United States and their cultural system is assimilated into the American cultural system. The biological system persists, however. The scientists of Huxley's *Brave New World* produce their alpha and beta types. Even the biological system has changed in this case. The examples are illustrative only. We are not stressing either a hierarchy in the systems illustrated or an absence of feedback between them. We stress here only the fact that nonsystematic discussions concerning system stability often cause confusion by failing to identify the system or systems about which statements are being made.

The preceding discussion also illustrates the fact that stability questions need to have reference to some research design. The concept of stability is meaningless until we specify, even if only imprecisely, the system, the variables whose equilibrium is of interest, the variation in values that will be considered to be consistent with equilibrium, and the length of time that has relevance. Thus the politician in a closely contested two-party district who is concerned with holding office will regard that situation as unstable. The party boss who selects the candidates may regard the system as quite stable, even though his candidates are elected alternatively with those of the opposite party and even though he may have to choose different candidates in different elections. Most Americans would find the American political system unchanged subsequent to the passage of the Communist Control Act. However, American Communists likely would not agree with this estimate. We would view the American and British political systems as stable. A visitor from Mars with a life span of 10,000 years might regard the changes in the two systems as kaleidoscopic. From the standpoint of an eternal observer, even the solar system is unstable, for eventually the sun will explode and destroy the solar system. The researcher cannot determine whether a system is stable or unstable until he establishes for himself the questions he desires to put to the subject matter. Stability always has reference to the framework of inquiries. There is no such thing as stability in and of itself.

Mechanical and Homeostatic Equilibrium

The physicist usually deals with systems in mechanical equilibrium. When the physicist says that two weights are equal, he has available independent methods that can confirm this statement. Thus his balance scales can be confirmed by his spring scales. If the spring scales do not confirm the balances, and if the elasticity of the springs is not at fault, the physicist will predict that the balance is asymmetrical. When a physicist says that two equal forces will cancel each other, he does not merely assume their equality from the cancellation. He has an independent measure for the equality. Thus the use of the concept of equilibrium with respect to mechanical equilibria is not merely descriptive but is also explanatory and predictive.

The statement that a system is in equilibrium is neither explanatory nor predictive in the case of homeostatic equilibria. Yet social and political systems manifesting some degree of equilibrium represent some kind of homeostatic equilibrium rather than of mechanical equilibrium. There are many different homeostatic equilibrium systems. The physiological system is homeostatic. Thus the temperature of the human blood is maintained by processes that compensate for environmental disturbances. For instance, in cold weather, constriction of the blood vessels occurs, whereas in hot weather perspiration takes place. The thermostatic system that maintains room temperature is also homeostatic. When the mercury reaches the desired range, the furnace is turned off. When the mercury goes below the desired range, the furnace is turned on. In both illustrative systems there are underlying mechanical systems where the equalities of physics are observed. However, homeostatic systems are not systems of equality. The process of perspiration continues until the required temperature change occurs. If for some reason this process cannot occur, as would be the case if the human body were covered with paint, either sickness or death will occur. There is no independent measure that will establish the equality between the perspiration and the lowering of temperature. Therefore, although naming the biological system one of homeostatic equilibrium tells us something about the general type of equilibrating process that characterizes the system, the statement that the system is in equilibrium is itself neither of explanatory nor predictive value. In the case of the biological system, we still require an explanation of the processes that characterize, for example, the system of temperature control.

This may help to explain why systems theory is not a general theory of all systems. Although general systems theory does attempt to distinguish different types of systems and to establish a framework within which similarities between systems can be recognized despite differences of subject matter, different kinds of systems require different theories for explanatory purposes. Systems theory not only represents a step away from the general theory approach but also offers an explanation for why such efforts will likely fail. Thus the correct application of systems theory to politics would involve a move away from general theory toward comparative theory. That is, using systems theory one would search for different theories for the explanation of different types of systems.

Types of Homeostatic Equilibrium

Discussion of the types of homeostatic equilibrium is important for several reasons. Knowledge of variations in homeostatic equilibria gives greater insight into the reasons why general theories are likely to fail in the social sciences. Political and social systems are variations of a particular type of homeostatic system, namely the ultrastable or multistable type. Moreover, the definition of a political system will be linked specifically to the concept of ultrastable regulation.

Some systems are merely homeostatic whereas others are ultrastable or multistable. Consider an ordinary homeostatic system such as the automatic pilot in an airplane. If a plane deviates from level flight while on automatic pilot, the automatic pilot will sense this and, by the application of negative feedback, will adjust the flight pattern of the plane back to level. Consider, however, the case in which the automatic pilot has been incorrectly linked to the ailerons of the plane. If the plane now deviates from level flight, the automatic pilot mechanism will sense this. It will now make an adjustment, but the adjustment, instead of bringing the plane back to level flight, will throw it into a spin.

In principle it would be possible to build an ultrastable automatic pilot the behavior of which was not critically dependent on the linkages to the ailerons. That is, the automatic pilot could be so built that it would reject its own behavior patterns if these increased the deviation from level flight. It could then "search" for a set of behaviors that would restore the level character of the flight and, when it found it, continue to use it so long as it maintained the critical variable within the established critical limits for variation. Such an ultrastable system would have distinct advantages for survival over a merely stable homeostatic system. Even ultrastability, however, is not sufficient for complex biological survival. Ashby, therefore, applies the term "multistability" to those cases where the part functions of the system are themselves individually ultrastable and where they can therefore "search" relatively independently for those critical behaviors consistent with the maintenance of the system. It is obvious that complex social systems must also be multistable.

Levels of Explanation in Systems Theory

A completely general theory would lack explanatory power. It would enunciate only the most elementary truisms about social and political structures or alternatively mislead by appearing to convey information about specifics—for example, equalities—that in its nature it could not provide. On the other hand, extreme particularization in social and political theories, or models, should also be avoided. In the first place, we cannot construct models that faithfully copy the particularities of the real world. The detail is too fine for us and, in addition, many of our variables must vary in their structure from their real-world counterparts. For instance, in calculating military interchanges we use numbers for which there are no exact counterparts in the real world. In the second place, even if we could match the fineness of the structure of the real world, our verbal, mathematical, and computer tools would be inadequate from the standpoint of representing the complex interrelationships between them. In the third place, the more complex a model becomes, if it is a feedback model, the more sensitive it is to slight variations either in loop directions or rates of flow. Thus highly complex models run the serious risk of being artifacts. That is, slight variations that we could neither detect nor measure in the real world might—and highly likely would—produce major differences in outcomes and in behaviors. Such highly particularized models lack both generality and relevance to any specific problem of social science.

The most productive level for systems theorizing will in all likelihood be that middle level where comparative theories can be evolved. Thus, for instance, Kaplan attempted a comparative theory of international systems based upon the conception that if the numbers, types, capabilities, motivations, and behavioral styles of the international actors vary, there should be systematic interrelationships among these variations. If one desired a systems theory of national systems, one would look not for a general theory of all national systems, let alone of all political systems, but for a comparative theory of different types of national systems. In the same way, a comparative theory of foreign policy might possibly be developed. It would seem likely that differences in national political systems should also make for differences in the styles or objectives of foreign policy behavior.

Such middle-level comparative theories have sufficient generality to be of scientific interest. That is, we speak about a given class of cases rather than merely about an individual or particular case. On the other hand, these comparative middle-level theories are sufficiently specific so that they say different things about distinguishable systems rather than the same thing about every system. If the variables that are treated in the comparative systems theories have sufficient importance for selective aspects of real-world behavior, they should then constitute reasonable first-order approximations that are useful for exploring those realities. At this level of generality, the fact that analogs and even counterfactual assumptions are sometimes employed does not contraindicate the validity of the enterprise.

Engineering of Systems Theories to Reality

The equilibrium models, or first-order approximations, of systems theory are useful heuristically for interpreting the real world. These equilibrium models, however, operate only under fixed parameter values. Events in the real world may be influenced by parameter values different from those assumed for the models. In this case, we can engineer the theory, or first-order approximation, by successive adjustments in order to account for individual cases, insofar as this is possible. As this occurs, generality is lost, for, with each successive approximation, we come closer to the particular and farther away from the general. This engineering process, however, remains relatively manageable because we do not consider every possible variation but only specific and important variations that we have some reason to believe occurred or might occur in particular cases.

An illustration of the way in which a theory may be engineered may be useful. Kaplan's "balance of power" theory indicates that alliances should shift rapidly and that wars should be limited. One of the reasons asserted for this is that within the framework of assumptions of the model it is more important to maintain the existence of a defeated state because of its potential importance as a future alliance partner than it is to secure the gains that could be obtained from its complete conquest. If one looks at the behaviors of the European national actors after 1870, they are inconsistent with the prescriptions of the model. Alliances tended to be long-term, to hinge around France and Germany, and the ensuing war was, according to the standards of time, unlimited.

One possible approach to this problem would be to define every descriptively different state of the world as representing a different system. Thus the European system after 1870 could be called a rigid "balance of power" system. Apart from being theoretically uninteresting —for by this method we would be forced to label every system that manifested different behavior a different system—this device is unnecessary. The "balance of power" model is a first-order approximation. The first-order approximation simplifies reality by extrapolating from considerations of internal politics in such a fashion that states are treated as if they were free to optimize according to international considerations only. When one applies a first-order approximation to reality, it is necessary to adjust for the specific boundary differences that play a role in the actual situation to which the application is being made. If one takes account of the actual temper of French politics after the seizure of Alsace Lorraine, it is evident that French public opinion became revanchist as a consequence of the seizure. Germany could neither cede Alsace Lorraine to France nor compensate France satisfactorily in other matters. As a consequence France and Germany could not be alliance partners for the foreseeable future. Thus they naturally became the poles of opposed alliances. Additionally the motivation that, according to the model, constrains the actors to accept limited objectives in war no longer operated with respect to these two states. Since neither was a potential alliance partner of the other, neither had this particular incentive to limit its aims against the other.

This example also illustrates the conditions under which one continues to employ a given theory or to adopt another theory. As long as the theory continues to explain behavior when suitable adjustments are made for the parameters of the system, that particular theory will continue to be employed even though the actual behavior is seemingly inconsistent with the prescriptions of the model under equilibrium conditions. When, however, one requires a different theory to explain the behavior, regardless of whether this is a matter of principle or of economy, then a different theory will be adopted. Obviously judgments as to when the same or different theories should be used will depend upon the state of the art as well as upon evaluation of the data.

Alternative Approaches

One may begin from different macrotheories—or first-order approximations—in order to explain the same microevents. Thus by suitable parameter adjustments, one may explain the events subsequent to 1870 either from the standpoint of a theory of international politics or from the standpoint of a theory of foreign policy. The different theories, however, will answer different sets of questions concerning these events. Thus, starting from the model or theory of international politics, we learn how public opinion produces behavior inconsistent with system stability and security optimization. If we start with a theory of foreign policy that explains how different types of polities produce different styles of external policy, we may learn how regime considerations under special circumstances produce variations in that style of behavior. In this case our primary focus is upon the foreign-policy process as a process within the national political system.

Whether we can use either or both levels of explanation depends upon the benignity of the data. Theories can be used only when their relevance is not swamped by external disturbances. There are cases where international behavior may be dominated by national considerations or, alternatively, where national regime considerations may be dominated by an international occurrence that overwhelms the actors. In the usual case, however, both sets of constraints operate and each first-order approximation serves as the best starting point to answer a particular set of questions.

One cannot build a theory of international relations, however, upon a theory of foreign policy; nor can one begin with a theory of international relations and derive theories of foreign policies from it. Either attempt would assume a general theory that encompasses both viewpoints. Either theory, however, may be useful in understanding the specific parameters to which the other theory needs to be adjusted.

There is still a third point of view which for some sets of questions may be the most productive. This is the cross-sectional or biographical slicing of history in order to delineate the dynamics of social change as a particular sequence of events unrolls and places inconsistent pressures upon actors holding critical role functions in several important systems. We are not speaking here of instability in the systems model, for presumably that would be revealed directly by the analysis of the model. Nor are we speaking of mere change, for every homeostatic system undergoes change in the process of maintaining the values of some critical variable. Thus the perspiration that supports the cooling function of the blood in summer is a change. We speak rather of those changes that are characterized by step functions—that is, by a basic alteration in the operation of the system. In the ultrastable systems designed by Ashby, disturbance of the system requires the system to "search" for some form of behavior that maintains the critical variables within the critical limits. If this cannot be done, then the system ceases to function.

Social and political systems differ from this example in at least one important respect. The actors are imbedded in social and political systems in such ways that it is a matter not merely of whether they tend to respond in the appropriate way but also of whether they will desire to. That is, in the usual case the actor can detach himself from any particular social system in which he is a participant. He must be motivated to act in ways consistent with the critical limits and the other actors must be motivated to induce him so to act.

The actors are imbedded in a web of systems. Thus John Jones has both nuclear and extended family relationships, a role in the business in which he is employed, a social and recreational role, and perhaps a religious role among many others. For some sets of environmental circumstances these roles may be not merely inconsistent but irreconcilable. Thus if Jones is a teller at a bank and if his wife desperately needs an operation and if he can get the money in no other way, he may have to choose between robbing the bank at the expense of his role as teller or failing his wife at this critical juncture. If Jones fails his wife, his family situation may be destabilized. It is unlikely that the failure of one clerk would destabilize the bank system. However, revolutions occur when critical numbers of key individuals respond to the demands of their other role functions at the expense of their functions in the state system. The conflicts that arise in cases of this kind are, along with the environmental changes that stimulate the problem, the cause of social change. This kind of cross-sectional problem can best be studied by examining how critical roles in different systems make critically inconsistent demands upon the critical actors who participate in the relevant set of systems. This is but another form of applied systems analysis or of engineering systems to the real world.

System and Subsystem Dominance

An important category for examining the problem of system stability or change is that of system and subsystem dominance. A system is system dominant to the extent that the behavior of the system functions as a parametric given for the actors within it. That is, a system is system dominant if the impact of individual behavior upon the system is negligible. For instance, in a perfect market, any individual buyer or seller will act as if price is a parametric given for him—that is, as if his entry into or staying out of the market has no effect whatsoever upon price. Cultural systems are in general system dominant. Although particular individuals may in some cases be cultural innovators, even so, with respect to both the general character of the culture and specific cultural norms, no individual is likely to be able to make any significant impact upon the culture. At the other extreme, that is, the subsystem dominant extreme, we might consider the Communist dictatorship under Stalin at the height of his power. Within broad limits, Stalin had the capability to tear the social and political system apart and to restructure it. Popular resistance, as when the kulaks slaughtered their cattle, could be treated somewhat as are price inelasticities in economics. Somewhere in between we would have a system like the "balance of power" system of international politics which, although toward the subsystem dominant end of the continuum, is no where near as far toward it as was the Communist system under Stalin. In the "balance of power" system, in the usual case, deviant actors would be induced into conforming behavior by the constraining actions of the other actors. Nonetheless each of the essential actors has a visible impact upon the system and the equilibrium is different from what it would be either in the system dominant case or farther along toward the subsystem dominant pole.

The Political System

A political system,

like many other social systems, has recognizable interests which are not identical—though not necessarily opposed and perhaps complementary—with those of the members of the system and within which there are regularized agencies and methods for making decisions concerning those interests. The rules for decision-making, including the specification of the decision-making roles and the general constitutional rules governing the society, are enacted with the political system.[2]

2. Morton A. Kaplan, *System and Process in International Politics* (New York: Wiley, 1957), pp. 13–14.

This definition of the political system is related directly to the systems theoretical method of analysis and, in specific, to the concept of ultrastability. The political system has the metatask capacity to act as the ultrastable regulator of the larger system in which it functions. It thus regulates the system by adapting it to environmental disturbances in such a way that the critical values of the system are maintained. In other words, it chooses the behaviors consistent with the critical values of the critical variables of the system. In the extreme subsystem dominant case—for example, Stalinist Russia—Stalin, and at most the Politburo, imposed decisions on the rest of the system.[3] In systems such as the British or American where the locus of the decision is in the governmental subsystem the decisions are modified by the activities of other actors within the over-all national system. (The larger system tends toward political multistability.) In subsystem dominant systems such as the "balance of power" system political decision-making is decentralized onto the essential actors; the norms of the system are imposed by their equilibrating behavior. Thus politics occurs in this system but there is no specific political subsystem. If we were to think of an international system with perhaps 10,000 or even 100,000 competing actors within it, and without any specific political subsystem, we would have approached the system dominant extreme for political activity. That is, if such a system were stable, the stability would result from the independent decision-making of the individual units in a system in which the behavior of no individual actor had discernible impact upon the behavior of the larger system. (This system would be multistable from a political standpoint.) It is rather difficult to imagine this extreme case, but it is less difficult to imagine international systems that come closer to it than any historical system has.

We note several things about the foregoing definition of the political system. It specifies neither power nor the allocation of values as central to the definition of the political system. The free market allocates values decisively. Pressure groups and criminal gangs exercise power. The attempt by Max Weber to overcome this problem, by using the word "legitimate" before the word "power," only obscures the problem, for the essence of the political in his definition lies not in the monopoly of power but in the concept of legitimacy. The definition used here stems directly from systems theory. Politics is the regulation of the system. It involves action manifesting capabilities or "power"; it may involve restructuring the relationship of the roles in the system or creating or eliminating roles; and it also allocates goods or values. The essential characteristic, however, is linked to that of ultrastable regulation. Where a distinctive subsystem (or actor) within the system fills this role, then

3. We omit discussion of the influence of extranational actors for reasons of simplicity.

the system is said to have a political subsystem. Its legitimacy or authority stems from its acceptance in this role by the other important actors in the system. Thus there may be nonlegitimate or illegitimate political systems. Where no such subsystem exists, or alternatively where the ultrastable regulation of the system occurs in a decentralized fashion, then we state that the system has no political subsystem but that politics occurs in it. Politics in this case consists of the efforts to influence those kinds of adjustments that the political subsystem (ultrastable regulator) would make if one existed.

Revolutions occur when subsystems outside the political subsystem disrupt or substitute for its ultrastabilizing activities, restructure or reorient it, take it over, or replace it. Imperial conquest occurs when the political subsystems of one or more other systems are absorbed after conquest by the surviving system. Political amalgamation occurs when the ultrastable political subsystems of several independent systems independently coordinate their subsumption within an overarching system with a political subsystem. Revolutionary amalgamation occurs when subsystems other than the political subsystem independently coordinate the process of amalgamation.

We hypothesize that systems will behave quite differently, depending upon whether a specific political subsystem exists and depending upon the degree of system or subsystem dominance in the larger system. Thus, although the delineation of these characteristics does not in and of itself provide sufficient information concerning the differences that will ensue, it does direct attention to one of the significant problems of political analysis: those characteristics of the system making for either system or subsystem dominance.

A Final Note on the Problem of System Stability

The duration of system and ultrastable regulator varies with our definitions of the systems. We can use definitions so broad that almost all changes including the replacement of one civilization by another will fit the definition. This does not seem useful. We will adopt the following constriction: when the system changes in such a way that a different theory is needed to account for its behavior, we will say that the system has changed. Thus the change from "balance of power" system to bipolar system will be called a system change. The change of a national system from democratic to authoritarian will be called a system change. For different research purposes, either broader or narrower definitions would be appropriate. In any case there is a limit to how much environmental disturbance any system can withstand. To state that an important characteristic of political and social systems is their ability to compensate for environmental disturbances and thus to persist through time is not to state that any system will persist regardless of the strength, duration, or multiplicity of environmental disturbances. An important difference between systems will be their capacity to overcome disturbances. And among the important research problems will be that of discovering which factors increase or decrease this capacity and how these factors vary with kinds of systems and kinds of environments.

9

An Evaluation of Systems Theory

HERBERT J. SPIRO

"THE IDEA of a system has been taken over from biological theory and adapted by some social scientists to the study of their subject matter. In biological theory it has been given a fairly complex and technical meaning."[1] Professor Beer may or may not be right about the biological origins of contemporary systems theory in political science, but a definition and classification of political systems was advanced more than three centuries before the current preoccupation with systems theory, in 1651, by the founder of modern political theory, Thomas Hobbes, at the beginning of Chapter 22 of his *Leviathan*: "By *systems* I understand any number of men joined in one interest. Some are *regular* and some *irregular*. Of the regular ones, some are absolute and *independent*, others are *dependent*, that is to say *subordinate*. Of the latter, some are *political* and some *private*. Of private systems, some are *lawful*, some *unlawful*." ("Of Systems, Subject, Political, and Private.")

I mention this not in order to promote that approach to the study of political theory which addresses itself to the question, "Who Said It First?"[2] but rather in order to emphasize that *anyone* who attempts to study politics scientifically must at least implicitly think of politics as though it were functioning as some sort of system. That is, he must assume that more or less regular relationships can be discerned among various aspects of politics and between phenomena he describes as political and certain other phenomena not so described. Morton A.

1. Samuel H. Beer, "The Analysis of Political Systems," in S. H. Beer and A. B. Ulam (eds.), *Patterns of Government: The Major Political Systems of Europe*, 2nd ed., (New York: Random House, 1962), p. 25.
2. See Andrew Hacker, "*Capital* and Carbuncles: The 'Great Books' Reappraised," *American Political Science Review*, Vol. XLVIII (September 1954) p. 779.

Kaplan expressed this thought more comprehensively and therefore more complexly:

> It is the thesis of this volume that a scientific politics can develop only if the materials of politics are treated in terms of systems of actions. A system of action is a set of variables so related, in contradistinction to its environment, that describable behavioral regularities characterize the internal relationships of the variables to each other and the external relationships of the set of individual variables to combinations of external variables.[3]

Professor Kaplan probably disagrees with my judgment that what he calls "a scientific politics" has been steadily developing at least since the time of Hobbes. Indeed, a convincing case could be made for Aristotle as the first systems theorist about politics, *inter alia* because his four "causes" foreshadowed the "functional requisites" of some contemporary systems theorists in the science which he founded.[4] My point is simply that not systems theory as such is a novelty within political science. The novelty consists rather in our tremendous self-consciousness about systems theory.

Having said this much, I should have made clear that my evaluation of the utility of systems theory is high—indeed, that I consider systems theory indispensable to political science, in all its branches. Whatever our central focus of inquiry, we can best approach answers to the questions we are asking by conceiving of politics in terms not only systematic but also systemic. We may address ourselves to very broad questions: What types of institutions and procedures are best designed to insure that policy corresponds to its makers' intentions? Are there criteria for evaluating political philosophies? How can one explain variations in the incidence of international violence? Or we may address ourselves to very narrow questions: Why was John Lindsay elected mayor of New York? How can we explain recent ideological changes in the Roman Catholic Church? Will the military of Black Africa play a role similar to that of their counterparts in Latin America? Regardless of the scope and thrust of our questions, they can best be answered through the comparison of analogous events, processes, and values when these are viewed within the context of a system.

However, though systems theory as such may be regarded as indispensable to political science, not all systems theories—perhaps I should say, not all the uses to which systems theory is put—are equally useful. Some contribute to the development of a "scientific politics" while others contribute confusion. Contemporary self-conscious systems theory—

3. *System and Process in International Politics* (New York: Wiley, 1957), p. 4.

4. See, e.g., *The Politics of Aristotle*, Sir Ernest Barker, editor and translator (New York: Oxford U. P., 1962), p. 304: "The history of Egypt attests the antiquity of all political institutions. The Egyptians are generally accounted the oldest people on earth; and they have always had a body of law and a system of politics."

largely because of the very self-consciousness with which it (quite unnecessarily) borrowed its concepts from biology, physics, and even
from economics and sociology, and other sciences generally believed
to be "harder" than politics—tends to lure political scientists into traps
that are often camouflaged by misplaced analogies.

The chronologically first of these traps is disguised by the term
system itself. Biological and physical systems at least *seem* to the observer to have an "objective" coherence. They appear as "natural" systems, though appearances may be deceptive, as David Easton has
demonstrated.[5] A single human body can "naturally" be perceived and
analyzed as a system. The same is true of solar systems. Similarly, but
with less clarity, most societies, especially premodern ones in relative
isolation from others, seem to the observer to have the "given" characteristics of a system, including coherence, endurance, interdependence.
They can be defined in terms of such "natural" features shared by their
members, as common language and customs, which distinguish these
members from those of other societies. All these systems share both
naturalness and givenness, though to varying degrees. They were not
explicitly "engineered" by men to serve certain purposes and perform
certain functions (except for some social systems, of which more later).
Those systems that are most frequently designated as political systems,
on the other hand, were brought into being, or are being affirmed and
reaffirmed, as results of more or less explicit and purposive human
action, to serve certain purposes and perform certain functions. The
imperfections in the analogy between "natural" and "voluntary" systems
imply that teleological systems analysis is more warranted for political
systems than for the others.

Most political scientists who use systems theory nowadays identify
the political system (wrongly, in my view) with the state, as it was
conceived of by Max Weber, no matter what language they may employ in order to synchronize this concept with their particular brand
of systems theory. For example, Easton asserts that

what distinguishes political interactions from all other kinds of social interactions is that they are predominantly oriented toward the authoritative allocation of values for a society. . . . Thus, we establish the two essential variables
for all and any kinds of political system as "the making and execution of decisions for a society" and "their relative frequency of acceptance as authoritative or binding by the bulk of the society.[6]

Gabriel A. Almond, too, proposes

that the political system is that system of interactions to be found in all independent societies which performs the functions of integration and adaptation

5. *A Framework for Political Analysis* (Englewood Cliffs, N.J.: Prentice-Hall,
1965), pp. 29, 63–65, and *passim*.
6. *Ibid.*, pp. 50, 96 ff.

(both internally and vis-à-vis other societies) by means of the employment, or threat of employment, of more or less legitimate physical compulsion. The political system is the legitimate, order-maintaining or transforming system in the society.[7]

If the political system is thought of in this narrow sense, i.e., basically as the state (almost The Hegelian State), then all political systems extant today were founded and/or are being maintained, by acts of human will, to serve more or less clearly specified purposes and to perform more or less clearly defined functions, for the society *or* societies that accept their allocation of values as "authoritative" or their physical compulsion as "legitimate." They can, in other words, be *studied* as systems precisely because they were set up to *be* systems. On the other hand, nonpolitical or prepolitical systems, including "natural" societies —but not politically created, i.e., "artificial" social systems—are always being anthropomorphized to some extent by systems analysis that ascribes or assumes functional requisites, goals, and the like. In this sense, as I have suggested elsewhere, the political system has served as a model for nonpolitical congeries described as systems, more often than "natural systems" have served as models for the political system.[8] This appears to have been true from the beginnings of Western philosophizing and psychologizing in classical Greece. Plato divided individual man up into three "elements," which might be in harmony or in conflict with one another. Analogously, other political categories, like the legal term "cause" (*aitia*), were projected unto nature and the universe.[9] These projections were made by the early political and natural philosophers for whom the most important entity was not the individual but the *polis*. They projected both upward and downward from their image of the political system, because man became conscious of it, before he became conscious of himself as an individual and of nature as entities distinct from the undifferentiated political system. Similarly today, the by now highly differentiated political system is more easily accessible to analysis than more natural systems—including, incidentally, nonpolitical systems of communications—which leads me to suspect that the political system is still (or again) *the* archetype, even when scholars explicitly assert the opposite.

The fact that all extant political systems conventionally studied as such are more or less "willed" systems does not, however, mean that they actually perform the functions which either their founders and

7. "Introduction: A Functional Approach to Comparative Politics," in Gabriel A. Almond and James S. Coleman (eds.), *The Politics of the Developing Areas* (Princeton, Princeton U. P. 1960), p. 7.

8. Herbert J. Spiro, *Government by Constitution: The Political Systems of Democracy* (New York: Random House, 1959), pp. 28 ff.

9. See Werner Jaeger, *Paideia: The Ideals of Greek Culture*, Vol. I (New York: Oxford U. P., 1944), pp. 160 ff.

elites, or their observers have "built into" them or discern in them. Nor does it mean that such functions, however described, are "universal political functional requisites." Most obviously, the so-called "output functions" adapted from the American version of the separation of powers (or differentiation of functions), rule-making, rule application, and rule adjudication, are not universally performed—in all systems, at all times—in this particular differentiated form. On the other hand, functions that are, as it were, "read into" the political system by false analogy from biological systems (which may in turn originally have been modeled upon older concepts of the political system, thereby compounding and amplifying the analogical errors) are likely to lead to even greater confusion. This applies with special force to "boundary maintenance."

Systems theory distinguishes between external and internal boundaries and their maintenance. One would think, offhand, that political systems are very much concerned with maintaining the integrity of their external boundaries—or to speak more plainly, that sovereign states protect and defend their frontiers, in ways analogous to a body's defenses against penetration from its outside. However, as Easton has pointed out (with intent different from mine here), even "geographic boundaries" have a "deceptive character," though this "does not weaken the utility of the concept 'boundaries' as an *analytical tool*."[10] If we use the concept of the political system by analogy to biological systems and think of the United States of America or Ghana as a political system, we should bear in mind what Professor Easton has to say about the apple:

An apple is an organic system isolated from its environment by a skin. We take it for granted that if our task is to understand the processes occurring within the apple itself as it matures and decays, we need to take into consideration factors outside of the skin itself. The soil in which the apple tree grows, the nature of the tree itself, and when parted from this, the humidity, temperature, and circulation of the atmosphere in which the apple is stored are all of decisive importance for the life of the apple as a system. Yet, from the point of view of the horticulturalist, these elements are variables external to the apple as an organic system. The boundary is well defined by the skin.[11]

Similarly *and* analogously, sovereign states, even at the height of the bygone period when sovereignty was the most important fact of international relations, were also subsystems of more encompassing international political systems. Today, states frequently set themselves goals, like a merger with other political systems in larger associations, or a sloughing-off of territory formerly within their boundaries. Tomorrow, conceivably, political systems may be able and willing to transfer them-

10. *Op. cit.*, pp. 67–68. Italics supplied.
11. *Ibid.*, p. 64.

selves from one territory and population to another. The conceptual feasibility of such a transfer again suggests that external boundary maintenance is not a universal function of political systems.[12] It also raises some questions about the scope of the political system in relation to the social and other overlapping nonpolitical systems and about the function of internal boundary maintenance.

While political systems theorists generally tend to be "horizontal imperialists," most of them are at the same time "vertical mice." They claim a horizontal monopoly of legitimate physical compulsion for "their" political system, but vertically they look upon the political system as a *sub*system of and in the social system. According to various systems theories, the political system must perform the function of maintaining its internal boundaries against penetration or overflow from or into the society, and against the economy, the culture and other less comprehensive, differentiated subsystems within (i.e., really aspects of) the society; or the political system performs this function of drawing, maintaining, and redrawing all internal boundaries between the various subsystems of the social system.

The organic analogy seems particular evident in this concept of internal boundary maintenance, since boundaries can be perceived between the various organs and other components of internally differentiated bodies. In contemporary as in classical Greek political systems, however, no such internal boundaries between "society" and "polity" exist. Nevertheless, much systems theory, forgetting what Easton calls the "analytic character of all systems,"[13] evaluates and classifies political systems according to their performance of this "function" of maintaining the "boundary" between the social and political systems. For example, so-called totalitarian systems are said to be directed deliberately by their rulers toward the destruction of this boundary, so that politics becomes "total," with the result that the "society" is "destroyed," or at least "atomized."[14] The roots of this notion of internal boundary maintenance, apart from the relatively recent misleading analogy from biology, must go back to the peculiarly Western Christian experience of the struggle between temporal and spiritual authorities, and the social contract theories formed, and informed, by this experience, which usually (though not in the case of Thomas Hobbes) assumed the existence of society as the precondition for the founding of "civil society," "civil government," or the "sovereign." Also, the fact that contemporary sociologists turned to self-conscious systems theory before political scien-

---

12. See also Wilbert E. Moore, "Global Sociology: The World as a Singular System," *American Journal of Sociology*, Vol. LXXI (March 1966), pp. 475–482.

13. *Ibid.*, p. 42.

14. For a critique of the concept, see my "Totalitarianism," in *International Encyclopedia of the Social Sciences*, in press.

tists did so undoubtedly contributed to the prevalent narrow view of the political system as a subsystem of the society.

This view mistakes the greater for the lesser, the more encompassing for the less encompassing, and I would add, the significant for the insignificant. The political system is more important, more encompassing, and "greater" than the social system. Many political systems in the world today consist of several societies that were joined together deliberately in order to achieve common, often newly forged goals. The patterns of most if not all social systems nowadays have been transformed as a result of deliberate political action (which is not to say that the effects of such action upon social patterns are usually as intended). Societies—and, as for that matter, economies, cultures, families, personality systems—"just grow," and they therefore deserve the designation of *system* less than political systems. Moreover, the moment more or less deliberate efforts are made to change society, including the family, economy, culture, or personality system, the given raw material of these "levels" or "aspects" of human existence is taken up by the political system and the political process. In this sense, the political system is the only "existential" system among so-called "social" systems. The others are merely analogic systems or anthropomorphized systems —unless their raw material is being absorbed by the political process, and then they may be looked upon and analyzed as subsystems of the political system. However, in order to avoid confusion, society, economy, and similar subordinate sets of relationships should be analyzed as political subsystems only to the extent that the political system treats them as such. This caveat is of relatively little practical importance *today*, because all contemporary political systems do in fact treat these patterns of other aspects of the lives of their members as political subsystems. It may be of slightly greater importance for the historical analysis of periods in which political, economic, spiritual, cultural, and other activities were believed to be carried on, as it were, in separate compartments—for example, when philosophers spoke of "economic man." But even for such periods we must not overlook that this belief in compartmentalization was the result of more or less deliberate decisions made in the political system—at least if we think of the scope of the political system in terms broader than the conventional ones cited on page 166.

The utility of systems theory, as of all else in political science, depends upon the understanding of politics with which it works, the notion of "the political" upon which it is based. Most systems theorists still identify politics ultimately with power, compulsion, violence, force, binding decisions, and the like. Many but not all—Professor Kaplan is an exception—identify the political system ultimately with the state in the Weberian sense. Even when they admit that a kind of politics goes on within families, firms, and churches, including communities of supranational scope that are not continuously or importantly affected by the actions of states, they prefer to focus upon the state as the political system—sometimes explicitly for reasons of analytical convenience, economy, and elegance. This focus tends to distort. It tends to distort the internal analysis of political systems, because it either leaves out of account too much of the allegedly "nonpolitical," or it takes for granted a causal sequence in which political phenomena are viewed as secondary or tertiary effects of "primary" economic or social factors. For example, such an approach studies the impact *upon* politics of economic, social, and cultural change in the politics of the developing areas, and thereby neglects the possibility that more or less deliberate efforts to bring about change—that is, politics—have more important consequences for the substantive conditions of life in these areas than vice versa.[15] Or it urges that "governmental authority patterns" be made congruent with social authority patterns in order to promote "stable democracy," without much attention to the possibility that men acting in politics are more likely to reform social authority patterns than vice versa.[16] It could be argued that one method to avoid this type of distortion would be to consider politics coextensive with all human relations, but this would be tantamount to the surrender of all focus in order to eliminate the distortions engendered by a particular and, as I believe, mistaken focus.

The focus upon the state as *the* political system tends to distort the analysis of international politics, by leading to a qualitative distinction between the politics that goes on within a "national" system and the relations that go on among national states. Kaplan avoids this kind of distortion by explicitly rejecting the focus upon power and by denying that the political system "is the coercive subsystem in the social system."[17] Instead, he focuses upon a political system whose geographical scope is defined by the purposes of a particular analysis. In his view, the main difference between conventional national systems and the global political system of our time is that the former are "system dominant," while the latter is "subsystem dominant."[18] "Politics is the contest to fill decision-making roles, to choose alternate political objects, or to change the essential rules of the political system."[19] Even this view of politics seems less than satisfactory, partly because of its definitional nature, partly because it does not entirely overcome the dangers of

15. See my "The Primacy of Political Development" in H. J. Spiro (ed.) *Africa: The Primacy of Politics* (New York: Random House, 1966) chap. 5.

16. See Harry Eckstein, *A Theory of Stable Democracy* (Princeton, Center of International Studies, 1961), *passim*.

17. *Op. cit.,* p. 12.

18. *Ibid.,* p. 16.

19. *Ibid.,* p. 14.

compartmentalization: "A political system exists when its constitution and laws are communicated successfully *within* a social system."[20]

How can we overcome these various disadvantages of systems theory, without moving toward the other direction of focuslessness? Very simply, I think, by remembering the classical statement that politics is the affairs—all the common affairs—of the *polis* and consists of the concerns of the citizens. This means that a political system can exist wherever people are concerned about common problems and are engaged in cooperation *and* conflict in their solution. The scope of a particular political system is defined by the extent of the population so engaged—not only by the scope of power or of authority or of the successfully communicated constitution, and not at all by the scope of a particular social system. Individuals or groupings are involved in politics with one another when they are trying to solve together their (several) problems (that is, often different sets of problems for different participants), because each recognizes he/it cannot solve these problems alone, without interaction with others. The political process[21] itself begins not with the recognition of problems, but with the *formulation of issues* arising out of the problems (which may be obstacles on the paths to quite different, even contradictory and mutually exclusive, goals). The political process continues with the *deliberation* of issues, that is, the weighing of the various alternatives contained in the statement of the issue. Deliberation normally, but not always, phases over into the *resolution* of the issue, which normally, but not always, is followed by the *solution* of the problems that originally gave rise to the issue—optimally the process finds a (very temporary) end in the removal of the obstacles on the road toward goals. Whether or not a political system exists depends not upon acceptance as legitimate or authoritative of the same goals by all, or by some proportion of, the participants; nor upon the capacity of any of the participants to compel others; nor upon the stability of the essential rules governing the process over a prolonged period of time. It depends, rather, upon the participants' awareness of their participation in the political process—in a sense, upon their willingness to take part, though this may be a highly reluctant willingness. My point is that the participants through their awareness impose upon their interactions the characteristics of a system. This means that a set of interactions of brief duration not only can be analyzed as a political system, but may actually be a political system.

The irreducible "existential" functions of political systems are the same as the four phases of the political process seen from another angle: (1) formulation, (2) deliberation, and (3) resolution of issues, and (4) solution of problems. They are irreducible in the sense that

20. *Loc. cit.;* italics supplied.
21. See my "Comparative Politics: A Comprehensive Approach," *American Political Science Review,* Vol. LVI (September 1962), pp. 577–595.

all are performed in all political systems (and, incidentally, by analogy to the model of the political system, in all personality systems).
Wherever there is human awareness of cooperation and conflict in the
solution of problems, these phases of the process are in fact performed.
But they are performed in a vast variety of ways, sequences, and combinations of relative attention paid to each. This range of differences
among systems can be systematically described by a typology of "political style," which is derived in turn from the basic goals to the pursuit
of which political systems are more or less deliberately directed, again
in a wide range of possible combinations. These four basic goals are
stability, flexibility, efficiency, and effectiveness. Individual human beings as individuals and as members, who "belong," with varying degrees
of intensity, to a multiplicity of political systems—at various "horizontal"
levels and, criss-crossing these, in "vertical" associations—assign different
and changing importance to these four basic goals in their pursuit of
their less basic goals (like prosperity or life and liberty or defense) and
in their pursuit of circumstantial goals like implementation of a particular policy. This means that, in addition to conventionally defined "national" political systems and the "cosmically" defined global political
system (whose boundaries do not have to be maintained but merely
grown into), there exists also at any moment a series of complex, intricate, overlapping networks of political systems that are brought into
being as a result of efforts, by individuals and by political systems, to
solve problems together. Men and political systems change their perspectives upon and their perceptions of problems and goals, partly
because they solve some of their problems and therefore approach
closer toward their goals. Consequently, a moving picture—as distinguished from the snapshot—taken of political systems would show kaleidoscopic patterns of expanding and contracting political systems, that
overlap with one another, and whose styles, as well as the styles of
their "intersystems" politics among each other, are forever changing,
except in the rare and pathological case of the exclusive pursuit of
stability.

This last-mentioned exception points to another shortcoming of much
of the literature on political systems, and of other systems theory, as
well: excessive preoccupation with stability.[22] Stability is only one of
several basic goals pursued by political systems. It can be achieved
through the institution of rigid, comprehensive, eternally anticipatory
legalism. Efficiency is another such basic goal, which can be achieved
through the quick, resolute use of all available power for purposes of
solving problems immediately as they are perceived. But in addition to

22. See Everett E. Hagen, "Analytical Models in the Study of Social Systems,"
in *On the Theory of Social Change* (Homewood, Ill., Dorsey Press, 1962), pp.
505–513; Marion J. Levy, Jr., "Structural-Functional Analysis," *International
Encyclopedia of the Social Sciences*, in press.

stability and efficiency, (the human beings who interact as) political systems also pursue flexibility and effectiveness. In addition to legalism and violence, their styles can also show pragmatism and ideologism. The combinations forever change, but this dynamism is rarely captured by systems theory with its built-in bias toward stability. This bias can be detected even in some systems theories that favor a "dynamic equilibrium," because they fail to take into account that very element which makes political systems not merely analogic but existential systems: human consciousness.

Human beings are aware of discrepancies between their present and some wished-for future condition. They try to work toward the future goals which they invent and set for themselves. On the road toward these goals, they encounter obstacles. In order to overcome these obstacles, to solve these problems, they engage themselves in politics, and they form and dismantle political systems. Sometimes they approach closer toward their goals, sometimes they move or are moved farther away from them, sometimes they forget about them as a result of changes in the perspective of their consciousness, and sometimes they substitute new goals for old ones. Usually all of this is going on simultaneously, all over the earth. And as men are engaged in the political process—actually, in many simultaneous political processes—they change their consciousness of the possible. Often they expand their awareness of that which they recognize as possible. In recent centuries, since the time of Hobbes, they have increasingly recognized the converse, namely, that whatever may be possible can be achieved ultimately only through politics. I am tempted to paraphrase the motto of a large chemical corporation: "Better things for better living through politics!"

Political systems are brought into being as direct or indirect results of more or less deliberate human actions upon nonpolitical reality (which *may*, in its various aspects, be conceived of for analytical purposes as composed of systems). Political systems reflect man's consciousness of the possible; their expansion—of the capacity to generate new goals and issues, to increase participation and to carry the increased volume of politics—normally contributes to the further expansion of consciousness. From this viewpoint, the continuous development of politics, both within and among systems, can be considered as an important value and could be considered as the human goal of highest priority.

Only systems theory can understand this, because only systems theory can understand politics in this existential sense. Systems theory has been understanding politics in this sense for some centuries. Perhaps because of a certain lack of historical perspective, recent advocates of systems theory in political science have stood it on its head. Here, I have tried to turn systems theory right side up once more.

10

The Theory of Decision-Making

JAMES A. ROBINSON and

R. ROGER MAJAK

DECISION AND DECISION-MAKING currently command increasing attention as objects of study in the social sciences. As Judith Shklar[1] has observed in tracing the development of the ideological phenomenon she calls "decisionism," "No one interested in social ideas can fail to notice how large a part the word 'decision' has, of late, come to play in the vocabulary of moral and political discourse." The social science literature—scientific research reports and intuitive, creative, and anecdotal essays—reflects this increased concern with decision. As illustration, Wasserman and Silander's first annotated bibliography of decision-making covering the period 1945 through 1957 contains 438 entries. A second edition covering 1958–63, contains more than 600 entries, despite more stringent selectivity.[2] The act of human decision, no longer regarded by social scientists as the constant complication of our study, has become a primary object of research aimed at unlocking the "secret" of human choice.[3]

The literature of decision-making is not merely vast; it is disparate as well. The concept is prominent in psychology, social psychology, sociology, economics, business administration, psychiatry, and other disciplines in addition to political science—and each discipline has its own

1. Shklar, Judith, "Decisionism," in Carl J. Friedrich (ed.), Nomos VII: *Rational Decision*. New York: Atherton Press, 1964, pp. 3–17.

2. Wasserman, Paul, and Silander, Fred S., *Decision-Making: An Annotated Bibliography*. Ithaca, New York: Graduate School of Business and Public Administration, Cornell University, 1958; *Decision-Making: An Annotated Bibliography, Supplement, 1958–1963*. Ithaca, New York: Graduate School of Business and Public Administration, Cornell University, 1964.

3. Soltau, Roger H., *An Introduction to Politics*. London: Longmans, Green, 1951.

particular emphasis. A description of theories of *political* decision making, therefore, must be selective in both the amount and the kind of literature surveyed. Criteria for selecting the latter are especially problematic. To confine oneself exclusively to theorizing about political decision-making would be to ignore the potential relevance of findings and formulations from non-political disciplines that, by analogy or adaptation, might usefully be applied to the study of decisions involving *political* issues or situations.[4]

One may, however, consider himself absolved of responsibility for reviewing all nonpolitical decision-making literature by the fact that much of it is adequately reviewed elsewhere.[5] We shall confine ourselves to discussing, in addition to the most important political writings on decision-making, only those items from nonpolitical writings that appear particularly useful for the study of *political* decision-making.

The degree to which one can justifiably transfer—whether substantively or heuristically—observations and generalizations about nonpolitical decision-making to political decisions is itself an intriguing question, one that leads ultimately to definitions of "political." Despite Merriam's[6] warning that "only confusion will be created by trying to draw too sharp and exclusive a line between political and other forms of organization," and that "on the contrary, a clearer view is gained by frankly recognizing the fundamental similarity between them, and the parallel and frequent interchangeability of functions," several analysts have taken pains to separate political from nonpolitical phenomena. Diesing[7] distinguished among economic, social, legal, technical, and political decisions on the basis of differences in rationality that, he suggests, are operative for each. He defined political decisions as those that concern "the preservation and improvement of decision structures." "All decisions," Diesing maintains, "occur within a decision structure of some sort, but political decisions in addition have decision structures as their special subject matter."[8]

In contrast to this rather narrow designation, other theorists have

4. The implication that "political" be distinguished in terms of issues or occasions—as opposed, for example, to processes or outcomes—will be explored more explicitly in a later paragraph.

5. For example, the psychological decision-making literature is reviewed by Edwards, Ward, "The Theory of Decision Making," *Psychological Bulletin*, 51 (1954), 380–417; "Behavioral Decision Theory," in Paul R. Farnsworth *et. al.* (eds.), *Annual Review of Psychology*, Vol. 12. Palo Alto, California: Annual Reviews Inc., 1961. Economic and business decision-making is abstracted by Wasserman and Silander, *op. cit.*

6. Merriam, Charles, *Political Power*. New York: McGraw-Hill, 1934.

7. Diesing, Paul, *Reason in Society: Five Types of Decisions and Their Social Conditions*. Urbana, Illinois: University of Illinois Press, 1962.

8. *Ibid.*, p. 198.

defined politics according to use and distribution of "power." Leoni,[9] for example, separates political decisions from nonpolitical ones on the basis that political decisions "result in the emergence of power" or the "modification of the previously existing power situation."[10]

Easton's[11] familiar definition of politics as "the authoritative allocation of values" has been linked to a decision-making focus by Riker (1962, p. 10):

Now if, as Easton asserts, politics is the authoritative allocation of values and if, as I interpret it, "allocation" refers not to a physical process but to the social process of deciding how a physical process shall be carried out, then the subject studied by political scientists is decision making.

The Easton definition, while it implies (through the use of the "authority" concept) that political decisions are distinguishable by the exercise or potential exercise of sanctions, does not distinguish between "public" and "private" decisions. Political decision-making as the term is used by most political scientists concerns *publicly* authoritative allocations of *public* values.

With respect to this public-private distinction, Wood[12] concludes that it is inappropriate to generalize findings about private decision behavior to public decision behavior. Public decisions differ from private "transactions," he maintains, in four ways: (1) In the political economy, the basic unit of decision-making is the formal or informal group, not the individual producer or consumer; (2) the "mechanism" at work in the public sector is the budgetary process rather than the price mechanism; (3) the "products" provided by government are public and thus are "indivisible" among persons; and (4) the "goals" of political decision-making include such factors as "votes and influences," not just "costs" and "production" as in private transactions. Public decisions are "collective"[13]; private decisions, noncollective. Thus, he con-

---

9. Leoni, Bruno, "The Meaning of 'Political' in Political Decisions," in *Political Studies*. Oxford: Clarendon Press, 5 (1957), 225–239.

10. Leoni's conclusions must be reviewed in the context of his definitions of "power" and the "power situation." The former he defines as "the possibility for individuals of their choices being identified with the decisions of the groups to which they belong," and the latter, he says, is "the status at a given point in time of the powers resulting from political decisions in a community conceived as a set of decision groups."

11. Easton, David, *The Political System*. New York: Knopf, 1953.

12. Wood, R. C. with Almendinger, V. V. *1400 Governments: The Political Economy of the New York Metropolitan Region*. Cambridge, Mass.: Harvard University Press, 1961.

13. *Ibid.*, p. 20.

cludes, "we could make no greater mistake than to suppose that the ways in which these political decisions are made parallels (sic) the behavior of firms and households."[14] Wheaton[15] analyzes the difference between public and private decisions in more specific terms, hypothesizing, for example, that "public policy actions involve far more complex chains of decision than private." Thus by emphasizing the group aspects of public decision-making as the source of differences between public and private decision-making, both Wood and Wheaton contrast political with nonpolitical decisions in terms of the collective, group processes hypothetically predominant in the former as opposed to the predominance (again, hypothetical) of noncollective, individual processes in private, nonpolitical decisions.

This view is in marked contrast to the work of Downs,[16] Bator,[17] Kuhn,[18] and others who tend to equate private and public decisions and to formulate concepts of political decision-making and decision-making in firms or households in the same terms.

If one cannot reach a conclusion on the generalizability of nonpolitical decision behavior to political decision behavior (and vice versa), he is at least prompted to generalize with caution and to recognize the need for retesting in political settings propositions derived from nonpolitical decision studies.

A review of political decision-making theories requires a framework in which to select and organize relevant materials. A useful way of looking at differences between political and nonpolitical decisions, as well as at differences among political decisions, is in terms of differences in certain variables and clusters of variables. This paper examines decisions and decision-making theory in terms of major "variable clusters," each composed of an indeterminate number of similar (though not necessarily dependently related) specific variables. These clusters are: (1) the decision *situation*; (2) the decision *participants*; (3) the decision *organization*; (4) the decision *process*; and (5) the decision *outcome*. Elsewhere[19] we have reviewed current theorizing about decision *situations* (characterized by surprise or anticipation, response time, and value

14. *Ibid.*, p. 17.

15. Wheaton, William L. C., "Integration at the Urban Level: Political Influence and the Decision Process," in Philip Jacob and James Toscano, *The Integration of Political Communities*. Philadelphia: Lippincott, 1964, pp. 130–132.

16. Downs, Anthony, *An Economic Theory of Democracy*. New York: Harper, 1957.

17. Bator, Francis M., *The Question of Government Spending: Public Needs and Private Wants*. New York: Harper, 1960.

18. Kuhn, Alfred, *The Study of Society: A Unified Approach*. Homewood, Illinois: R. D. Irwin, 1963.

19. Robinson, James A., and Snyder, Richard C., "Decision-Making in International Politics," in Herbert Kelman (ed.), *International Behavior: A Social-Psychological Analysis*. New York: Holt, Rinehart, and Winston, 1965, pp. 435–463.

implications), *participants* (characterized by their personalities, social backgrounds and experiences, and values or preferences), and *organization* (characterized by roles and units). Here we confine our attention to the decision process and its outcomes.

The Decision Process Cluster— "How" Decisions Are Made

If, as Easton suggests, politics is a process of allocating values through the making of decisions, *the* political process must be regarded as the intersection of numerous lesser processes (which we refer to as subprocesses), the final, cumulative outcome of which is the allocation of values. We use "process" to refer to the sum of the particular techniques, methods, procedures, and strategies—conscious or unconscious— by which a given decision is made. "Process" comprises the "how" of decision making as distinct from "who" decides (the "decision participant cluster"), under what conditions or upon what occasion (the "situation cluster"), in what organizational context (the "organizational cluster") or what the results of the decision might be (the "outcome cluster").

We consider the central fact of decision processes to be that any decision can be made in a number of different ways. For some decision makers, the manner in which a particular decision will be made (i.e., the techniques to be used) is a matter of conscious choice. Yet it has been common to speak of *the* decision process, implying a universal process by which all decisions are taken. Classic economic theory, for example, assumes that, in any decision, participants formulate all possible alternatives and select the best one on the basis of known utilities for each alternative and ordered preferences among them. In contrast to this "rationalistic" model, Simon[20] theorizes that the decision process involves only "bounded rationality." For the classic *optimizing* model, he substitutes "satisficing," which predicts that a decision will be adopted when an alternative seems to meet minimal standards, or is "good enough," and that a decision is not dependent on the availability of all possible alternatives from which the best may be selected. Satisficing theory has been studied primarily in industrial rather than in government organizations.[21] The satisficing model has been illustrated in a case

20. Simon, Herbert, *Models of Man: Social and Rational*. New York: Wiley, 1957.

21. March, James G., and Simon, Herbert, with Guetzkow, H., *Organizations*. New York: Wiley, 1958; Feldman, Julian, and Kanter, Herschel, "Organizational Decision Making," in James G. March (ed.), *Handbook of Organizations*, Chicago: Rand-McNally and Co., 1965, pp. 614–49.

study of the adoption of new data-processing equipment in a business firm,[22] and it is central to current behavioral theories of firms.[23] There is no reason, however, to expect such theories to be any less applicable to government decision-making than to that of business.

Lasswell[24] identifies seven "functional" stages through which all decisions are processed. The stages comprise information (problem identification and information search); recommendation (formulation of alternatives); prescription (sanctioned selection of alternatives); invocation (provisional enforcement); application (specific implementation); appraisal (monitoring and review of the decision and its effects); and termination (renewal, revision, or repeal).

Rather than searching for a universal formulation of the decision process, which might be achieved only at so broad a level as to be of little analytic utility, one may concentrate on elements of variation in ways of making decisions. This approach moves in the direction of a typology of decision processes and a set of process variables.

March and Simon,[25] for example, distinguish four processes of decision-making: (1) problem-solving; (2) persuasion; (3) bargaining; and (4) "politics." Two or more of these processes, they believe, are combined in the making of decisions. Braybrooke and Lindblom,[26] in presenting "disjointed incrementalism" as a decision "strategy," postulate a continuum of decision-process types ranging from the rational economic model, which they label "synoptic," to such less rationalistic types as "incrementalism," which involves the consideration of only a selected variety of alternatives in making decisions. They suggest that each "strategy" is useful (and therefore "rational") under particular conditions (i.e., decision situations) with regard to the degree of change in the environment represented by the decision situation and the amount and certainty of information available.

Another typology of decision subprocesses distinguishes among the *intellectual, social,* and *quasi-mechanical* aspects of decision-making. The *intellectual* part of the process is the analytic aspect of decision-making, which is performed largely by individual and group thought processes. These thought processes, in turn, may include such specific elements as "subjective probability," insight, creativity, intuition, perception, cognition, and the like—each of which represents a specific variable or group of variables within the process cluster. Optimizing,

22. Cyert, Richard M., Simon, Herbert, and Trow, D. "Observation of a Business Decision," *Journal of Business*, 29 (1956), 237–48.

23. Cyert, Richard M., and March, James A., *A Behavioral Theory of the Firm.* Englewood Cliffs, New Jersey: Prentice-Hall, 1963.

24. Lasswell, Harold, *The Decision Process: Seven Categories of Functional Analysis.* College Park: University of Maryland, 1956.

25. March, James A., and Simon, Herbert, *op. cit.*, pp. 129–131.

26. Braybrooke, David and Lindblom, Charles, *A Strategy of Decision.* New York: Free Press, 1963.

satisficing, and several stages of Lasswell's functional concept of decision-making emphasize the intellectual dimension. Problem-solving, collecting and analyzing information, defining situations, formulating alternatives, and similar activities are primarily intellectual processes. Certain *social* processes may also operate in the making of a given decision. Several of these have been treated extensively by others but they have not always been placed in the context of the total decision process. These social processes include coalition formation,[27] interest group interaction,[28] and interest aggregation,[29] among others. Boulding[30] has defined the political process as "the mutual modification of images through the process of feedback and communication," and Deutsch[31] has described communication as a social process in the context of political decision systems. Dahl and Lindblom[32] have identified four basic social control processes: hierarchy (control of nonleaders by leaders); bargaining (control of leaders by other leaders); polyarchy (control of leaders by nonleaders); and the price mechanism (qualitative but decentralized combination of control by leaders and nonleaders). Lindblom[33] has refined and expanded this typology of social decision processes in his study of "mutual adjustment" as a social component of the decision process in which he especially emphasizes "coordination" as a factor in decision processes involving more than one group or organization. Types of mutual adjustment include manipulation, negotiation, and bargaining.[34]

Social aspects of the decision-making process appear to be particularly significant in (to use Lasswell's convenient categories) the prescription, invocation, and application stages, in which various "disjointed" individuals, groups, and organizations must consolidate their interests and arrive at a common decision.

In addition to the intellectual and social aspects of the process by

27. Riker, William, *The Theory of Political Coalitions*. New Haven: Yale University Press, 1962.

28. Bentley, Arthur F., *The Process of Government*. Chicago: Chicago University Press, 1908; Truman, David, *The Governmental Process*. Chicago: Chicago University Press, 1951.

29. Almond, Gabriel, and Coleman, James, *The Politics of the Developing Areas*. Princeton: Princeton University Press, 1960.

30. Boulding, Kenneth, *The Image*. Ann Arbor: University of Michigan Press, 1956.

31. Deutsch, Karl W., *The Nerves of Government: Models of Political Communication and Control*. New York: Free Press, 1963.

32. Dahl, Robert and Lindblom, Charles E., *Politics, Economics, and Welfare*. New York: Harper, 1953.

33. Lindblom, Charles E., *The Intelligence of Democracy: Decision Making Through Mutual Adjustment*. New York: Free Press, 1965.

34. The most notable applications of Lindblom's ideas to political process is in the work of Wildavsky, including his case study of the Dixon-Yates controversy (Wildavsky, Aaron, *Dixon-Yates; A Study in Power Politics*. New Haven: Yale University Press, 1962) and his essay on budgeting (*The Politics of the Budgetary Process*, Boston: Little, Brown, 1964).

which a given decision is made, a third dimension may be operative. Riker[35] suggests that the authoritative allocation of values may be made in whole or part by *quasi-mechanical* processes. The most notable example is the market and price system, although Riker[36] observes that quasi-mechanical processes alone rarely produce decision outcomes.

It is relatively rare that a society debases itself as abjectly to mechanical decisions as, for example, the United States did in the latter part of the nineteenth century. More typically, authority is believed to rest in determinate persons and the automatic allocations by institutions are believed to be subject to review by those in authority.

Quasi-mechanical processes are characterized particularly by decision-makers unconsciousness of their decision-making roles. It appears, in fact, that the process by which most decisions emerge includes two or three of the subprocesses—that is, a decision rarely emerges from intellectual processes alone, without, for example, related and complementary social and/or quasi-mechanical processes. The literature on decision process, considered as a whole, strongly supports the interpretation that the process by which a given decision is made should be viewed as a combination of these subprocesses. This implies, in turn, that the classic optimizing model and Simon's "satisficing" modification of it, sometimes viewed as competing, full-fledged "theories" of decision-making, should be regarded as partial theories (dealing with particular aspects of the *intellectual* dimension), which are "competing" only in the sense that they are mutually exclusive (i.e., if "satisficing" occurs in the decision process, "optimizing" may not occur). Likewise, the pluralist theory of policy formulation and decision-making offers a theoretical explanation of only a part of the social dimension; it is inadequate as a grand theory of the policy process because it ignores intellectual and quasi-mechanical dimensions.

Bentley[37] introduced the idea that interest or pressure groups decisively explain governmental policies, thus arguing that social processes are more important in the decision process than "intellectual" or "quasi-mechanical" subprocesses. Truman[38] revived the Bentleyan formulation with some modifications, but still suggested that individual behavior accounts for less than group activity. Hilsman[39] applies this approach in his analysis, using a conflict-consensus model, of United States foreign policy. Related concepts emphasizing social rather than

35. Riker, William, *op. cit.*
36. *Ibid.*, p. 12.
37. Bentley, Arthur F., *op. cit.*
38. Truman, David, *The Governmental Process.* New York: Knopf, 1951.
39. Hilsman, Roger, "Congressional-Executive Relations and Foreign Policy Consensus," *American Political Science Review*, 52 (1956), 725–744; "The Foreign-Policy Consensus: An Interim Research Report," *Journal of Conflict Resolution*, 3 (1959), 361–382.

intellectual processes include "veto groups,"[40] countervailing forces, influence as credit[41] overlapping games,[42] access, and communication.

Some of these perspectives are refined and extended in a study of the adoption of a new trade-agreement program by the United States.[43] This case emphasizes foreign policy decision-making as a social process rather than as an intellectual process and it identifies mechanisms of group and intergroup interaction that tend toward decision.

In this context, various "legalistic" approaches to political outcomes popular in American political science in the late nineteenth century (and in certain circles at present) may be viewed as explanations only of certain "quasi-mechanical" components of the decision process, if law and constitutions can be considered as established decision guidelines intended to provide a framework for "programming" in a "quasi-mechanical" manner certain substantive types of decisions. The limitation of these "legalistic" and "formal institutional" approaches was that they did not view law in conjunction with the intellectual and social dimensions of the policy process—an oversight that twentieth-century political scientists have been intent upon remedying to the extent perhaps of going to the opposite extreme. Snyder[44] and others have begun to develop conceptions of the decision process that combine "intellectual" and "organizational" process dimensions.

It may be that Riker, Snyder, and others have undervalued quasi-mechanical processes in decision-making. The definition of decision occasions (i.e., the "information" stage) is often quasi-mechanically determined through custom, "routine," or established rules in organizations, and through tradition or law in broader contexts of the social system. Kuhn[45] notes, for example, that

Many organizations have periodic decision built into their routines. Some are

40. Riesman, David, *The Lonely Crowd*. New Haven: Yale University Press, 1950; Birnbaum, N., "David Riesman's Image of Political Process," in S. M. Lipset and L. Lowenthal (eds.), *Culture and Social Character: The Work of David Riesman Reviewed*. New York: Free Press, 1961, pp. 207–225.

41. Banfield, E. C., *Political Influence*. New York: Free Press, 1961.

42. Long, Norton, "The Local Community as an Ecology of Games," *American Journal of Sociology*, 44 (1958), 251–261; *The Polity*. Chicago: Rand-McNally, 1962.

43. Bauer, Raymond, Pool, Ithiel, and Dexter, Lewis A., *American Business and Public Policy: The Politics of Foreign Trade*. New York: Atherton Press, 1963.

44. Snyder, Richard C., Bruck, H. W., and Sapin, Burton, *Decision-Making as an Approach to the Study of International Politics*. Princeton: Foreign Policy Analysis Project, 1954; *Foreign Policy Decision-Making as an Approach to the Study of International Politics*. Princeton: Foreign Policy Project, 1954; *Foreign Policy Decision-Making: An Approach to the Study of Internatioanl Politics*. New York: Free Press, 1962; Snyder, "A Decision-Making Approach to the Study of Political Phenomena," in R. Young (ed.), *Approaches to the Study of Politics*. Evanston, Illinois: Northwestern University Press, 1958, pp. 3–38.

45. Kuhn, A., *op. cit.*

regular audits which ask in appropriate detail, "Are we doing as well as possible?" or "Is there a better way?" In a less obvious way annual reports, financial statements, or budget making may reopen questions for decision.

Often, then, "deciding to decide"[46] is "automatically" done, lending a quasi-mechanical aspect to the total decision process.

One finds the complementary interaction of intellectual, social, and quasi-mechanical processes in most political decisions illustrated in the types of analysis used to study judicial decisions have been studied. Schubert[47] indicates that judicial decision-making has been studied in terms of (1) individual judges; (2) courts as small groups and the interest group and social context in which the courts operate; and finally (3) the judiciary in the context of formal legal institutions. Each of these approaches emphasizes one of the types of process just outlined. The study of individual judges encompasses the analytic, intellectual thought processes of the judicial mind. Studies of courts as small groups and of the social context within which judges and the courts function emphasize the social aspects of judicial decision-making. Finally, the study of the judiciary as part of a formal framework of rules, precedents, and laws emphasizes the quasi-mechanical influences upon judicial outcomes. Similarly, Eulau[48] has stressed the importance of precedents as a factor in determining judicial outcomes and, analogously, the importance of "routine" as a factor in determining legislative outcomes. In the final analysis, decision-making cannot be understood adequately or decision outcomes predicted without taking into account all three process types. It is the interaction of these processes, and their cumulative effects, that best explain decision outcomes.

The Outcome Cluster—
Characterizing Decision "Products"

Three concepts need to be distinguished and clarified in reviewing the "outcome" cluster: (1) "output," (2) "outcome," and (3) "effect." In many instances these terms are used synonymously to refer to the products of a process or chain of processes. Decision-making, as we have noted, may be regarded as a total process composed of distinguishable

46. Engel, Alan S., "Non-Decision: The 'Decision' Not to Decide," unpublished monograph, Northwestern University, Evanston, Illinois, 1958.

47. Schubert, Glendon (ed.), *Judicial Decision-Making*. New York: Free Press, 1963; *Judicial Behavior: A Reader in Theory and Research*. Chicago: Rand-McNally and Co., 1964.

48. Eulau, Heinz, and Sprague, John D., *Lawyers in Politics, A Study in Professional Convergence*. Indianapolis, Indiana: Bobbs-Merrill Co., 1964.

subprocesses. It is sometimes convenient, therefore, to employ "output" to refer to the products of the various subprocesses in decision-making, and to reserve the use of "outcome" to designate the final product of the decision-making process as a whole. The product of each of Lasswell's seven decision-making steps, for example, might be considered "outputs," but the sum of these "outputs" would represent the decision "outcome." Thus, the distinction between "outputs" and "outcomes" is twofold: (1) it is a difference between *intermediate* and *end* products, and (2) it is a difference in usage—"outputs" being used *within* the decision unit to produce other "outputs" and, eventually, "outcomes." "Outcomes" in turn are imposed upon the environment external to the decision unit. The "implementation," or "consequences," of decision "outcomes" may be referred to as decision "effects."[49]

As Gross[50] has noted, products of individual, group, or organizational processes may be either "goods" or "services," and it is particularly difficult to characterize the "intangible services" that typically constitute political outcomes. Despite this "intangibility," however decision outcomes as "products" of individual, group, and organizational decision processes have been characterized in several ways: by their *complexity, quantity, effectiveness, rationality,* and *stability,* among others. More specifically, some researchers have devised substantive outcome types based upon "degree of hostility," "degree of risk acceptance," or, in the case of voting studies, the distribution of the vote among political parties or their candidates.

Still another way to classify outcomes and their effects is by reference to their value implications. Lasswell and Kaplan[51] propose a comprehensive check list of value categories embracing and classifying virtually any human demand, preference, or goal. This list includes values of power, respect, rectitude, affection, wealth, skill, enlightenment, and well-being. An outcome may refer to one or to several value categories. That is, a decision may affect any one of these values; for example, a legislative act (outcome) that increases aid to dependent children is classified as pertaining to well-being. The imposition of a sales or income tax affects wealth, and so on.

The outcomes of political processes may be described, in one way,

49. Lasswell's prescription for a "basic data survey" (Lasswell, Harold, *The Future of Political Science.* New York: Atherton Press, 1963, pp. 43–94) takes the position that even intermediate outputs may precipitate "effects," as for example when C.I.A. intelligence functions are "uncovered" by foreign governments and produce international incidents. There can be no quarrel with this position. Lasswell, however, refers to "outcomes" at each of his seven stages of decision-making, using the term less restrictively than we do.

50. Gross, Bertram, *The Managing of Organizations.* New York: Free Press, 1964.

51. Lasswell, Harold and Kaplan, Abraham, *Power and Society.* New Haven: Yale University Press, 1950.

according to the relative attention they accord different value categories. The decisions of a community, state, nation, or transnational unit may affect some values more than others. Government legislation, a systematic inventory would most likely show, pertains more frequently to the values of wealth, skill, enlightenment, and well-being (the so-called "welfare state" values) than to other values. Legislation to repeal or reduce government regulation of rectitude and affection has been approved in many advanced societies. And with contemporary emphasis on changing patterns of race relations, governments are increasingly active in affecting the value of respect.

Decision-making analysis explores the extent to which variations in the decision process account for variations in governmental attention to some values rather than others. (We take for granted that processes other than decision-making also operate to affect governmental activity and that decision-making analysis alone cannot provide complete explanation in any comprehensive value analysis.) Beyond analyzing the relative attention decisions give to certain values rather than others, the decision-making orientation is concerned with ways in which variations in the decision process relate to the content and effects of decision outcomes. For example, does one kind of decision process result in a more liberal sharing of power than another? Are decisions made through one chain of processes more likely to favor demands for wealth by a given interest group than decisions taken through another chain of processes? Do certain ways of making decisions serve demands for welfare (i.e., for skill, enlightenment, and well-being) more than others?

As one surveys scientific research on decision process and decision outcomes, he must be impressed by the paucity of empirical research that correlates variations in one with differences in the other. We assume, as we think most political scientists do, that political analysis strives ultimately to understand, predict, and influence the distribution of values—that is, the outcomes and effects of decisions. Few studies of decision processes, however, demonstrate whether process makes a difference for outcomes and effects and, if so, in what way. Dawson and Robinson[52] examined variations in decision processes in the American States and showed how they are related to differences in state expenditures for welfare, including aid to dependent children, old-age assistance, aid to the blind, aid to the permanently disabled, and aid to the unemployed. These comparative and longitudinal studies confirm the observations by V. O. Key and Duane Lockard (among others) that

52. Dawson, Richard, and Robinson, James A., "Inter-Party Competition, Economic Variables, and Welfare Policies in the American States," *Journal of Politics*, 23 (1963), 265–289; "The Politics of Welfare," in Herbert Jacob and Kenneth Vines (eds.), *Politics in the American States.* New York: Little, Brown, 1965, pp. 371–410.

the greater the competition between a state's political parties is, the more extensive its welfare efforts will be. The same research reveals that other factors in decision processes, such as the extent of political participation and the articulation of ethnic group demands, are also related to welfare outcomes. Such factors in decision-making are not, however, the only predictors of a state's welfare policies: nondecision-making variables such as state wealth (defined by per capita income) also partly determine the size of welfare programs.

Among the most important tasks of decision-making studies is the extension of research to the process-outcome nexus. To date, the greatest part of decision analysis has been "within the process" rather than on the relation of process to outcomes. In part, this shortcoming results from increasing process complexity in modern societies, especially in systems such as our own in which decision authority is widely dispersed among local, state, and federal levels, and among separate branches, institutions, and agencies at each level. Increased complexity of decision-making processes is implicit in such trends as "collectivism"[53] and "service class proliferation"[54] (Dahrendorf, 1959) in government. These trends are marked by the growth of bureaucracies and the extension of channels of communication and influence (both formal and informal) to increasing numbers of individuals and groups outside government. Thus Frankel[55] has observed that

We seem to have allowed to grow up around us a decision-making process in which those who make key decisions are invisible, and in their invisibility do not themselves know that they are making such decisions. The result is a kind of organized irresponsibility built out of the decisions and actions of countless disciplined and responsible men. . . .

The apparent increase in departmentalization and collectivism in decision making is, in itself, a way of characterizing decision processes, whose effects on decision outcomes might usefully be explored more systematically than they yet have been. At the same time, however, these trends complicate the task of tracing decision processes, make the study of process-outcome relationships more difficult, and place heavy demands upon efforts to build a comprehensive decision-making theory.

Many things pass for "theory" in political science. Among other things, "theory" may refer to a set of categories that constitutes an "approach" or "conceptual scheme";[56] or, at a more sophisticated level,

53. Beer, Samuel H., *British Politics in the Collectivist Age.* New York: Knopf, 1966.

54. Dahrendorf, Rolf, *Class and Class Conflict in Industrial Society.* Stanford: Stanford University Press, 1959.

55. Frankel, Charles, *The Democratic Prospect.* New York: Harper and Row, 1962.

56. Van Dyke, Vernon, *Political Science: A Philosophical Analysis.* Stanford: University Press, 1960.

theory may consist of a set of statements that specify relationships among variables tending toward determinacy. At present, decision-making most nearly fits the former definition, and its value lies in the degree to which it can inspire the building of theory in the latter sense. The breadth of the decision-making approach forces us to cast our theory-building nets widely to account for the interaction of intellectual, social, and quasi-mechanical processes, involving large segments of the political strata of societies that affect outcomes in an increasing range of value categories. If its breadth is a weakness of the decision-making approach, perhaps it is a source of strength as well. The search for decision-making theory, for example, provides a framework within which the findings of psychologists, sociologists, and economists may be applied to the study of political phenomena.[57]

The tendency of decision-making studies to concentrate on process and to stop short of the process-outcome nexus, then, appears to result both from the breadth of the decision-making approach and from the pervasiveness of decision processes in the modern polity. Indeed, the observation of some analysts that decision processes have become so complex and diffuse that it is no longer possible to identify the origins of decisions serves better as an argument for continued intensive process studies than as a deterrent to them.

But process analysis alone neither constitutes nor builds theory. Theory-building hinges upon our ability to relate the growing store of descriptive knowledge about *how* decisions are made to the *outcomes* and *effects* of those decisions. The immediate challange is to search the process data for patterns and characteristics that make a difference for outcomes. Further efforts in this direction promise to inspire propositions upon which to build from the decision-making approach a *theory* of political decision-making that will enhance our understanding of "who gets what, when, how."

57. Recent efforts to apply social-psychological findings to the study of international politics (Singer, J. David (ed.), *Human Behavior in International Politics.* Chicago: Rand-McNally, 1965; Kelman, Herbert (ed.), *International Behavior: A Social Psychological Analysis.* New York: Holt, Hinehart, Winston, 1965.), for example, have been facilitated by looking at international affairs in terms of a decision-making system.

11

The Premises and Promises of Decision-Making Analysis*

JAMES N. ROSENAU

LIKE COUNTRIES in the twentieth century, the sciences of human behavior seem to pass through several stages as they move toward modernization. During the *traditional* stage the practitioners in a field of inquiry rely on ambiguous concepts and untested theories to guide their impressions of the dynamics of their subject matter. Unrestrained by standards of reliability and unconcerned about the relationship of data to theory, the practitioners do not hesitate to attribute human characteristics to abstract entities and then to equate their insights into the behavior of these entities with human behavior itself. At this stage, consequently, knowledge is not cumulative. Being free to pursue their own interests in their own way, the various researchers do not build on each other's work. Case studies proliferate, but do not converge. New concepts and theories are advanced, only to go unheeded. What stands out are practitioners with a capacity for impressive insights, rather than insights with an impressive capacity for explaining an ever-widening range of phenomena.

At a certain point, however, a few practitioners become dissatisfied with the procedures and assumptions of the traditional stage and develop the aspiration to modernize. The absence of progress toward unified knowledge provokes them into protesting the reliance on ambiguous formulations, reified entities, and undisciplined modes of inquiry. Human behavior is not, the modernizing practitioners contend,

* I am indebted to the Research Council of Rutgers University for providing the time to prepare these reflections, to the Center of International Studies of Princeton University for placing the facilities appropriate to reflection at my disposal, and to my wife Norah for supplying the counsel and support that makes reflection possible in the first place.

189

abstract, mystical, or capricious, but is undertaken by concrete and identifiable actors whose behavior can be observed. Rather than being capricious, this behavior is the result of causal processes and thus exhibits regularities and patterns. Hence it is capable of being measured and quantified. Measurement and quantification, however, require explicit theory and operationalized concepts. Data do not fall into place on their own, but must be rendered meaningful by models and constructs that clearly identify how the components of behavior are structured and how they relate to each other. What is needed, the protest concludes, is greater attention to the accumulation of quantified data, to the formulation of empirical theories to explain the data, and to the utilization of scientific procedures which make both the data and the theories independent of those who use them.

Although the traditionalists in the field tend to feel threatened by the modernizing practitioners and to dismiss their protests as impracticable and misleading, the appeal of a more empirically based science cannot be denied and as the ranks of the protesters grow, the field moves into the *take-off* stage of development. Hence, as in the countries that move into this stage, the air becomes charged with excitement and commitment. A self-generating sense of change emerges and, with it, a headlong rush into uncharted areas of inquiry. No phenomenon is too minute to be considered; no fact is too established to be questioned; no abstraction is too sacrosanct to be challenged. Previously unrecognized sources of behavior are recognized and explored, giving rise to the identification of previously unidentified actors and the discernment of previously undiscerned relationships. New concepts, theories, models, frameworks, approaches, formulations, and hypotheses are proposed and modified. Schools of thought abound and factions within them emerge. Propositional inventories are compiled and philosophical underpinnings are contested. Sister disciplines are ransacked for relevant materials. Articles and arguments on methodology multiply. Untapped sources of data are discovered and exploited. Seemingly ungainly words are coined to designate the phenomena revealed by the new data or indicated by the new formulations. Diagrammatic presentations, replete with linking arrows and proliferating categories, are introduced to accommodate the new materials and depict their interrelationships.

Like the leaders of protest movements in traditional societies, however, the modernizing practitioners are not able to contain their revolutionary fervor once they overcome the forces of tradition and shoulder the responsibilities of leadership. The surge of innovative activity is too exciting and the vision of its ultimate potential is too exhilarating to temper enthusiasm with perspective, involvement with restraint, and creative formulations with scientific procedures. In the name of greater discipline the field comes to be marked by undisciplined inquiry. Freed of the traditional rules and as yet unconcerned about the need for modern ones, its newly ascendant practitioners are receptive to almost any innovative framework, irrespective of whether it is capable of yielding reliable empirical findings. Despite the welter of activity, therefore, knowledge is no more cumulative in the take-off stage than in the preceding one. Rather than building on each other's work and converging around accepted concepts and standardized procedures, the practitioners support each other's innovativeness even as they pursue their own. What stand out are insights that encompass an ever-widening range of phenomena, rather than an ever-widening range of phenomena that have been reliably explained.

The take-off stage lasts perhaps a decade or two—long enough for it to become apparent that the initial burst of activity has not resulted in a solid and expanding body of reliable knowledge. To be explicit and innovative about observable phenomena is not to engage in the painstaking task of actually observing them and then making the theoretical revisions that the observations require. Nor does the avoidance of impressionistic and reified analysis lead automatically to the formulation of viable frameworks and researchable propositions. As the modernizing practitioners slowly become aware that a science of human behavior cannot be built overnight and that instead slow, patient, and disciplined inquiry is required, the field moves into the third or *mature* stage of development. The innovative frameworks are scaled down to manageable proportions, the new concepts are rendered operational, and the resulting hypotheses are tested, revised, and tested again. As a result, the school of thought gives way to the empirical finding, the grandiose theory to the rigorous study, the propositional inventory to the research design, the philosophical challenge to quantitative analysis, and the all-encompassing insight to the precise formulation. Equally important, as the field becomes a mature science the criteria of relevance are toughened and the standards for processing data are raised. Where theories proposed during the take-off stage were accepted or rejected on the basis of speculation about their utility, those offered in the mature stage are broken down into their component parts and subjected to the test of empirical validation. Where journals were once filled with diagrammatic presentations, now they are characterized by tabular data tested for statistical significance. And, with this greater discipline, the practitioners begin to take cognizance of each other's hypotheses, to use each other's methods, to carry each other's work one step further, to replicate each other's findings—in short, to build on each other's research. Consequently, knowledge cumulates, even explodes, and the practitioners settle into a sustained period of growth that is satisfying even if not exhilarating.

Since it is crucial to the central theme of the ensuing discussion, stress must be laid on the necessity for the take-off stage to intervene between the traditional and mature stages. It cannot be by-passed. There is no shortcut. The creativity must precede the discipline, the seminal thinker must precede the patient researcher, and the compelling scheme must precede the refined theory. Ofttimes the premises, concepts, and procedures that permitted the take-off are so thoroughly reworked as to be unrecognizable in the later stage, but without them maturity could not ensue.

The Paradox of the Decision-Making Approach

The foregoing considerations have not only helped me to resolve my personal ambivalence (noted below) toward the concept of decision-making, but, more importantly, they also serve to summarize the paradox and controversy that have marked the concept since its introduction into American political science after World War II. Stated most succinctly, the paradox is that as a wide consensus formed over the utility of the concept, so did a deep dissensus develop over its contents, boundaries, and premises. Unlike, say, the extensive efforts at empirical validation that followed the initial enthusiasm which the introduction of the theory of cognitive dissonance aroused in social psychology,[1] the advent of the decision-making approach in political science evoked immediate attention and provoked considerable excitement that were not accompanied by endeavors to clarify its contents, eliminate its ambiguities, and trace the limits of its relevance. Rather than perfecting the concept of decision-making and narrowing its empirical meaning through subsequent inquiry, political scientists found it to be relevant in a variety of contexts. As a result, the concept has come to stand for an inconsistent set of diverse individual and group processes. For some, especially those attracted to game-theoretical formulations, decision-making phenomena connote rational calculations undertaken by hypothetical political actors. For those who find psychoanalytical notions persuasive, such phenomena pertain to the irrational drives that underlie the choices of real political actors. For still others, including both the probers of historical documents and the users of simulation techniques, the concept embraces all the factors, both rational and irrational, that enter into the process whereby empirical

1. The theory was introduced in Leon Festinger, *A Theory of Cognitive Dissonance* (New York: Harper, 1957). For a summary of the extensive efforts at empirical validation that followed, see Jack W. Brehm and Arthur R. Cohen, *Explorations in Cognitive Dissonance* (New York: Wiley, 1962).

political actors select one course of action from among several possible alternatives.

For me both the history and the contents of the concept have always had a special meaning. In the early 1950's I had the good fortune of closely observing, as a graduate student at Princeton, Richard C. Snyder's attempts to develop what subsequently became the first systematic treatment of decision-making phenomena in the study of foreign policy and international politics.[2] Those were exciting days. Over and beyond the usual enthusiasm of a graduate student for a stimulating teacher, one was keenly aware of being in the presence of a modernizing practitioner at the very moment when his protest against traditional modes was being launched. Snyder went out of his way to be tactful and to avoid offense to the traditionalists. The emphasis was on the worth and potential of new concepts, not on the ambiguous and misleading nature of old ones. Yet there was no mistaking that a major skirmish in the battle for modernization was being joined. This was not to be merely a reformulation of a few marginal concepts. Rather the new concepts were conceived to be inextricably interrelated and, as such, to constitute nothing less than a full-fledged "approach" to the study of international political phenomena. The inexperienced graduate student may have been perplexed by the virulence of the controversy that the approach occasionally aroused in the Princeton community even before its publication, but he could hardly fail to recognize that Snyder's assumptions were a departure from the past and that acceptance of them necessitated a rejection of certain long-standing ways of thinking about international actors and processes.

Having had the introduction of the concept of foreign policy decision-making into American political science conjoined with the start

2. After initially formulating an approach to decision-making processes in foreign policy and international politics, Snyder outlined ways in which it might be broadened to encompass virtually any political process. However, I have confined my attention here mainly to the initial formulation, since it is the more elaborate of the two versions and has occasioned much more discussion than the broadened outline. In addition, since Snyder was the main creator of the approach, I have not included in the analysis references to the two junior colleagues who assisted him in developing the initial formulation and who are also listed as its authors. For the initial formulation, see Richard C. Snyder, H. W. Bruck, and Burton Sapin, *Decision-making as an Approach to the Study of International Politics* (Princeton: Foreign Policy Analysis Project, Organizational Behavior Section, Princeton University, June 1954), later reprinted in Richard C. Snyder, H. W. Bruck, and Burton Sapin, (eds.), *Foreign Policy Decision-Making: An Approach to the Study of International Politics* (New York: Free Press, 1962), pp. 14–185. For the broadened version of the formulation, see Richard C. Snyder, "A Decision-Making Approach to the Study of Political Phenomena," in Roland Young (ed.), *Approaches to the Study of Politics* (Evanston: Northwestern U. P., 1958), pp. 3–38. Still another version, simplified for comprehension by undergraduate students, can be found in Richard C. Snyder and Edgar S. Furniss, Jr., *American Foreign Policy: Formulation, Principles, and Programs* (New York: Holt, 1954), Chap. 3.

of my own professional career, I have followed the evolution of the concept subsequent to its publication with particular care, rejoicing when a consensus formed and lamenting when dissensus also developed. Even more personally, the history of the concept since its publication has been the cause of considerable ambivalence. On the one hand, Snyder's framework so brilliantly clarified for me the nature of certain key aspects of international politics that I feel an enormous indebtedness to it and still fall back on it for stimulation. On the other hand, only one empirical application of the framework has ever found its way into the literature of the field,[3] and with each passing year I have increasingly come to doubt the merits of a framework that fails to spark empirical inquiry and thereby to meet the ultimate test by which any analytic scheme must be assessed. Only lately, and with the help of the analogy between the modernization of nations and intellectual disciplines, have I been able to resolve this ambivalence and evaluate the history and utility of the concept in a coherent way. What follows are the essential elements of this evaluation. The format is somewhat autobiographical and the tone is occasionally aggressive, but the commitment is to accuracy and balance. To anticipate the main thrust of the analysis, the decision-making approach is conceived as having been a crucial front in the behavioral revolution in political science and, like its parent movement, to have become the victim of its own achievements.[4] In effect the ensuing pages etch another epitaph onto another monument to the same successful protest.

Decision-Making Variables

At the heart of Snyder's original decision-making framework is the simple notion that political action is undertaken by concrete human beings and that comprehension of the dynamics of this action requires viewing the world from the perspective of these identifiable actors. The observer may regard the action as unwise and it may in fact prove disastrous, but neither the judgment nor the outcome serves to explain why the actors proceeded as they did. Only by transcending his own judgments and adopting the perspective of the actors can the observer engage in explanatory analysis. To facilitate reconstruction of the world

3. Richard C. Snyder and Glenn D. Paige, "The United States Decision to Resist Aggression in Korea: The Application of an Analytic Scheme," *Administrative Science Quarterly*, Vol. 3 (December 1958), pp. 342–378.

4. For a history and analysis of the behavioral revolution, see Robert A. Dahl, "The Behavioral Approach to Political Science: Epitaph for a Monument to a Successful Protest," *American Political Science Review*, Vol. LV (December 1961), pp. 763–772.

of the actors, Snyder suggested that all their activities can be examined in terms of one main form of behavior, the decision to pursue one course of action rather than many others that might be pursued. Whatever the actors do, and however sound their actions may be, they proceed on the basis of prior choices, and the presence of this decision-making activity at the core of all political action provides a common focus for the analysis of otherwise disparate political actors, situations, and processes. Decision-making sustains bureaucracies, dominates legislatures, preoccupies chief executives, and characterizes judicial bodies. Decisions lead to policy, produce conflict, and foster cooperation. They differentiate political parties and underlie foreign policies, activate local governments and maintain federal authorities, guide armies and stir international organizations. To explain any sequence of political actions, therefore, the analyst must ascertain who made the key decisions that gave rise to the action and then assess the intellectual and interactive processes whereby the decision-makers reached their conclusions.

To facilitate further the reconstruction of the world decision-makers, Snyder outlined and categorized the main factors that operate on them and give structure and content to their choices. In the case of foreign-policy choices, he subdivided the world of officials into three main sets of stimuli—those that emanate from the society for whom officials make decisions, those that arise out of circumstances or actions abroad, and those that are generated within the governmental organizations of which they are a part. Labeled, respectively, the "internal setting," the "external setting," and the "decision-making process," these categories were further subdivided in terms of certain major types of factors —nonhuman as well as human, attitudinal as well as behavioral—that each encompassed.[5] The internal setting was conceived to subsume not only such standard political phenomena as public opinion, but also "much more fundamental categories: major common-value orientations, major characteristics of social organization, group structures and function, major institutional patterns, basic social processes (adult socialization and opinion formation), and social differentiation and specialization."[6] The external setting was posited as comprising such phenomena as "the actions and reactions of other states (their decision-makers), the societies for which they act, and the physical world."[7] The decision-making process was envisioned to consist of three main

---

5. When he recast the framework to account for decision-making at any governmental level, Snyder understandably abandoned the external-internal distinction and referred instead to the "social" and "political institutional" settings (cf., Young, *op. cit.*, p. 22). Here I have chosen to confine myself to the framework for the analysis of foreign-policy decisions because it has been more fully elaborated.

6. *Ibid.*

7. Snyder, Bruck, and Sapin (eds.), *op. cit.*, p. 67.

subcategories: spheres of competence, communication and information, and motivation. Taken together, these decision-making subcategories include the roles, norms, goals, and functions within both the government in general and the particular unit making the decisions being subjected to analysis. In a diagrammatic presentation of the main categories and subcategories, and using a series of two-way arrows to link them together, Snyder demonstrated that the framework embraces a complex and interdependent set of social, political, and psychological processes. Most notably, he drew on a vast array of concepts developed in sociology, social psychology and psychology to show how the internal, external, and organizational worlds acquire structure and content—as well as how the links among them are fashioned—through the perceptions, motives, experiences, and interactions of the decision-makers.

Many years later all of this may seem so obvious as to be trite. But when photo-offset copies of the original formulation of the decision-making approach were distributed to a selected list of political scientists in the field of international politics in June, 1954, its basic premises were neither obvious nor trite. At that time, for example, precision about the identity of international actors and the sources of their behavior was not a dominant characteristic of research. Instead, the prevalent tendency was to regard the state as the prime actor and to look for the sources of its behavior in what were regarded as the objective realities of its position in the world. But who or what was the state? And how could the analyst, who inevitably had to rely on some degree of subjective interpretation, ever know what constituted the objective reality of its position? These troublesome questions had long been ignored. Many analysts were still quite content to treat the abstract state as if it were a concrete person and, in so doing, to impute to it the entire range of aspirations and traits normally associated with individual human actors. The fears of France and the hopes of India were treated as no less real and empirical than the quirks of a Charles de Gaulle and the idealism of a Jawaharlal Nehru.

Similarly, not being inclined to examine the attitudes and actions of concrete human beings, researchers still tended to search for the goals and sources of a state's behavior in geographic, historical, political, and technological circumstances, and these circumstances always seemed so unmistakable that the state was conceived to be subservient to them. Geography, history, politics, and technology were not conditions to be subjectively evaluated by officials, but rather were objective realities to which they had to pay heed. To know the goals of a state and identify its national interest, therefore, the analyst had only to discover the objective circumstances in which it was situated at any moment in time. That the "discovered" circumstances might be nothing more than the analyst's own subjective interpretation never gave much pause: in the absence of procedures for rendering findings independent of those who uncovered them, the inclination to equate reality with one's perceptions of it exerted a powerful and understandable hold on even the most dispassionate observers.[8]

With the publication of the decision-making approach, however, these long-standing habits of analysis could no longer be practiced with blissful unconcern. Whatever one may have thought of Snyder's scheme, there was no denying that it constituted a serious challenge to prevailing assumptions. In a decision-making context, reification of the state and objectification of its circumstances are neither necessary nor desirable. By definition, the state becomes its decision-makers, those officials of a society who have the authority and responsibility for preserving its integrity and enhancing its values through the selection of appropriate courses of action. To be sure, officials speak in the name of abstract entities and many may even act as if such entities do have a concrete existence, but whatever the content of the speeches and actions, they constitute empirical phenomena that allow the analyst to come down from the rarefied atmosphere of abstractions to the observable world of interacting human beings.

In searching for the goals and interests of a state, moreover, analysts no longer had to run the risk of equating their subjective interpretations with objective realities. The decision-making approach offered a clear-cut operational solution to the problem: national interests and aspirations are neither more nor less than what the duly constituted decision-makers conceive them to be, and while ascertaining the aims and values of officials can be extremely difficult, at least it is possible.[9] Stated differently, the reality of any situation is what the decision-makers, as aware (or unaware) of geographic, historical, political, and technological considerations as they may be, perceive it to be, and while the actions resulting from their perceptions may prove to be disastrous, such an outcome is due to the observable miscalculations of fallible men and not to the unknowable impact of inexorable forces.

Does this mean that the decision-making approach compels the analyst to ignore all the needs and wants of the members of the society and thus to posit a national interest that bears no relation to the hopes and fears of either the public in general or the particular segments of which it is comprised? Not at all, as no group of decision-makers that in fact has the authority to bind the society to a course of action can ever be totally cut off from its demands and aspirations (or else it will

8. For an elaboration of this reasoning, see Hans J. Morgenthau, *Politics Among Nations: The Struggle for Power and Peace,* 2nd ed (New York: Knopf, 1954), Chap. 1.

9. For an elaboration of this conception, see my "The Concept of National Interest," in the *International Encyclopedia of the Social Sciences,* in press.

lose the authority). Indeed, one of the innovative virtues of the decision-making approach was that it provided a way of empirically tracing the role of domestic variables as sources of foreign-policy behavior. Traditionally, students of the subject tended to assume that international actors were moved primarily by each other and, as a result, they dealt only superficially, if at all, with the processes whereby the history, composition, structure, and dynamics of a society condition its international behavior. Viewed in a decision-making context, however, domestic factors are, along with those located in the external setting and the decision-making organization, a major source of foreign policy and cannot be ignored. Just as the analyst is led to ask how perceptions of events abroad condition the choices that decision-makers make, so is he inclined to probe how developments at home enter into the formulation and selection of policy alternatives.

The fact that the decision-making process is itself treated as a major source of the policies adopted constituted still another clarifying innovation fostered by Snyder's framework. Previously analysts had been inclined to assume a simple one-to-one relationship between the stimuli to which officials are exposed and the decisions whereby they respond. But, Snyder contended, what the contents of a decision are, depends partly—and sometimes crucially—on how it is formulated as well as on the circumstances to which it is a response. At least in large industrial societies, which necessarily have evolved complex bureaucratic structures for making decisions, external events and internal demands must be processed as well as perceived by officialdom if decisions are to be made, and in this processing—in the rivalries of agencies, the procedures for convening and conducting committees, the techniques for collecting and distributing intelligence, the role requirements of particular policy-makers, the general structure of authority, the accepted style of framing and winnowing alternatives, the precedents for resolving conflicts, the modal backgrounds and career motivations of top officials—factors are introduced that shape the contents, direction, and adequacy of the resulting decisions. Most of Snyder's framework is devoted to an elaboration of these organizational variables and the many ways in which they can affect the choices that emerge from a decision-making organization.

Reasoning and Motivation in Decision-Making Analysis

That the decision-making approach constituted a radical departure from traditional practices at the time of its publication is perhaps best demonstrated by the nature of the criticisms it evoked. While some critics properly noted that the framework suffered from an absence of theory,[10] others were so provoked that they misunderstood its basic premises and criticized the scheme for proposing research strategies that in fact it explicitly rejected. As noted below, the approach is not lacking in severe limitations, but to criticize it for the assumptions it makes about the rationality or irrationality of officials and the policy-making process is to fail, in the most profound way, to grasp the central thrust of the analysis. Indeed, it is a measure of the extent of this failure that some of Snyder's least sympathetic critics rejected his approach on the grounds that it posited the decision-making process as too rational and that some condemned it for exaggerating the irrationality of the process. The former, apparently appalled by the proliferation of categories and subcategories in the discussion of the decision-making process, somehow concluded that the scheme viewed decision-makers as carefully weighing the pros and cons subsumed in each subcategory before framing alternative courses of action and of then giving serious consideration to every possible alternative before finally choosing one of them. Such a process, the critics rightly noted, involves a degree of rationality that bears little relationship to the world in which officials conduct their deliberations. Neither the time nor the resources are available to identify and relate all the ends and means that might be relevant when a situation requiring a decision arises.[11] As I read it, however, Snyder's formulation does not suggest that foreign-policy decision-making necessarily unfolds in a rational and conscious fashion. It merely asserts that officials have some notion, conscious or unconscious, of a priority of values; that they possess some conceptions, elegant or crude, of the means available and their potential effectiveness; that they engage in some effort, extensive or brief, to relate means to ends; and that, therefore, at some point they select some alternative, clear-cut or confused, as the course of action that seems most likely to cope with the immediate situation. Game theory may posit rational actors, but the decision-making approach does not. In effect, Snyder left the question open. In his approach it is an empirical question: intellectual and interactive processes necessarily precede decision, but whether they do so rationally or irrationally is a matter to be determined through the gathering and analysis of data.

Much the same can be said about the proliferation of categories.

10. Cf. Herbert McClosky, "Concerning Strategies for a Science of International Politics," *World Politics,* Vol. VIII (January 1956), pp. 281–95; and Vernon Van Dyke, *Political Science: A Philosophical Analysis* (Stanford: Stanford U. P., 1960), p. 153.

11. For a specific criticism of Snyder for positing "highly conscious moves and choices which can be analyzed in terms of neat categories," see Stanley H. Hoffmann, "International Relations: The Long Road to Theory," *World Politics,* Vol. XI (April 1959), p. 364. For a general critique of the decision-making literature that elaborates this theme, see Charles E. Lindblom, "The Science of 'Muddling Through,'" *Public Administration Review,* Vol. 29 (Spring 1959), pp. 79–88.

While the decision-making approach assumes that the antecedents of decision do occur in terms of a wide variety of role requirements, communication processes, and motivational determinants, the relevance of these variables to the choices that are made is not assumed in advance. If empirical investigation indicates that some of the subcategories will not yield particularly significant findings, then they are passed over and more fruitful matters considered. For example, if in certain situations stimuli in the external setting prove more central to the responses of officials than those arising within the decision-making organization or internal setting, then in those situations the latter are not examined as thoroughly as the former. By calculating the relative strength of the different sets of variables, however, the analyst has at least made sure that he searches for the sources of behavior in the only place where they can be found, namely, in the responses of officials to the external setting and not in the external setting itself. To proliferate categories is not to make a commitment to divide attention equally among them. Rather it is to ensure that no relevant considerations are overlooked.

While some analysts discerned an assumption of rationality in the fact that stimuli inherent in the decision-making process received considerably more attention than those located in the internal or external settings, others responded to this perceived imbalance by objecting to Snyder's framework for exactly opposite reasons. These critics concluded that the decision-making approach required the researcher to proceed as an amateur psychoanalyst in search of personality traits, private prejudices, and uncontrolled drives that might underlie the behavior of officials.[12] This line of criticism seems even more unwarranted than the one which posits the decision-making approach as overly preoccupied with rational actors. For not only did Snyder avoid an assumption of irrationality, he explicitly and emphatically rejected it. In what is unquestionably one of the most incisive and thorough translations of the psychological literature on motivation into a political context,[13] Snyder stresses that while students of foreign policy cannot afford to ignore motivational factors if they are to explain the behavior of concrete international actors, they need not be concerned with the entire range of motives that might be operative. Motives are conceived to be of two kinds, those that an official acquires through membership and participation in the decision-making organization and those he develops as an individual in a vast array of prior experiences during childhood and adulthood. The former are what Snyder calls *in order to* motives, since

12. For an example of a critic who concluded that "those who hold to the decision-making approach . . . consider it necessary to probe into the personal events that take place within the psyches of men," see Arnold Wolfers, "The Actors in International Politics," in William T. R. Fox (ed.), *Theoretical Aspects of International Relations* (Notre Dame, Ind.: U. of Notre Dame Press, 1959), esp. p. 92.

13. Snyder, Bruck, and Sapin (eds.), *op. cit.*, pp. 137–173.

they impel officials to act in order to achieve or maintain a future state of affairs in the decision-making organization, in the internal setting, or in the external setting. The latter are labeled *because of* motives, since the behavior to which they lead can be said to occur because of idiosyncratic predispositions acquired in the course of past experience. Political scientists, Snyder emphasized, may not have to devote equal attention to both types of motives. Students of foreign policy are not interested in the official as a whole human being, but only in that part of him that gives rise to his behavior as an official. Hence, while psychologists and historians might have reason to examine the idiosyncratic aspects of his personality and past experience, political scientists may be able to develop sufficient explanations of his behavior without ever investigating the "because of" motives that gave rise to it. Indeed, in what comes closest to an explicit theoretical proposition in the entire formulation, Snyder contends that usually the behavior of officials can be satisfactorily explained through an exploration of the motives derived from their decision-making organization, from their interpretations of the society's goals, and from their reactions to demands of situations in the internal and external settings—and that therefore it is usually not necessary to investigate their "because of" motives. Ordinarily, for example, one does not need to know the details of a chief executive's upbringing or the profession in which he was trained after completing his formal education in order to explain his decision to arm allies and otherwise contest the aggressive behavior of a potential enemy. The decision is entirely comprehensible in terms of the perceptions and values which any occupant of the role is likely to have.

Yet this is not a rigid proposition. Even as he asserts it, Snyder acknowledges that the analysis of "in order to" motives may not always yield a satisfactory explanation, that there may be circumstances in which the idiosyncratic variables are so strong that "because of" motives must be investigated if an adequate assessment is to be made. If this should be the case, the decision-making approach does not preclude such an investigation. Snyder argues only that since "because of" motives are likely to be least relevant, considerable time and energy can be saved by examining the "in order to" motives *first*. Idiosyncratic variables, in other words, are treated as a residual category which the researcher considers only if there is a residue of behavior that is unaccounted for. Proceeding in this way the researcher not only avoids in most instances the difficult task of searching for personality data, but he also isolates, in the remaining cases, "what area of behavior must be accounted for in terms of idiosyncratic factors, that is, self-oriented needs not prompted by the system."[14]

14. *Ibid.*, p. 161.

Plainly this reasoning is not the equivalent of assuming that comprehension of the decision-making process requires exploration of the psyches and irrational impulses of officials. Again the question is left open. Motives are operative and they must be examined, but whether they are rational or irrational is a matter to be determined by the accumulation and inspection of empirical data.[15]

The Impact of
the Decision-Making Approach

Despite the critical preoccupation with the rationality problem, Snyder's emphasis upon decisional phenomena stirred widespread thought among political scientists, especially those in the fields of international politics and foreign policy. Of course, it would be patently false to argue that he was alone responsible for the shift away from the analysis of reified abstractions and toward the investigation of empirical choices. Intellectual ferment never stems from only one source, and there was no lack of protest against the traditional modes of analyzing international actors prior to 1954. Not until the decision-making approach was published in that year, however, did a shift in analytic practice become manifest. Perhaps the shift and the publication of the approach were mere coincidence, but I have always felt that the coherence and thoughtfulness of Snyder's formulation served to crystallize the ferment and to provide guidance—or at least legitimacy—for those who had become disenchanted with a world composed of abstract states and with a mystical quest for single-cause explanations of objective reality.

In any event, whatever the historical relation between the publication of the decision-making approach in 1954 and subsequent practice, in the ensuing years decisional phenomena did become a central concern of students of politics. Signs of this shift were everywhere—in the language analysts employed, in the phenomena that they studied, in

15. Furthermore, there is nothing in the decision-making approach which suggests that "in order to" motives are rational and "because of" motives irrational. It was the critics of the approach that introduced the criterion of rationality. Snyder himself never distinguished between the two types of motives in terms of this criterion nor even implied that one type is likely to be more rational than the other. On the contrary, the dynamics of organizational decision-making are conceived to be just as capable of fostering inappropriate behavior as are the psychological processes of individuals. One can readily imagine circumstances under which the idiosyncratic experiences of an official will give rise to choices that are more consistent with the analyst's criterion of rationality than are the choices provided the official by his organization. For a cogent discussion of these matters, see Sidney Verba, "Assumptions of Rationality and Non-Rationality in Models of the International System," World Politics, Vol. XIV (October 1961), pp. 93–117.

the concepts they developed, and in the methods they used to generate data. The most obvious of these signs, of course, was the acceptance of the terminology of decision-making. The phrase itself began to appear in the titles of books and articles as well as in their contents,[16] and soon became a permanent fixture in the vocabulary of political analysis. Indeed, the phrase even overcame the layman's tendency to dismiss the scholar's terminology as unnecessary jargon and found its way into the vocabulary of politics. It is one of the few technical terms of political science that occasionally appears in the speeches of presidents, the appeals of candidates, the debates of Congressmen, and the editorials and headlines of newspapers. It seems more than a mere accident of style that led a recent President of the United States to refer to "the dark and tangled stretches in the decision-making process."[17] Like political scientists—and, I believe, because of them—many top officials have been attracted by the substance as well as the terminology of decision-making analysis.[18]

The impact of the decision-making approach could even be discerned in the work of scholars who continue to use some of the traditional terminology. For several years subsequent to 1954 it became quite commonplace for analysts to preface their use of abstract terms with qualifying footnotes that took note of the dangers of reification and that recast the traditional language into a decision-making context. The following is a typical expression of this qualification:

Although there are frequent references in this study to such collective nouns as the "nation," "country," "state," and "government," it is to be clearly understood throughout that these terms are used merely for the sake of convenient exposition. Only individuals have motives, expectations, and interests, and only they act or behave. Strictly speaking, it is not the "state," in the above reference, which substitutes its schedule for that of private persons, but certain officials who, with the acquiescence of other persons, shift resources to new goals and away from others valued highly in peacetime.[19]

16. For example, see Donald R. Matthews, *The Social Background of Political Decision-Makers* (Garden City: Doubleday, 1954); Dwaine Marvick (ed.), *Political Decision-Makers* (New York: Free Press, 1961); and Karl W. Deutsch, "Mass Communications and the Loss of Freedom in National Decision-Making: A Possible Research Approach to Interstate Conflicts," *Journal of Conflict Resolution,* Vol. I (June 1957), pp. 200–211.

17. John F. Kennedy, "Foreword," in Theodore C. Sorensen, *Decision-Making in the White House: The Olive Branch or the Arrows* (New York: Columbia U. P., 1963), p. xiii.

18. For a multitude of evidence along this line, see U.S. Senate, Committee on Government Operations, Subcommittee on National Policy Machinery, *Organizing for National Security* (Washington, D.C.: Government Printing Office, 1961), Vols. I–III; and Charles J. Hitch, *Decision-Making for Defense* (Berkeley: U. of California Press, 1965), *passim.*

19. Klaus Knorr, *The War Potential of Nations* (Princeton: Princeton U. P., 1956), p. 64.

More significantly, the terminological shifts were accompanied by changes in the way political scientists structured their subject matter and the concepts they used to probe it. The substantive shifts were subtle and gradual, but in retrospect they are clearly discernible. Students of foreign policy, for example, were not only less disposed to posit abstract actors, but they also spoke less of compelling realities and more of conflicting alternatives, less of the formalities of diplomacy and more of the dilemmas of diplomats, less of the demands of situations and more of their limits and opportunities, less of the primacy of international affairs and more of the competition between domestic and foreign-policy goals. To be more specific, during the decade subsequent to 1954 the literature of the field was swollen by a veritable flood of new inquiries that, coincidentally or otherwise, reflected the premises of the decision-making approach: the origins of World War I were probed in terms of the perceptions which key officials in the various countries had of their capabilities and their adversaries;[20] the production of information for the makers of foreign policy was examined in terms of a conflict between the perspectives of the gatherers and users of intelligence;[21] the capabilities available to policy-makers were conceived in terms of a distinction between those perceived by officials (the "psychological environment") and those that existed irrespective of whether they were perceived (the "operational environment");[22] the evolution and choice of policy alternatives were analyzed in terms of the requirements and processes of consensus-building among executive agencies,[23] military services,[24] and nongovernmental leaders;[25] the development and change of policy goals were assessed in terms of shifting motivational patterns among participating officials;[26] the relationship between executive and legislative policy-makers and agencies was posited and probed as a communications process,[27] as were the relations

20. Dina A. Zinnes, Robert C. North, and Howard E. Koch, Jr., "Capability, Threat, and the Outbreak of War," in James N. Rosenau (ed.), *International Politics and Foreign Policy* (New York: Free Press, 1961), pp. 469–482.

21. Cf. Roger Hilsman, *Strategic Intelligence and National Decisions* (New York: Free Press, 1956).

22. Harold and Margaret Sprout, "Environmental Factors in the Study of International Politics," *Journal of Conflict Resolution*, Vol. 1 (December 1957), pp. 309–328.

23. Roger Hilsman, "The Foreign-Policy Consensus: An Interim Research Report," *Journal of Conflict Resolution*, Vol. III (December 1959), pp. 361–382.

24. Samuel P. Huntington, *The Common Defense: Strategic Programs in National Politics* (New York: Columbia U. P., 1961).

25. James N. Rosenau, *National Leadership and Foreign Policy: A Case Study in the Mobilization of Public Support* (Princeton: Princeton U. P., 1963).

26. Vernon Van Dyke, *Pride and Power: The Rationale of the Space Program* (Urbana: U. of Illinois Press, 1964).

27. James A. Robinson, *Congress and Foreign-Policy Making: A Study in Legislative Influence and Initiative* (Homewood, Ill.: Dorsey Press, 1962).

between policy-makers and their publics,[28] between officials and the press,[29] and between legislators and interest groups;[30] psychological warfare was seen in terms of the intellectual and organizational context of those who conduct it as well as those toward whom it is directed;[31] the role of delegate to the United Nations was conceived in terms of the stimuli experienced by its occupants;[32] the role of legislator was conceptualized in terms of the conflicts between internal and external variables[33] and between role and idiosyncratic variables;[34] the relevance of personal experience and professional training for the foreign policy outlooks of academics,[35] scientists,[36] military officers,[37] Southerners,[38] and other role occupants[39] was subjected to searching inquiry, as was the socialization of legislators,[40] foreign-service officers,[41] and secretaries of state[42] into their roles; and the relevance of goals in different

28. Bernard C. Cohen, *The Political Process and Foreign Policy: The Making of the Japanese Peace Settlement* (Princeton: Princeton U. P., 1957); also see Karl W. Deutsch and Lewis J. Edinger, *Germany Rejoins the Powers: Mass Opinion, Interest Groups, and Elites in Contemporary German Foreign Policy* (Stanford: Stanford U. P., 1959).

29. Bernard C. Cohen, *The Press and Foreign Policy* (Princeton: Princeton U. P., 1963).

30. Raymond A. Bauer, Ithiel de Sola Pool, and Lewis Anthony Dexter, *American Business and Public Policy: The Politics of Foreign Trade* (New York: Atherton, 1963).

31. Robert T. Holt and Robert W. van de Velde, *Strategic Psychological Operations and American Foreign Policy* (Chicago: U. of Chicago Press, 1960).

32. Chadwick F. Alger, "United Nations Participation as a Learning Experience," *Public Opinion Quarterly*, Vol. XXVII (Fall 1963), pp. 411–426.

33. Roland Young, *The American Congress* (New York: Harper, 1958).

34. James N. Rosenau, "Private Preferences and Political Responsibilities: The Relative Potency of Individual and Role Variables in the Behavior of U.S. Senators," in J. David Singer (ed.), *Quantitative International Politics: Insights and Evidence* (New York: Free Press, 1967).

35. Gene M. Lyons and Louis Morton, *Schools for Strategy: Education and Research in International Security Affairs* (New York: Praeger, 1965).

36. Robert Gilpin, *American Scientists and Nuclear Weapons Policy* (Princeton: Princeton University Press, 1962). See also Robert Gilpin and Christopher Wright (eds.), *Scientists and National Policy-Making* (Columbia U. P., 1964).

37. Morris Janowitz, *The Professional Soldier: A Social and Political Portrait* (Glencoe, Ill.: The Free Press, 1960), and John W. Masland and Laurence I. Radway, *Soldiers and Scholars: Military Education and National Policy* (Princeton: Princeton U. P., 1957).

38. Alfred O. Hero, Jr., *The Southerner and World Affairs* (Baton Rouge: Louisiana State U. P., 1965).

39. R. Joseph Monson, Jr., and Mark W. Cannon, *The Makers of Public Policy: American Power Groups and Their Ideologies* (New York: McGraw-Hill, 1965); and Hans Speier and W. Phillips Davison (eds.), *West German Leadership and Foreign Policy* (New York: Harper, 1957).

40. James David Barber, *The Lawmakers: Recruitment and Adaptation to Legislative Life* (New Haven: Yale U. P., 1965).

41. James L. McCamy, *Conduct of the New Diplomacy* (New York: Harper, 1964), Part III.

42. W. Lloyd Warner, Norman H. Martin, Paul P. Van Riper, and Orvis F. Collins, *The American Federal Executive: A Study of the Social and Personal*

issues-areas as a source of differential behavior on the part of the same actors was explored.[43]

As even this small sample of illustrations indicates, however, the post-1954 concern with decisional phenomena was scattered over a vast range of diverse and unrelated problems. Decisional phenomena served as a common concern, but they did not serve to foster coherence in research. Few analysts probed different aspects of the same problem and even fewer built upon the findings of others. Comparison of the foreign-policy-making of different nations became a widespread preoccupation,[44] but the comparisons generally lacked uniformity and, in effect, were little more than single-nation analyses juxtaposed with each other.[45] Spurred by the application of game theory to the problems of deterrence in a world of nuclear superpowers, efforts to develop formal models of the utility-probability calculations made by foreign-policy actors also attracted a number of practitioners,[46] but these too failed to achieve uniformity as many of the analysts became restless in face of the difficulty of estimating the subconscious and subjective factors that underlie the calculations of utilities and probabilities in a particular situation.[47] Anxious to account for these subjective factors under various circumstances, other analysts turned to simulating international phenomena in a laboratory,[48] but the wide use of the technique of simulation has yet to yield a coherent body of findings.

Characteristics of the Civilian and Military Leaders of the United States Federal Government (New Haven: Yale University Press, 1963), and Dean E. Mann, with Jameson W. Doig, *The Assistant Secretaries: Problems and Processes of Appointment* (Washington, D.C.: Brookings Institution, 1965).

43. Theodore J. Lowi, "American Business, Public Policy, Case-Studies, and Political Theory," *World Politics,* Vol. XVI (July 1964), pp. 677–715. See also James N. Rosenau (ed.), *Domestic Sources of Foreign Policy* (New York: Free Press, 1967), *passim.*

44. For example, see Joseph E. Black and Kenneth W. Thompson (eds.), *Foreign Policies in a World of Change* (New York: Harper & Row, 1963); Roy C. Macridis (ed.), *Foreign Policy in World Politics,* 2nd ed. (Englewood Cliffs, N.J.: Prentice-Hall, 1962; and Kurt London, *The Making of Foreign Policy: East and West* (Philadelphia: Lippincott, 1965).

45. For an elaboration of this point, see James N. Rosenau, "Pre-Theories and Theories of Foreign Policy," in R. Barry Farrell (ed.), *Approaches to Comparative and International Politics* (Evanston: Northwestern U. P., 1966), pp. 34–37.

46. For example, see Bruce M. Russett, "The Calculus of Deterrence," *Journal of Conflict Resolution,* Vol. VII (June 1963), pp. 97–109; and J. David Singer, "Inter-Nation Influence: A Formal Model," *American Political Science Review,* Vol. LVII (June 1965), pp. 420–430.

47. Cf. Martin Patchen, "Decision Theory in the Study of National Action: Problems and a Proposal," *Journal of Conflict Resolution,* Vol. IX (June 1965), pp. 164–176; and Bruce M. Russett, "Pearl Harbor: Deterrence Theory and Decision Theory" (mimeo., n.d.).

48. Among the many who moved in this direction was the main author of the decision-making approach himself: see Richard C. Snyder, "Experimental Techniques and Political Analysis: Some Reflections in the Context of Concern Over Behavioral Approaches," in James C. Charlesworth (ed.), *The Limits of Behavior-*

Least of all did the post-1954 lines of inquiry yield any extension of the original decision-making approach itself. Stimulating as Snyder's scheme was, as of this writing (May 1966) it has yet to arouse widespread attempts at conceptual modification or empirical validation. Thought was provoked and decisional phenomena came to be emphasized, but the approach itself remains unamplified. There has been no rush of graduate students to expand its propositions in Ph.D. dissertations and no accumulation of case studies utilizing its categories. As previously noted, only one direct effort to apply the approach has been undertaken and even this failed to yield amplification or clarification of foreign-policy decision-making process in other than the single situation to which it was applied. To be sure, the approach has been widely excerpted in anthologies[49] and students in undergraduate and graduate programs still receive an introduction to its premises. Otherwise, however, the approach as such has tended to disappear from sight. The original formulation no longer recurs in the footnotes of professional articles or in discussions at professional conferences.

The Need for Theory

How can we explain the decision-making approach's apparent lack of durability? How do we resolve the contradiction between the claim that its impact was pervasive and the conclusion that it failed to generate theoretical elaboration or even empirical case studies? If the impact was so extensive, why are traces of the original formulation vanishing from present-day literature and research? Is it that Snyder was so far ahead of the field that it is still catching up and that the *next* decade will witness attempts to apply and expand his formulation? Or, more personally, is it that I have engaged in wishful thinking and allowed my assessment of the merits and impact of the decision-making approach to be distorted by the way it enriched my own graduate training? Could it be that the approach never was capable of elaboration and that I have been blinded by attachments to a favored teacher?

alism in Political Science (Philadelphia: American Academy of Political and Social Science, 1962), pp. 94–123; and Harold Guetzkow, Chadwick F. Alger, Richard A. Brody, Robert C. Noel and Richard C. Snyder, *Simulation in International Relations* (Englewood Cliffs, N.J.: Prentice-Hall, 1963).

49. For example, see Heinz Eulau, Samuel J. Eldersveld, and Morris Janowitz (eds.), *Political Behavior: A Reader in Theory and Research* (New York: Free Press, 1956), pp. 352–359; Stanley H. Hoffmann (ed.), *Contemporary Theory in International Relations* (Englewood Cliffs, N.J.: Prentice-Hall, 1960), pp. 150–165; and James N. Rosenau (ed.), *International Politics and Foreign Policy: A Reader in Research and Theory* (New York: Free Press, 1961), pp. 186–192, 247–253.

The answer to these questions has two dimensions which, taken together, serve both to explain the discrepancies in the previous analysis and to justify indebtedness to Snyder and his approach. One dimension concerns the lack of theory in the original formulation and the other posits a justification for this lack. While many of the criticisms of the approach were ill-founded, it is certainly true that Snyder identified the existence of a number of relationships without attempting to theorize about their components and structure. Nothwithstanding the vast array of categories and subcategories, the links among them remain unspecified. As previously indicated, only the place of idiosyncratic variables —"because of" motives—are the subject of predictive assessment and even here the prediction is cast in such broad terms as to have little relevance for specific situations. To posit decision-making as a central activity and the internal, external, and organizational settings as prime sources of this activity is not to suggest the relative strength of these sources under varying conditions or the interaction between them. To indicate that the strengths of the relevant variables have to be assessed and compared is not to outline a method for assessing them or a basis for comparing them. Yet, self-admittedly, Snyder did not carry his analysis to these lengths. He identified unexplored phenomena, but did not indicate how they might unfold. He called attention to new premises and concepts, but did not specify when, where, and how they might be used. He suggested problems that could be fruitfully researched, but did not provide substantive guidance as to how the researcher should proceed.[50]

Conspicuously missing from the decision-making approach, in other words, are any "if-then" hypotheses—propositions which indicate that *if* certain circumstances are operative, *then* certain decisions and actions are likely to ensue. The difficulty with all the categories and subcategories subsumed by the approach is not that they have been proliferated, but rather that they have been isolated from each other. Our computer technology is fully capable of coping with the proliferation problem. But the computer has to be programmed. It cannot in itself handle the problem of cross-tabulating and analyzing the subcategorized data. For this, theory—or, if theory is too stringent a requirement, simple if-then propositions—is needed that instructs the computer how to process the

---

50. Some years later Snyder, with another colleague, somewhat offset this deficiency by outlining fifty-six research projects that could usefully be undertaken. However, again there was a shortage of theoretical propositions and the guidance provided for carrying out each project was mainly in the form of questions that might be considered and bibliographical sources that might be consulted. Cf. Richard C. Snyder and James A. Robinson, *National and International Decision-Making: A Report to the Committee on Research for Peace* (New York: Institute for International Order, 1961).

data in terms of the interaction that is presumed to take place within and among the categories.

The main reason for the lack of theory is clear. While the organization variables are elaborated at length, those in the internal and external settings are merely identified. Anxious to demonstrate the relevance of the decision-making process to the contents of foreign-policy decisions, Snyder explicitly passed quickly over the domestic and foreign sources of motivation, pausing only long enough to note their existence and the necessity of viewing them from the perspective of officials in an organizational context. But to theorize about the decisions that officials are likely to make, one must have some notion of the nature of the stimuli to which they are exposed. Variables within the decision-making organization may be crucial, but they are variables, and events or trends outside the organization are key determinants of the way in which they vary. Domestic demands and national aspirations may be increasingly important sources of foreign policy, but the conditions under which they are salient for officials can fluctuate markedly. External demands are perhaps subject to even wider and more erratic fluctuation. Since Snyder did not enumerate any of the factors in the internal and external settings to which decision-makers might respond, naturally he was not led to hypothesize about the choices that they might make in different types of situations.

Theories of political decision-making, in other words, can never be exclusively comprised of propositions about the officials who make choices. Processes located in the environment toward which officials direct their decisions are no less relevant than those which occur in their minds and interactions. To reconstruct the world from the perspective of the decision-maker, the researcher must examine the world itself in order to comprehend the dynamics and limits of the decision-maker's perspective. To predict the direction, timing and nature of political decisions, one must include and interrelate variables pertaining to the targets of the decisions, the actors making them, and the relationship between the targets and the actions. To expect decisional phenomena to provide the sole basis for if-then propositions about politics is thus to establish an unattainable goal. There can be no theory of political decision-making that is divorced from the political environment with respect to which decisions are made. The decision-maker may serve as the organizing focus, but propositions about his behavior are bound to be as diverse and discontinuous as the targets of his behavior and the circumstances under which he makes his choices. A unified theory of political decision-making would be nothing less than a theory of the entire political process.

Little wonder, then, that students of foreign policy did not converge upon the decision-making approach in an effort to apply and extend it. Lacking theoretical propositions and all the materials out of which such propositions must be fashioned, it contained no encouragement to application and extension. The premises were clarifying and the concepts new and useful, but there were no loose ends to tie, no intriguing hypotheses to challenge or empirical observations to test. One could only adapt the premises and concepts to whatever substantive problems and phenomena one might be interested in—say, to the origins of World War I, to the conflicts between gatherers and users of intelligence, to the analysis of capabilities, to the role of UN delegate.

But hindsight is easy. Reconstructing the world of political science from the perspective of its author, another, more justifiable reason emerges as an explanation of why Snyder settled for the decision-making approach rather than attempting a theory of international politics and foreign policy. Comprehension of international phenomena at the time he developed his scheme was rudimentary. Since international action had previously been conceived to be undertaken by abstract actors, data on interaction among decision-makers, their organizations, and their internal and external settings had not been systematically developed. For Snyder to have enumerated, assessed, and compared the strength of the relevant variables in 1954 would thus have been to engage in sheer guesswork. He could not turn to a body of reliable findings as a basis for articulating theoretical propositions. For such findings to come into existence a break with traditional modes of analysis had to be made. Reification had to be undermined. The quest for insight into reality had to be redirected. The nature of decisional phenomena had to be brought into focus. The existence of organizational and domestic variables had to be established. The case for inquiring into motivation had to be made and the legitimacy of importing concepts from other social sciences had to be demonstrated. In short, the field had to pass into and through the take-off stage before its practitioners would be in a situation to evolve theoretical propositions that would assess and compare the relevant organizational, internal, and external variables.

The study of foreign policy has since advanced well into the take-off stage and is rapidly approaching the transition to maturity. Almost every day—or at least every issue of the professional journals—brings fresh evidence that practitioners are beginning to assess the relative strength of internal and external variables as sources of international behavior undertaken by officials whose deliberations occur in different types of governments and societies. In so doing they take for granted that action is sustained by concrete and identifiable persons, that the goals of this action arise out of a need to balance internal and external demands, that the way in which officials experience these demands is a consequence of organizational as well as intellectual processes, and that therefore the researcher must investigate both the nature and processing of the demands if he is to comprehend, explain, and predict the quality and direction of the action.

The decision-making approach, in other words, had been absorbed into the practice of foreign-policy analysis. The habits it challenged have been largely abandoned and the new ones it proposed have become so fully incorporated into the working assumptions of practitioners that they no longer need to be explicated or the original formulation from which they came cited. Unencumbered by mystical concepts, unconcerned about reified abstractions, disinclined to search for objective reality, and willing to settle for replicable findings, practitioners are now free to devote themselves to the painstaking tasks of constructing and testing hypotheses about the behavior of international actors. Now they can utilize the technique of simulation and pursue the logic of game theory in meaningful and productive ways. Now they are free to enjoy the prime pleasure of empirical research: that endless sequence whereby new theoretical propositions exert pressure to gather new data which, in turn, initiate pressure for still newer theory. None of these opportunities or pleasures would have been available if an earlier generation had not cleared the way by calling attention to the centrality of decision-making phenomena.

12

What Is Game Theory?

T. C. SCHELLING

You ARE on the station platform, ready to board the train, and meet an old friend who has reserved a seat in a different car from yours. You agree to meet in the diner. After you board the train a steward comes through making reservations, and you discover that there is a first-class diner and a second-class buffet car. You'd somewhat rather eat in first class, you suspect that your friend would prefer the buffet car, but mainly you want to make a reservation that coincides with his. Do you elect the diner or the buffet car?

Again you are on the platform and meet a friend you are trying to avoid; he is going to coax you onto some committee. Your reservations are in different cars, but he suggests meeting in the diner. When the steward comes through you discover to your relief that there are two diners, first-class and buffet, and if you choose correctly you may "innocently" miss your friend. You have to be careful; he can guess that you'll evade him if you can. Normally you'd dine first class and he knows it. For which car do you make your lunch reservation?

Once again, you are on the train without a reserved seat. You find a seat but a few passengers are left standing. When the steward announces lunch, the standing passengers watch eagerly to see who will vacate a seat in favor of lunch. If you go to the diner you will have no claim to your seat when you return. If you do not vacate your seat you cannot eat; if you do not eat nobody gets your seat, not even for the time you would like to be in the diner. What arrangement can you work out?

Finally, you are in your air-conditioned parlor car when the steward gives you your ballot. Passengers are asked whether they wish smoking to be permitted in these cars. You suspect it will be a close vote. A second item on the ballot asks whether, if smoking is permitted in response to the passengers' wishes, it should be confined to cigarettes.

You'd love a cigar, which is all you ever smoke, would evidently answer no to the second question, but suspect that all nonsmokers and some cigarette smokers would vote to exclude cigars. How do you vote? Can you make a deal with someone?

As you leave your parlor car at the station, the steward stands expecting his tip. Fifty cents would be a reasonable tip, but the steward disposes of enough favors to make it worth some small expense to be among his favorites. You suspect that some of the other regular commuters try to tip a little above average. You'd like to tip a little above average. How much do you give the steward?

Interdependent Decisions

Game Theory is the formal study of rational decision in situations like these. Two or more individuals have choices to make, preferences regarding the outcomes, and some knowledge of the choices available to each other and of each other's preferences. The outcome depends on the choices that both of them make, or all of them if there are more than two. There is no independently "best" choice that one can make —it depends on what the others do.

For some problems, like choosing the route that minimizes distance from home to office, you can reach a solution without solving anybody else's problem at the same time. To drive through an intersection, though, you want to know what the other driver is going to do—to stop, slow down, speed up, or just keep going—and you know that a main element in his decision is what he thinks you are going to do. Any "solution" of a problem like this is necessarily a solution for *both* participants. Each must try to see the problem from the other's point of view, but when he does he sees himself trying to reach a decision.

What game theory did was to identify this class of situations as one of practical importance and intellectual challenge, and to propose that any satisfactory solution for rational participants ought to be a solution for them jointly. Each must base a decision on his expectations. Unless we are willing to suppose one or more among them merely to expect wrong—and then we have to decide *ad hominem* who is going to be wrong—there must be some consistency, not only of their choices with their expectations but among their expectations of each other. Game theory is the formal study of the rational, consistent expectations that participants can have about each other's choices.

It is, though, abstract and deductive, not the empirical study of how people make decisions but a deductive theory about the conditions that their decisions would have to meet in order to be considered "rational," "consistent," or "noncontradictory." Of course, defining "rational," "consistent," or "noncontradictory" for interdependent decisions is itself part of the business of game theory. Take the case of the man whom we do not want to meet in the diner: could there be a theory that tells us unequivocally which diner to choose in order not to meet him? Only if we deny our opponent access to the theory. If logic could tell us which diner to choose, the same logic could tell him which diner we would choose, and as von Neumann and Morgenstern said in the monumental work that launched game theory two decades ago, we can hardly be satisfied with the generality of any theory whose success depends on its not becoming known!

Strictly speaking, this kind of theory is not predictive. It is what is sometimes called "normative" theory in contrast to predictive or explanatory theory. Still, it is doubtful whether theorists would put forth so much energy and receive so much attention if their deductions were not felt to provide some bench mark for the analysis of actual behavior. This method, which might be called "vicarious problem-solving," has been traditional in economics; for the study of how business firms maximize profits, even for the study of whether they try to, it is helpful to know how they would behave if they actually tried and succeeded.[1]

Solving the Problem

Let us look, now, at how the problems that began this essay are approached through game theory. First, with an exception to be noted later, from the point of view of game theory none of these problems involves dining cars. The dining cars are merely an interpretation; the man I did not want to meet in the diner could as well be a disarmament inspector along whose route I do not want to leave evidence of violation, or a submarine commander about to fire a torpedo in the direction he thinks my ship will go. Second, the problem does not involve par-

1. Impressive support for this approach is in Jerome S. Bruner, Jacqueline S. Goodnow, and George A. Austin, A Study of Thinking (New York: Wiley, 1957). In studying experimentally the process of "concept attainment" the authors use the term, "strategy," to refer to a "pattern of decisions in the acquisition, retention and utilization of information that serves to meet certain objectives, i.e., to insure certain forms of outcome and to insure against certain others [p. 54]." Furthermore —and this is an interesting step beyond the restrictions of game theory—the authors do not demand that the subject be conscious of his strategy. "Psychology has been celebrating the role of 'emotional factors' and 'unconscious drives' in behavior for so long now that man's capacity for rational coping with his world has come to seem like some residual capacity that shows its head only when the irrational lets up. . . . Man is not a logic machine, but he is certainly capable of making decisions and gathering information in a manner that reflects better on his learning capacity than we have been as yet ready to grant." (p. 79.)

ticular individuals; game theory eschews solutions based on personal idiosyncracy or the ability of one individual to outguess another. Third, in game theory one does not care why the one individual wants to meet the other and the second wants to avoid the first; they are treated as "rational" in the way they try to achieve their goals, but their goals are *their* business, and game theory takes them as data.

In the case of *opposed interests*, if either of us has to make his choice first, in a way that the other can see, the solution is easy: the first loses, however he chooses, and the second wins. This result is trivial but its implications are not. It points to the value of postponing decision, of gaining intelligence about the choice another has already made and denying intelligence in case one has to move first.

This dining-car case is simplified by the occurrence of only two possible outcomes, *meet* and *don't meet*, and using S and F for success and failure, the problem can be depicted in a 2 × 2 matrix:

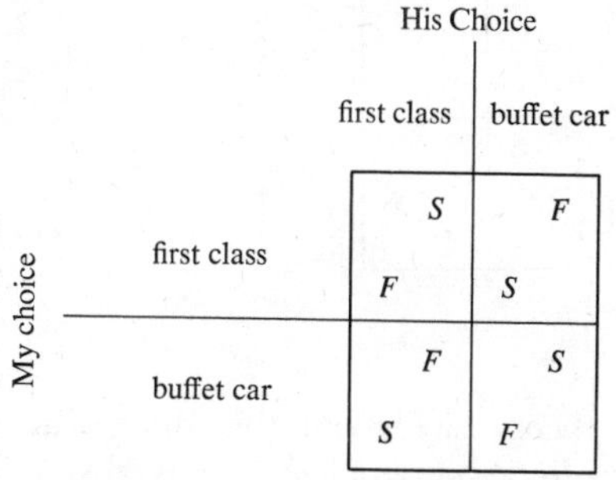

His Choice

	first class	buffet car
first class	S / F	F / S
buffet car	F / S	S / F

FIGURE 12.1

In the lower left corner of each cell is the outcome from my point of view, I being the one whose decision corresponds to choosing the upper or lower row; and in the upper right corner of each cell is the outcome from his point of view, his decision corresponding to the choice of the left or right column. We can make the problem look somewhat quantitative by using numerical scores in place of S and F—a 1 for success and a 0 for failure, or perhaps a −1 for failure, choosing numbers for sheer mnemonic and typographic convenience, just remembering that the larger of the two numbers means success. We may as well use the same pair of numbers for both players, although this again is just for convenience. We can now say that each player tries "to maximize his score," but this merely means that he tries to achieve success or to maximize his chances of success.

This is one of the situations that in game theory is known as "zero-sum." It is often described as a situation in which he loses what

I gain and vice versa, but actually in game theory the scoring systems of the two individuals are invariably treated as incommensurate. If two feudal noblemen play a game of cards, one to lose his thumb if he loses and the other to lose his eyesight, the game is "zero-sum" (as long as neither cares about the other's loss) though nobody's loss is the other's gain and there may be no way of comparing what they risk losing. It is precisely *because* their value systems are incommensurable that, if their interests are strictly opposed, we can arbitrarily represent them by scales of value that make the scores or pay-offs add up in every cell to zero. Visually it is often more convenient to use positive numbers and zeros; the sum then will be some positive number.

His Choice

		First Class	Buffet Car
My Choice	First Class	1 — 0	0 — 1
	Buffet Car	0 — 1	1 — 0

What, now, does game theory say about this dining-car or dis-armament-inspection or torpedo-target problem that is abstractly represented in our matrix? The reader can probably guess: it says that each participant should have a fifty-fifty chance of succeeding. Why? Because the positions are symmetrical, and in game theory we agree not to pick favorites. Is it quite true that their positions are symmetrical, when one wants to meet and the other wants not to meet? Yes, the same situation arises in matching pennies; one wants both coins heads or tails and the other wants a head and a tail, but if we match a nickel against a penny it is arbitrary whether we call the Indian or the buffalo "head." So we not only eliminate the dining car, we eliminate the concept of "meeting." We can interchange columns in the matrix and get another that is superficially changed but essentially the same; "meet" and "not meet" are only labels, and in game theory we ignore the labels unless there are special reasons for using labels as part of the communication process.

We might say that it is a "tossup" who wins this game and indeed one may as well flip a coin. But I can flip the coin for either of two reasons, because I just don't care and, like a person who doesn't know which shoe to put on first, want some arbitrary way to decide, or alternatively because if I deliberately flip a coin you cannot guess what I will do, any better than you can guess the toss of a coin. In game theory it is discovered that some games of wits (usually, "zero-sum" games of pure conflict) can be converted into games of chance by appropriate randomization of one's decision.

There is a consistency here: if I flip a coin you can have no better than a fifty-fifty chance at meeting me, and if you flip a coin I can have no better than a fifty-fifty chance of avoiding you. In game theory, this fifty-fifty chance of success or failure for each participant is considered the "value of the game," and the "solution." This does not quite say that a person should flip a coin. What it says is that two rational participants, in this situation with alternative outcomes, cannot rationally expect more than a fifty-fifty chance of success unless there are special reasons for supposing that one of the opponents just does not understand the game. If you can think of any line of reasoning by which to choose one car or the other with a better than fifty-fifty chance of meeting me, I can spoil your strategy by flipping a coin. No mediator could talk the two of us into any scheme that gave odds of less than, or more than, a fifty-fifty chance of meeting, because one of us could always do better by flipping a coin.

Where is all the mathematics? The mathematics is of two sorts. One relates to logical generalization: it is interesting to know whether every problem of this kind has this kind of solution, and what kinds may not. Second, if we complicate the problem it may take some practical mathematics to figure out what kind of coin to flip. Suppose for example that there is one dining car in which your acquaintance is bound to find you but another in which he has only a fifty-fifty chance even if you both go to that car. The latter is like two dining cars coupled together, and to decide where to go you must choose among the equivalent of three dining cars, rolling dice to determine which of the three to go to. He then has one chance in three of finding you, and could himself guarantee one chance in three by choosing one or the other dining car with odds of two to one. Complicate the problem all you please, the principle remains the same; complicate it all you please, and the services of a mathematician or a computer become necessary. The intellectual achievement is in recognizing which complicated problems of disarmament inspection, torpedo fire control, and dining-car selection can be reduced to the general principle of flipping a coin or using random numbers. For generations people presumably chose safe combinations at random in order not to be outguessed by burglars, but it was game theory that saw the same principle (with the odds suitably chosen) in the allocation of a quota of on-site disarmament inspections among the months of a year or the sections of a territory.

Notice that communication is of no significance in this strictly adversary relation. The submarine commander and the captain of the target ship can have no rational interest in sending each other messages; any message worth sending is not worth reading, unless somebody thinks that he is a little smarter than his adversary and can think one step further in a game of mutual deceit.

Alternative Solutions

Now turn to the two friends who want to meet in the same dining car. They succeed or fail together. (If we want symmetrical terminology we can call the situation a "zero-difference game" in exactly the same sense as the pure-conflict situation is called a "zero-sum game.") Their choices are represented in the following matrix:

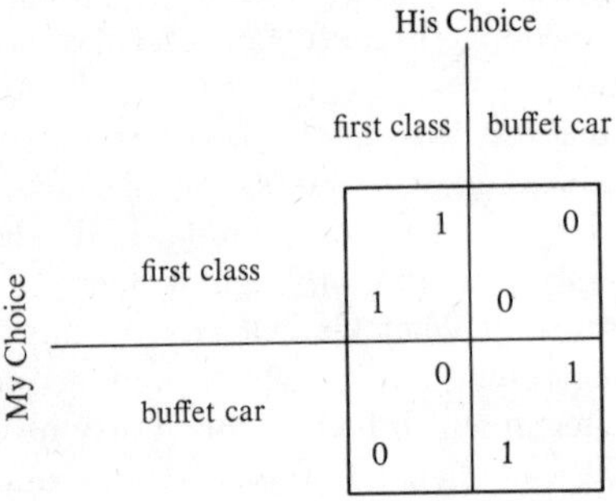

His Choice

		first class	buffet car
My Choice	first class	1 — 1	0 — 0
	buffet car	0 — 0	1 — 1

FIGURE 12.3

Their problem is an "embarrassment of solutions." There are two, and they do not know which to choose. If either can move first, letting the other follow, the situation is trivially easy. This is a "team" situation (to use Jacob Marschak's term) and it takes only one-way communication, or a leader-follower relation, or a "rule" known to both participants, to solve their problem.[2] If they flip coins they guarantee the same fifty-fifty chance that the adversaries did. What they might do is search for clues; a clue is a kind of signal that each can recognize as an

2. Jacob Marschak, "Theory of an Efficient Several-Person Firm," *American Economic Review: Papers and Proceedings,* 50 (May, 1960), pp. 541–548. The cost of information in the presence of coinciding preferences is a central part of Marschak's theory of organization.

arbitrary instruction worth following in the interest of getting together. Here is the place where "labels" can make a difference, but only as a kind of surrogate for an instruction or a communication. If one dining car is named "The Rendezvous" and the other "Solitaire," they may agree tacitly that they have the signal they need. Members of a squad separated in combat, two people with a lunch date who failed to mention where to meet, or two cars keeping to opposite sides of the road need such clues and signals. Communication makes the problem trivial, but communication is not always available. What is interesting conceptually about this problem is that there are too many "solutions," posing a problem.

Consider now the man who will lose his seat if he goes to the diner. His interest, and that of the man who wants his seat, are neither strictly opposed nor wholly coincident. Both will be better off if the man can reclaim his seat when he returns, because if he can he will eat, and the other will get to sit down for a while. The "solution," if the man would rather sit than eat and has no way of reclaiming his seat, is an *inefficient* one: he goes without lunch, the other stands up all the way. What is needed is a one-way promise that the man who sits down will get up, or an enforceable contract, or a scheme to rearrange the incentives of the man who takes the seat (such as his going to the dining car second, not first, and being hungry enough to vacate his seat when the first returns). Game theory helps to discover some of these "inefficient" situations; it can also try to discover some rules or procedures, legal arrangements, or enlargement of the range of strategies available, to achieve better outcomes for both participants. Game theory also provides a framework for studying the bargaining that then occurs if there are two or more such outcomes and they discriminate differently among the participants.

A Framework for Analysis

So far I have mentioned only some rudiments of game theory, and none of the subtle or elaborate analysis that has attracted the attention of mathematics. But what may be of most interest to a social scientist is these rudiments. The rudiments can help him to make his own theory, and make it in relation to the particular problems that interest him. One of the first things that strike a social scientist when he begins to experiment with illustrative matrices is how rich in variety the relationships can be even between two individuals, and how many different meanings there are for such simple notions as "threat," "agreement," and "conflict." He is struck by how many configurations of information and misinformation there are, how many different communication systems, and what a variety of alternative "legal" constraints on bargaining and tactics. Even the simplest of situations, involving two individuals with two alternatives apiece to choose from, cannot be exhaustively analyzed and catalogued. Their possibilities are almost limitless. For this reason, game theory is more than a "theory," more than a set of theorems and solutions; it is a framework for analysis. And for a social scientist the framework can be useful in the development of his own theory. Whether the theory that he builds with it is then called game theory, sociology, economics, conflict theory, strategy, or anything else, is a jurisdictional question of minor importance.

Consider two individuals with two choices each, four possible outcomes. For each participant, rank the four outcomes from first choice to fourth, without yet using numbers to represent the intensity of preferences; eliminate ties, that is, assume that no two outcomes are equally attractive or unattractive for either of the participants. How many different 2 × 2 situations can we get? The answer is 78. Furthermore, in 66 of these situations the positions of the two participants are different; and there are a total of 144 different positions a man can be in vis-à-vis his partner.

This number is large enough to surprise most people; but if it seems manageably small, we need only to make allowance for some tied preferences and the number of distinguishable 2 × 2 matrices exceeds a thousand. Just give each participant three alternatives to choose among, rather than two, with nine outcomes that can result from the joint decision, and the number of distinguishable positions a man could be in vis-à-vis his partner is more than a billion. That is to say, if we prepare a table with three rows and three columns and put, in each of the nine cells, one of the numbers from one to nine for the player who chooses column, and similarly for the one who chooses row, there are more than a billion different ways of inserting those numbers, even after we eliminate all the duplications that result from arbitrarily rearranging rows and columns. (To be more exact: the number is $[9!]^2 \div [3!]^2 = 3,659,830,400$.)

No wonder there is no exhaustive catalogue of even the simplest kinds of interdependence that can exist between the decisions of two people. Add a third person, or add for each person his estimate of the other person's preferences, or add an opportunity for one person to make his choice conditional on the other's choice, and the number of different possibilities quickly becomes astronomical. Let the population explosion go to any imaginable extreme and form all the possible pairs of human beings on this planet; there will not be enough pairs to illustrate the full variety of the situations that can occur when two people contemplate between them a dozen possible outcomes they jointly determine by choosing, in a brief sequence of moves, among three or four alternatives each.

These numbers are not meant to daunt the theorist but to encourage him. Since a definitive catalogue of even the simplest situations and their analyses could not be physically provided nor humanly read if it could be, and since evidently not all differences are important differences, one needs a system, or some criteria, for handling whole classes of situations that, though different, need not be distinguished. One needs to identify the models that have the greatest generality or some unique interest. And one needs a few theorems that permit him to make general statements based on a few salient characteristics of a model, without having to examine all the possibilities.[3]

Some Illustrative "Moves"

The use of matrices and explicit preferences can be helpful both in discovering and in communicating distinctions that need to be made (and in recognizing false distinctions or inessential ones). How does one distinguish a threat from a warning? How does one distinguish the potency of a threat from its credibility? How does one distinguish a bluff from an insufficiently credible threat? When does a threat need to be coupled with a reassurance to be effective? In what situations can both parties be interested in threats, in what situations can only one party have an interest? When is misinformation of value to both parties, when is it of value to one party, and when harmful to both? What is the minimum communication system required for the effectiveness of a threat, of a promise, of a threat coupled with a promise; and what kinds of insurance against failure will enhance the credibility of a threat, what kinds will degrade it? What definitions break down, or have to be replaced by more complicated notions, if the number of relevant alternatives increases from two to three, or from three to some larger number?

3. Interesting attempts to characterize and classify two-person situations, by reference to some kind of pay-off matrix, are in Kellogg V. Wilson and V. Edwin Bixenstine, "Forms of Social Control in Two-Person Two-Choice Games," *Behavioral Science*, Vol. 7 (1962), pp. 92–102, reproduced in Shubik (see bibliographical note); and in John W. Thibaut and Harold H. Kelley, *The Social Psychology of Groups* (New York: Wiley, Inc., 1959). There are many twofold classifications that can be combined; the original distinction between zero-sum and nonzero-sum is one, the distinction between "cooperative" and "noncooperative" games another. See Luce and Raiffa (bibliographical note), esp. Chaps. 4, 5, and 6. Two-by-two and larger games can also be classified according to the type of "solution" they admit, to their symmetry or asymmetry, to the order of moves, to the dominance of strategies, and so forth. The "best" method of classification will usually depend on what the analyst wants to bring out.

It turns out that many of these concepts and distinctions can be operationally defined by reference to an explicit "pay-off matrix" that shows the preferences of two parties among the several outcomes. It also turns out that some cannot, and it is useful to see explicitly why they cannot. Some concepts can be operationally defined, and quite simply represented, as a change in a single number or preference ranking in a single cell of a matrix; some can be defined as simultaneous changes in two or more of the pay-offs—two pay-offs of the same person in different cells, or one pay-off for each of the players.

This is hardly high-powered theory, and surely does not yet involve mathematics, but it can lead to discoveries and it can reduce ambiguity in communication.

We can make threats that are bluffs or bets that are bluffs: does "bluff" have the same meaning in both cases? My dictionary says that to bluff is to frighten someone by threats that cannot be made good. What about "will not" be made good? Is there a difference? What is it if I make a threat that I want you not to believe will be made good? Am I bluffing if I try to make you underrate either my capability or my willingness to do what I said? As von Neumann and Morgenstern pointed out (p. 189; see bibliographical note at end of chapter), in situations like poker one may not only bluff to win an occasional hand on poor cards but also, quite rationally, bluff to be occasionally caught bluffing, so that a partner may think one is bluffing when one is not and put more money in the pot. It is extraordinary how rich in alternative meanings some of these apparently simple concepts are; the surest way I know to identify the necessary distinctions, to get away from verbal ambiguities, even to discover significant motives and actions that one had not thought of, is to use some of the rudimentary paraphernalia of game theory in making a model that one can manipulate.

Another superficially simple concept is *immunity*. An important problem in a rebellious area is to get people to give information that they want to give but are afraid to. The same problem arises in getting Negroes to testify when their rights have been violated, or hotels integrated whose owners are afraid of reprisal. Medical authorities have the same problem in getting dope addicts to seek medical advice, since disclosure of the addiction makes the patient subject to prosecution. Grand juries often have to grant a witness immunity from self-incrimination. (A committee can even give an immunity that a witness does not want, to deny him the excuse that otherwise resides in the danger of self-incrimination.) In elections the secret ballot is mandatory, not an optional privilege, so that no one can give evidence of how he voted and thus cannot be made to comply with a bribe or a threat. This concept of immunity is susceptible to formal analysis, and the analysis could lean on some of the concepts and techniques of game theory. The situation is a "game" of *n* persons, where *n* is typically three or more but can be as small as two; there are pay-offs to be identified, channels of communication and a structure of information, a distinction between verbal communication and evidence, and a set of choices that go in a certain sequence. There are alternative ways of providing immunity, such as privacy, protection, and coercion. Privacy can be personal or statistical; the protection can be based on defense against third parties or deterrence of them; the coercion can be secret, or it can be made visible to third parties to discourage countercoercion. These situations do not especially belong to economics, law, political science, criminology, strategic intelligence, or any of the traditional disciplines; it cuts across them.

Still another example is the interesting subject of locks, alarms, warnings, and safety catches. We usually do not need much theory to help us buy a lock for the garage door, but a lock on nuclear weapons is rich in its theoretical possibilities. There are many kinds of locks and many motives, and even a classification of them requires something that looks a little like game theory. A lock on radium in a doctor's office has, among its purposes, the anomalous one of protecting the thief himself. A lock on the bathroom door is intended to keep people out who prefer to stay out and is equivalent to a sign saying "occupied"; and in bathrooms in some new buildings, to keep children from locking themselves in, there is an anomalous lock that can be unlocked from either side of the door. A lock on an ammunition chest may be designed to keep the contents from being used by somebody, and a mechanism that destroys the contents when the box is violated is almost as good as one that keeps the thief out; if the lock is to keep someone from destroying our ammunition, though, a destruct mechanism merely eases his task. A lock that makes the ammunition explode when the mechanism is joggled will not protect the ammunition if it works secretly, but if the burglar knows that it will explode in his face it can deter him. Some locks are designed only to measure the urgency of entry and are designed to give way under stress; fire alarms and emergency brakes are protected by a piece of glass to which a small metal hammer is conveniently attached. Some locks are meant to catch the intruder by blocking escape, some to catch his identity by photograph, some merely to report his intrusion by giving an "alarm," and they are hidden or made conspicuous according to whether one wants to trap the burglar or to deter him. And some, like the time lock on a bank vault, are designed to keep the owners themselves from being able to open them, so that they are immune to coercion during times of day that the place is unprotected.

And so on. Similar problems arise in handling confidential information, the reaction to a radar alarm and the authority to launch warfare, systems to guard the legal rights of apprehended suspects, and disciplinary systems. What we are discussing is devices or institutions that can be construed as a "move" in an n-person game, where interesting values of n may be anywhere from one up to half a dozen and the game can profitably be described by reference to the pay-offs, the information structure, and the strategies available to the participants. The garage door, as I said, may be an easy one, but designing an appropriate device for a nuclear weapon, a fallout shelter, or an ammunition convoy in Vietnam requires explicit attention to the rich array of alternatives, the trade-offs and compromises, the probabilities of contingent events, the relative magnitudes of pay-offs, and what needs to be communicated, what guarded against revelation. The richness of the problem, and the value of explicit analysis, is occasionally brought home to us on those occasions when we lose a credit card, lock ourselves out of a house, or can't find something we hid to keep it away from the children.

I am not trying to advertise something called "game theory" that will provide instant insight into these interesting problems, but rather to make vivid the kind of problem that stimulated the development of game theory and to show how ubiquitous these problems are.

Voting Strategy as an Example

Voting schemes provide nice illustrations of the domain of game theory. Voting is notorious for inviting strategy—the calculation of how one ought to cast his ballot in view of how others may cast their ballots. Someone who dislikes public housing may vote in favor of a civil rights amendment he despises, knowing that only with the amendment can the bill itself be killed on a subsequent ballot. Voting also invites coalitions; and implicit coalitions can be exploited by designing "package" proposals to be voted all at once as a means of enforcing the coalition. "Packages" eliminate alternatives; a rule obliging the President to enact or to veto an appropriations bill in its entirety permits the Congress to exploit the President's preferences.

I am going to work through an example, and to keep it simple I shall restrict the number of voters to two. I can do that if I use a rule of unanimity. You and I are members of a two-man committee to determine the career of an employee who would normally be considered for promotion but has been charged with a blunder that he might be fired for. Our committee has to decide two things. First, is the man's over-all record so excellent that, leaving the blunder aside, we ought to promote him? Second, is he guilty of this blunder? If his record is excellent and he is innocent he will be promoted; if his record is only ordinary and he is guilty he will be fired. If we find him guilty, but find his record excellent, he will be demoted but not fired; if we find him innocent but of ordinary record he will be kept but neither promoted nor demoted.

I have been through the evidence and reached the conclusion that, all things considered, the man ought to be demoted, but I'd rather keep him than fire him, even promote him than fire him. You are convinced the man ought to be fired; if you can't fire him you'd like him demoted, least of all promoted. Under the rules we must vote on both issues, his record and his innocence. Under the rules, it takes two to find him guilty of the blunder, and two to award him an excellent. Under the rules, we do not vote whether to promote, keep, demote or fire the man; we vote these two issues.

The normal procedure is to vote first on guilt or innocence and, having that out of the way, to proceed with whether his record is excellent or ordinary. If both of us prefer, however, to take his record up first, we may. So together we first vote on which question to take up first, unanimity being required to take up his record first.

Both of us are interested in the *outcome,* not in the abstract notions of innocence and excellence. And both of us have made no secret of our preferences.

We can sketch this problem in the form of a branching tree:

There are eight ways that the balloting can go in arriving at one of these four results. The first branching point at the top determines which issue is taken up first; the second determines the answer on that first issue and the third the issue voted last. The numbers in the sketch refer to how many votes it takes to determine the choice; at the top of the diagram the 2 means that it takes two favorable votes to elect the right-hand procedure (under which his record is voted before his innocence or guilt), the 1 means that it takes only one vote to have his guilt taken up first. It would take three unanimous ballots to reach the right-hand outcome where the man is promoted; either of us can bring about the outcome on the left because it takes only one vote for guilt to be considered first, one vote to find him innocent, and one vote to deny him an excellent rating. Under one procedure if I vote him guilty you can alone decide to have him fired; under the alternative procedure, if you vote him a good record I can get him promoted by finding him innocent. How should we expect each other to vote?

One way to work this problem is to start from the final votes and work up. At the far left (at the point reached if either of us votes for the normal procedure and if either of us votes him innocent) the final ballot (nominally on his excellence) is a choice between *promote* and *keep,* and it takes two to promote him. Evidently we'll both vote to keep him. At the final vote second from the left the choice is between firing and demoting, and it takes two to find his record excellent and thus to demote him; you prefer to fire him, and your vote would do it. Foreseeing this, at the preceding stage when we vote innocent or guilty, we know that the choice is between keeping him and firing him, so I shall vote him innocent, after which we shall both find his record ordinary. This means that if either of us supports the normal procedure on the first ballot the result will be that the man is kept.

Similarly, on the far right if we have found him excellent, we shall both vote to demote him; if instead we have found him ordinary I shall vote to keep him. So when we vote on his rating we know we are voting to demote or to keep him, and we both vote "excellent" in order to demote him at the next stage.

So, if we both vote to reverse the normal procedure and take up his record first, we can expect the man to be demoted. Since we both prefer his demotion to his merely being kept, we should both vote to reverse the normal procedure, then to find his record good, then to find him guilty.

There are several points to note. First, *the procedure makes a difference;* the man is demoted or merely kept according to which of

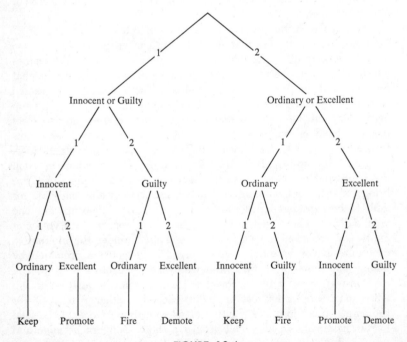

FIGURE 12.4

the two questions we vote first. Second, one of the two procedures is *less satisfactory for both of us* than the other procedure, even though our interests do not coincide. Third, the reason why voting first on guilt or innocence leads to this less satisfactory outcome is that I must expect you to find his record poor after we both find him guilty. Because I do, I have to find him innocent. It is your power of decision on the final ballot that diverts me down another branch, to an outcome that we both like less than demotion. If you could promise in advance to vote his record good, I could go ahead and vote him guilty and we'd both be better off. The alternative procedure, down the right-hand branch, can be thought of as a way for you to give me that promise; by voting a good record in advance, you deny yourself the possibility to get the man fired after I vote him guilty, leaving me free to vote him guilty.

Each of us would have to re-examine his strategy if the other's preferences were switched. If you knew that I really wanted him promoted, for example, you would not dare to vote as you just did; nor would I if I knew that you wanted him promoted.

A Matrix of Strategies

One technique of game theory is to identify all of these "strategies" —all of the different contingent plans that the voter may have for deciding along the way how to vote next. If I had to be absent, and sent a deputy to represent me, I could not simply tell him how to vote on each ballot. Each vote should depend on how the preceding ballot went. I can, however, if I'm willing to be sufficiently explicit, anticipate all possibilities and tell my deputy what to do in each case that could arise. I could say, for example, "Vote yes on the first ballot; if that loses vote no on the next two ballots but if it wins vote yes on the next ballot and yes again if it wins or no if it fails."

This is a *sufficient* instruction; it tells him how to do everything I would have done as the situation unfolds. In the language of game theory, this is a "strategy." Every such contingent instruction, if it covers all possible contingencies, is a "strategy." In this voting problem, the number of different strategies is limited, and any advance plan or instruction that covers every contingency can be thought of as a selection of one strategy from among all the possible strategies. If we identify all of the alternative strategies, we can construct a matrix consisting of all possible plans that the two of us might have, and thus convert our dynamic sequential problem to a static simultaneous-choice equivalent, in which I merely choose a strategy in advance, considering all the strategies open to you, and you do the same, and the outcome is the joint result of these two strategies.

To see how this is done, without cluttering the page with too large a matrix, suppose that we have already voted to reverse the usual procedure and to take up excellence first, and are about to decide on our remaining strategies. Since a no vote is decisive while a yes vote can carry or lose, I have one completely definite strategy: voting no on both ballots with the result that the man is kept, independently of how you vote. I also can vote no on the first ballot and yes on the second; if I want him fired, this may be a way of achieving my aim. If I vote yes on the first ballot there are four possible plans I could have for continuing: (1) to vote him guilty whether or not the first ballot finds his record excellent, (2) to vote innocent however the first ballot comes out, (3) to vote guilty if his record is found excellent, otherwise innocent, and (4) to find him innocent if his record is found excellent, otherwise guilty. I have, then, a total of six possible ways of playing the game when two ballots remain. You have the same alternatives, so there are thirty-six different ways our contingent plans can combine in reaching one of four possible outcomes. These are shown in Figure 12.5.

The numbers have to be explained. To represent my preferences I have arbitrarily given a score of 3 to *demote*, 2 to *keep*, 1 to *promote*, 0 to *fire*. Since your preference order is *fire, demote, keep, promote*, I've scored you with 3 if he is fired, 0 if he is promoted, etc. These numbers just remind us of our preference order, the magnitudes do not matter. (A little later we shall see where numerical values would make a difference.)

Neither of us has a "dominant" strategy, that is, a strategy that he would be satisfied to have chosen no matter what the other chose. Row 6 looks good to me unless you choose Column 3 or 4, in which case I'd rather have chosen Row 1. Column 5 looks good to you if I choose Row 2, bad if I choose Row 3 or 4, pretty good if I choose Row 5. There are some columns you might choose that leave me indifferent—Column 1, for example. There are some columns in which my score can be anything from 0 up to 3 according to what row I pick.

Though no row or column is an obvious "best" choice, we can still ask whether there is a pair of expectations we can have about each other that will lead us to choices that confirm those expectations. Is there a column such that if I expect you to choose it I will choose precisely the row that, if you expected it, would lead you to choose that column? Yes, Row 6 and Column 5 have that "equilibrium" property. If I expect you to choose Column 5 I am content with Row 6, and if you expect me to choose Row 6 you are content with Column 5. We cannot quite say that I "prefer" Row 6 when you choose Column 5, because I would do just as well in Row 5, but if you expected me to choose 5 you would choose Column 2. The intersection of Row 6 and Column 5 is an "equilibrium point," or an "equilibrium pair" of strategies. It has the property that if we both make the corresponding choices, each expecting the other to do so, each has behaved correctly in accordance with his expectations and each has confirmed the other's expectations.

Furthermore, the intersection of Row 6 and Column 5 is an "efficient"

Your Strategies

My Strategies		No No		No Yes		Yes No		Yes No/ Yes *		Yes Yes		Yes Yes/ No **
No, No		1		1		1		1		1		1
	2		2		2		2		2		2	
No, Yes		1		3		1		3		3		1
	2		0		2		0		0		2	
Yes, No		1		1		0		0		0		0
	2		2		1		1		1		1	
*Yes, No/Yes		1		3		0		0		0		0
	2		0		1		1		1		1	
Yes, Yes		1		3		0		0		2		2
	2		0		1		1		3		3	
**Yes, Yes/No		1		1		0		0		2		2
	2		2		1		1		3		3	

*Vote *yes,* Followed by *no* if it carries, *yes* if it fails.

**Vote *yes,* followed by *yes* if it carries, *no* if it fails.

Outcomes:

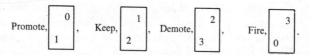

Promote, $\begin{array}{c}0\\1\end{array}$, Keep, $\begin{array}{c}1\\2\end{array}$, Demote, $\begin{array}{c}2\\3\end{array}$, Fire, $\begin{array}{c}3\\0\end{array}$.

FIGURE 12.5

outcome, as economists use the term. There is no other cell in the matrix that can improve the outcome for one player without worsening it for the other. The same cannot be said for the cell in the upper left corner, which is also an equilibrium point but a weak one. (It is a "weak" one, a kind of "neutral equilibrium," because neither of us has an actual preference for that cell above any others in the corresponding row or column.)

If we draw up the corresponding matrix for the two-stage ballot under the normal procedure, with guilt or innocence being decided first, we get the matrix in Figure 12.6.

This matrix differs from Figure 12.5 in several ways. One is that you now have a dominant strategy: Column 3 in every row is as good as any other column and sometimes better. You can eliminate the other 5 from consideration. Since you can, I can assume you will, and I choose Row 1 or 2.

But though 3 dominates, your outcome is not especially favorable. Knowing your choice, I pick a row that gives me a score of 2 and you but 1. You cannot wish that you had chosen differently, all you can wish is that I could have expected you to. Then I might have chosen differently.

If Columns 3 and 4 could be suppressed I would have a dominant strategy, Row 6, and you could choose Column 5 or 6 and both of us would be ahead. But in the matrix as it stands, the two of us cannot hold a consistent pair of expectations that would lead us to Row 6, Column 5. This pair of strategies has not the equilibrium quality; there is no line of reasoning by which we can reasonably expect each other to expect it.

The Complete Matrix

The very first ballot, then, deciding the order in which to take up the two questions, can be construed as a ballot for deciding which of these two matrices to confront. We could of course construct a matrix corresponding to the whole three-ballot game. It would be hard to get on a single page, but we can at least ask what it should look like.

How many rows and columns would it have? A complete strategy has to indicate how to vote on the first ballot and how to vote thereafter in either of two cases. Since it takes two of us to reverse the normal procedure, one to keep it, a vote of no on the first ballot need only be coupled with a choice of a row (or column) in the matrix (Figure 12.6) corresponding to the left-hand branch. So there are six complete strategies corresponding to a vote of no on the first ballot. If I vote yes on the first ballot, my strategy must specify a row in each matrix, since I shall have to choose a row in whichever matrix the first ballot selects. There are, thus, 36 possible strategies containing a yes vote on the first ballot. Altogether, then, there are 42 strategies for me and the same number for you. This 42×42 matrix has 1764 cells, each containing one of the four outcomes. What else do we know about it without taking the trouble to draw the matrix?

Your Strategies

	No No	No Yes	Yes No	Yes No/ Yes *	Yes Yes	Yes Yes/ No **
No, No	1 / 2	1 / 2	1 / 2	1 / 2	1 / 2	1 / 2
No, Yes	1 / 2	0 / 1	1 / 2	0 / 1	0 / 1	1 / 2
Yes, No	1 / 2	1 / 2	3 / 0	3 / 0	3 / 0	3 / 0
*Yes, No/Yes	1 / 2	0 / 1	3 / 0	3 / 0	3 / 0	3 / 0
Yes, Yes	1 / 2	0 / 1	3 / 0	3 / 0	2 / 3	2 / 3
**Yes, Yes/No	1 / 2	1 / 2	3 / 0	3 / 0	2 / 3	2 / 3

My Strategies

**Vote *yes,* followed by *yes* if it carries, *no* if it fails.
**Vote *yes,* followed by *yes* if it carries, *no* if it fails.

Outcomes:

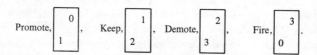

Promote, | 0 / 1 |, Keep, | 1 / 2 |, Demote, | 2 / 3 |, Fire, | 3 / 0 |.

FIGURE 12.6

We know, without any more theory, that the outcome is bound to be asymmetrical; no outcome has the same rank in our two preference scales. We might guess, and with a little more theory we would know, that this large matrix shows an equilibrium pair of strategies corresponding to a yes on the first ballot for both of us and Row 6, Column 5, of the matrix in Figure 12.5. That is, the solution we arrived at by working backwards from final outcomes corresponds to an equilibrium pair in our larger matrix.

Actually, there is a further characteristic that game theory tells us to expect. There is at least one "dominated" row or column in the matrix—a row or column that is inferior to some other row or column in at least one cell and nowhere superior. If we strike out dominated rows and columns, compressing the matrix, we shall still find dominated rows and columns (because some that were originally not dominated are dominated after the eliminations). We can go on doing this until the residual matrix contains only cells with the *demote* outcome. Game theory is interested in which kinds of problems generate matrices that have various properties, like this one.

A few more things can be observed in this example. One is that a "dominant" strategy is not necessarily a good strategy *to have*. It is necessarily a good strategy *to play*, because no matter what the partner does the dominant strategy proves never to have been inferior to any other choice. But its mere availability can induce the other player to make a choice that condemns one to a poor outcome.

Another point, not illustrated in our matrix, is that in general a matrix need not show an equilibrium pair of strategies; it may show more than one; if it shows more than one they may differ, and they may differ by both pay-offs' being lower in one cell than another or by one pay-off's being lower, the other higher. (Game theory also tells us that if a matrix shows no equilibrium pair of strategies one can be generated by a randomized choice, with suitable odds, among some or all of the strategies in the matrix; this procedure, though, requires that there be a suitable interpretation of the numerical values of the pay-offs.)

Collective Decisions

This voting example illustrates that a "gamelike" situation can be viewed as a *collective-decision* process—a process by which two or more individuals jointly decide on an outcome. The analysis also has ethical implications: we assumed the voters to be concerned with outcomes, not with strategies for their own sake; with consequences, not actions; with ends, not means; with justice, not truth. A voting scheme also illustrates how the organization of authority, leadership, and bargaining arrangements can affect the outcomes—can affect whether an outcome is efficient, can affect in whose favor the outcome discriminates. And evidently if we had been willing to enlarge our committee and have a majority-vote procedure, coalitions would have been important; communication might have been important to coalitions, and so might discipline. And it is evidently important what people know, or think they know, about each others preferences.

The "legal" arrangements are important. If binding promises can be enforced, the alternative voting procedure is unnecessary; you merely promise to vote the man excellent if I will join in finding him guilty. In fact, the first ballot can be thought of as a "bargain" that you have an incentive to keep because I have a credible incentive to vote for promotion if you back out of the bargain.

Probabilistic Uncertainty and Numerical Preferences

The numbers in our matrices had only ordinal significance. To illustrate how the numerical values could assume importance, and how numerical values are assigned in game theory, suppose that any award of excellence or verdict of guilty is subject to a review procedure that we believe to have only a fifty-fifty chance of confirming our unanimous vote. If a man is found innocent and excellent there is a fifty-fifty chance that he will be kept or promoted; if a man is found guilty and excellent there are equal probabilities of .25 that he will be promoted, kept, demoted or fired.

To handle the problem we now need a more complicated set of preferences. It is not enough to know that I prefer demoting to keeping the man, keeping to promoting, and promoting to firing. We now have to know whether I'd rather keep the man or take a fifty-fifty chance between demoting and firing. And we may have to know whether I'd prefer a fifty-fifty chance between demoting and firing or a four-way split over the four outcomes. We can assume a few things, such as that if I prefer demoting the man to keeping him I prefer a fifty-fifty chance between demoting and keeping to the certainty of keeping him, and prefer any odds between demoting and keeping to any odds between promoting and firing.

Two points are worth mentioning. First, not only can these "critical odds" or "critical risks" be subjected to certain consistency postulates in a way that may permit us to go ahead and solve our problem, but it even turns out to be possible and convenient (though not necessary) to derive numerical values for the different outcomes from a limited number of expressed critical-risk preferences. These numbers can be operated on *as though* one were trying to maximize the mathematical expectation, i.e., the expected value in a probabilistic sense. One can alternatively just postulate that a decision maker associates numerical values with all the outcomes and tries to maximize expected value; but the postulate need not be that heroic. It needs only to be that he can answer a few simple questions like those we asked above about the critical odds between a pair of outcomes that would make him just willing to settle for the certainty of a third that lies between the other two. If our man then obeys a few other "consistency" rules to avoid some kind of contradiction, we can often handle the problem. For convenience we can attach numerical values to outcomes, based on these critical odds, even calling these numbers "utilities" or something of the sort, but this is only a convenience for combining and compounding a limited set of expressed preferences in the form of critical odds.

The second point is that the need for numerical values arises only in the presence of uncertainties of this sort (and only when the number of alternative outcomes is at least three), when one has to place his bets in a probabilistic environment. (The uncertainty may be about another's choice or, in case of deliberate randomization or faulty control, about one's own.) If there is no such uncertainty, numerical values prove unnecessary (as they were in our original voting situation). And in the face of uncertainty one *has* to make choices of this kind, so it is not an outlandish assumption that one actually can. "Numerical utilities," though often thought unique to game theory, are by no means peculiar to game theory; they arise in the same fashion in any theory of decision under uncertainty.[4]

These numerical values are arrived at separately for all the participants, and there is no intended interpersonal comparability among value scales. In some calculations it may appear that arithmetic is done on the numerical values of two or more players together, but it invariably turns out in game theory that an expression involving the "utilities" of two participants contains only *ratios of increments,* from which any units of measure would cancel out.

It is of some philosophical interest whether the value scales of two individuals are *assumed* inherently incommensurable, or instead we just mean that we don't yet *know how* to compare them. Game theory typically assumes the first position. Some writers treat this as a limita-

---

4. See, for example, Robert Schlaifer, *Probability and Statistics for Business Decisions,* New York, McGraw-Hill, 1959, esp. Chap. 2. Luce and Raiffa (see footnote 7) give an excellent account of "numerical utilities" in their Chap. 2; and a highly persuasive presentation is in Armen A. Alchian, "The Meaning of Utility Measurement," *American Economic Review,* Vol. 43 (March, 1953), pp. 26–50.

tion of the theory and look forward to some way to compare the scales of value between people. I know of none, though, that has indicated how he would use such knowledge if it were available. Just as absolute-cost comparisons in international trade are unnecessary and usually meaningless—the notion of "comparative advantage" or "comparative cost" being sufficient to solve every problem of interest in international-trade economics—the notion of *comparative* ratios of *utility increments* (in which any absolute scales would cancel out) is sufficient in game theory. In fact, so far as game theory is concerned, there really are no "utility scales" to compare. There are merely preference rankings among outcomes that have to incorporate numerical probabilities when some of the outcomes themselves are probabilistic. To say that a rational individual "maximizes utility" is a little like saying that nature "conserves" momentum or that water "seeks" its own level. These figures of speech save a lot of circumlocution; but when we forget that they are figures of speech and try to compare actual measures of utility, or to measure the "frustration" of water when a valve opposes it, it is time to abandon the metaphor and get back to operational statements.

An Apotheosis of "Rationality"?

The question is often raised whether game theory restricts its empirical applicability by postulating mental giants with nerves of steel —perfectly rational amoral deciders who have access ex officio to the theoretical results of game theory.

The answer is: not quite. In principle there is no difficulty in imputing misinformation rather than true information, in supposing that calculation is costly or that people make mistakes or suffer from bad memories or display idiosyncrasies in their choices. In our voting scheme, for example, we can easily suppose that when a man votes on excellence he cannot remember whether or not a vote has already been taken on guilt or innocence; and in fact our review-board procedure can easily be interpreted as the likelihood that a vote will be recorded wrong or that one of the voters will shy away from the word "guilty" for unconscious reasons.[5]

But to handle these departures from perfection one has to specify them explicitly. And it greatly complicates the problem to depart from

5. A perfect example is in the work of Bruner et al., referred to in footnote 1 in which the limitations on memory show up in the difference between "in the head" and "on the board" records. They even allow for the "comforting" quality of certain strategies. Their work is impressive evidence that one of the best ways to study "irrational" (or, better, "imperfectly rational") decisions is to look at specific departures from perfection rather than to start from no base line at all.

perfection, whether it be perfect memory or perfect absence of memory, perfect knowledge or perfect absence of knowledge, perfect calculation or perfectly random choice. The man with the perfect memory and the man without a memory are the easiest to handle in abstract analysis. To allow for an imperfect memory requires that we specify precisely how his memory misbehaves (and whether he knows how it misbehaves, whether his partner knows how it misbehaves and whether he knows whether his partner knows how it misbehaves, and so forth). Pretty soon we are tempted to give him either a perfect memory or no memory at all, or perhaps to provide him a simplified and idealized "imperfect" memory such that exactly half the time he forgets everything, knows that he does, and his partner knows it too.

But this is not a limitation of game theory; it is a limitation of any theory that tries to deal with the full multidimensional complexity of imperfect decision-makers. Game theory indeed usually assumes perfect knowledge or perfect absence of knowledge, because these are simple and unambiguous assumptions to make. Anything between the two extremes requires detailed specification, and game theorists can at least be forgiven for solving the simpler problems first and saving the more complicated ones for later.

Game theory usually supposes a few other things, such as that a man's ethics are what have recently been called "situation ethics"; he is concerned with *outcomes*, not intermediate processes. (In our voting example he is not seeking "truth" as to guilt or excellence, but defines justice in terms of what is done with the man.)[6] The decision-maker is assumed not trying to be bold or novel for the sake of boldness or novelty, not trying to surprise us for the sake of surprise itself; he is not concerned with *why* his partner may choose a particular strategy, but what strategy his partner will choose. Nothing but the *outcomes* enter his value system. If a man has good will or malice towards his partner, a conscience or a bent for mischief, it is all assumed to be reflected in his valuation of the final outcomes. It is assumed that all the elements of his value system are displayed—everything that matters

---

6. Lying, murder, abortion, suicide, violence and nonviolence, adultery, and presumably voting, are to be judged by their consequences, not by reference to absolute laws (which, if plural, are bound to conflict occasionally), in "the new morality," which Joseph Fletcher characterizes as "a method of 'situational' or 'contextual' decision-making." Joseph Fletcher, *Situation Ethics* (Philadelphia, Westminster Press, 1966), esp. pp. 11–39, 64–68, 71–75. The question whether "deterrence" is evil if it threatens something awful (massive retaliation, capital punishment) and it works, so that what is threatened need not be done (and indeed is not expected to be done), is a question to which "situation ethics" will give a different answer from the more traditional ethics. In some of these questions the central issue is how the consequences of an action depend on the way it influences someone else's choice; thus not only does game theory typically assume a "situation ethics," but "situation ethics" needs game theory. (Fletcher, p. 188, even supports a game-theoretical attempt "to assign numerical values to the factors at stake in problems of conscience.")

to him is allowed for—in the ranking or valuation of cells in the matrix.

How much a limitation this is depends, as in any theory, on whether an abstract, somewhat perfectionist bench mark can be helpful, and whether we can keep in mind that the result is only an abstract perfectionist bench mark. Newton's laws don't work if atmospheric resistance is present; purely inertial motion is hard to observe in the earth's gravitational field; some voters are shrewd parliamentarians, some are naïve or inept. Game theory runs the same danger as any theory in being too abstract, even in the propensity of theorists to forget, when they try to predict or to prescribe, that all their theory was based on some abstract premises whose relevance needs to be confirmed. Still, game theory does often have the advantage of being naked so that, unlike those of some less explicit theories, its limitations are likely to be noticeable.

Games, Theories, and Social Science

A word needs to be said about the name of this discipline, "game theory." The name has frivolous connotations. It is also easily confused with "gaming," as in war gaming, business gaming, crisis gaming—confused, that is, with simulations of decision or conflict.

The name arises from the observation that many parlor games have the key quality of interdependence among players' decisions. The best move in a chess game, the best way to bid or the best card to lay down in a bridge game, depends on what one's opponents are likely to do, even on what one's partners are likely to do. Furthermore, these games are usually well defined; there is an explicit and efficient set of rules; the information available to the players is specified at every point (even if in a probabilistic sense); and the scoring system is complete. If we had a more general name for the subject now known as "game theory" it would be found that a great many parlor games fit the definition. It was this that led the authors of the first great work in the field to call their book, *Theory of Games and Economic Behavior*, and "game theory" stuck like a nickname.

Two decades of usage have got professionals so used to the name that they occasionally forget that "game" is not only a technical term but a word in the English language. If they say that war is a *game*, elections are a *game*, industrial disputes or divorce negotiations are *games*, they usually have nothing playful in mind but are merely using a term that grew out of the recognition that some games, too, are *games*.

There is another problem of nomenclature: *game theory* already has the word "theory" in its name. We find it useful to draw distinctions between economics and economic theory, statistics and statistical theory, decisions and decision theory; but there is no accepted name for whatever the field is of which "game theory" refers to the theoretical frontier. Most game theory in fact has been substantially mathematical; some people prefer even to define it as the application of mathematics to this subject, and any bibliography of the discipline is almost dominated by accomplished mathematicians. Often the mathematicians have been more interested, for natural professional reasons, in mathematics than in law, social structure, diplomacy, economics, or sociology. Game theorists, and social scientists who deal with the subject of which game theory is the mathematical frontier, are out of touch with each other in a way that, say, economists and economic theorists are not, for a number of reasons including, often, the absence of a sufficient common interest to keep them in touch. The mathematical barrier is not the only one. There is an unusual dichotomy between the subtle, elegant, mathematical accomplishments of game theorists and the interests of social scientists.

Nothing in this essay begins to describe what mathematical game theorists actually do or even to give the flavor of it. For the social scientist, what is rudimentary and conceptual about game theory will be, for a long time, the most valuable. And it will be valuable not as "instant theory" just waiting to be applied but as a framework—one with a great deal of thought now behind it—on which to build his own theory in his own field.

Take the pay-off matrix itself. This is hardly "theory," although a good deal of theory underlies the definition of strategies and the interpretation of pay-offs. Yet by itself, as a way of identifying alternatives and ordering choices, of laying out the structure of a situation to facilitate analysis, comparison and communication, the pay-off matrix may be, for the analysis of interdependent decision, what double-entry bookkeeping was for accounting, national-income accounts for economics, the truth table for logic, or even the equation for mathematics.[7]

7. *Bibliographical note:* The definitive survey of game theory is still R. Duncan Luce and Howard Raiffa, *Games and Decisions* (New York: Wiley, 1957); though ten years old it has not been surpassed and is not likely to be. A good sampling of game theory pertinent to social science is in Martin Shubik (ed.), *Game Theory and Related Approaches to Social Behavior* (New York: Wiley, 1964); the 75-page introduction by Shubik should be read by anyone who found this essay worthwhile. A professional treatment of zero-sum games, with illustrative applications to military tactics, is Melvin Dresher, *Games of Strategy: Theory and Applications* (Englewood Cliffs, N.J.: Prentice-Hall, 1961). For some of this author's work see T. C. Schelling, *The Strategy of Conflict* (Cambridge: Harvard U. P., 1960). *The Journal of Conflict Resolution* and, somewhat less, *Behavioral Science*, are the journals to watch for suggestive uses of the concepts and apparatus of game theory in the social sciences. The original classic is John von Neumann and Oscar Morgenstern, *Theory of Games and Economic Behavior* (Princeton: Princeton U. P., 1944); it is a stunning architectural achievement even if not, now, the best route of access for most social scientists.

13

The Uses of Game Theory

MARTIN SHUBIK

Introduction

THIS PAPER presents simultaneously both an optimistic and a pessimistic view of the uses of game theory in political science in particular and in the behavioral sciences in general.

One of the greatest sources of misunderstanding between mathematically inclined and verbal-analysis oriented political scientists is the role of the formal and mathematical model in political science. Both the extreme opponents and proponents of mathematics have a valid basis for their criticism of the actions of each other. Mathematics and methodology with little understanding of the substantive content of political science can easily become a sterile and unrewarding pastime.

The arrogance and incomprehension displayed by the rabid methodologist and mathematizer are only equaled by the arrogance and incomprehension of the belle-lettrist to whom any formal or mathematical schema is anathema.

Game theory has provided new methodology and mathematics. It is not a cure-all and there are no a priori reasons to suspect that a blind application of it to political science would yield results of significance. It is far more than a generator of oversimplified homely examples based on analogies between international affairs and adolescents playing "chicken" or shoppers trying to meet or find each other in downtown New York. It is also far less than a developed theory of political science. The remainder of this article is devoted to examining its uses and limitations when applied to political science.

The precision and greater resolving power of the game-theoretic model are often bought at the cost of narrowing the field of vision. It is easy to destroy nuances and subtleties when employing mathematical notation. The language of mathematics is poor in adjectives; complex qualifying statements cannot be made with the ease of the essayist. In spite of these drawbacks a good mathematical model is amenable to a depth of analysis that would be extremely difficult if not impossible for the essayist. We need knowledge, insight, and breadth of view. These must be coupled with clear logic and analytical ability. The type of mathematical thinking exemplified by the theory of games provides the analytical support needed to examine many basic questions of political science.

What Is Game Theory?

Although our prime concern is to discuss the utility of game theory, before doing so a digression on what is meant by game theory is given. Those who have used the term have used it sufficiently loosely that a certain amount of confusion exists. This has been excellently illustrated in the article by A. Wohlstetter entitled "Sin and Games in America"[1] which contains a survey of literature purporting to deal with the theory of games, which most serious students of the topic would find hard to recognize as such.

Game theory is a mathematical method for the study of some aspects of conscious decision-making in situations involving the possibilities of conflict and, or cooperation. It deals with processes in which the individual decision-unit has only partial control over the strategic factors affecting its environment. The decision-unit may be an individual, a firm, a government or any formal or informal institution.

In the context of political science the game may involve generals engaged in battle; diplomats involved in bargaining and negotiations; politicians attempting to influence their voters; legislators trying to put together the appropriate coalitions; medieval princes concerned with power or modern mayors fighting their way through the morass of municipal affairs. In economics or political economy the conflict situation may be labor unions striking against the firm; firms in oligopolistic competition; members of a cartel negotiating market shares or legislatures devising "fair" taxation schemes.

The essence of the "game" is that it involves decision-makers with goals and objectives whose fates are intertwined. They have some control, but the control is partial. Each group or individual faces a cross-purposes optimization problem. His plans must be adjusted not only to his own desires and abilities but also to those of others.

1. A. Wohlstetter, "Sin and Games in America" in M. Shubik (ed.), *Game Theory and Related Approaches to Social Behavior* (New York: Wiley, 1964), pp. 209–225.

The term "theory of games" was possibly a quite unfortunate choice. There are too many undesirable connotations. The mathematician may immediately observe in a dispassionate manner the formal strategic analogies between any problem of strategy and poker or bridge or some other formal game. Political scientists and other behavioral scientists are perhaps more sensitive to or less detached from their environment. Thus, they would argue that diplomatic relations or wars are not games. The participants are not players attending for amusement or enjoyment. Certain abstractions can be made, but the analogies with formal games are not sufficient to encompass the basic aspects of political affairs.

We will discuss the caveats further. However at this point we make the several heroic assumptions and simplifications which enable us to present the basic elements of game theory. The elements which describe a bridge game are the players, the rules describing how the game is to be played and with what, together with the definition of winning and losing positions. There are beyond the formal rules of the game several aspects of the situation which are not handled in a game-theoretic treatment, which nevertheless are obviously important. Are the players friends, are they intelligent, do they expect to play frequently, are there special social relationships among them? These extrarational features are far more important in the analysis of political affairs than they are for games or even for economics. Heroism at the bridge table or even on the production line or at the yearly audit, is rarely called for; in political and social life it may be of critical importance.

Let us assume that the *players,* be they individuals or institutions, are rational entities with well-defined objectives. Each player has at his disposal some set of resources. The *rules of the game* describe how the resources may be utilized.

An extremely shorthand way of describing the *play* of a game is by means of *strategies*. Consider chess; given the rules we can examine every one of the set of first moves for White (there are 20), we could then examine all possible replies by Black and so forth until the game is over. If the computation of alternatives and contingencies were costless and infinitely fast, a player in chess could work out a complete strategy before playing. A *strategy* may be viewed as a book of instructions which a player could give to a delegate telling him what to do under all contingencies. It is a general plan of action worked out in complete detail.

In politics and other human affairs individuals rarely if ever, are in a position to plan in the detail indicated by a strategy. When a general uses a strategy he accounts for the major contingencies leaving much of the fine detail to be delegated to his subordinates.

Assuming that there are n players, each player i, has a set of strategies S_i from which to choose, then the outcome of the game will depend upon the strategies chosen by all of the players. Suppose that each player i, selects a specific strategy s_i from the set S_i, then associated with every array of n strategies (one for each player) will be a *pay-off function* $P_i (s_1, s_2, s_3, \ldots ,s_n)$ for each player i.

There are two fundamentally different ways in which a game can be represented. They are known as the *normalized* and the *extensive form*. The normalized form is the most compact and does not display the details of the game. The actions of the players are examined only in terms of their strategies.

In most of the popular writings a particular example of the game in normalized (or strategic) form has been used; that is the 2 by 2 *pay-off matrix* as is illustrated below:

		Strategy for Player 2				
		1	2		1	2
Strategy	1	5,5	−4,10	1	5	−4
for Player 1	2	10,−4	0,0	2	10	0

In the matrix to the left the numbers in the vertical left margin stand for the set of strategies for Player 1. In this example he has only two strategies available and must choose between them. Similarly the numbers in the top horizontal margin represent the strategies available to Player 2. Each of these numbers may stand for a very complicated set of facts. For example the translation of the statement: "Player 1 chooses strategy 1" into plain English might be: "The English decide to bomb the Suez Canal if the Egyptians attack the Israelis after having been warned."

The numbers in the matrices are pay-offs. The first matrix employs a notation somewhat more compact than the second. It has the pay-offs for both players. In each cell, for example in the cell given by (1,1) the first number is the pay-off to the first player and the second number is the pay-off to the second; in this case 5 and 5 respectively. The second matrix displays only the pay-offs to the first player.

If we use $\pi_1 (s_1, s_2)$ and $\pi_2 (s_1, s_2)$ to stand for the pay-offs to Players 1 and 2 respectively when they employ strategies s_1 and s_2, then $\pi_1 (1,1) = 5$ and $\pi_2 (2,1) = -4$. In the first instance $s_1 = 1$ and $s_2 = 1$ and in the second $s_1 = 2$ and $s_2 = 1$.

The game of "chicken" can be illustrated with a 2×2 matrix. In this game two individuals drive towards each other at great speed each with one set of wheels on the center line of the road. If neither veers off course they will crash. Whoever veers is "chicken." The pay-off matrix might look as follows:

	Stay on course	Veer
Stay on course	−10, −10	+5, −5
Veer	−5, +5	−1, −1

The numbers are merely suggestive for this form of "brinkmanship." These numbers suggest that both sides would much prefer joint "dishonor" to joint death as $\pi_1\,(1,1) = \pi_2\,(1,1) = -10$ and $\pi_1\,(2,2) = -1\ \pi_2\,(2,2) = -1$. This might not be the case. Furthermore it is highly unlikely that we can attach too much meaning to the numbers −10 and −1; at least not to the extent that we would wish to believe that joint dishonor is exactly ten times preferable to death.

Another example, this time using a 4×2 matrix, will both provide an introduction to the concept of threat and serve to illustrate the relationship between the normalized and extensive forms.

Let us suppose that one country wishes to stand by one of its allies who is in danger from a third party. Suppose that Spain were threatening to invade Andorra and that General de Gaulle (acting as a surrogate for le Comte de Foix) decides to guarantee the independence of Andorra. Let us limit him to two strategies. He may give a "strong" guarantee or a pro forma guarantee of support for Andorra. The difference between the two might be that the first (to within the limits of human fallibility) is understood by all to be an absolute commitment whereas the second might be interpreted as sufficiently lukewarm that the betting odds are, say 2 : 1 that if an attack took place France would not send aid to Andorra.

We may assume that the French are given the opportunity to make their announcement before the Spaniards have taken action. Even before the French announcement, the Spaniards may have completed their plans. If they are thorough, the Spanish might wish to examine the contingencies arising from any one of four plans they could adopt. These plans are as follows:

1. If the French make a strong guarantee we will not attack;
   If the French make a pro forma guarantee we will not attack.
2. If the French make a strong guarantee we will not attack;
   If the French make a pro forma guarantee we will attack.
3. If the French make a strong guarantee we will attack;
   If the French make a pro forma guarantee we will not attack.
4. If the French make a strong guarantee we will attack;
   If the French make a pro forma guarantee we will attack.

We call the strong guarantee strategy 1 for the French and the pro forma guarantee, strategy 2. The pay-off matrix is:

	1	2	3	4
1	2, 0	2, 0	—3, —5	—3, —5
2	3, 0	—7/3,1	3, 0	—7/3,1

The values are suggested by the following considerations. The French regard the keeping of the status quo as having a positive worth. Maintaining it by a strong guarantee is somewhat more costly than by a pro forma guarantee (it requires more display of troops, attention and general diplomatic activity) hence we assign values of 2 and 3 to maintenance of the status quo under these two conditions. The Spaniards (in their value system, which may not be comparable with the value system of the French) regard the status quo as their "break-even point" worth 0. If war breaks out, although both will suffer losses, let us suppose that it is more costly to the Spaniards than to the French; we give them values of —5 and —3 respectively.

Suppose that if the Spaniards were able to occupy Andorra without French interference this would be worth +4 to them and that the French evaluate this possibility at —2. *If* we are willing to consider expected values as an appropriate way to evaluate events involving probabilities then the values in the cells (2,2) and (2,4) of the pay-off matrix are obtained in the following manner:

Both are outcomes of situations in which the French give a pro forma guarantee and the Spaniards attack. When they attack they expect that two-thirds of the time the French will not interfere and one third of the time they will. Thus the expected value of this course of action to the Spaniards is $2/3 \ (—5) + 1/3 \ (4) = 1$, and to the French is $2/3 \ (—2) + 1/3 \ (—3) = —7/3$.

An examination of the matrix suggests that the optimal strategies for each are respectively 1 for the French and 2 for the Spaniards. We return to the discussion of optimal behavior later.

We may utilize the example just given to illustrate the extensive form of representing a game. In order to do so we employ a diagram known as a *game tree*. It is called a tree because it has branches, and to those to whom orientation does not matter, it looks like a tree.

The vertices in the game tree represent choice points and the branches indicate alternatives. All vertices bear the label of the player to whom they belong. Hence vertex *0* (where the game starts) also is labeled P_1 indicating that the French are being called upon to make the first move which is a choice between two alternatives. After the French have made their move, the Spaniards have the choice between two alternatives: to attack or not to attack.

It is important to note that they have only two alternatives at their

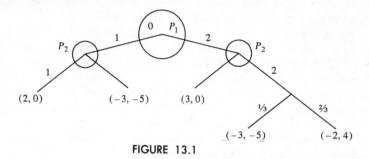

FIGURE 13.1

move but they have four strategies. The reason for this is that a strategy is a global plan for accounting for all contingencies. A move is a local decision which is made given whatever knowledge is available at that time. The availability of information during the play of a game is illustrated by means of curves enclosing *information sets*. In the game tree drawn above we note that the vertices labeled P_1 and P_2 are each surrounded by curves. In this game this means that throughout the course of the game each player knows exactly "where he is." In particular it means that before the Spaniards invade or fail to invade they will have found out whether the French had made a strong or a pro forma guarantee.

When moves are made in secrecy or simultaneously then more than one choice point may belong to the same information set. Suppose that the Spaniards had not been informed of the French decision before they had to make their move. The first part of the game tree would look as indicated below:

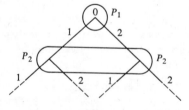

FIGURE 13.2

That both the vertices labeled P_2 are enclosed in the same curve indicates that Player 2, the Spaniards, when called upon to move do not know where they are, in the sense that they cannot distinguish whether the French have selected alternative 1 or 2.

Examining the fully drawn game tree for the original game we note that if the French had selected their first alternative then after the

Spaniards make their move the game terminates. Depending upon the move the game terminates with pay-offs of $(2,0)$ or $(-3,-5)$. If however the French chose their second alternative and the Spaniards likewise, then the game continues. We note that it continues at a vertex which is not labeled and that the branches instead of being labeled with integers indicating alternatives have numbers which sum to 1. These numbers represent the probability of occurrence of the various alternatives which are assumed to be under the control, or in the hands of "nature" rather than any specified player. Referring back to the pay-off matrix for the normalized form of this game we observe that the outcomes from the Spanish attack after the French pro forma guarantee are weighted averages.

In this example we have described a situation as a game in two different ways. We have discussed neither how individuals *should* nor *do* behave. This is a different aspect of game theory which we discuss below. Prior to examining *solution* concepts it should be stressed that the normalized and extensive forms for describing any situation involving interacting decision-makers provide a useful language for describing and analyzing key elements in cooperative or competitive behavior. The very attempt to give precision to concepts such as strategy, pay-off, choice, information and so forth can be counted as successful and worthwhile if all it did were to help to discover difficulties and ambiguities in previous usage and to help to separate out new variables. For many problems to which game theory can be applied, in fact it does far more.

Types of Game Theory

Before one can be in a position to judge the worth of a game theoretic approach it is necessary to realize that there are several types of game theory each with a considerable amount of literature of its own. The first major division of importance is into:

> 1. Two-person zero-sum games,[2]
and 2. Two-person nonconstant-sum games,
> 3. n-person nonconstant-sum games for $n > 2$.

The second division is into:

> 1. Games of finite length,
> 2. Games of an indeterminate duration.

2. Speaking more strictly, we should say constant-sum games, but it can be shown that they are strategically equivalent to zero-sum games. Those who wish to pursue this technical point are referred to R. D. Luce and H. Raiffa, *Games and Decisions* (New York: Wiley, 1957).

The third division concerns solutions rather than structure and is dealt with in detail in a later section of this chapter. The major branches are:

1. Cooperative solutions,

and

2. Noncooperative solutions.

Two-Person Zero-Sum Games

The most elemental and completely studied game from the viewpoint of mathematics is the two-person zero-sum game. It has the property that whatever one individual wins the other *must* lose. Many formal games such as chess or two-person poker have precisely this property.

A two-person zero-sum game is a game of pure opposition. It is strictly competitive. There is no need for communication, discussion or bargaining. There is no joint gain or savings to be had from reasoning or cooperation. It is completely meaningful to call the participants in such a struggle opponents.

Military applications to tactical situations involving "duels"[3] such as air combat; local battles or guerrilla activity are obvious. Wars considered as a whole are never strictly competitive (or constant sum); it is easy for both sides to lose. Negotiations and communication beyond the battlefields are often important. Individual battles however can be fairly realistically modeled as strictly competitive games. Both duelists in a fight to the death might be persuaded, in a larger context, that they should shake hands and refrain from dueling. However once they have decided to fight it out we may consider the action on the dueling ground as one involving pure opposition.

A simple (and obviously highly oversimplified) example is provided by a 2×2 matrix where we consider that a group of guerrillas are going to strike at one of two locations. The defenders have only enough manpower to offer full protection to one. If they meet the guerrillas they will destroy them. If they fail to do so, a town will be destroyed. The pay-off matrix may look like the following:

		Guerrillas	
		1	2
Defenders	1	+4, −4	−3, +3
	2	−3, +3	+4, −4

3. See M. Dresher, *Games of Strategy: Theory and Application* (Englewood Cliffs, N.J.: Prentice-Hall, 1961).

We note that $\pi_1(s_1, s_2) + \pi_2(s_1, s_2) = 0$. Hence as soon as the pay-offs have been specified for one player, the pay-offs for the other are known.

Apart from appreciating the two-person zero-sum game as the definition of a strictly competitive situation, the general political scientist will not gain too much insight from an intense study of this topic. There is a large literature, a well-developed body of mathematical theory and of applications.[4] There is also a considerable amount of misinterpretation concerning the role in general game theory of the famous result concerning two-person zero-sum games known as the *minimax* or *saddle-point theorem*[5] Zero-sum games are of extremely limited interest in the behavioral sciences in general. Those who desire to follow an exposition of the mathematics of two-person zero-sum games are referred to that of Luce and Raiffa.[6]

Two Person Nonconstant-Sum Games

The earlier examples were of two-person nonconstant-sum games. In the fanciful example involving strained relations between France and Spain over Andorra both sides could lose as a result of mutually undesirable actions. The optimal joint pay-off occurs when the Spaniards do not invade and the French do not have to spend much time and attention to guarantee assistance to Andorra. It is conceivable that both sides could gain by "a settlement out of court"; i.e., some type of quid pro quo arrangement in which other concessions or side-payments are made between the two antagonists so that they can both benefit from following a cooperative solution to their differences.

If we could add together the pay-offs in each cell (in general we may not be able to do so unless we can justify value comparisons) a measure of the amounts at stake to both is given by the war pay-offs of $\pi_1(1,3) + \pi_2(1,3) = -8$ and the best peace pay-offs of $\pi_1(2,1) + \pi_2(2,1) = +3$.

N-Person Nonconstant-Sum Games (for $n > 2$)

The games we have discussed above all have two players. For strictly competitive games it is meaningless to talk of coalitions; for two person nonconstant-sum games either no coalitions are formed or there is a coalition of the whole. As soon as we wish to consider three

---

4. Dresher, *op. cit.*
5. Dresher, *Ibid.*
6. R. D. Luce and H. Raiffa, *op. cit.*

or more players the coalition possibilities (even for zero-sum games) become large and complex.

As most human affairs of interest cannot be described adequately as zero-sum games[*] we confine our remarks to nonconstant sum games.

It can be shown easily that for n players there will be $2^n - 1$ coalitions to be considered. Table 13.1 presents a few values:

TABLE 13.1

n	number of coalitions
2	3
3	7
4	15
5	31
.	.
.	.
.	.
10	1,023
20	more than 10^6

Included in the coalitions are the coalitions consisting of the individual, thus the two-person game has three coalitions, consisting of players 1 or 2 and players 1 and 2. Coalition structure and formation play an important role both in international affairs and in party and cabinet politics. In most instances it is not necessary to consider more than 10 to 20 separate entities as individual players (usually far fewer will do). Furthermore, it may not be necessary to consider all coalition structures, as other information may be sufficient to rule them out. This means that the investigation of the coalition possibilities in detail is a large but not unmanageable task.

Many game theoretic solutions utilize the *characteristic function* description of a game; this specifies the amount that every coalition can obtain for itself if it does not cooperate with the others. Returning to the example of France and Spain the characteristic function has three values:

$$v\,(\overline{1})\ = -7/3$$
$$v\,(\overline{2})\ =\ \ \ 0$$
$$v\,(\overline{1,2}) =\ \ \ 3$$

The notation $\overline{1}$ means "the set of players consisting of Player 1." We need to distinguish between the name of the player (here Player 1 and France are equivalent names) and the name of the set or coalition consisting of the players.

The values $v\,(\overline{1}) = -7/3$ and $v\,(\overline{2}) = 0$ were obtained by con-

[*] Except by the fiction of introducing an extra player "Nature" who wins or loses all that the actual players lose or win.

sidering the sets of strategies for each player and observing what is the best outcome he can guarantee to himself assuming that the other is out to damage him.

In the mathematical analysis it is often useful to "normalize" the characteristic function, i.e., to transform it so that we assign the value 0 to every coalition consisting of a single player. This helps in studying the amount to be gained from cooperation and does not distort the analysis.

The characteristic function serves as the basis for several solution concepts and applications to political science as is discussed later in the chapter.

Games of Finite or Indefinite Length

The game-theory models described so far have been presented in the context of a situation with known duration. Although chess games vary both in the number of moves taken and the time to play, they do end in a finite amount of time and both sides do know when the game is over. In many political and diplomatic actions this is not the case. The pay-offs are not necessarily at the end of the game but are being made continuously. The length of time during which negotiations may take place and moves be made is theoretically unlimited. The life of a corporation or nation state may be considerably longer than that of an individual. Although history appears to indicate that sooner or later all states and empires die, the process is harder to define than it is for an individual and often an empire may have a high enough expectation of lasting sufficiently long that a model with life of indefinite duration may be best.

A highly simplified example of the process of guarding the frontier against the barbarians is given; first in the extensive form by means of a game tree of indefinite length, then by means of a flow diagram. For simplicity in exposition we assume that the Romans have two policies and that the policy of the barbarians is given. Let the chances for success with policy 1 at time t_1 be $p_{1,t}$; failure $q_{1t} = 1 - p_{1,t}$ and similarly $p_{2,t}$ and $q_{2,t}$ for policy 2. Here we see that the barbarians are represented as "nature." There is a probability of beating them which depends upon the policy adopted. If they are beaten they can be taxed, this is a positional pay-off and the game continues. If they win the empire is destroyed and for purposes of analyses the game ends. The probabilities p_{1t} and p_{2t} undoubtedly depend upon previous events but we do not discuss them at this time.

Another and even more compact way of representing this process is

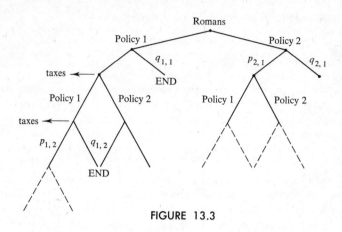

FIGURE 13.3

by means of a flow diagram which is not only highly useful in mapping out processes during the construction of computer programs but is by itself valuable in describing decision-making in political, psychological or sociological contexts. This diagram indicates that after a policy has been chosen we must assess the possibilities of winning or losing. After this the consequences of each outcome are analyzed. If there is a defeat there is no more to be analyzed. Given a victory, taxes may be collected after which as is indicated by the symbol $1 \leftarrow$ the situation (although advanced in time) returns to where a new policy must be picked and the frontiers defended once more.

A certain amount of work has been done on games of indefinite

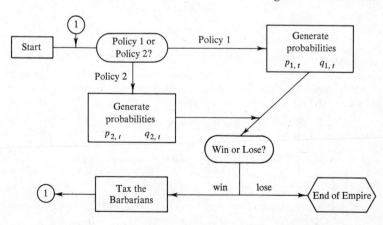

FIGURE 13.4

length under the title of games of social and economic survival, for
further discussion the reader is referred elsewhere.[7]

Solutions

In all of the preceding discussion the emphasis has been upon the
description of the situation and not upon its resolution. We have defined moves, strategies, pay-offs and information conditions; the amounts
that groups of players acting together can obtain, have been specified.
We have indicated neither what they *do* obtain nor what they *should*
obtain.

The various concepts of solution to a game are addressed normatively or behavioristically to what players should or do obtain. Both
viewpoints can be and have been adopted. It may be argued that a
positive political science may be more concerned with how people
should conduct their political life and control their government than
how they actually behave. The merits of the different approaches are
not discussed here; both have been suggested when applying game
theory to political science.

There are four broad groups of solution concepts:

1. Noncooperative equilibrium.
2. Cooperative: Stable set theories.
3. Cooperative: Value theories.
4. Quasi-cooperative dynamic bargaining process solutions.

Solutions of type (1) and (4) are usually justified from a behavioristic
viewpoint; solutions of type (2) both behavioristically and normatively
and (3) mainly normatively.

Noncooperative Equilibrium

A noncooperative equilibrium point in a two-person game consists
of a pair of strategies, one for each player which are stable with respect
to each other in the sense that if either player knows the strategy
chosen by the other, he will not be motivated to change his own strategy.

We may state this formally as: An equilibrium pair of strategies
(s_1, s_2) has the property that

$$\max_{s_1} P_1(s_1, s_2^*) \quad \text{implies} \quad s_1 = s_1^*$$

and

$$\max_{s_2} P_2(s_1^*, s_2) \quad \text{implies} \quad s_2 = s_2^*.$$

7. M. Shubik, "Game Theory and the Study of Social Behavior: An Introductory
Exposition" in M. Shubik (ed.), *op. cit.*, pp. 61–70.

Referring to the pay-off matrix for the game of chicken there is no simple noncooperative equilibrium solution. If one knows that the other is staying on course he should veer, and vice versa. But this holds for each of them simultaneously and there is no simple way for them to resolve their dilemma. This is not the case in the example of the French Spanish confrontation. Looking at the 2×4 matrix once more we can explain the choice of the strategy pair $(1, 2)$ in terms of noncooperative theory. Given that the Spaniards know that the guarantee by the French is strong and given that the French know that the Spaniards know it and know the relative costs of war and peace to both they can calculate that strategy 2 is the *individually rational* choice for the Spaniards. In a like manner we could reason from the Spanish side and show that strategy 2 chosen by the Spaniards would be countered by strategy 1 chosen by the French.

It is important to realize that individual rationality does not imply *joint rationality* in many human affairs. By cooperating usually both sides can agree on an outcome which is or can be made more favorable to both sides than that obtained from the noncooperative equilibrium. The important difference is that a cooperative solution very often calls for a level of trust far higher than that required or expected in the equilibrium.

The individual advocating the cooperative theory may often justify it by saying that people *should* jointly optimize; the supporter of the noncooperative theory will say that although joint optimization might be a desirable *norm*, in this vale of tears it is not necessarily reached by more or less individually rational but fallible and not terribly cooperative people.

In a two-person zero-sum game the paradoxical difference between individual and joint rationality does not exist. This is because there is no room for cooperation. By definition the amount won by one must equal the amount lost by the other. It is easy to see that in this instance the noncooperative equilibrium will be the equivalent of the minimax strategy. We know (s_1, s_2) is an equilibrium point if:

$$\max_{s_1} P_1 (s_1, s_2^*) \quad \text{implies} \quad s_1 = s_1^* \tag{1}$$

and

$$\max_{s_2} P_2 (s_1^*, s_2) \quad \text{implies} \quad s_2 = s_2^*. \tag{2}$$

We know that

$$P_2 (s_1, s_2) = -P_1 (s_1, s_2). \tag{3}$$

Hence

$$\max_{s_2} P_2 (s_1^*, s_2) = \min_{s_2} P_1 (s_1^*, s_2).$$

Conditions (1) and (3) taken together give us a description of an equilibrium point in a zero-sum game such that (s_1^*, s_2^*) must satisfy

$$\max_{s_1} \min_{s_2} P_1 (s_1, s_2)$$

Our examples for noncooperative solutions were limited to two players because in political affairs although when there are only two players a noncooperative or quasi-noncooperative approach may occasionally seem reasonable when there are more than two it rarely appears to be reasonable (this is not the case in game theory applications to economics).[8]

Cooperative Solutions: Stable Sets and Related Theories

If we start with the assumption that people tend to be or should be jointly as well as individually rational we must describe how individuals work out the means for dividing the joint proceeds. Von Neumann and Morgenstern originally defined a cooperative solution in terms of a concept of social stability.[9] Use is made of the characteristic function to determine the bargaining power of all groups. There is now an extensive literature dealing with different but allied solutions. Among the better known are the stable sets of Shapley;[10] the core[11] and the bargaining set of Aumann and Maschler.[12]

The easiest solution to describe is the core. We describe it and the stable set by giving a three-person example. The characteristic function is given as:

$$v(\theta) = 0 \,\dagger$$
$$v(\overline{1}) = 0 \qquad v(\overline{2}) = 0 \qquad v(\overline{3}) = 0$$
$$v(\overline{1,2}) = .6 \qquad v(\overline{1,3}) = .2 \qquad v(\overline{2,3}) = .2$$
$$v(\overline{1,2,3}) = 1.0$$

Together all players can obtain 1.0. We define an imputation as a division of the total proceeds which can be gained by cooperation among the players where each obtains at least as much as he could get by himself, i.e., it is at least individually rational for any player to consider any imputation. An example of an imputation in this game

8. See M. Shubik, *Strategy and Market Structure* (New York: Wiley, 1959).

9. J. von Neumann and O. Morgenstern, *Theory of Games and Economic Behavior*, 3rd ed. (Princeton: Princeton U. P., 1944).

10. L. S. Shapley, "Notes on the N Person Game III: Some Variants of the von Neumann-Morgenstern Definition of Solution," Rand RM 817 (April 1952).

11. L. S. Shapley and M. Shubik, "Concepts and Theories of Pure Cognition" Rand RM 3553 (May 1963).

12. R. J. Aumann, and M. Maschler, "The Bargaining Set for Cooperative Games" in No. 52, Annals of Mathematics Studies (Princeton: Princeton U. P., 1963).

† For formal completeness it is sometimes desirable to include a value for the coalition consisting of no one. This is denoted by $v(\theta) = 0$.

would be the triplet of numbers $\alpha = (0.8, 0.1, 0.1)$. We observe that the three numbers sum to 1 which is the amount that all acting together can obtain.

A set of players S is effective for an imputation β if the members of S can by independent action obtain at least as much for themselves as they are being offered in β. Suppose $\beta = (.3, .2, .5)$; then the set $(1,2)$ is effective against β as they can together obtain .6 without any cooperation from 3.

An imputation β dominates an imputation α if there exists a set of players S which is effective for β and every member of S obtains more in β than he does in α. For example consider $\alpha = (.2, .1, .7)$. If α is ever suggested as an outcome, as a manner for dividing the proceeds of cooperation, the coalition $(\overline{1,2})$ can reject it in favor of β because they are effective for and both obtain more from β than from α.

The von Neumann and Morgenstern stable-set solution consists of a set of imputations which has a special form of internal stability. A set V of imputations is a solution if no imputation α in set V dominates any other imputation α in set V and if for any imputation β not in V there exists an imputation α in V which dominates β.

The stable-set solution has little predictive value in many instances as many imputations may belong to the same stable set. Furthermore the same game may have many different stable-set solutions. Certain solutions nevertheless reflect the richness of sociopolitical possibilities which are consistent with basic forms of stability. These include, for example, nonsymmetric solutions to games which are symmetric. Phenomena such as the systematic exclusion of or discrimination against a specific set of players can be recognized, and these are consistent with social stability.

A stronger criterion for stability is suggested by the *core* to a game. This consists of the set of imputations which is undominated by any other imputations. An imputation in the core has the property that no coalition can argue effectively against it. No group can guarantee themselves more. Two simple three-person examples will serve to illustrate a game with a core and a game without a core.

Consider two games each with three players; in each game a coalition of a single player obtains nothing and a coalition of all three players obtains 1. In the first game a coalition of any two players obtains .5 and in the second game a coalition of any two players obtains .8.

In the first game any imputation $(\alpha_1, \alpha_2, \alpha_3)$ such that:

$$\alpha_1 + \alpha_2 \geqslant .5$$
$$\alpha_1 + \alpha_3 \geqslant .5$$
$$\alpha_2 + \alpha_3 \geqslant .5$$

is in the core. No subset of players can effectively argue against a distribution such as (.3, .3, .4) which satisfies all three conditions.

In the second game the three conditions which must be satisfied simultaneously are:

$$\alpha_1 + \alpha_2 \geqslant .8$$
$$\alpha_1 + \alpha_3 \geqslant .8$$
$$\alpha_2 + \alpha_3 \geqslant .8,$$

but there is no possible way of dividing the unit available so that some two-person coalition does not get less than the amount .8 which it could get by "going into business for itself."

Games without a core appear to be at the basis of sociopolitical processes. At any time there will always exist some (possibly all) groups who will be able to argue that (at least in the immediate short run) they can obtain more than the amount they are offered by society by failing to cooperate. It is not only feasible but likely that the demands of all groups based upon the threats they perceive that they can carry out will be mutually inconsistent. Social codes and political compromise may be directed towards establishing the conditions for groups to cooperate even though they are apparently obtaining less than individual noncooperation would net.

When a game does have a core, the intuitive appeal that the outcome should be in the core, is great. The existence of the core depends heavily upon the power of coalitions. The power of coalitions can best be understood in terms of their threats. We return to discuss threats later in the chapter.

Cooperative Solutions: Value Theories

Neither the stable set nor the core solutions to a game suggest or predict a single outcome except in relatively trivial instances. The various value theories in general do. Nash,[13] Shapley,[14] and Harsanyi[15] have presented the best known work on value and they are all closely related to each other. The major differences among them involve the treatment of threats and questions concerning the comparison of the intensity of preference among different individuals.

13. J. F. Nash, "Two Person Cooperative Games" *Econometrica*, Vol. 21 (1953), pp. 128–140.

14. L. S. Shapley, "A Value for N-Person Games" in H. W. Kuhn and A. W. Tucker (eds.), *Contributions to the Theory of Games*, Vol. II (Princeton: Princeton U. P., 1953).

15. S. C. Harsanyi, "Measurement of Social Power, Opportunity Costs, and the Theory of Two-Person Bargaining Games," *Behavioral Science*, Vol. 7, No. 1 (January 1962), pp. 67–80.

Mainly because it is the easiest to illustrate and because of an application of the value formula of Shapley to voting schemes in order to obtain an a priori index of the power of individuals under different rules of voting[16] only this value formula is discussed and demonstrated.

Intuitively behind such a phrase as "one man, one vote" is an appeal to an innate belief in the symmetry, justice and equality of the democratic voting procedure. Before the mathematically inclined political scientist becomes too enamored with his axioms and general rules it is well to heed the warning of Robert Dahl:

> Moreover propositions stated in universal terms are rarely assumed by men of common sense to imply universality in practice; to the frequent dismay of logicians, a common tendency of mankind—and not least of Americans—is to qualify universals in application while leaving them intact in rhetoric.[17]

Given this observation, is it still reasonable to attempt to seek general rules and measures? Not only does this problem exist in political science but it is fundamental in the consideration of the law. The fine general rules for justice and equality must be tempered by the introduction of *equity*[18] to provide guidance for settling the myriads of special cases which do not fall neatly into the general categories handled by the rules.

The value solutions are based upon very general axioms. They supply trivially simple yet intuitively reasonable solutions to situations which are simple. Thus, for example, if two identical individuals were called to divide an easily divisible item to which they had equal claim, the value solutions would reward each one half. The axioms, however, provide a rule not only for the simple cases but for the complex as well. Without going into a detailed discussion of the development of the value from the basic assumptions, an insight can be provided by considering an example applied to measuring voting "power."

Intuitively the value assigns to an individual as his reward for cooperation an amount which is the average of his incremental worth to every coalition that could form in the society. It is an extension of the economists' rule of rewarding each individual by his marginal productivity. Consider a club with four members and five votes distributed 2, 1, 1, 1. How much "power" does the man with two votes have? Or, what value should we assign to him in recognition of his special role as an individual who is more vital and necessary for the success of any vote than is any other member? If he had three of the five votes he would have complete control; if on the other hand there were five

16. L. S. Shapley and M. Shubik, "A Method for Evaluating the Distribution of Power in a Committee System" *American Political Science Review* 48 (1954), pp. 787–792.

17. R. A. Dahl, *Who Governs? Democracy and Power in an American City* (New Haven: Yale U. P., 1961), pp. 318–319.

18. C. K. Allen, *Law in the Making* (New York: Oxford U. P., 1958), Chap. V.

members each with 1 vote, it would be reasonable to say that they all are equally important.

Suppose that the club operates by a simple majority of the votes. We can consider a very simple characteristic function which assigns a worth of 1 to every winning coalition and a worth of 0 to every losing coalition. In a situation involving a simple majority and an odd number of votes it is easy to observe that any coalition that does not win, loses; there are no ties or stalemates.

Let us consider all the ways in which a winning coalition could be formed and examine the voting to see which individual is "pivotal," i.e., turns a coalition without enough votes to win into a winner. There are 24 different ways (4!) in which a winning coalition can be formed. These are illustrated below:

$$
\begin{array}{ccc}
\underset{\ }{\dot{1}} & 6 \\
\dot{2}, & \dot{1}, 1, 1 \\
3 & 1 & 2 \\
1, & \dot{2}, 1, 1 \\
6 & 1 & 1 \\
1, & 1, \dot{2}, 1 \\
6 & 1 \\
1, & 1, \dot{1}, 2 \\
\end{array}
$$

In the first instance we may consider that the two-vote man votes first. He may be followed in any one of six ways by the three individuals who have one vote each. If their names were A, B, and C, their voting order could be ABC, ACB, BAC, BCA, CAB and CBA. In the second instance any one of the single-vote men votes first, followed by the man with two votes, followed by the others.

We note that there is a dot placed above the vote that is pivotal, i.e., changes a coalition to winning. It occurs as soon as there are three or more votes. In the first block of six a single-vote individual is pivotal in the second and third, the two-vote man and in the fourth a single-vote man. The two-vote man is pivotal in 12 out of 24 cases hence we assign him a value of $12/24 = \frac{1}{2}$. The single-vote individuals are each pivotal in 4 out of 24 cases hence are assigned a value of $1/6$ each.

Every game has a value, regardless of whether it has a core. This means that even when no core exists and hence the claims of all coalitions will be mutually inconsistent the value may serve as a potential arbitration scheme for dividing the overall product of cooperation in the light of the potential threat of noncooperative behavior by every group.

Games for which the characteristic function consists only of the values 0 or 1 are known as *simple games*.[19] Many voting processes can be modeled in this manner. A coalition which controls enough or more than enough votes to win is known as a *winning coalition*. A winning coalition consisting of a group of individuals such that a single defection by any member would turn it into a losing coalition is known as a *minimal winning coalition*. Riker has suggested[20] that in the political process of gaining power, groups try to form minimal winning coalitions because although they want to be large enough to win, the smaller they are the less they have to divide the gains in the form of rewards and side-payments to the faithful.

The investigations of Leiserson[21] do not show much evidence that the value is a good predictor of how rewards are divided. Nevertheless the value and allied fair division schemes provide considerable aid in the analysis of some aspects of the structure of political power and rewards.

Quasi-Cooperative Dynamic Bargaining Process Solutions

The noncooperative and cooperative game solutions described above are not sufficient for the study of several of the more important problems of political science. They are not adequate for guiding us through the maze of instinct, quasi-cooperation, bluff, trust, misperception, poor information, and unclearly perceived values which go to make up the anatomy of a bargaining or negotiation process. Learning models such as those noted by Rapoport,[22] behavioral models as sketched by March and Simon[23] and Ikle[24] appear to be as relevant if not more relevant than strict game theory. The eventually successful models will undoubtedly be a blend of these many different but complementary approaches. Those parts of the system in which conscious strategic decision-making is called for under conditions of known relatively fixed preferences and information about the outcome resulting from the selection of the various alternatives are amenable to game-theoretic analysis. Beyond that we

19. L. S. Shapley, "Simple Games: An Outline of the Descriptive Theory" *Behavioral Science*, Vol. 7, No. 1 (January 1962), pp. 59–66.

20. W. H. Riker, *The Theory of Political Coalitions*, (New Haven: Yale U. P., 1962).

21. M. A. Leiserson, "Coalitions in Politics: A Theoretical and Empirical Study" (New Haven: Yale University, unpublished Ph. D. thesis, 1966).

22. A. Rapaport and A. M. Ghammah, *Prisoner's Dilemma* (Ann Arbor: U. of Michigan Press, 1965).

23. J. G. March and H. A. Simon, *Organizations* (New York: Wiley, 1958).

24. F. Ikle, *How Nations Negotiate* (New York: Harper, 1964).

must ask several fundamental questions before we risk lavishing a sophisticated but only tangentially relevant methodology on the wrong problem.

1. Are the goals of the decision-units well defined?
2. Do they remain constant over time or do they change in accordance with some known law such as reinforcement or change in aspiration levels?
3. Are the players completely informed about "the rules of the game" or are there important gaps in their information which can only be filled by searching procedures?
4. Are there any major problems in the misperception of values of outcomes or in the misperception of moves? If so, what error correction and adjustment mechanisms or institutions exist?
5. Is there any difficulty in the "coding" and interpretation of moves, i.e., can one "say what one means, and mean what one says"? Formal game theory can help somewhat in the study of this but much of it belongs to the general problem of coding discussed below.

If, as is often the case, goals are not well defined but are evolving and being resolved; if players are not completely informed and if problems of misperception and coding are important then methods other than that of game theory are probably of more value.

Some of the fair division procedures noted earlier have dynamic processes behind them as a rationale. Notable are those of Harsanyi[25] and Zeuthen,[26] but they depend upon the existence of known fixed goals and complete information without misperception by the players.

There remains the observation that the so-called "noncooperative" solution described above does not necessarily remain noncooperative when applied to situations of indeterminate length such as those which best characterize negotiations and international affairs. The resultant equilibria can be best described as "quasi-cooperative" as is shown later in the discussion of variants of the well-known Prisoners' Dilemma Game.

Coding, Threats, and Signaling

Coding and Threats

In keeping with the usual practices in the development of a new body of knowledge, difficulties have been divided and simplifications made in the work on game theory. A natural but very critical simplification was made in the treatment of language. The possibility that words

---

25. J. Harsanyi, *op. cit.*
26. F. Zeuthen, *Problems of Monopoly and Economic Warfare* (London: Routledge, 1930).

or statements might be used as moves in a game is expressly avoided in all formal game theory analysis. Moves are best conceived of as physical acts such as moving a knight in chess; playing a card in poker; bombing an enemy airfield or producing a good for the market. In the original work of von Neumann and Morgenstern[27] it is specifically stated that the bargaining, haggling, and discussion among the players—the dynamics of coming to an agreement—are excluded from the analysis. For many aspects of economic life, for war, competitive sports, board games and duels this simplification is sufficient. In two-person strictly competitive games there is no need for bargaining; in many economic situations although discussion and agreements could play a role, for the most part the moves are actions such as production, pricing or advertising.

Unfortunately when we come to the study of international affairs and for that matter other forms of negotiation, words play a critical role as moves. Pieces of paper, treaties, threats, bluffs, statements in the press are very often important as moves. Neither game theory nor for that matter any other theory has successfully been able to solve the *coding problem* of relating words to acts. The limitations of game theory have served to clarify the problem but no solution has yet been supplied.

In the formal body of game theory, a game is described by its rules. Individuals know and *abide* by the rules. Although the rules may provide for certain forms of bluffing as in poker, the players nevertheless abide by them and are not affected by "sweet talk," oratory, unclear statements, and so forth. In poker a player must "put his money where his mouth is" if he wishes to carry out a bluff. If he is called, "the cards speak for themselves." He does not have the opportunity to smile at his opponents, take his money back from the pot, and say that he did not really mean to bet.

It is possible to define a game in which verbal statements are moves. At the level of pure formalism it can be done. However until we know how to attach a degree of belief to statements; how to decide what statements mean in terms of deeds; when promises will be kept; how to judge the trustworthiness of a commitment or the credibility of a threat the formal description of the process as a game is of limited aid.

In game theory as it exists today there is no equivalent to a threat as the word is usually used to describe this type of hostile statement often made during negotiations. A threat in a game theoretic sense is merely part of a strategy. It is an *absolutely enforceable* commitment which states in an unequivocal manner what will happen if certain contingencies come to pass. The player is completely locked in; his Doomsday machine has been set in motion and there is nothing that he can

---

27. J. von Neumann and O. Morgenstern, *op. cit.*, Chap. 1.

do about it. Consider the simple game in which the first player has one strategy which is: "agree to my terms or we fight." The second player can choose to agree or fail to agree. This apparently can be described by a 1×2 matrix as is shown below:

	Yes	No
Agree or I fight	10, −5	−15, −15

In this formulation the threat is assumed to be completely believed and enforceable. But is this reasonable? Suppose the second player said no, there still might be time for the first to try some other approach short of war.

In the process of negotiation not only are words hard to interpret but sometimes acts themselves become symbolic and part of the discourse. Thus for example we may need to consider "token bombings" or reprisals where the act is more a continuation of the conversation than an act in itself. A reprisal may be carried out, not to burn an enemy village per se but merely to show them that we are not fooling. We need a calculus of credibility and neither game theory nor anything else has yet supplied us with it.

The concept of threat is insufficiently understood and yet is basic to the satisfactory application of n-person nonconstant-sum game theory to almost any part of political science. The characteristic function of a game, or for that matter any other representation of the worth of coalitions depends upon deciding what a group can obtain for itself if it refuses to cooperate with the rest. This amount depends upon the damage that they will be likely to do to each other if they fail to cooperate. Often this damage is extremely large *if* one is willing to assume paranoid pathological behavior by the players. But it is not necessarily reasonable to assume that a player is actually going to suffer considerable losses in order to inflict smaller losses on his opponents.

The word "threat" is used in many different disciplines in many different ways. Yet each different use appears to be relevant to the understanding of political process. In psychiatric work we may talk of a patient "feeling threatened"; in law if one individual threatens another with physical violence there may be grounds for an action. In the courting and fighting behavior of animals there are elaborate sets of gestures for threats and in some cases for submission. Mobs threaten to turn ugly, the economy threatens to go into a slump. The Chinese, feeling threatened owing to a deep-seated inferiority complex in international affairs, threaten to invade Taiwan. The wolf threatens the flock and the shepherd's boy "cries wolf"; and in game theory, a threat is merely part of a strategy. It is usually distinguished by the feature that it contains the statement of the noncooperative action to be followed if some suggestion for the division of the proceeds to be obtained from cooperation is not agreed to. This is not necessarily the case. The phrase: "Is that a threat or a promise?" serves to indicate that the operational meaning of this word is by no means clear.

Bluffing and Signaling

Although formal game-theory analysis does not provide us with a means to estimate the credibility of verbal statements it does provide considerable insight into problems of bluffing and signaling. Even if it were always possible to code verbal statements accurately so that they could be treated as moves the possibilities for bluffing and signaling would still remain. Poker and bridge provide examples where the games can both be completely described numerically however in the first bluffing plays an important role and in the second the partners use a formalized bidding system for signaling.

Suppose two nations wish to sign a disarmament treaty but there is no third party to enforce it. They each maintain sovereignty and the inspection process will certainly not be sufficient to guarantee that each will honor its promises. If as a first approximation we can describe this as a formal game, how should it be played and what role if any will bluffing play?

Recent but as yet unpublished work by Harsanyi, Aumann, and Maschler has been able to provide some insights. A simple model serves to illustrate the approach. Consider two players A and B; suppose that A knows B's preferences, but that B is not sure of A's preferences. We can model this by imagining that B thinks that A can be any one of several people. For simplicity we assume that B thinks that A can be either A_1 or A_2. Let us assume that initially B has beliefs as to the identity of A and that these beliefs can be expressed by a probability distribution known both to A and B. For example B's preferences for the outcome of the game are shown in the pay-off matrix below:

	1	2
1	-2	2
2	2	-2

He has a belief of $(1/2, 1/2)$ that A is A_1 or A_2. The pay-off matrices are respectively:

A_1 A_2

	1	2
1	2	−2
2	−2	2

	1	2
1	10	0
2	0	−1

If both players knew that the game were A_1B this would be a fair zero-sum game with an expected value of zero to each. If both knew that the game were A_2B this would be a nonconstant sum game in which it is easy to show that the noncooperative equilibrium pair of strategies is $(1,2)$. By inspection it is easy to see that A_2 prefers his first strategy to his second. Player B will obviously counter with his second strategy. However, B does *not* know if he is facing A_1 or A_2. A knows who he is. Suppose in fact he is A_2. It is in his interest to play in such a manner that B cannot easily deduce this from his behavior (all that B finds out on each play of the game is what A did). If B is not sure who A is he will occasionally use his first strategy and hence A will have a chance to win 10. If this game is repeated many times, gradually B will be in a position to try to improve his estimate of the identity of A by using his information on A's previous moves. A must calculate how to intermix the short-term considerations of optimal play in the one-period game versus the long-term gains through possible concealment of identity. This process is very much at the heart of disarmament procedures. If one side destroys a certain number of ICBM's with witnesses from the other side present the latter still have the problem of divining the true intentions and the former still have the problem of deciding whether they want to and are in a position to reveal their intentions by this act.

Paradigms

If they are used with care and employed mainly to help to sort out and clarify difficulties simple 2×2 examples can be of use. Three simple examples are given below.

The Prisoners' Dilemma

Perhaps the most famous and illustrative nonconstant-sum game example is the so-called Prisoners' Dilemma. It owes its name to the scenario often supplied to justify the selection of the pay-offs. Two prisoners are in the custody of the police. They are cross-examined separately. They both know that if they both remain silent the worst that can happen is that they will be booked for vagrancy, a relatively minor charge. If one turns state's evidence and the other remains silent the former will go free while the latter will get a stiff sentence. If both squeal both will draw a fairly stiff sentence. In its most general form the pay-off can be described as follows:

	1	2
1	a,a	b,c
2	c,b	d,d

where $2a > b + c$, $c > a > d > b$. A specific instance is:

	1	2
1	10, 10	$-5, 15$
2	15, -5	0, 0

Obviously the jointly optimal solution is for each to use his first strategy and each to obtain 10. However the noncooperative equilibrium point has each play his second strategy and obtain 0. A simple application of a principle of individual rationality can be suggested in defense of this paradoxical nonoptimal result. Consider the first player. Suppose he knows that his opponent will use his first strategy. He can obtain 10 of 15 depending upon his choice of his first or second strategy. Suppose that he knows that his opponent will use his second strategy, depending upon his choice he can make -5 or 0 by selecting his first or second strategy. In each case the second strategy appears to be the best, yet if both select it the result is mutual disaster.

There are many situations in which conditions more or less analogous to the Prisoners' Dilemma exist; price-cutting in economic competition being an important example. The main lesson to be learned from this game is that individual rational choice may lead to mutual disaster when the fates of the individuals are intertwined.

Consider a modification of the game just exhibited as is indicated below:

	1	2
1	10, 10	0, 9
2	9, 0	0, 0

In this instance individual rational choice results in a joint maximum. Each player selects his first strategy. This game has a very desirable feature. The joint optimum is also a self-policing point. In other words, it is not only desirable by society as a whole; given its existence, no individual is motivated to move away from this equilibrium. The design of self-policing systems is a central problem in treaty-making, disarmament, and in obtaining social stability in general.

Reverting to the example of the Prisoners' Dilemma, many experiments under varying conditions have been performed with it. In one-shot plays, especially if the stakes are high, it is indeed possible to show that players actually use their second strategies and obtain the resulting low pay-offs. Rapoport and others[28] have investigated the results of repeated plays. It is when we examine these results together with the mathematical analysis and model-building that game-theory and gaming raise new problems and provide insights.

If we use no imagination whatsoever but merely apply mathematical analysis to the iterated game—that is, suppose that the players are to play the same game for a specified number of time k (in several experiments k has been as high as 300)—we obtain a paradoxical result. The noncooperative equilibrium will call for the players to double-cross each other on every play and to use as an over-all strategy the rule "always select your second move in each subgame, that is, each period." This can be seen immediately from a backward induction. Suppose that the players have played $k - 1$ times and are now playing the last time. The analysis of the one period game indicates that it is individually rational to double-cross. Each will expect the other to play 2. Given that they both have deduced that they will play 2 on the kth repetition of the game they will also do so on the $k - $1st. This can be argued because as their behavior for the last period is determined they can regard the strategically important part of the game to involve only $k - 1$ trials with the $k - 1$st being effectively the last. We may keep applying this argument until we reach the first play.

Do players actually play so noncooperatively? It depends; sometimes yes, sometimes no. There are varying degrees of cooperation and non-cooperation observed among actual players. Does this mean that they are foolish or that the theory is not too good and that this is manifested in the foolishness of the mathematical result?

Actually a mathematical difficulty encountered in the analysis of the many period game raises questions which call for the reconsideration of the basic model. Suppose that the game were to be played for an indefinitely long time, what would the theory predict about the players' behavior? The mathematical model is not yet completely defined because if the game can conceivably last for an indefinitely long time with the prizes being the same each period the sum of the pay-offs could

28. A. Rapaport and A. M. Ghammah, *op. cit.*

become arbitrarily large; this is both behavioristically unreasonable and mathematically unmanageable. There are two simple ways to avoid this difficulty. They suffice individually or together. We may suppose that there exists a probability p that the game will continue after any particular trial k. If this is the case, then the greatest conceivable expected pay-off from playing the game is:

$$\pi = 15\,\{1 + p + p^2 + p^3 + \cdots p^t\} = 15\,\left\{\frac{1}{1-p}\right\}.$$

For $p = .99$, $\pi = 1,500$; for $p = .5$, $\pi = 30$. As long as $0 \leq p < 1$ these amounts are limited. We could also consider that the individual has a discount factor that he applies to "pie-in-the-sky." He is more interested in his winnings now than later. Let this discount be ρ, where $0 \leq \rho < 1$. The greatest value attached to the best possible sequence of winnings is:

$$\pi = 15\,\{1 + \rho + \rho^2 + \cdots \rho^t + \cdots\} = 15\,\left\{\frac{1}{1-\rho}\right\}.$$

If both effects were relevant simultaneously then the value of the largest pay-off would be $\pi = 15\,\{1/(1 - p\rho)\}$.

When we consider the game with either a probability of continuing or with a discount factor the paradoxical behavior called for by the analysis of the noncooperative solution to the game played k times no longer applies. As there is never an absolutely certain last period we cannot use the backward-induction argument. This may actually be a better representation of human affairs than the model with a finite length. Although we may all die eventually, no matter how small the chances are, there is always some probability that we will live for a few seconds more.

An examination of the strategy pair in which both players play only 2 for ever shows that this is still an equilibrium point. If one knows that the other intends to play 2, then he will do so as well and vice versa. However this is by no means the only noncooperative solution. Suppose that $p = 0.99$ and that the matrix is that for the Prisoners' Dilemma given previously. Consider the following strategy:

I will start with 1 and will continue to play 1 as long as my information tells me that my opponent has played 1. If at some time t he plays 2, then at time $t + 1$ I will play 2 and continue to do so for the rest of the game.

If the other player is informed of this strategy and believes it he will be able to deduce that he faces only two alternatives; either to play 1 for all time, or to double-cross immediately. If he believes that as soon as his using 2 has been discovered the other player will switch to 2 for good, then he might as well play his double-cross as early as

possible in order to get the greatest benefit from it. His two sets of
actions are:

1. Never double-cross, play 1 only $\pi = 10 \left(\dfrac{1}{1 - .99} \right) = 1,000.$

2. Double-cross immediately and continue with $2\pi = 15 + 0 \left(\dfrac{.99}{1 - .99} \right) \cong 15.$

It is evident that the double-cross does not pay and the joint optimum
has been enforced as a noncooperative solution by means of the threat
in the strategy which calls for retaliation if there is a departure from
playing 1.

At this point that we can review several basic concepts. We have
a noncooperative self-policing system for enforcing the joint optimum.
This type of solution might more properly be called "quasi-cooperative."

A threat was formalized as part of a strategy, warning the com-
petitor of the dire consequences of not conforming to the plans of the
player wishing to *enforce* the joint optimum outcome. In the strict
game-theoretic sense any strategy played by a player is enforced by the
rules and should be viewed as a firm commitment. However in a situation involving individual bargainers or nations there is no tournament
committee such as is to be found in a chess match. There is much
leeway and uncertainty concerning the rules of bargaining. In particular
leaving aside coding and the uncertainties of language, if in the example
above the two players were nation-states and one of them had sent the
other a message containing his strategy as written above, why should
the other believe it? There is no outside agency enforcing contract; this
is a mere declaration concerning the possibility of future acts. In a
formal game because of the adherence to rules the problem of belief
does not arise. Here it does.

The task of developing an adequate theory of threats calls for a
mixture of game theory, learning theory, observation and experimentation, and behavioral science of every variety. No single approach has
offered a satisfactory theory.

I believe that a combined game-theory and learning-theory approach
can still go much further than it has. We can usefully consider a taxonomy of threats such as "weak," "strong" killing and suicidal; where
the carrying out of the threat is more or less costly to the individual
than not carrying it out; or where its execution kills the opponent or
kills the threatener.[29] At least between relatively rational institutions or
individuals we should be able to obtain a ranking on the plausibility of
threats in terms of short and long term expected costs and effects.

In spite of the optimistic observations above, there remains a large
group of problems that would still be unanswered by the work sug-

---

29. M. Shubik, *Strategy and Market Structure*, op. cit., Chaps. X, XI.

gested. What are the effects of instinctual behavior; the actions of large bureaucracies; madmen and morons? On the whole we do not know. Was Hitler mad or "crazy like a fox"? Where does the writing of *Uncle Tom's Cabin* fit into a strategic model? A random sniper can run amok with a carbine and is difficult to control. Will a single madman be able to influence national policy by being able to control, say, a small atomic device or the means for bacteriological warfare?

Games of Coordination and Salient Points

In the past few years, a certain amount of attention has been given to games of coordination[30] and to features such as salient points[31] and "natural solutions." These games indicate the importance of cues and conventions which serve to simplify strategic problems and provide natural coding schemes which lessen uncertainty in the interpretation of either words or deeds. For example, rivers and mountains or seacoasts are "natural boundaries," whereas lines dividing an open plain with no distinguishing features are not.

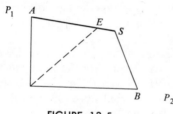

FIGURE 13.5

Consider the 'game' in which two players are told individually that if they can each pick a number x and y such that (x,y) is a point on the curve *AESB* they will obtain rewards $P_1(x,y)$ and $P_2(x,y)$ otherwise they will both obtain nothing. The situation is illustrated in the figure above. Let us assume that the points *A*, *E*, *S*, and *B* are not labeled because that would call extra attention to them. What do we expect to happen? *S*, even without a label attached, is a salient point although it favors player 2. The "equal split" point *E* is a possibility and is even more likely if we were to have letters on the diagram calling attention to it.

The game of chicken can be considered as a special violent case of the rules of the road. Suppose we have two cars approaching each other on a two-lane highway.

30. T. C. Schelling, *The Strategy of Conflict* (Cambridge: Harvard U. P., 1960).
31. J. J. Stone, "An Experiment in Bargaining Games" *Econometrica*, Vol. 26 (1958), pp. 286–296.

	Keep Right	Keep Left
Keep Right	5, 5	—50, —50
Keep Left	—50, —50	5, 5

Either the *convention* of driving to the right or the left will work. Otherwise chaos will result. Convention and institutionalization are methods for the solution of games entailing coordination. A game of coordination (if we wish to consider it as a separate category) may be said to have the properties that all parties involved recognize the value of obtaining a jointly optimal solution. Furthermore, even though the solution selected may be somewhat nonsymmetric, other considerations make it worthwhile for all to accept it. People are taught by their society that this is the solution until it becomes instinct and beyond the realms of ordinary conscious rational calculation. We do not have to calculate or engage in deep thought every time we drive on the right side of the road in the United States.

If at some point some members of society feel that the simplicity and ease in following convention do not offset the inequity, "unfairness" or "wrong" in the solution, then indeed a conscious game-theoretic problem must be solved.

National boundaries have changed throughout history, yet men always have been concerned with defending their "natural territorial rights." Many animals who are otherwise peaceful will fight if their territorial claims are infringed upon. Is it instinct, learning, or both that define the concept of "my territory"?

The Lynch Mob, Social Psychology, and Technology

Game theory deals with actions in cold blood. Lynchings, mob hysteria, riots, many of the acts on the battlefield, vendettas, acts of heroism and acts of cowardice can scarcely be described as such. What are the factors that make the mob turn ugly? When does morale go to pieces; when does an atmosphere of distrust cause negotiations to break down? These are all relevant questions which have no simple answer that can be supplied by game-theoretic analysis. Yet before we abandon all investigation, leaving it to the sociopsychologist or historian, there are some observations that can be made.

Consider a lynch mob which has cornered a suspect. If he is caught in the open without a weapon the odds are that he will be strung up immediately. If he has a revolver, he still probably will be rushed and although he might kill one or two he will still be hanged. Suppose, however, he is on the other side of a gulf over which there is a rickety bridge only wide enough for one man at a time. In this situation he may be able to hold them off long enough to be able to reason with them, to wait until they have calmed down, or until others have arrived. The outcome will be a function of the width and stability of the bridge, the armament of the possible victim and the communication system.

Faster communication systems may *increase* rather than decrease the instability of a political situation. Better communications allow for a speeding up of the transmission of error as well as understanding. They permit actions to be taken in hot blood, when otherwise enough time would have lapsed for a more balanced approach to have been adopted.

Model-Building, Simulation, and Gaming

Closely related to the developments in game theory and partly caused by them are simulation and gaming. Although many people use these two words more or less interchangeably, at least for the purposes of this discussion a distinction will be made.[32,33]

A *simulation* of a system, organization or organism is the operation of a simulator or model of the system. By studying the behavior of the model, the behavior of the relevant parts of the actual system is inferred.

Gaming is an experimental, operational, teaching or training method (which may or may not utilize a simulated environment) which involves humans playing their own, or simulated roles.

A simulation need not involve participation by anyone. It can be a pure mathematical or computer model. It is used when other methods for studying the behavior of a system or organism are too expensive, impracticable or impossible to perform.

Gaming is invariably concerned with human behavior. It does not necessarily need complex formal models or computer programs to simulate the background or the "scenario" for the exercise.

As has been noted, game theory has helped to provide a better language with which to portray decision-making processes. It has raised and helped to define far more questions than it has answered. Simulation and gaming have been employed to start to answer some of these questions. The mere increase in the ability of individuals to construct formal models, games, and simulations has probably more than justified the time and effort spent.

32. M. Shubik, "Simulation of Socio-Economic Systems: Part I," Gowles Foundation Discussion Paper No. 203, Yale University (March 1966).
33. R. A. Brody, "Political Games for Model Construction in International Relations," Department of Political Science, Northwestern University (June 1961).

Although this chapter does not directly deal with gaming or simulation, it is important for the student of political science at least to be aware that these are topics closely related to but different from game theory.

Conclusion

A new methodology rarely if ever can be applied as a magic solution device for many of the problems in any science. Game theory has been of some value and can be of further use to political science. Yet it is not easy to apply it meaningfully without considerable care. There has been considerable misapplication and misunderstanding of game theory. It is a broad difficult technical subject that has been developing along many branches. A reasonable degree of sophistication both in political science and mathematics is required for its application in anything more than a conversational mode or to demonstrate simple paradigms.

Given a sufficient understanding of both political science and formal game theory, its uses are many though not necessarily all of spectacular import. At the level of political philosophy formal game models help in the investigation of concepts such as power, freedom, and equity. In the study of bureaucratic process they help in investigating communication, information and centralization or decentralization of decision-making. In the study of bargaining and negotiation they help to explore the meaning of concepts such as threat. They also raise questions concerning the meaning of social and political stability.

Perhaps in some of the failures of formal game theory lies some of its major successes. It helps to answer the question, "How far can one go with formal rational models of political man?" In helping to set the limits and to provide an understanding of why they exist, game theory serves to point out how it connects naturally with other methods in the behavioral sciences.

14

Communication Models
and Decision Systems

KARL W. DEUTSCH*

THE RECENT MODELS of communication and control may
make us more sensitive to some aspects of politics that have often been
overlooked or slighted in the past. This, as we know, is a major function
of models in their early stages. Well before they permit quantitative
inferences, they may already aid in adding new criteria of relevance:
What kinds of facts are now interesting for us, since we have acquired
a new intellectual context for them?

Here we propose to deal with such possible areas of relevance. We
will survey two of the major concepts—information and feedback—then
offer a short discussion of the politics of growth.

The Concept of Information

Let us remember the distinction made by theorists like Norbert
Wiener between communication engineering and power engineering.
Power engineering transfers energy which then may produce gross
changes at its place of arrival. In power engineering, these changes are
in some sense roughly proportionate to the amount of energy delivered.
Communication engineering transfers extremely small amounts of energy
in relatively intricate patterns. It can produce sometimes very large
changes at the point of arrival, or in the "receiver" of the "message,"
but these changes need in no way be proportionate to the amount of

* Adapted by Karl Von Vorys and K. W. Deutsch from selections from Deutsch's
The Nerves of Government, revised ed. (New York, Free Press-Macmillan, 1966).

energy that carried the signal, much as the force of a gunshot need not be proportionate to the amount of pressure needed to set off the trigger.

Power, we might say, produces changes; information triggers them off in a suitable receiver. In the example just given, the most important thing was not the amount of pressure on the trigger, once it had reached the required threshold, but rather the fact that it was delivered at the trigger—that is, at one particular point of the gun. Similarly, the information required for turning the gun to a particular target need not be carried by any amount of energy proportionate to the energy delivered to the target by the gun. The important thing about information is thus not the amount of energy needed to carry the signal, but the *pattern* carried by the signal, and its relationship to the set of alternatives available in the same information-carrying channel of communication. (The meaning of this information is something else again: it depends on the relationship of the pattern of the signal to the set of patterns stored in the receiver.)

Generally, *information* can be defined as a patterned distribution, or a *patterned relationship between events*. Thus the distribution of lights and shadows in a landscape may be matched by the distribution of a set of electric impulses in a television cable, by the distribution of light and dark spots on a photographic plate, or on a television set, or by the distribution of a set of numbers if a mathematician had chosen to assign coordinates to each image point. In the case of photography or television the processes carrying this information are quite different from each other: sunlight, the emulsion on the photographic plate, the electric impulses in the cable, the television waves, the surface of the receiving screen. Yet each of these processes is brought into a state that is similar in significant respects to the state of the other physical processes that carried the image to it.

A sequence of such processes forms a *channel of communication,* and information is that aspect of the state description of each stage of the channel that has remained invariant from one stage to another. That part of the state description of the first stage of the channel that reappears invariant at the last stage is then the information that has been transmitted through the channel as a whole.[1]

1. George A. Miller states the same point in somewhat different language:

The "amount of information" is exactly the same concept that we have talked about for years under the name of "variance." The equations are different, but if we hold tight to the idea that anything that increases the variance also increases the amount of information we cannot go far astray.

The advantages of this new way of talking about variance are simple enough. Variance is always stated in terms of the unit of measurement—inches, pounds, volts, etc.—whereas the amount of information is a dimensionless quantity. Since the information in a discrete statistical distribution does not depend upon the unit of measurement, we can extend the concept to situations where we have no metric and we would not ordinarily think of using the variance.

The Reception of Information

The effectiveness of information at the receiver depends on two classes of conditions. First of all, *at least some parts of the receiving system must be in highly unstable equilibrium,* so that the very small amount of energy carrying the signal will be sufficient to start off a much larger process of change. Without such disequilibrium already existing in the receiver, information would produce no significant effects.

This obvious technical relationship might have some parallels in politics. The extent of the effect of the introduction of new information into a political or economic system might well be related, among other things, to the extent of the instabilities that already exist there. A crude empirical expression of this problem is found in the perennial debate concerning the relative share of "domestic instabilities" versus "foreign agitators" in strikes or political disturbances. On a somewhat more sophisticated level, the problem reappears as the question of the role of ideas in inducing or prompting social change, and it has relevance for studies of the conditions favoring political reform or technological in-

---

And it also enables us to compare results obtained in quite different experimental situations where it would be meaningless to compare variances based on different metrics. So there are some good reasons for adopting the newer concept.

The similarity of variance and amount of information might be explained this way: When we have a large variance, we are very ignorant about what is going to happen. If we are very ignorant, then when we make the observation it gives us a lot of information. On the other hand, if the variance is very small, we know in advance how our observation must come out, so we get little information from making the observation.

If you will now imagine a communication system, you will realize that there is a great deal of variability about what goes into the system and also a great deal of variability about what comes out. The input and the output can therefore be described in terms of their variance (or their information). If it is a good communication system, however, there must be some systematic relation between what goes in and what comes out. That is to say, the output will depend upon the input, or will be correlated with the input. If we measure this correlation, then we can say how much of the output variance is attributable to the input and how much is due to random fluctuations of "noise" introduced by the system during transmission. So we see that the measure of transmitted information is simply a measure of the input-output correlation.

There are two simple rules to follow. Whenever I refer to "amount of information," you will understand "variance." And whenever I refer to "amount of transmitted information," you will understand "covariance" or "correlation."

The situation can be described graphically by two partially overlapping circles. Then the left circle can be taken to represent the variance of the input, the right circle the variance of the output, and the overlap the covariance of input and output. I shall speak of the left circle as the "amount of transmitted information," you will understand "covariance" or formation, and the overlap as the amount of transmitted information.

George A. Miller, "The Magical Number Seven, Plus or Minus Two: Some Limits on Our Capacity for Processing Information" *Psychological Review,* Vol. 63 (March 1956), pp. 81–82.

novations in different countries. In all such cases a search for "promising instabilities"—that is, instabilities relevant for possible innovation—should be rewarding.

Richness of Information and Selectivity of Reception

The second class of conditions involves the *selectivity* of the receiver. What patterns are already stored in the receiver, and how specific must be the pattern of the incoming signal in order to produce results? A simple example of this problem is furnished by the relationship of lock and key. How many tumblers and notches have been built, let us say, into a particular Yale lock, and what restrictions do they impose upon the distribution of notches on any key that is to turn it? Clearly, the effectiveness of any key in turning a particular lock depends only slightly on the energy with which it is turned (beyond a minimum threshold), and far more on the correspondence of the configuration of its notches with the configuration of the tumblers in the lock.

This crude example shows that there is a measurable difference between locks that are simple and those that are elaborate. Simple locks may have few tumblers in them, and may be turned by a wide variety of differently patterned keys, as long as each of these keys corresponds to the others and to the lock at the few relevant points determined by the distribution of the tumblers. A more elaborate lock will have more tumblers and thus is likely to impose more restrictions on the patterns of keys able to turn it. The selectivity of receivers, then, is related to, among other things, the richness and specificity of information already stored in them.

Similarly, there is a measurable distinction between the richness of information contained in different images. The amount of detail that a photographic film can record is limited by, among other things, the fineness of the grain. Reproductions of photographs in ordinary newspapers are made with halftone screens with less than a hundred lines to the inch, and are thus much poorer in detail and cruder in appearance than the original photographs or magazine reproductions using much finer screens. The same is true of pictures in television, and of details of the human voice in telephoning or recording. In all these processes details can be lost, and the amount of lost information can be measured. Altogether a large amount of thought and experience has gone into the measurement of information, of the possible losses of information under certain conditions, and of the carrying capacity of certain communication channels in terms of quantities of information.

The Measurement of Information and the Fidelity of Channels

The upshot of all this work has been the emergence of information as a quantitative concept. Information can be measured and counted, and the performance of communication channels in transmitting or distorting information can be evaluated in quantitative terms. Some of these measurements in electrical engineering have reached high levels of mathematical sophistication.[2]

Other methods of measuring information may be simpler. Information could conceivably be measured in an extremely crude way in terms of the percentage of image points transmitted or lost on a line screen of a given fineness, or in terms of the number of outstanding details lost as against the number of outstanding details transmitted; or perhaps in a slightly more refined way, information could be measured by the number of such details lost or transmitted in terms of their probability in the context of the possible alternative states of the communication channel; and their meaning could be estimated in the context of the probabilities of the set of details already stored in the receiver.

The fact that social scientists may have to use some of the cruder rather than the more refined methods for measuring the amounts of stored or transmitted information should not obscure the importance of being able to measure it at all. In the investigations of Gordon Allport and L. J. Postman on the psychology of rumor, quantitative measurements of information were used to good effect: a subject was shown a picture for a short time and then told to describe it to a second person who had not seen it. The second person then had to tell a third, and so on through a chain of ten, and the amount of details lost or distorted at each stage was recorded. When each successive stage of retelling was plotted along a horizontal axis, and the number of details retained correctly were plotted vertically, the result was a curve of the loss of details that paralleled strikingly a well-known curve of the forgetting of details by individuals in the course of several weeks. In both cases the details were flattened and sharpened—that is, simplified and exaggerated—and were assimilated by distortion to the prevailing opinions and cultural biases of the individuals carrying the memories or rumors.[3]

2. Y. W. Lee, *Statistical Theory of Communication* (New York: Wiley, 1960).
3. G. W. Allport and L. J. Postman, "The Basic Psychology of Rumor," *Transactions of the New York Academy of Science*, Ser. II, VIII, 1945, pp. 61–81, reprinted in Wilbur Schramm, ed., *The Process and Effects of Mass Communication* (Urbana: U. of Illinois Press, 1954), pp. 141–155. Cf. also F. C. Bartlett, "Social Factors in Recall," in T. M. Newcomb and E. L. Hartley (eds.), *Readings in Social Psychology* (New York: Holt, 1947), pp. 69–76, esp. on "The Method of Serial Reproduction," *ibid.*, p. 72; C. I. Hovland, I. L. Janis, and H. H. Kelly, *Communica-*

Information and Social Cohesion

If we can measure information, no matter how crudely, then we can also measure the cohesion of organizations or societies in terms of their ability to transmit information with smaller or larger losses or distortions in transmission. The smaller the losses or distortions, and the less the admixture of irrelevant information (or "noise"), the more efficient is a given communications channel or a given chain of command.

If we think of an ethnic or cultural community as a network of communication channels, and of a state or a political system as a network of such channels and of chains of command, we can measure the "integration" of individuals in a people by their ability to receive and transmit information on wide ranges of different topics with relatively little delay or loss of relevant detail.[4]

Similarly, we can measure the speed and accuracy with which political information or commands are transmitted, and the extent to which the patterns contained in the command are still recognizable in the patterns of the action that are supposed to form its execution.

The difference between a cohesive community or a cohesive political system, on the one hand, and a specialized professional group—such as a congress of mathematicians—on the other, consists in the multiplicity of topics about which efficient communication is possible. The wider this range of topics, the more broadly integrated, in terms of communications, is the community, or the "body politic." In traditional societies this range of topics may be broad, but limited to topics and problems well within the traditional culture; the ability to communicate widely and effectively on nontraditional topics may be relevant for the cohesion and learning capacity of peoples and political systems in countries undergoing rapid industrialization.

All this is not to say that the measurement of losses in the transmission of information on different ranges of topics is the only way in which the predisposition for political or social cohesion can be measured. Approaches in terms of interlocking roles and expectations might be another way. It is suggested, however, that the information approach offers an independent way of measuring basic cohesion, however crudely, and that it can do so independently from the current political sympathies of the participants. Such sympathies or conflicts might show up sharply in the execution of controversial commands, such as, let us say, between Northerners and Southerners in the United States in the 1850's and

---

tion and Persuasion (New Haven: Yale U. Press, 1953), pp. 245–249; and C. I. Hovland, "Human Learning and Retention" in S. S. Stevens (ed.), *Handbook of Experimental Psychology* (New York: Wiley, 1951), pp. 613–689.

4. K. W. Deutsch, *Nationalism and Social Communication* (Cambridge-New York: M.I.T. Press-Wiley, 1953), pp. 70–74.

again during the Reconstruction period, or between nationalists and Social Democrats in Germany before 1914. Measurements of the accuracy and range of topics of information transmitted in a state or a political or social group would also show the extent and depth of the remaining area of effective mutual communication and understanding among its members. In this manner we might gain important data for estimating the chances for strongly unified behavior of the political system, as well as of the underlying population, in later emergencies.

The Concept of Feedback

It may be useful here to refer to a description of its essentials by Norbert Wiener:

> This control of a machine on the basis of its *actual* performance rather than its *expected* performance is known as *feedback,* and involves sensory members which are actuated by motor members and perform the function of *tell-tales* or *monitors*—that is, of elements which indicate a performance. . . .
> Something very similar to this occurs in human action. If I pick up my cigar, I do not will to move any specific muscles. Indeed in many cases, I do not know what those muscles are. What I do is to turn into action a certain feedback mechanism; namely, a reflex in which the amount by which I have yet failed to pick up the cigar is turned into a new and increased order to the lagging muscles, whichever they may be. In this same way, a fairly uniform voluntary command will enable the same task to be performed from widely varying initial positions, and irrespective of the decrease of contraction due to fatigue of the muscles. . . .
> It is my thesis that the operation of the living individual and the operation of some of the newer communication machines are precisely parallel. Both of them have sensory receptors as one stage in their cycle of operation: that is, in both of them there exists a special apparatus for collecting information from the outer world at low energy levels, and for making it available, in the operation of the individual or of the machine. In both cases these external messages are not taken *neat*, but through the internal transforming powers of the apparatus, whether it be alive or dead. The information is then turned into a new form available for the further stages of performance. In both the animal and the machine this performance is made to be effective on the outer world. In both of them, their *performed* action on the outer world, and not merely their *intended* action, is reported back to the central regulatory apparatus. This complex of behavior is ignored by the average man, and in particular does not play the role that it should in our habitual analysis of society.[5]

Some Applications of Negative Feedback

As we know, applications of this feedback principle in modern control engineering surround our lives. The thermostats in our homes,

5. Norbert Wiener, *The Human Use of Human Beings* (Boston: Houghton, 1950), pp. 12–15 (italics in original).

the automatic elevators in our office buildings, as well as the automatic gun directors in antiaircraft batteries, and the guided missiles now existing or under development, all represent applications of this principle.

In all these cases, an electric or mechanical system first of all is given a major internal imbalance or disequilibrium that functions as its *drive,* in the sense that the system tends to move toward a state in which this internal disequilibrium will be reduced, or more loosely expressed, in which its internal "tension" will be lowered. Moreover, this inner disequilibrium must be of a particular kind, such that it can be reduced by bringing the whole system into some particular situation or relation vis-a-vis the outside world. This situation of the system to the outside world we may call a *goal situation,* or briefly, a *goal:* once the system has reached such a goal its inner disequilibrium will be lower.

Second, in order for the system to approach the goal effectively, the feedback condition must be given. The system must receive information concerning the position of the goal and concerning its own distance from it; and it must receive information concerning the changes in its distance from the goal brought about by its own performance. The messages are often negative in that they *oppose* the previous actions of the system, so as to oppose overshooting of the target.

In the third place, the system must be able to respond to this information by further changes in its own position or behavior. With these facilities, and given sufficient freedom, the system will therefore tend to approach its goal.

Finally, if these changes are effective and the system reaches the goal, some of its drive or inner tension usually will be lowered.

There is an obvious similarity between these steps in the process of goal-seeking, and the concepts of "drive," "cue," "response," and "reward," which are familiar from the psychology of learning.

Similar patterns of behavior have been found in the performance of the nervous system of animals and human beings. Feedback processes seem to represent the particular machinery of *homeostasis* by which certain essential states or functions of an organism, such as body temperatures or breathing rate, are maintained at an even level. The maintenance of even states, and the seeking and approaching of external goals, are thus performed essentially by the same configuration of processes.

The similarity of these processes of steering, goal-seeking, and autonomous control to certain processes in politics seems striking. Governments may seek goals in domestic or foreign policies. In order to approach these goals they must guide their behavior by a stream of information concerning their own position in relation to these goals; their remaining distance from them; and the actual, as distinct from the intended, results of their own most recent steps or attempts to approach them.

In addition to seeking goals, governments or political organizations may try to maintain some state of affairs they deem desirable, such as prosperity in economics or tranquility in politics. In so doing, they must receive information concerning the extent and rate of disturbances in order to guide the magnitude and speed of their countermeasures. If they react too much or too soon, they will overshoot the mark and themselves create a disturbance in the opposite direction. To the statesman, guiding a difficult program to success may thus resemble the art of driving an automobile over an icy road: his problem is to anticipate the skids quickly enough so that he can still control them by small corrections at the steering wheel, where slowness of the action or oversteering would provide worse skids and might wreck the car.

An Alternative to the "Equilibrium" Approach

In its application to politics, the feedback concept permits a more sophisticated approach than does the traditional mechanistic concept of equilibrium, and permits a far wider range of analysis and measurement.[6] If we think of a political system in terms of a classic mechanistic equilibrium, we are forced to think in terms of a system that is isolated from its environment and receives nothing important from the outside except disturbances. If these disturbances are small, the equilibrium will simply be restored through the automatic reaction of the system. If the disturbances are somewhat larger, we should expect them to elicit proportionately greater reactions tending to restore the same status

6. For the continued interest in equilibrium models see, for example, George Liska, *International Equilibrium,* Cambridge, Harvard U. P., 1957, and the criticism in Stanley H. Hoffman (ed.), *Contemporary Theory in International Relations* (Englewood Cliffs, N.J.: Prentice-Hall, 1960), pp. 50–52. For a critical discussion of the limits of the "the analogy between a market and a balance of power situation," cf. also Charles P. Kindleberger, "International Political Theory from Outside," in William T. R. Fox (ed.), *Theoretical Aspects of International Relations* (Notre Dame, Ind.: Notre Dame U., 1959), pp. 69–82. For other examples of the use of concepts of equilibrium or the balance of power, cf. Charles de Visscher, *Theory and Reality in Public International Law,* trans. Percy E. Corbett (Princeton: Princeton U. P., 1957), p. 92; Kenneth W. Thompson, *Political Realism and the Crisis of World Politics* (Princeton: Princeton U. P., 1960, pp. 144–166; and George Modelski, *A Theory of Foreign Policy* (New York: Praeger, 1962), p. 129. For another critical discussion of balance-of-power theory and its limitations, see Hans Morgenthau, *Politics Among Nations,* 3rd ed. (New York: Knopf, 1960), pp. 167–216. It is interesting to note that both Thompson and Morgenthau compensate for some of the limitations and rigidities of the equilibrium and balance-of-power model by stressing heavily the need for normative theories of international morality. Cf. Thompson, *loc. cit.,* and pp. 166–173; Morgenthau, *op. cit.,* pp. 216–223.

quo. If the disturbances are too great, we can only imagine that the system will somehow be overthrown or destroyed, but the equilibrium concept gives us little or no information as to just what will happen from then on, except vague indications of disaster. In short, the equilibrium concept is incapable of describing an important range of dynamic phenomena and it can indicate no time path for substantial change. With no help from the equilibrium concept in analyzing major processes of social change, statesmen would either have to hope that "every action must be followed by an equal and opposite reaction," or they must rely on general experience or intuition.

To be sure, some of the more sophisticated dynamic theories of processes of change also speak of "equilibrium," but they are using the word as a description of a certain state of equilibrium that may be achieved or lost; but unlike classic mechanistic theory, they no longer envisage equilibrium itself as a process by which this state is maintained or restored. Rather they are describing this process in other terms—for example, through differential equations—and are then asking under what conditions a state of equilibrium will be one of its results.[7] In short, where classic mechanism often thought of equilibrium as a suitable over-all description of an entire large system, the concepts of equilibrium and disequilibrium are now most useful as descriptions of temporary states of small components of such systems, while the systems themselves are recognized as engaged in dynamic processes of change which go well beyond the classic equilibrium image. It is this classic image, however, that often lingers on in the folklore of social science and political thought and even in minds of statesmen trying to defend or restore some classic image of the balance of power.

At first glance the process of goal-seeking that we described above may seem similar to the process of restoring simple equilibrium. Actually, it is very different in at least four ways. First of all, in feedback processes, the goal situation sought is outside, not inside, the goal-seeking system. Second, the system itself is not isolated from its environment but, on the contrary, depends for its functioning upon a constant stream of information from the environment, as well as upon a constant stream of information concerning its own performance. Third, the goal may be a changing goal. It may change both its position, as a flying bird or an airplane, and even its speed and direction, as a rabbit pursued by a dog. Suitable feedback processes could in principle catch up with a zigzagging rabbit, just as in principle suitable automatic gun directors can track and shoot down an airplane taking evasive action.

7. Cf. the use of the concept by Anatol Rapoport, *Fights, Games and Debates* (Ann Arbor: U. of Michigan Press, 1960), pp. 25–43.

In the fourth place, a goal may be approached indirectly by a course, or a number of possible courses, around a set of obstacles. This problem resembles our notion of *purpose:* a major or strategic goal, preference, or value that is to be pursued through a set of intermediate movements toward intermediate goals, or avoiding intermediate obstacles. In a simple form this problem has appeared in the design of automatic torpedoes and guided missiles. In politics, it appears as the problem of maintaining a strategic purpose throughout a sequence of changing tactical goals.

In addition to these four differences between feedback and the equilibrium concept, feedback analysis permits us to identify and in principle to measure a number of elements in either goal-seeking or homeostatic processes. We can evaluate the efficiency of a feedback process in terms of the number and size of its mistakes, that is, the under- or overcorrections it makes in reaching the goal. If the series of such mistakes should increase rather than decrease, the goal will not be reached at all. The system will go into a series of increasing oscillations, and may break down. Whether this will happen or whether, on the contrary, the goal will be approached successfully through a number of diminishing mistakes depends on the mutual relationship between four quantitative factors:

1. The *load* in terms of information—that is, the extent and speed of changes in the position of the target relative to the goal-seeking system. In the cases of a moving ship or airplane, or of a darting rabbit, this load may be quite high.

2. The *lag* in the response of the system—that is, the amount of time between the reception of information concerning the position of the target and the execution of the corresponding step in the goal-seeking behavior of the system. This is the time between the reception of the information concerning the position of an enemy airplane and the actual pointing of the antiaircraft gun barrels to the spot designed for interception; or it might correspond to the time between a dog's seeing the hunted rabbit change its course, and the corresponding change in the course of the dog. Clearly, this lag may be influenced by a number of factors, such as slowness in the reception of target information, or in its interpretation or transmission; or by delays in the response of parts of the system in executing the new course; by the inertia of the system; and so on. The greater its lag in relation to its load, the less likely is a system to reach a changing goal or moving target.

3. The *gain* in each corrective step taken by the system—that is, the amount of actual change in behavior that results. Thus the more we turn the steering wheel of an automobile during a given time the greater should ordinarily be the gain in the resulting change of the

course of the car. A high rate of gain increases the probability of *over-steering*—that is, of departing from the correct course in the opposite direction.

4. The *lead*—that is, the distance of the accurately predicted position of the moving target from the actual position from which the most recent signals were received. In this manner, sportsmen "lead" flying ducks and clay pigeons: they fire at the target's predicted rather than at its perceived position by aiming somewhat ahead in the direction of its previously observed course. The greater this lead in terms of time, so long as the prediction remains accurate, the greater is the probability of hitting the target or reaching the goal. The amount of lead, in turn, depends on the efficiency of predictive processes available to the goal-seeking system, and on the amount of inaccuracy that can be tolerated. For this reason, duck hunters use duckshot rather than bullets, and antiaircraft guns fire their shells in a pattern calculated in terms of probability.

The chances of success in goal-seeking are thus always inversely related to the amounts of *load* and *lag*. Up to a point, they may be positively related to the amount of *gain*, although, at high rates of gain, this relationship may be reversed; and they are always positively related to the amount of *lead*.[8]

A feedback model of this kind permits us to ask a number of significant questions about the performance of governments that are apt to receive less attention in terms of traditional analysis:

1. What are the amount and rate of change in the international or domestic situation with which the government must cope? In other words, what is the *load* upon the political decision system of the state? Similarly, what is the load upon the decision system of particular interest groups, political organizations, or social classes? What is the intellectual load upon their leadership? What is the load upon the facilities to ensure participation from their members?

2. What is the *lag* in the response of a government or party to a new emergency or challenge? How much time do policymakers require to become aware of a new situation, and how much additional time do they need to arrive at a decision? How much delay is imposed by broader

---

8. Cf. W. S. McCulloch: "Feedback was defined as an alteration of input by output; gain was defined as ratio of output to input; feedback was said to be negative or inverse if the return decreased the output, say by subtracting from the input. The same term, inverse or negative feedback, was used for a similar effect but dissimilar mechanism, wherein the return decreased the gain. The transmission of signals requires time, and gain depends on frequency; consequently, circuits inverse for some frequencies may be regenerative for others. All become regenerative when gain exceeds one." From "Summary of the Points of Agreement Reached in the Previous Nine Conferences on Cybernetics," Appendix I, in Heinz von Foerster (ed.), *Cybernetics: Circular Causal and Feedback Mechanisms in Biological Social Systems* (New York: Macy Foundation, 1955), p. 71.

consultation or participation? How much time is required to transmit a series of changing orders to the officials, soldiers, and citizens who are to execute them, and how much time do these persons require to readjust their previous behavior patterns, habits, and values, so as to be able to comply effectively? What is the corresponding lag in the response of particular political parties, interest groups, or individuals? What is the lag in the response to new information that is brought into the political decision system through one channel rather than another— for example, the lag in the reaction to information that is reported more or less "straight to the top" (as the possibility of an atomic bomb was reported to President Roosevelt in 1940), in contrast to the information that is first accepted among some particular social or occupational groups? What is the relationship between the accessibility of a government to the amount of lag observed in its reactions? If it is known that armies and totalitarian governments can cut down their rate of lag by ensuring the quick transmission of orders from the top *down*, to what extent is this advantage lost, and the amount of lag increased, by possible difficulties in such systems in getting new information *up* to the top? What attempted solutions for this problem have been adopted in practice in various countries? What differences in this respect can be observed in the structure and performance of different dictatorships, such as Spain and Nazi Germany, or of, say, Yugoslavia, Cuba, Poland, China, and the USSR? What differences in this respect can we observe among various democracies such as France, Great Britain and the United States?

3. What is the *gain* of the response—that is, the speed and size of the reaction of a political system to new data it has accepted? How quickly do bureaucracies, interest groups, political organizations, and citizens respond with major recommitments of their resources? To what extent do authoritarian regimes have an advantage in enforcing a massive response to new policies, once they have been adopted? To what extent can democracies have a high rate of gain? What factors account for the vast and quick response of the United States to Pearl Harbor—a response utterly unexpected by the Axis governments?

4. What is the amount of *lead*, that is, of the capability of a government to predict and to anticipate new problems effectively? To what extent do governments attempt to improve their rate of lead by setting up specific intelligence organizations, strategy and planning boards, and other devices? What is the effect of free public discussion, including freedom for unorthodox opinions, upon the predictive efficiency of a political decision system? What is the relationship of the institutions, organizations, or practices that produce forecasts to those that control their selection, evaluation, and acceptance for action?

The over-all performance of political decision systems will depend upon the interplay of all these factors. Since gain is related to power, governments or organizations with little power may have to try to compensate for their low rates of gain by trying to increase their foresight and the speed of their response—that is, to cut down their lag and to increase their lead. Great powers, on the other hand, may often succeed in coping with a situation by the sheer size of their response, even though their reactions may be slow and their predictions poor. Again, governments or political organizations, whose rates of lag, gain, and lead were sufficiently adjusted to each other for dealing with moderate rates of change in their environment, may find themselves unable to control their behavior effectively in times of rapid change that may put an excessive load upon their decision-making system.

Considerations of this kind may be of some help in the long and seemingly unpromising debate concerning the "superiority" of this or that political system. Such debates have often been held in terms of a vague all-round superiority, in which cultural, ethical, religious, and political values were inextricably mixed and which tended to end as exercises in ethnocentrism. At the other extreme, attempts could be made to evaluate political systems operationally in terms of a single function, in which case the outcome depends largely upon the selection of the function. If we assume, however, that all governments are trying to maintain some control over their own behavior, to maintain as long as possible the conditions for the existence of their political systems, and to get nearer to, rather than further away from, the goals that they have accepted, then it would be possible to evaluate different configurations of political institutions in terms of their capacity to function as a more or less efficient steering system.

While the evaluation of political systems as steering systems ought to be technically possible, it would be quite one-sided. Both Pericles and John Stuart Mill might remind us that states should not merely be evaluated in terms of their ability to function efficiently as states, but far more in terms of the types of personality and character they produce among their citizens, and of the opportunities they offer to all their citizens for individual development. In the final section of this chapter we shall deal with some of these broader concepts of growth in relation to individuals as well as to communities and government. At this point, let us note only that over-all steering performance is an important aspect of political decision systems but that it is by no means an exhaustive one.

Another word of caution should be added. Thus far our discussion has been in terms of *goals* and not of *goal images*. We defined goals in terms of the actual configuration of the steering or decision system, and in terms of the configurations of its environment. In this manner we discussed the goals the system appears to be seeking in its observable behavior, as in the case of a ship steered by an automatic pilot. In the case of a ship steered by a single human pilot, we would have to treat the memories of the pilot as part of the ship. A psychiatrist dealing with the personality and the nervous system of an individual might similarly look for the goals that he might in fact be pursuing, as distinct from the goals that the patient contemplates in his imagination. The goals actually sought and the goal images carried in the minds of some or all of the participants may of course coincide, but they need not in fact do so. Wherever one's goals are pictured in goal images that are distinct form the actual process by which goals are sought, information derived from such images may be fed back into the steering process and influence its outcome.

Some Applications of Amplifying Feedback

Thus far we have discussed patterns of negative feedback. In all these, information concerning the performance of a decision system is returned to it and may serve to negate, oppose, or reverse its current action if that action had been leading the system away from its goal. In other situations, however, we may meet positive or amplifying-feedback patterns. In cases of amplifying feedback, information about the response of the system serves to reinforce that response in the same direction, and information about this reinforced response may produce further reinforcement of this behavior. Panics in crowds, market panics, cases of runaway inflation, armament races, the escalation of wars, or the growth of bitterness in an extremely divided community are examples of amplifying-feedback systems in social or political life. The sequence of military mobilizations by the various powers in July-August, 1914, showed the features of an amplifying-feedback system on a grand scale—features that to some extent came as a surprise to all participants.[9] Since amplifying-feedback situations may under certain conditions get out of control, and may damage or wreck the system in which they arise, their better understanding should be of great interest to social scientists.

Perhaps the decisive quantitative consideration in evaluating the probable behavior of an amplifying-feedback system, or the course of an amplifying-feedback sequence, is the increasing or decreasing character of the series of increments in response to the mutual stimuli at each cycle of operation. If the sequence of reinforcements of behavior, due to the feedback phenomenon, forms a uniform or even an increasing

9. Cf. Russett, "Cause, Surprise, and No Escape," *Journal of Politics*, 24:1 (February, 1962), pp. 3–22. A larger study of the 1914 crisis is currently being conducted by Prof. Robert C. North and his associates at Stanford University. Compare also Herman Kahn, *On Escalation: Metaphors and Scenarios* (New York, Praeger, 1965)

series, then the total response must grow until it exceeds the limits of the system and ends in some form of breakdown. If, on the contrary, this sequence of reinforcements forms a decreasing series, so that, on the whole, each new reinforcement tends to be smaller than the ones that went before, then the total reinforcement will tend to approach an upper limit that need not be beyond the capacities of the system. In this latter case, amplifying feedback would bring the system up to some maximum level of performance, and would tend to keep it there. In the earlier case of uniform or increasing amplifying feedback, there would be no such upper limit within the system: performance would increase without limit until stopped by breakdown, external constraint, or exhaustion.

Situations of bitter domestic or international conflict may easily assume the characteristics of amplifying feedback situations. Each side may feel obliged to answer the threats, encroachments, or insults of the other by reprisals in kind, or by precautionary measures that are in fact competitive and are interpreted as threats by the opponent. If each side is convinced that it must have a margin of superiority over the other, amplifying feedback may result for the whole system of which the two contending groups or states are parts. The course of the resulting amplifying-feedback sequence could be forecast and perhaps even controlled, however, by observing and, if possible, controlling the growth or decline of the amount of gain at each cycle, that is, the size of successive increments in performance, of which it is composed. If gestures are answered by more vigorous gestures, and threats with more vigorous counterthreats, but if care is taken to keep the competitive increase at each stage somewhat below the increase during the stage that preceded it, then it should be possible for both contending sides to "keep themselves covered" at each step, and, without ever accepting inferiority to the rival, to reduce the sequence of wage-price rises, military threats, and so on, to some foreseeable and perhaps tolerable maximum level. President Kennedy's announcement in March, 1962, that the United States would respond to the earlier series of Russian nuclear weapons tests in the atmosphere with a *smaller* series of such tests of its own, unless a nuclear test ban should be agreed on within a short time, may have represented an attempt to use such tactics of "underretaliation," or of decreasing increments, in the amplifying-feedback situation of the nuclear weapons race.[10]

If no control over the increments is possible, then the uniformity, or increase, or decrease, in the observable rate of gain of the system could be used for predictive purposes. Many amplifying-feedback processes depend on some external supplies or facilities in maintaining

10. *New York Times*, March 3, 1962, pp. 1–2.

their rate of gain, such as forest fires that require fuel, or arms races that require economic resources. In such situations we may find a phase of constant or increasing gain, and thus accelerating performance, followed by a phase of slowly or rapidly decreasing gain, as the limits of available supplies or facilities are approached. The resulting sequence of behavior may be pictured somewhat in terms of the well-known "logistic" curves of growth. These S-shaped curves show a slow rise in growth or performance, accelerating later to a phase of very rapid growth, and decreasing gradually in the end so as to remain below a definite upper limit.

Some aspects of conflict situations can be analyzed in terms either of an amplifying or of a negative-feedback process. The interchange of threats, or acts of retaliation, has been a topic of study by a number of theorists of "deterrence."[11] One might conceive, for instance, of a deliberate policy of "underretaliation," which would aim at inflicting on the opponent only four-fifths or nine-tenths of the damage one's own side has received, in the hope that the subsequent counterretaliation of the enemy will again remain limited to four-fifths or nine-tenths of one's own action, so that the series of moves will quickly converge to a new and tolerable level.

Some Implications of Goal-Changing Feedback

Thus far we have discussed goal-seeking and steering systems in which the goals were assumed as fixed. If the thermostat in our home has been set for 68 degrees, the heating or air-conditioning system will then go through a series of operations to maintain this temperature. In the preceeding section we discussed, in principle, the ability of such a system to seek one particular goal, or to maintain one particular state, such as this one temperature under rapidly changing weather conditions outside.

It is, however, quite possible for the goal itself to be changed. This may occur gradually, through a drift in the characteristics or behavior of some parts of the system. Gradual changes in the culture patterns or personality structures of a population, or in the personnel of a political elite, may thus change the goals sought by a political decision system. Studies of the political effects of changes in the "national character" or in prevailing personality patterns, such as the change toward

---

11. E.g., Rapoport, *op. cit.;* Morton A. Kaplan, *The Strategy of Limited Retaliation,* Policy Memorandum No. 19, The Center for International Studies (Princeton: Princeton U. P., 1959); Thomas C. Schelling, *The Strategy of Conflict* (Cambridge, Harvard U. P., 1960); and Herman Kahn, *On Thermonuclear War* (Princeton: Princeton U. P., 1960) and *On Escalation,* cited in note 9, above.

"other-directedness" suggested by David Riesman, might be developed in this direction.[12]

In some organizations, goal-changing is a part of the pattern of feedback processes itself. In such cases, if goal A has been approached to the extent of a given threshold value, the reaching of the threshold will trigger a rearrangement of some elements in the communication system, so as to give priority to another feedback circuit steering the system in the direction of another goal B. If B is reached, the system may return to the search for A, or go on to a third goal-seeking circuit steering it toward goal C; and so on. In this manner, animals may alternate between hunger and thirst, and machines have been built that move toward sources of light as long as their own energy supply is high, but move toward sources of energy when their own energy supply falls below a certain level.

Isolated instances of goal-changing are well known in politics. Literature is replete with descriptions of the changes in the behavior of former political "outs" that have become "ins," or of new men who have "arrived" and who, as the French say, "do not send the elevator down." How, when, and how quickly goals are changed by individuals, groups, and organizations might be a fruitful subject for political research.

A more specifically political problem arises in situations where a major strategic goal must be achieved through a sequence of intermediate or tactical goals. According to Adolf Hitler's view of mass psychology, the art of mass leadership in such cases consists in the ability to make each intermediate goal appear as the ultimate one, and to convince the rank and file that everything depends upon their ability to gain this particular objective here and now, regardless of all else. Only ultimate goals, in this view, have the capacity to elicit the total commitment of all available resources from large numbers of persons. Despite vehement disagreement with other theories of Adolf Hitler, Communist agitation often shows a similar pattern: each particular and transitory goal is represented for the time being as the be-all and end-all of political activity, until it is replaced by another. Similar psychological strategies have been employed to some extent by democratic governments in wartime, and in some of the protracted contests of the "cold war."

12. Cf. also David M. Potter, *People of Plenty: Economic Abundance and the American Character* (Chicago, U. of Chicago Press, 1954), pp. 3–72; Alex Inkeles and Daniel J. Levinson, "National Character: The Study of Modal Personality and Sociocultural Systems," in Gardner Lindzey, (ed.), *Handbook of Social Psychology* (Reading, Mass.: Addison-Wesley, 1954), II, 977–1020; and Margaret Mead, "National Character," in A. L. Kroeber (ed.), *Anthropology Today* (Chicago: U. of Chicago Press, 1953), pp. 642–667. Cf. also David Riesman, Nathan Glazer, and Rueul Denny, *The Lonely Crowd: A Study of the Changing American Character* (New Haven: Yale U. P., 1950), esp. pp. 17–31; and Washington Platt, *National Character in Action* (New Brunswick: Rutgers U. P., 1961).

Despite their occasional empirical usefulness, such psychological "all-out" tactics are fraught with serious political costs. Thucydides early noted one of their drawbacks: since each tactical goal is represented as all-important, and virtually as ultimate, all disagreement about tactics becomes treason. Since, moreover, the most recklessly chosen tactical objectives can be most easily represented as ultimate goals, or as equivalent to victory, the most reckless tactics may seem to be the most appealing; and since, at the same time, they may evoke a larger measure of dissent, they may form an excellent pretext of purges of dissenters. Under suitable conditions, such as those prevailing in Athens during certain stages of the Peloponnesian War, the most reckless foreign policy or military tactics thus tended to be selected by the political decision process. The gradual hardening of war aims in modern wars involving mass participation, such as the last two world wars, may be related to a similar political process.[13] It might be worth investigating to what extent totalitarian dictatorships are subject to this process, and thus to the danger of the loss of control over their own strategy, and whether, and to what extent, and by what devices, differnt regimes of this kind have succeeded in dealing with this problem.

Exalting each of a series of changing tactical goals to the temporary status of a final goal may also exact a somewhat subtler price. Both Hitler and Lenin drew a technical distinction between the mere adherents of political parties, who agreed with the party's announced objectives, voted for its candidates, and possibly gave it some limited support, and the fully active members of the organization—sometimes called the "activists"—who committed to the party a major part of their time, resources, and imagination. Within the ranks of those "activists," in theory, little further distinction was made. If a political party, however, demands all-out commitment to a succession of changing tactical goals, and at the same time invites persons to become activists, it is apt to impose precisely upon those activists an almost intolerable psychological strain. They must commit themselves completely to each transitory goal. They may find it impossible, therefore, to devote much time and attention to considering the strategic course of which the goal may be a minor part, and thus to considering the probability of a change in the goal in the future. Many of them may well feel "let down" when this change in fact arrives. Since this experience is repeated every time the goal is changed, such parties are apt to have a high turnover of disgruntled former activists. These activists may eventually leave their party almost regardless of the supposed intrinsic merits of each change in policy, even in terms of their own previously held ideology. They

13. For a thoughtful study of an important case—the employment of atomic bombs against Japanese cities—see Robert C. Batchelder, *The Irreversible Decision, 1939–1950* (Boston: Houghton, 1962), esp. pp. 190–210.

may leave the movement, not because the particular change in tactics was iniquitous, but rather because for each of them personally it was one change too many—the straw that broke the camel's back.

In addition to producing a high turnover, this "idolization of ephemeral goals"—if we may adopt one of A. J. Toynbee's terms again—may have a peculiar effect on the type of persons who remain faithful to the parties or governments that resort to such tactics. On the one hand, there will remain a larger or smaller number of eternal activists, who accept each change without question, and who give their all to each goal in its day. On the other hand, the functions of planning strategy, of choosing sequences of tactical goals, and of timing the switches between them must still be fulfilled. Since many of the unquestioning activists may become psychologically unsuited to fulfilling this second group of functions, another structure may have to be developed to fulfill it: a strategic party or "inner circle"—a group of "insiders" who commit their own attention in part to data inconsistent with the all-out policy of the moment, and who carry on among themselves some of the deliberation and discussion needed for its future change.

Parallels to this functional split may even occur in business organizations. The folklore of sales organizations and advertising staffs is full of the distinction between the "Boy Scout" or "eager beaver" type of employee who commits himself completely to every sales campaign, and the "insider" or "executive type" who does his bit in a respectable fashion but who avoids all undue enthusiasm about tactical goals he knows will soon be changed.

Where democratic governments use tactics on an all-out scale, as they did during World War II, they may face the risk of a similar split between cynics and believers, with a gradual increase in the number of cynics as time goes on. David Riesman's assertion that the "inside dopester" may have replaced the crusading reformer as the political model for many persons in our time may not be unrelated to this problem.[14]

Most elements of this analysis should lend themselves to research. How sharp a change in goals or policies has been imposed on how many people, in how short a time, and with what consequences? How noticeable is the split between outsiders and insiders in a particular political party or government? What methods and devices have been adopted to control this type of disintegration, and with what success?

One possible way of controlling this split between tactical and strategic goals, and the corresponding split between outsiders and insiders, has been suggested to the writer by Professor Franklin Scott. If it were possible to publicize at all times the strategic goal of the

14. Riesman et al., *op. cit.*, pp. 199–209.

government or organization, and to publicize the particular relation
of the day's tactical goals to that strategic goal, then it might be easier
for citizens or soldiers, or for the members of an organization, to maintain their emotional commitment to the strategic goal and to avoid
emotional commitment to the changing tactics, while at the same time
giving full operational support to these tactics, not for their own sake,
but for the sake of the strategic goal they are held to serve. This, it will
readily appear, represents to some extent a more elaborate disguise for
the well-known "means-ends" problem; but the actual extent to which
such methods have been used, or could be used, in politics might be
an interesting topic for research.

A last aspect of goal-changing feedback might involve fundamental
changes in goals. An organization, having pursued one kind of goal,
might come to pursue a very different kind of goal. In this manner, the
Swedish political system changed from the pursuit of military power
in the seventeenth century to the pursuit of neutrality and social welfare
in the twentieth. This may involve more than the change of just one
or several values. Rather, where such changes in major goals occur, we
may find at work a process of long-range reconstruction; and where they
occur in a relatively short time we may face the phenomena of renova-
tion, reformation, revolution, or conversion, all of which are forms of
systems transformation. All these involve a major change in over-all
function and behavior, as well as major structural rearrangements of the
political decision system, and usually of the rest of the society. If we
ask, "How likely are such major changes to occur in a particular political
or social system? And how likely are they to occur without self-destruc-
tion on the part of the system?"—then we have gone beyond the problem
of simple goal-changing feedback. We are asking about the learning
capacity or innovating capacity of that society. In fact, we enter the
politics of growth.

The Politics of Growth

It is often said that it is the task of politics to promote the "public
interest" or the "common good" of a nation or of a larger society over
and above all special or lesser interests. If we admit that there can be
such a common good and that social life is not exhausted by group conflicts, we must ask what this good is. Despite wide differences in cultures
and values, we may assume provisionally that one of the most widely
accepted values is the *survival* of the family, community, people, or
nation. In terms of their probability of survival, we may divide all
political systems or organizations into four categories:

1. *Self-destroying systems,* which are apt to break down eventually even in relatively favorable environments.

2. *Nonviable systems,* which are unlikely to survive under the range of difficulties found in most environments (though they need not be likely to be self-destructive).

3. *Viable systems,* which are likely to preserve their original probability of survival over a limited range of environmental conditions; and

4. *Self-developing or self-enhancing systems,* which are able to increase their probability of survival and their ranges of possible action over an increasing variety of environments.

While social organizations are radically different from organisms, the last three of these categories happen to parallel somewhat the medical notion of "health," and to parallel closely the biologist's concept of "evolutionary progress."[15] This latter concept is also based on the notion of probable long-run survival and on the probability that in the long run most environments may change very considerably, so that only self-changing and self-enhancing systems and organizations are apt to survive eventually, thanks to their ability to cope with many different environments and to increase their relative independence from any one of them.

Neither the biologist nor the social scientist need deny that there may arise on occasion some nonviable organisms or some nonviable or self-destructive organizations. All they need say is that such highly self-destructive organizations will tend in fact not to survive, even though they may function as a dangerous environment for those organizations and individuals committed in some way to the values of life and survival. In the legislative control of the behavior of individuals, we similarly draw up laws on the assumption that most persons value life, and desire the survival of individuals and communities dear to them; and we treat suicide and attempts at suicide as exceptions that, though real, are not likely to change the basic rules of the game for the survivors.

The consequence of these notions, from Émile Durkheim's notion of social health to Julian Huxley's concept of evolutionary progress, is the recognition of growth, of adaptability, and of learning capacity as essential for the survival of societies and cultures. What are the dimensions of this growth, and what can politics contribute to it?

Dimensions of Growth

As the first dimensions of growth of a political system, we may count the growth of *manpower* and population included in it, as well as gains in their physical and mental health. In the second place, we may count *economic growth.* Without trying to summarize the literature on eco-

---

15. Julian Huxley, *Evolution, the Modern Synthesis* (New York: Harper, 1943), pp. 556–578; Huxley, *Man in the Modern World* (New York: New American Library, 1951), pp. 7–27.

nomic growth, we may merely note that this would include particularly the amounts of disposable factors of production, such as capital goods, land, and labor, as well as the growth of skills and technical knowledge. A further condition would be that the rate of growth of the second category, economic resources, should exceed in the long run the rate of the growth of population. The meeting of these conditions requires the maintenance of rates of savings and of investment in capital-goods industries, which without government aid have been attained only in a few countries, and only for limited periods, and which often may require political decisions.

In the third place, we may list the criteria of growth that bear on the availability of material and human resources for recommitment to new uses. Particularly we may list here the development of *operational reserves* in the system that may be committed to the pursuit of new goals or to the meeting of new stresses or new challenges from the environment.

The fourth group of criteria of growth refers to the growth of autonomy, or *self-determination.* This implies, on the one hand, a growth in the resources and functions that bear on social cohesion, that is, the growth, range, speed, and effectiveness of internal communications, both among individuals and among institutions or parts of the society or the political system. On the other hand, it implies growth in the steering performance of the system, in the effectiveness of its use of data recalled from memory, and of information received from outside. It will require, therefore, a growth in the facilities of memory and recall, and thus of institutions of learning, record-keeping, and the like; a growth in the variety and effectiveness of channels for the intake of new ranges of information from the outside world; an improvement in goal-seeking operations, through increases in the gain and lead, and through the cutting down of lag by reducing the delays due to either slowness of communication or to inertia or inner resistance in response.

A possible fifth criterion is implied in the fourth. A growing organization, and hence also a growing state or government, must be able to change its own patterns of communication and organization so as to overcome the results of the "scale effect," that is, the effects of the changing proportions produced by increased size. It must resist the trend toward increasing self-preoccupation and eventual self-immolation from its environment; and it must reorganize or transform itself often enough to overcome the growing threats of internal communication overload and the jamming up of message traffic. One of the most effective responses to these threats—highlighted by such writings on politics and administration as "Parkinson's Law"—consists in *strategic simplifications.*[16]

16. C. Northcote Parkinson, *Parkinson's Law, and Other Studies in Administration* (Boston: Houghton, 1957).

Often in history, growth in organization and progress in technique appear to imply just such a simplification of some crucial link or coupling in the chain of interlocking and self-sustaining processes by which the organization is kept going. Thus the maintenance of an ever-growing written tradition is facilitated by the invention of increasingly simple alphabets and increasingly simple methods of writing and, eventually, printing. The many tasks of modern languages are facilitated by the sloughing off of many of the ancient inflections and the replacement of their semantic functions by means of word position and context. Other examples of this process of strategic simplification are the replacement of trolley tracks by rubber tires; of telegraph wires by radio; and many other processes of this kind, ranging all the way to the increasingly simple symbol structures of the central theories of physics from the cumbrous models of Ptolemy and Copernicus to the simpler and more general formulations of Newton and Einstein.

Cases of this sort are cited by A. J. Toynbee, but the interpretation proposed here is somewhat different from his. In none of the cases of simplification which he cites do we find a simplification—or a reduction in the number of elements—for any of the systems cited *as a whole*, be they systems of transportation, communication, or theoretical physics. On the contrary, each system as a whole is becoming more complex; what is becoming simpler are particular links in it, which are crucial or strategic. Thus a modern radio station is a far more complicated piece of electric equipment than the original wire telegraph of Samuel Morse; but its ability to transmit signals without telegraph wires permitted man to put its increased complex of resources to other and more fruitful uses. With this qualification, however, there seems to be a good deal of evidence supporting Toynbee's surmise that some such strategic or crucial simplifications may well be essential for any extended process of growth.

An important special case of such strategic simplifications might perhaps be seen in the replacement of gross operations or experiments with major physical resources by much simpler and quicker operations or experiments by means of symbols. An increasing shift from operations with gross resources toward a growing proportion of operations by means of symbols is thus another possible criterion of growth; and most of the cases of what Mr. Toynbee has called "etherealization" as an important aspect of growth could be brought perhaps under this heading.

All these elements of growth, taken together, may go far to meet one of the tests for growth once proposed by Simon Kuznets: the ability of an organization, an economy, or a state to approach the goals it happens to have chosen. In this sense, growth as the ability to approach previously chosen goals is closely related to the increase in the will and power characteristics of the system. The more rigorously the system is able to exclude all outside resistance in its way, the more likely it may be to reach the particular goal chosen. In this sense, will and power represent the ability to harden and deepen the temporary commitment of attention and resources, and are essential instruments of short-run steering performance, autonomy, and growth.

The sixth group of criteria deals with long-run growth. These include increases in *goal-changing* ability, in the range of different ends the society, culture, or political system is able to choose and to pursue. Here we find learning capacity, not merely in terms of limited operational reserves but also in terms of the capacity for deep rearrangements of inner structure, and thus for the development of radically new functions. Here we list the growth in the possibility of producing genuine *novelty*, of applying some of the resulting new combinations of information to the guidance of behavior as *initiative*, and of producing eventually new patterns in the physical or social environment in processes of *creativity*.

Thus far, all criteria derived from our growth model have applied primarily to the decision system as a whole. However, an essential characteristic of any human organization, in contrast to an anthill, is the interplay between the dimensions of growth of the organization and the growth of the individuals and of the more or less autonomous subgroups that compose it. In this sense the growth of human organizations is always the growth of several levels of autonomous systems, and the autonomous growth and enhanced self-determination of individuals is one of its touchstones. To a lesser but still very real degree, this may apply to the growth of lesser autonomous organizations within the system. The growth of the whole decision system may thus also be "measured" in terms of progress in articulation and multiple autonomy, and thus as progress in what some psychologists have called "integrative behavior." Gains in the capacity for *integrative behavior*—which does not destroy the autonomy of the units integrated—may in turn be related to the ability of a society or state to deal with other societies or states without suicide or mutual destruction. A combined growth in power and in the awareness of limits; in depth of memory and in openness to new ranges of information; in social, intellectual, and emotional resourcefulness and creativity; and in the capacity for integrative behavior; these, taken together, may well be most conducive to survival in international politics.

The Task of Politics: Accelerating Needed Innovation

If we accept provisionally this sketch of the criteria of growth, politics can contribute much to fulfill them. Within the general field of social innovation and social learning, politics can function as the sphere of decision. If we define the core area of politics as the area of enforceable decisions or, more accurately, of all decisions backed by some combination of a significant probability of voluntary compliance with a significant probability of enforcement, then politics becomes the method par excellence for securing preferential treatment for messages and commands and for the reallocation of human or material resources. Politics thus appears as a major instrument for either retarding or accelerating social learning and innovation, and it has been used in both functions in the past. Politics has been used to increase the rigidity of already semipetrified social systems, and it has been used to accelerate ongoing processes of change.[17]

Examples of the conservative function of politics can be found in many cultures. Perhaps it has been a peculiarity of Western politics to have developed a range of significant techniques for accelerating innovation. Perhaps three of the most important of these techniques are majority rule, the protection of minorities, and the institutionalization of dissent.

Autonomous organizations may be prone to overvalue internal or parochial information, as well as familiar data from the past, as against data and information derived from new or wider ranges of experiences. Resistance to change and innovation may thus be one of the "occupational risks" of autonomous organizations. Political patterns requiring unanimity—as does much of Oriental village politics—may tend to slow down the rate of change to a very low level. Majority rule in the Western manner permits, on the contrary, a change to be carried out much earlier and thus much faster. At the same time, Western traditions for the protection of minorities may prevent majority-imposed rates of change from disrupting the integrity and dignity of dissenting individuals or groups, or of breaking the bonds and communication channels of social cohesion. Finally, the institutionalization of dissent, and the provision of acceptable channels and modes for the expression of criticism and self-criticism, of counter-proposals and of new suggestions, protect not merely the majority of yesterday but also provide potential growing points for the majorities of tomorrow. Taken together, majority rule, minority protection, and institutionalized dissent, reinforced by highly conscious, analytical, critical, and combinatorial modes of thought, provide Western societies and political systems with an unusually wide range of resources and instrumentalities for rapid learning and innovation. Even though other cultures may not copy these institutions in their Western shape, they will have to provide by some means for the functions of wide

---

17. For a stimulating discussion of psychological and other aspects of growth and innovation; cf. David C. McClelland, *The Achieving Society* (Princeton: Van Nostrand, 1961), esp. Chap. 10, "Accelerating Economic Growth," pp. 391–437.

exploration and rapid recommitment these Western institutions have performed.

Politics, like all techniques of making and implementing decisions, is not an end in itself. Indeed, we have a range of generous visions, from early Christianity to H. G. Wells, envisaging a state of social development where all social compulsion, and with it all politics, will become obsolete. Whatever one may think of these hopes, politics in the world of today is an essential instrument of social learning. It will be more likely to function as an instrument of survival and growth, rather than destruction, if it is guided by cognitive insights. All studies of politics, and all techniques and models suggested as instruments of political analysis, have this purpose: that men should be more able to act in politics with their eyes open.

This perspective is no less relevant to those among us who see politics chiefly as a contest rather than as a process of awakening. Competition in world politics in the second half of the twentieth century resembles less a tug-of-war than a race; less a hundred-yard dash than a marathon; less a marathon than a slalom; and less a slalom than a combined course in survival, and persuasion, as well as in learning and discovery. In this contest, too, government and politics will long remain indispensable instruments for accelerated social learning, by which mankind in its various subdivisions, still organized in states, can adapt more quickly to the dangerous but hopeful tasks of growing up.

15

The Analytical Prospects of Communications Theory

ROBERT C. NORTH

COMMUNICATION REFERS to a body of basic concepts underlying several contemporary approaches to human behavior—including the interaction of nation states. As used by Warren Weaver, the word includes "all the procedures by which one mind may affect another."[1] This, of course, involves not only written and oral speech, but all human behavior. In an even broader sense it may be used with reference to the ways in which the physical environment excites signals in the central nervous system—together with the ways in which the human being operates upon the physical environment. In these terms the organism and the environment form a single system: the organism affects the environment and the environment affects the organism.[2]

Among pioneers in communication theory was the mathematician, Norbert Wiener. In developing his theory of messages, Wiener used the word *cybernetics,* which he derived from the Greek *kubernētēs,* or "steersman," the same word from which "governor" derives.

Cybernetics, as developed by Wiener and others, is fundamentally a body of theory and technique for the study of probabilities in different but analogous universes such as certain types of machines, animals, individual human beings, societies, and nation-states—and the ways in which message transactions function to control such universes.[3] W. Ross Ashby referred to cybernetics as the study of "all possible machines," the word *machine* being construed to include men and animals as well as inanimate systems.[4]

1. Claude E. Shannon and Warren Weaver, *The Mathematical Theory of Communication* (Urbana: U. of Illinois Press, 1959), p. 95.
2. W. Ross Ashby, *Design for a Brain* (New York: Wiley, 1960), p. 87.
3. Norbert Wiener, *The Human Use of Human Beings* (Garden City: Doubleday, 1956), p. 15.
4. *Ibid.,* p. 2.

Wiener was primarily concerned with the characteristics and processes of feedback systems[5]—systems controlled on the basis of comparing an actual state with some prearranged norm or preferred state and then releasing energy to reduce the difference.[6] "The process of receiving and of using information," Wiener wrote, "is the process of our adjusting to the contingencies of the outer environment, and of our living effectively with that environment."[7]

On mechanical levels a controlled feedback system may be illustrated by thermostatic controls for maintaining desired temperatures within a house, by the self-aiming device of an antiaircraft artillery piece, or the automatic pilot in a ship or aircraft. By force of analogy several of the basic functions of such servomechanisms can be compared with certain minimally necessary, if not sufficient, functions of living systems such as the individual human being, the work team, the corporation or the nation-state. Once these processes are identified, moreover, it should be possible to describe organizations on each level in terms of the probability that its components will perform their appropriate functions. In the long run it should also be possible—with tolerance for insufficient information and random phenomena—to predict the system's behavior and also the conflictual and cooperative or integrating transactions between or among systems.

In his book *The Image*, Kenneth Boulding suggests the ways in which a human being operates according to analogous, complex, highly sophisticated, frequently illusive feedback or cybernetic principles. Each of us maintains an image of *what is* (the thermometer, so to speak) and an image of *what ought to be* (the preferred thermostat temperature setting). In highly oversimplified terms, we behave in various ways in an effort to reduce the gap between these two parts of the image.[8]

Associations, organizations, societies, and the nation-state itself are built upon and held together by communications—by perceptions, by decisions, by the expectations which people maintain of each other, by transactions, and by their willingness to validate a considerable portion of the expectations by appropriate reciprocal behaviors. Politics could not exist without communications, nor could wars be fought. In these terms a modern nation-state may be viewed essentially as a decision and control system which relies upon the exchange of messages in both its domestic affairs and its foreign relations.

Wiener classed communication and control together. "Why did I

5. Cf. Alfred Kuhn, *The Study of Society: A Unified Approach* (Homewood, Ill.: Dorsey Press, 1963), pp. 40–43.

6. Wiener, p. 24.

7. *Ibid.,* p. 18.

8. Kenneth Boulding, *The Image* (Ann Arbor: U. of Michigan Press, 1956), pp. 5, 6, 11.

do this? When I communicate with another person, I impart a message
to him, and when he communicates back to me he returns a related
message which contains information primarily accessible to him and
not to me. When I control the actions of another person, I communicate
a message to him, and although this message is in the imperative mood,
the technique of communication does not differ from that of a message
of fact. Furthermore, if my control is to be effective I must take cognizance of any messages from him which may indicate that the order
is understood and has been obeyed."[9] A state may be viewed as that
part of a society whose function it is to maintain a superordinate decision and control apparatus over the other constituent parts.

The systematic study of communication and control represents, according to Karl Deutsch, "a shift in the center of interest from drives
to steering, and from instincts to systems of decisions, regulation and
control . . ."[10] It is a viewpoint suggesting that all organizations are alike
in certain fundamental characteristics, that every organization is held
together by communication, and that no two or more individuals or
organizations have touch with each other except through channels of
communication, including the human central nervous system. In these
terms, a "society can only be understood through a study of messages
and the communications facilities which belong to it . . ."[11]

How does one go about studying international relations by way of
communications? A first step may involve a mapping of the system to
provide a picture of the actual flows of information within and through
it.[12] In addition to describing the communications network and channels
through which the information flows, an observer may want to know also
about the procedures and rules governing communications within the
system; the instruments of communications; the kinds of information
and messages; the intensities of feeling, and so forth.[13] A great deal
can be learned about an individual, an organization, a nation-state or
other system by examining the configurations and other characteristics
of the environment in which it is embedded, the ways in which that
environment limits, constrains, and otherwise influences the system's
behavior, and how the system operates upon its surroundings.

Elman Service, an anthropologist, has discriminated means of integration on five levels of social-political organization: (1) familistic bonds
of kinship and marriage which integrate the relatively small and simple
societies called bands; (2) pantribal sodalities—such as clans—which
integrate several bandlike societies into a single tribe; (3) functions of

9. Wiener, p. 16.
10. Karl W. Deutsch, *The Nerves of Government* (New York: Free Press,
1963), p. 76.
11. Wiener, p. 16.
12. Deutsch, *op. cit.*, pp. 75–97.
13. Richard C. Snyder, H. W. Bruck and Burton M. Sapin (eds.), *Foreign
Policy Decision-Making* (New York: Free Press, 1962), p. 88.

specialization, redistribution, and related centralization of authority which integrate still more complex societies into what he calls chiefdoms; (4) the state, which is further integrated by a specialized bureaucracy or decision and control system employing a monopoly of legitimized or legal force; and (5) a presumably emerging industrial society, integrated not only by a state decision and control apparatus, but also through a complex network of specialized, interdependent occupations.[14] In this paper we are primarily concerned with nation-states—though Service's propositions raise fundamental questions about the evolution of the state from the more primitive organizational levels.

To a large extent the level and characteristics of social-political organization seem to depend upon the nature of the environment (including the availability of resources), the numbers and density of population, and the level of technology; that is, the extent of the organization of knowledge and skills. Human beings—especially in environments which are neither too hostile nor too benign—increase their knowledge and skills over time by responding to the environment and operating upon it by cybernetic, more or less trial-and-error processes.

Whenever human beings interact in a sustained way we tend to observe the phenomenon of hierarchical peaking, which seems to be characteristic of most organizations including nation-states and coalitions of nation-states. This suggests that under demands and pressures of interaction, human beings are likely to become structured into something like a pecking order, or leadership hierarchy, each more effective individual (or organization) tending to inhibit the initiative of less effective individuals (and organizations) which tend, in turn, to contribute power to the more dominant one. This seems to take place both inside and outside various organizational structures, producing factions, interest groups, political parties, bureaucracies, and bureaucratic echelons (inside); and coalitions, alliances, or blocs (outside, as among relatively sovereign nation-states). At any given juncture such hierarchies (bands, tribes, chiefdoms, states, coalitions of states, and so forth) —together with the frequency and content of communications among them and among their components—are important features in the environmental configuration.[15] Activities of member states in the world community tend to alter and sometimes to transform such configurations.[16]

14. Elman R. Service, *Primitive Social Organization* (New York: Random House, 1962), p. 181; see also George Peter Murdock, "World Ethnographic Sample," *American Anthropologist*, Vol. 59, No. 4 (August 1957), pp. 664–687.

15. William H. Riker, *The Theory of Political Coalitions* (New Haven: Yale U. P., 1962); see also Karl W. Deutsch and J. David Singer, "Multipolar Power Systems and International Stability," *World Politics*, Vol. XVI, No. 3 (April 1964), pp. 390–406.

16. Morton A. Kaplan, *System and Process in International Politics* (New York: Wiley, 1957); see also J. David Singer and Melvin Small, "The Composition and Status Ordering of the International System: 1815–1940," *World Politics*, Vol. XVIII, No. 2 (January 1966), pp. 236–282.

On the nation-state level the individual head of government (and those cabinet members or other advisers and aides who immediately assist him in making policy) constitutes one subsystem in a complex "system of component systems." We might imagine the "head of state system" as lodged in the center of concentric circles of other systems, the outer circle representing the total society of which the nation-state is a specific manifestation—the decision and control component. Beyond the outermost circle lies the foreign environment. This means that the head of state—in the center, so to speak—is the recipient of and responder to a wide range of communications from the domestic subsystems that surround him—from various sectors of his own executive, from other agencies of government, from political parties (including his own), from pressure groups, news media, and the broadly dispersed values of the society itself. How the head of state responds to communications from the foreign environment will depend considerably upon the nature and strength of the communications he receives from these domestic sources—and vice versa.

In undertaking alterations and transformations of the surroundings both individual human beings and interpersonal organizations, including nation-states, respond to environmental events or stimuli (S), including the behavior of other actors, with activities (R), which to one degree or another alter the previous state of affairs. Intervening between the stimulus event (S) and the overt response (R) are various encoding and decoding procedures.

By *decoding* we mean the way the individual or the interpersonal organization receives and processes information from the situation or environment—his internal responses to stimuli (S). These decoding processes include: information translation, that is, the translation of stimuli (S) into neural impulses; information transmission from the periphery of the nervous system toward the decision-making center; information integration in terms of past experience and other information "stored" from the past; and information interpretation and the arousal of feelings about it.

Encoding processes refer to efforts on the part of an individual or an organization to select and execute a response (R) to the environmental event (S) which has excited him. The first set of encoding processes includes the selection of a response plan or response hierarchy and the emotional charged activation of it. These policy and decision-making processes involve the comparison—in terms of appropriateness—of various possible plans or strategies or means-end hierarchies of response on the basis of (a) goals, (b) past experience and habit, (c) emotions and feelings, and the like. Involved also is the activation or emotional charging of one plan or strategy above the others, which then provides a basis for behavior.

The second, third, and fourth sets of encoding processes are the integration of the decisions in terms of specific instrumentalities, the transmission of the decision toward the periphery of the nervous system, and translation of the decision from the code of neural impulses into actions upon the environment.[17]

Among mediating elements within the individual human being we are likely to infer some perception of the universe, of man's role in it, and of the particular position and interactions of the individual himself. There will be habits, preferences, attitudes, identifications, loyalties, perceptions of what is, what ought to be, and what can and cannot be. There will be expectations of "self" and of various "others." Insofar as these perceptions, identifications, loyalties, and habits are shared and reciprocated or complemented by other individuals in the environment we have a basis for community, for custom, for what Durkheim called the *conscience collective*,[18] for law, and for institutions. Indeed, laws and institutions can ve viewed as expectations of interactions validated by more or less habitual responses.

If we ignore internal feedbacks between processes, the typical sequence of events in any human system at any level of complexity would be: (a) exposure to some input pattern; (b) translation of this information into the form or code which this system as a whole is equipped to handle; (c) transmission of this information further into the system along established channels of communication; (d) integration of this information in terms of past experience with the pattern of informational elements available; (e) more or less simultaneous interpretation of and feeling about this information; (f) generation of intent and preliminary activations as the first step in decision-making; (g) integration of these decisions in terms of established instrumentalities and under continuing purposeful guidance of the intention-activation pattern; (h) transmission of these decisions outward toward the periphery of the system along established channels of communication; (i) translation of these decisions out of the code of the system and into actions upon the environment; and (j) emergence of these actions or events into the physical world as a specific output pattern from the system.[19]

With respect to an individual human being, the stimulus (S) and response (R) represent overt observable events—both verbal and nonverbal—in the external environment. The intervening and mediating decoding and encoding processes are normally nonobservable, and consequently their operation and the principles governing them are

17. Charles E. Osgood and Robert C. North, "From Individual to Nation" (Urbana, Ill., and Stanford, Calif., 1963). Mimeographed for limited private distribution only. The definitions are paraphrased from Osgood's original.

18. Emile Durkheim, *The Division of Labor in Society* (New York: Free Press, 1933).

19. Osgood in Osgood and North, *op. cit.*, p. 55.

largely inferred.[20] Basically they are electrochemical in nature. Inherent in the mediating processes are phenomena of perception (or, more precisely, discrimination, interpretation, and evaluation), emotion or affect, memory, values, goals, purposes, intention, selection or intention, activation decision and so forth.

On the nation-state and other interpersonal levels—as with the individual human being—the stimulus (S) and response (R) represent overt observable events—both verbal and nonverbal—in the environment external to the system itself. With respect to such *interpersonal* organizations, moreover, there are possibilities for observing directly many aspects of the internal processes that are not directly observable within the individual.

The decoding and encoding processes that intervene and mediate within a nation-state or other interpersonal system are a combination of electrochemical phenomena occurring within (individual) human evaluators, decision-makers, and the like, together with sign and symbol communications transmitted from person to person orally, in writing, or by gesture, facial expression, or other observable activity. With respect to the behavior of such interpersonal systems, the electrochemical phenomena occurring within individual human components of each system must be inferred to a large extent, rather than directly observed—as with respect to the individual human being as a system. On the other hand, many aspects of the information translation, transmission, integration, interpretation, and other processes (on the input or decoding side), and the intention, activation, decision integration, transmission, and translation processes (on the output or encoding side) are carried out interpersonally and overtly by individual human beings in more or less open communication with each other within the interpersonal system. Many of these can be studied by observing a wide variety of manifest human activities.

A thorough analysis of the decision-making and behavior of a nation-state would thus require examination of many communication channels and of many offices and institutions where information is collected, evaluated, or integrated and where policies or plans and alternate policies or plans are shaped. But depth studies of the personalities, attitudes, and behavior of key individuals in various parts of the nation-state system would also be appropriate, and in many instances basic.

Stimuli (S) serve as inputs into the system, whereas responses (R) constitute the outputs. A stimulus is an event that takes place objectively, without regard to the way in which it is perceived or responded to. A response, on the other hand, is an action of an actor without respect

20. For an appreciation of some of the problems involved see Kenneth Mac-Corquodale and Paul E. Meehl, "On a Distinction Between Hypothetical Constructs and Intervening Variables," *Psychological Review*, Vol. 55 (1948), pp. 95–107.

to his intent or how either he or other actors may perceive or feel about it. Thus, both S's and R's are nonevaluative and nonaffective; that is, there is no good or bad residing in them inherently—they merely exist. The "good" or "bad" (and other evaluative qualities) are bestowed upon them or attributed to them by various perceivers—or "charged into" them by their perpetrators.

In any case, it is not the stimulus event, per se, that we respond to, but its action upon us plus *our interpretation* of that action. This means that an actor's response will be shaped *by his perception* of the stimulus and not necessarily by qualities objectively inherent in it.[21] "What the decision-makers 'see' is what they act upon."[22] My behavior—in terms of my perceptions—may appear perfectly rational and appropriate to me (subjective rationality), whereas you (and indeed the whole of society)—*in terms of your perceptions*—may consider my behavior utterly mad.

The elements of the decoding sector of the individual system are at once discriminative, affective or emotional, and evaluative.

In the nation-state the perception of the stimulus (S) within a decision system corresponds to the "definition of the situation" in the decision-making literature.[23] On the other hand, the encoding sectors include the actor's expressions of his own intentions, plans, predispositions or attitude toward another actor. This portion of the model is similar to the Miller, Galanter, and Pribram[24] concept of the Plan.

The system model includes perceptions of past events "stored," so to speak, in memory or habit structure, and also perceptions of events that may occur, or are likely to occur, or which the actor hopes will occur in the future. Hull refers to the latter antedating situations of this class as expectative. Similarly, the encoding sector refers not only to perceptions of current intent but also to perceptions of what the actor perceives he may intend to do in the future. Thus, "We often know what we are about to do before we perform an act, sometimes long before."[25] This phenomenon is commonly known as goal, or purpose.

Values are public to the extent that discriminative, evaluative, and affective elements are shared by two or more individuals. As such elements are shared by more and more people they tend to become organizational, societal values, or cultural values. A shared plan emerges whenever two or more individuals try to cooperate in order to pursue a

21. Cf. John Locke, *An Essay Concerning Human Understanding*, Vol. I (New York: Dover, 1959), pp. 122–123.

22. Snyder, Bruck, and Sapin, *op. cit.*, p. 66.

23. *Ibid.*; James G. March and Herbert A. Simon, *Organizations* (New York: Wiley, 1958).

24. George A. Miller, Eugene Galanter and Karl H. Pribram, *Plans and the Structure of Behavior* (New York: Holt, 1960).

25. Clark L. Hull, *A Behavior System* (New Haven: Yale U. P., 1952), p. 152.

purpose which they seemingly cannot achieve alone. Each member thus assumes responsibility for the performance of some part of the public plan and thus incorporates it into his personal plan. The sharing of values, preferences, plans, and responses depends upon communication.

In carrying out any part of a personal plan—including relatively simple physical movement—the central nervous system of the individual compares and recompares preparatory activations with recollections of previous similar or analogous movements and also with each other—taking trial sightings, so to speak, "bracketing in" on the desired activity. "The action," according to Miller, Galanter, and Pribram, "is initiated by an 'incongruity' between the state of the organism and the state that is being tested for, and the action persists until the incongruity . . . is removed."[26] According to this view, the fundamental building block of the nervous system is the feedback loop.

By feedback we mean, according to Karl Deutsch, "a communication network that produces action in response to an input of information, and *includes the results of its own action in the new information by which it modifies its subsequent behavior.*"[27] Or, as suggested by Snyder, Bruck, and Sapin, "Feedback refers to the messages about the actions or state of the system which are returned to the system. By means of a continuous flow of such messages it is possible for the decision-makers to have a more or less current picture of the success or failure of their actions and the relative adequacy of the system."[28]

In organizations—including nation-states—as well as within the central nervous system, feedback loops operate within feedback loops, and more feedback loops operate within these.

A communication approach suggests the measurement of transactions of one state (or group) with other states (or groups) by "metering" certain pertinent channels of the system.[29] It also enables the investigator to locate an individual decision-maker within a number of nesting systems—the foreign minister within the cabinet and within the state, for example—and to relate data from each of these levels in an orderly fashion. One may, in effect, install "meter boxes"—any one of a variety of measuring techniques—at four points in the state system: (1) just outside the input gate, so to speak, in order to measure objectively

26. Miller, Galanter, and Pribram, *op. cit.*, p. 26.

27. Deutsch, *op. cit.*, p. 88.

28. Richard C. Snyder, H. W. Bruck, and Burton M. Sapin, *Decision-Making as an Approach to the Study of International Politics* (Princeton: Organizational Behavior Section, Foreign Policy Analysis Project, Foreign Policy Analysis Series No. 3, 1954), p. 88.

29. See also Chadwick F. Alger, "Interaction and Negotiation in a Committee of the United Nations General Assembly" (mimeo.), Third North American Peace Research Society (International), Philadelphia, Pennsylvania, November 14–16, 1965.

existent stimuli from the environment (especially the behavior of other states); (2) "inside" the foreign decision-making group, measuring the leadership's perceptions of and attitudes toward the stimulus events taking place outside; (3) "inside" the foreign decision-making group, measuring the leadership's perceptions of their own state's past, present, and future attitudes, intents, purposes, and preferences toward other actors "outside"; and (4) just "outside" the output gate, in order to measure the overt behavior that the decision-makers put in motion. Of course, it is also possible, whenever appropriate, to measure communications among component parts of a single nation-state system—between the Congress and the President, for example, or between pressure groups and an arm of the government, and so forth.

With respect to measurements, a number of *caveats* need to be mentioned, however. Partly these become necessary because the "outside" stimulus event (S) and the overt behavior (R) can be either verbal or nonverbal. This state of affairs presents us with certain difficulties.

First, even a purely physical, nonverbal "outside" event such as the attack on Pearl Harbor or the establishment of Soviet missile bases in Cuba reaches the decision-maker—and eventually the research investigator—in symbolic, verbal form. There is no way of avoiding this: often our only access to nonverbal, purely physical events lies through symbolic, verbal representation.

Second, overt, physical, nonverbal behavior such as mobilizing an army or mounting an attack is frequently initiated verbally by the decision-maker, the plan or order or command being transmitted through many hands and frequently much elaborated upon. In such instances the verbal commands must be viewed as internal messages between the leader and those agents deputized to perform the physical acts. Thus the plan initiated by the head of government or other top decision-maker with respect to the state system is just that—a statement of intent, not overt behavior (R) *until the order is activated.*

Third, either a stimulus event (S) or a response event (R) may be wholly verbal and symbolic in that it does not—and was not intended to—represent or translate into a physical event. The message *if you do not remove your embargo, we shall attack* is a strictly verbal event which achieves its status through transference of symbolic meaning. It does not command a gun to be fired nor an army to invade. No matter what the recipient may do in response, there is no physical act for which it was the foreshadowing verbal command—the activating message. The total value lay in the meaning of the verbal message, and therefore it is a response (R) of its initiator, and a stimulus (S) for the recipient.

On the other hand—and this is the fourth point—the conditional, purely verbal message *if you do not remove your embargo* is only the initiator's plan or intent *until it is articulated outside the boundaries of the state that issued it.* Thus, unless a top decision-maker transmits it himself directly to the recipient by telephone or voice radio or announces it publicly, it may well be delivered—as with a nonverbal act such as the firing of a gun or dropping of a bomb—by an agent, an ambassador, or other representative deputized to perform this function. The distinction becomes clear in the case of a message from a head of state which is not delivered, or which is transmitted in garbled or otherwise altered form.

The fifth consideration is that a stimulus (S) or a response (R) event usually consists of a complex set of subsidiary events. An attack along a front embraces dozens or hundreds of sector attacks, and a speech with implications of violence can be subdivided into paragraphs or themes or words with more or less implication of violence. This means that the boundaries of an "event" are frequently difficult to define, and whatever designation is used may be wholly arbitrary.

And, finally, the same speech, for example, may qualify as an action (R for the asserting nation and S for a receiver nation) and at the same time contain perceptions of "other" and perceptions of intent from which perceptual, evaluative, and affective data may be inferred for the actor nation. Under these circumstances great care must be taken not to confuse the function of data which are being subjected to a given procedure of analysis—that is, is it action or perceptual, evaluative, or affective content that is being measured, and to which actor is it properly attributed?

Various objections to the communication approach are frequently raised. Since such studies often require primary diplomatic and decision-making documents for analysis, the question is often asked, how can one be certain of the reliability of the documents? The answer is that one uses the same time-honored canons and techniques of verification that the historian uses. A second question frequently raised is, how can you be sure whether or not a decision-maker or diplomat is bluffing or lying? Clearly, one cannot be certain at first glance whether or not *anyone* is bluffing or lying. Indeed, the objective truth is difficult to establish no matter what research technique one is using. However, a well-designed communication study should measure systematically the correlation over time of *what is said* with *what is done,* and it should also uncover—impartially—consistencies and inconsistencies, congruencies and incongruencies, sequiturs and nonsequiturs in all that each actor for whom there is adequate data says and does.

The objection is raised that nation-states and their circumstances differ too much from place to place, culture to culture and time period to time period for comparative analyses to be useful or feasible. However, as pointed out by David Singer, ". . . there is a world of difference between *identical* and *comparable,* and if we could only generalize on the basis of *identical* cases, conditions or experiments, all science would be impossible. . . . All we ask is that the cases be similar enough to be comparable in terms of the specific variables that concern us in any particular inquiry."[30]

The problem of sampling can present very real difficulties. In some types of content analysis, the only safe way is to include *all* the documentation that is available for a given crisis or other decision-making or interaction situation under study. Even if this precaution is taken, there remains the possibility that some unknown quantity of pertinent documentation has been lost, destroyed, or withheld. Not much can be done about this problem other than to monitor alternate channels of communication, if they exist and documents are available, and to compare the correlation of variables with outcomes in a number of similar situations—or in both similar situations and opposed situations (crises, for example, which eventuate in war, as contrasted with crises which have not eventuated in war).

If sources are reasonably adequate, modern techniques for the measurement of both verbal and nonverbal behavior can handle large bodies of data with discrimination, precision, reliability, and replicability. The raw data have to meet certain criteria, however, and procedures have to be followed with care and strict discipline. Valuable statistical tests and controls are available—many of them computer-programmed—but their usefulness can be severely limited by inadequate data or faulty procedure. It is particularly important for the investigator to be exceedingly rigorous in distinguishing intervening variables from hypothetical constructs.[31] Undeniably, too, the techniques tend to be expensive.

Only a few years back a major disadvantage lay in the large number of people—the intellectual serf labor—who had to be employed in content analysis and other communication research techniques. The work was exacting, psychologically debilitating, and neurosis-producing. No one liked to do it, fatigue and disaffection produced errors, and errors were difficult if not impossible to control. Now much of this work has been taken over by computers which—if properly programmed—perform the same functions more rapidly, far more accurately (the margin of error is likely to be negligible), with high replicability, and without the same psychological wear and tear. But the techniques continue to be expensive.

Content analysis offers several standard ways of measuring the mediating sectors of the model. A number of automated systems are now available, and the possibility of running the same data—once punched

30. J. David Singer, *Human Behavior and International Politics* (Chicago: Rand McNally, 1965), p. 11.

31. MacCorquodale and Meehl, *op. cit.*, pp. 95–107.

on cards—through two or more competing programs represents an attractive feature of this type of analysis. A pioneer automated content analysis tool is the General Inquirer, developed by Philip Stone and his associates at Harvard University and M.I.T.[32] The Stanford General Inquirer was adapted from the Stone system for the analysis of diplomatic and decision-making documents.[33] The basic unit of analysis for the Stanford system is the *perception,* which consists of: a perceiving actor (Kennedy, U.S.A., Khrushchev, U.S.S.R., etc.), a perceived actor (Mao, Communist China, Madam Gandhi, India, etc.), an attitude or an action, and a target (Cuba, Castro, Great Britain, Wilson, the Communist Bloc, NATO, etc.). The computer is programmed to isolate these units (together with whatever words are included in them or associated with them), count them, store them, and measure them in terms of emotional or affective content.

By means of the Stanford General Inquirer—among a wide range of possibilities—any dyadic relationship can be measured through time in terms of perceptual combinations like the following:

In his relationship with B, Actor A perceives		In his relationship with A, Actor B perceives	
Self	B	A	*Self*
positive ←	→ positive	positive ←	→ positive
strong ←	→ weak	strong ←	→ weak
active ←	→ passive	active ←	→ passive

or

In his relationship with B, Actor A perceives		In his relationship with A, Actor B perceives	
Self	B	A	*Self*
positive ←	→ positive	positive ←	→ positive
strong ←	→ strong	strong ←	→ weak
active ←	→ active	active ←	→ passive

In the first instance we would expect that A and B would not only like each other, but also that B would lean on A and A would behave supportively toward B. In the second instance, however, B's need and expectation of support from A would probably not be forthcoming. The relationship might prove even more unsymmetrical, of course, if both A and B saw "self" as passive and weak, each depending on the "other"

32. Philip J. Stone, Robert F. Bales, J. Zvi Namenwirth, and Daniel M. Ogilvie, "The General Inquirer: A Computer System for Content Analysis and Retrieval Based on the Sentence as a Unit of Information," *Behavioral Science,* VII (1962), pp. 484–494; and Philip J. Stone *et al., The General Inquires: A Computer Approach to Content Analysis* (Cambridge: The M.I.T. Press, 1966).

33. Ole R. Holsti, "An Adaptation of the 'General Inquirer' for the Systematic Analysis of Political Documents," *Behavioral Science,* IX (1964), pp. 382–388.

for support. An unsymmetrical relationship appears inherently unstable —and under many circumstances—is unlikely to persist for a long period of time.

Another dimension of analysis is added if one examines not only current perceptions, but *expectations of the future.*

The S and R parts of the model can be investigated—and correlated with perceptual, evaluative, and affective data—in a number of different ways. In general, these measurements can be considered properly as two problems: The aggregation of data which are reported in "natural numbers," and the scaling of data for which natural numbers do not exist.

With respect to aggregations reported in natural numbers, we can use communication flows (numbers of letters, numbers of telegrams and the like), financial indices, troop movements, and so forth—provided the appropriate data are available on a more or less daily basis. Studies of the six weeks before the outbreak of war in 1914 have shown that both these types of data are useful. Flows of gold across international boundaries, stock-market fluctuations within the major powers (but *not* in uninvolved nations), commodity futures, and interest rates all revealed high correlations with perceptual, evaluative, and affective changes. Similarly, troop mobilizations and movements also correlated —though it was evident that some affective variations were in response to verbal threats rather than to military and naval maneuvers.

Charles A. McClelland has pioneered in developing objective quantifiable methods of interaction analyses—particularly in studies of the Quemoy and Matsu confrontations.[34] As one aspect of a wide range of investigations, Karl Deutsch has studied transaction flows or indicators of relations between states (and also relations of components within states). He has also used content analysis to gauge distribution of attention and of favorable and unfavorable judgments and value patterns.[35] In his Dimensionality of Nations Project, R. J. Rummel has used factor analysis and other quantitative methods for studying both the conflictual and the cooperative and integrative behavior of states.[36]

34. Charles A. McClelland, Daniel P. Harrison, Wayne R. Martin, Warren R. Phillips, and Robert A. Young, *The Communist Chinese Performance in Crisis and Non-Crisis: Quantitative Studies of the Taiwan Straits Confrontation, 1950–1964.* Final report of completed research under contract for Behavioral Sciences Group, Naval Ordnance Test Station, China Lake, California (W60530-11207), Los Angeles, Calif., December 14, 1965.

35. See, for example, Karl W. Deutsch, "Shifts in the Balance of International Communication Flows," *Public Opinion Quarterly,* Vol. XX (Spring 1956), pp. 143–160; also Bruce M. Russett, Hayward R. Alker, Jr., Karl W. Deutsch, and Harold D. Lasswell, *World Handbook of Political and Social Indicators* (New Haven: Yale U. P., 1964); and Philip E. Jacob and James V. Toscano (eds.), *The Integration of Political Communities* (Philadelphia: Lippincott, 1964).

36. Rudolph J. Rummel, "Unrotated Factor Tables for 236 Variables" (mimeo.), Dimensionality of Nations Project, Yale University, July 1964; R. J. Rummel, "Or-

At the University of Pennsylvania, Philip E. Jacob and associates have been studying the acts of politically relevant persons who make decisions "which either trigger or jam integrative relationships."[37] Chadwick Alger, at Northwestern University, has made numerous studies of interaction and negotiations within the United Nations.[38] There are various other promising techniques and approaches.[39]

One alternative—or supplementary—approach is to look for one or more common dimensions underlying a body of action data. A dimension which is relevant in the study of international relations is the level of *violence* or potential violence in the act. Or an investigator might wish to compare the data along the dimension of generality to specificity of actions. The problem here is somewhat analogous to comparing apples, oranges, and bananas. Although these are all qualitatively different, they share some common characteristics. One can compare them for weight, a relatively simple task. They might also be compared for somewhat harder-to-define characteristics: texture, sweetness, pleasantness of shape, and so on. The latter may be accomplished by one of many available techniques of scaling in which the judge or judges assign ordinal numbers to the various items.

Scaling has at least one major advantage for the student of international relations: Most relevant action data are not reported in quantitative form; for example, "Khrushchev denounced Mao Tse-tung at his

thogonally Rotated Factor Tables for 236 Variables" (mimeo.), Dimensionality of Nations Project, Yale University, July, 1964; R. J. Rummel, "Dimensions of Foreign and Domestic Conflict Behavior: A Review of Empirical Findings" (mimeo.), Yale University, August 1964; R. J. Rummel, "Correlations Between Foreign Conflict Behavior 1955–57 and 1955 National Characteristics" (mimeo.), Dimensionality of Nations Project, Yale University, September 1964; R. J. Rummel, "Dimensions of Dyadic War, 1820–1952" (mimeo.), Research Report prepared in connection with research supported by the National Science Foundation (NSF G-536 and NSF GS-0956), Yale University, January 1966.

37. Philip E. Jacob, "The Influence of Values in Political Integration," in Jacob and Toscano, *op. cit.*, p. 209.

38. Chadwick F. Alger, *op. cit.*; see also "Interaction in a Committee of the United Nations General Assembly," in J. David Singer (ed.), *"Quantitative International Politics," International Yearbook of Political Behavior Research*, Vol. VI (New York: Free Press 1967).

39. Raymond Tanter, "Dimensions of Conflict Behavior Within and Between Nations, 1958–60," *Journal of Conflict Resolution*, Vol. 10, No. 1 (March 1966), pp. 41–64; see, for example, Dina A. Zinnes, "A Comparison of Hostile State Behavior in Simulate and Historical Data" (mimeo.), Department of Political Science, The University of Indiana, 1965; Dina A. Zinnes, "The Expression of Perception of Hostility in Pre-War Crisis: 1914," in J. David Singer (ed.), *"Quantitative International Politics," op. cit.*; see also Martin George Zaninovich, "An Empirical Theory of State Response: The Sino-Soviet Case," Ph.D. Dissertation (Stanford University, 1964); and Robert C. North, Ole R. Holsti, and Richard A. Brody, "Perception and Action in the Study of International Relations: The 1914 Crisis," in J. David Singer (ed.), *International Yearbook of Political Behavior Research* (New York: Free Press, 1967).

news conference of April 15, 1964," or, "Austria-Hungary declared war on Serbia July 28, 1914." But even such apparently disparate items can be quantified along a dimension of shared characteristics.

A common type of scaling is one in which the investigator defines his categories in terms of certain relevant criteria. Each category is then assigned a scale value, and the data are then scaled according to this measure. One might wish to construct a twelve-point scale, for example, to assign rank-order values on a conflict-integration scale. Such a scale, no matter how carefully each category is defined, probably will not avoid the need for some scaling judgments. The advantage of this type of scaling is that, assuming the scale is properly constructed, the measure will yield results which are comparable across two or more cases. A second type of scaling is exemplified by the Q-Sort[40] which has proved useful in a variety of problems ranging from psychiatric research to problems of international relations.[41]

Simulations offer a third broad approach to communication studies —especially the type developed by Harold Guetzkow and his associates.[42] In this connection, the simulation devised by Hermann and Hermann[43] to combine the technique with historical data ought to be particularly useful.

Currently, the communication approach—and appropriate, still developing techniques of measurement—looks extremely promising. At this point it would be premature, however, to settle upon any single model, paradigm, pretheory, or particular set of tools. The most rewarding procedure seems to require, for the time being, at least, the encouragement of alternative models and alternative methods and techniques with the hope that various investigations will serve to cross-check each other—and perhaps reveal important convergences.[44] It is almost

40. Jack Block, *The Q-Sort Method in Personality Assessment and Psychiatric Research* (Springfield, Ill.: Thomas, 1961).

41. Robert C. North, Ole R. Holsti, M. George Zaninovich, and Dina A. Zinnes, *Content Analysis: A Handbook with Application for the Study of International Crisis* (Evanston, Ill.: Northwestern U. P., 1963), pp. 56–77; see also Lincoln E. Moses, Richard A. Brody, Ole R. Holsti, Joseph B. Kadane, and Jeffrey S. Milstein, "Scaling Inter-Nation Action Data" (Stanford Univ., mimeo., 1966).

42. Harold Guetzkow, "A Use of Simulation in the Study of International Relations," Behavioral Science, Vol. IV (1959), pp. 183–191; Harold Guetzkow (ed.), *Simulation in Social Science* (Englewood Cliffs, N.J.: Prentice-Hall, 1962); and Harold Guetzkow, Chadwick F. Alger, Richard A. Brody, Robert C. Noel, and Richard C. Snyder, *Simulation in International Relations: Developments for Research and Teaching* (Englewood Cliffs, N.J.: Prentice-Hall, 1963).

43. Charles F. Hermann and Margaret G. Hermann, "On the Possible Use of Historical Data for Validation Study of the Inter-Nation Simulation," report prepared for the U.S. Naval Ordnance Test Station, China Lake, California (Department of Political Science, Northwestern University, 1962).

44. Robert C. North, "International Relations: Putting the Pieces Together," *Background*, Vol. 7, No. 3 (November, 1963), pp. 119–130; see also Herbert C.

self-evident that communication approaches and general systems and decision-making approaches are complementary. In the long run several competing measurement devices are likely to prove reciprocally reinforcing in somewhat analogous ways.

Kelman (ed.), *International Behavior: A Social-Psychological Analysis* (New York: Holt, 1965); Dean Pruitt, "An Analysis of Responsiveness Between Nations," *Journal of Conflict Resolution*, VI (1962), pp. 5–8; Elton B. McNeil (ed.), *The Nature of Human Conflict* (Englewood Cliffs, N.J.: Prentice-Hall, 1965); and Herbert A. Simon, *Models of Man, Social and Rational* (New York: Wiley, 1957).

16

The Theory of Political Development

FRED W. RIGGS

THE EMERGENCE during the last two decades of a swarm of new states born out of the holocaust of World War II and the collapse of empires has presented political science with a great challenge —a challenge which we are, indeed, only numbly beginning to appreciate. These emerging states have confronted political scientists in America with a range of qualitatively new problems which have already begun to influence every traditional field of governmental studies and may some day lead to a restructuring of the whole discipline.

An essay on the "theory of political development" can be used to survey some critical problems in the methodology and theory of political science. In doing so the preliminary and provisional character of the survey must be stressed. It is too easy to jump from a suggestive phrase to an unfounded conclusion. The mere enunciation of a topic, "theory of political development," already seems to imply that there is such a "theory," and that we are talking about something real when we refer to "political development." In fact, of course, there is as yet no such theory, although there are a host of speculations and even hypotheses. Nor is there any consensus on the meaning of the word *development* in this context, or even, for that matter, of the word *political*.

Yet the phrase remains attractive, even useful, as a sign pointing to recesses where hidden treasures may lie. It is faith in the existence, nay, the accessibility, of these riches which lures adventurous political scientists on this venture into the unknown. The study of political behavior in the "new states" and the "old societies" of Asia, Africa, and Latin America promises not only intrinsic attractions but extrinsic rewards for our discipline.[1] It has interdisciplinary attractions also, es-

1. For an alluring prospectus, see Edward Shils, "On the Comparative Study of the New States," in Clifford Geertz (ed.), *Old Societies and New States: The Quest for Modernity in Asia and Africa* (New York: Free Press, 1963), pp. 1–26.

pecially when the topic is defined as the "politics of modernization," and for scholars committed to the campaign for a better world, the appeal may be to "nation-building."[2]

It is in this sense, not that any theory has yet been fashioned or even that an area of inquiry has yet been clearly marked out, but rather in the confident hope with which one embarks on a treasure hunt—perhaps better, on a "fishing expedition"—that this essay is written. It will have three parts: first, an examination of the primary impact of the interest in new states on the study of comparative government as redefined by the term "comparative politics"; second, an assessment of the idea of "political development" as a recently defined focus of attention; and third, some thoughts on a possible direction for the generation of relevant theory.

The Forward Thrust in
Comparative Politics

Perhaps the most notable impact on political science from the study of politics in the "third world"—to borrow from the Europeans a term which seems more apt than such phrases as "developing countries" and "transitional societies"—has already been made in the field of comparative government. A provocative blast, which served to launch this revisionist movement, was set off by Roy Macridis in 1955. The study of comparative government, he argued, was parochial, insufficiently theoretical in orientation, and formalistic.[3]

Macridis' ideas were based on discussions held during the summer of 1952 at a seminar at Northwestern University sponsored by the Social Science Research Council. The interest provoked by this seminar led to the formation by the SSRC of a Committee on Comparative Politics under the chairmanship of Gabriel Almond. This committee has undoubtedly exerted a major influence on the whole field of comparative government, primarily by bringing the political problems of the third world within the range of vision of students who had previously focused

2. See, for example, David E. Apter, *The Politics of Modernization* (Chicago: U. of Chicago Press, 1965) and Karl W. Deutsch and William J. Foltz (eds.), *Nation-Building* (New York: Atherton, 1963).

3. Roy C. Macridis, *The Study of Comparative Government* (New York: Doubleday, 1955). Macridis subsequently presented his ideas at a meeting of the International Political Science Association, provoking Gunnar Heckscher to write his critical reactions and assessments in *The Study of Comparative Government and Politics* (New York: Macmillan, 1957). The work of the SSRC seminar at Northwestern University on which this statement was based is reported in "Research in Comparative Politics," *APSR*, Vol. XLVII, No. 3 (September 1953), pp. 641–657.

their attention primarily on the "first world" of the Western democracies and the "second world" of the Soviet bloc. In the years which followed, the study of comparative politics became both fashionable and intellectually exciting. Although the established approach to comparative government as an examination of salient institutional and behavioral characteristics of the major foreign powers persisted, a new focus of attention arose based on studies in the non-Western countries.[4]

Interest in the politics of the third world branched off in two divergent though interrelated directions, reacting not only on the study of comparative government, but also on other subfields of political science. These trends involve first, the use of quantitative and behavioral methods, and second, the strengthening of "area studies" and cross-disciplinary integrations.

Quantitative Methods in Comparative Politics

The rise of interest in political behavior, including the use of survey data and studies of public opinion and voting patterns, antedates the rise of comparative politics. However, modes of quantitative analysis seem to have taken a long time to become established in the study of comparative politics. Yet the logical necessity of this approach should have been apparent from the beginning. As the number of countries subjected to analysis increased, it became increasingly clear that no one could be expected to learn and remember the mushrooming array of information about each of the more than 130 members of the United Nations. Could not measurable information about each of these states be compiled and used to provide in compact and truly comparable form a way of studying and understanding these numerous polities? Even more, would not such quantitative methods at least provide a means to validate general propositions about political systems at the macro level, enabling political science to progress from the idiographic description of a few states to the nomothetic analysis of many? Through analytic quantitative approaches, indeed, political behavior and comparative government might even merge into a single whole.

One of the first men to promote quantitative studies in this fashion was Karl Deutsch. He announced his program in 1961,[5] proposing to

4. Among the early landmarks in this new literature were George Mc.T. Kahin, Guy J. Pauker and Lucian Pye, "Comparative Politics of non-Western Countries," *APSR*, Vol. XLIX, No. 4 (December 1955), pp. 1022–1041; Lucian W. Pye, "The Non-Western Political Process," *The Journal of Politics*, Vol. XX (August 1958), pp. 468–486, and most influentially, Gabriel A. Almond and James S. Coleman (eds.), *The Politics of the Developing Areas* (Princeton: Princeton U. P., 1960).

5. Karl Deutsch, "Social Mobilization and Political Development" *APSR*, Vol. LV, No. 3 (September 1961), pp. 493–514. The basic theoretical framework had been spelled out earlier by Deutsch in *Nationalism and Social Communication* (New York: Wiley, 1953).

utilize the measurable indicators of "social mobilization" for cross-national comparisons, in conjunction with other indices which could be related to political development. One sequel was the establishment of the Yale Political Data Program and the subsequent publication by this Program of several important volumes.[6] A comparable effort, started quite independently, led to the publication in 1963 of the *Cross-Polity Survey* by Banks and Textor.[7]

The work of Banks and of Deutsch and his associates involves the use of parametric or aggregate data that characterize whole political systems. Clearly these methods can be used for subpolities as well. Thus they can be extended to the comparative study of state and local government in the United States and, for that matter, to the examination of subnational jurisdictions in other countries as well. By this means the study of local government, which had been languishing, has already started to show signs of new vitality, and the boundaries between "local government" and "comparative government" have been eroded.

Quantitative methods have also been particularly useful in the study of individual political behavior. As yet the effective utilization of survey data for cross-national studies is in its infancy. Despite many acknowledged weaknesses, however, the pioneering study by Almond and Verba of a few of the more "developed" polities has already established a model for others to follow.[8] Almond himself has now launched a more ambitious follow-up study of some of the "less-developed" countries.

The Center for International Studies at M.I.T. has also taken a lead in promoting cross-cultural studies based on survey data. Daniel Lerner's studies utilizing survey data from Middle Eastern countries have proven a landmark in this regard.[9] Fred Frey and his colleagues at M.I.T. have continued to carry out and promote field research in selected countries utilizing returns from increasingly sophisticated survey methods.[10]

The Inter-University Consortium for Political Research, with its head-

6. Most notable has been the *World Handbook of Political and Social Indicators* by Bruce M. Russett, Hayward R. Alker, Jr., Karl W. Deutsch, and Harold D. Lasswell (New Haven: Yale U. P., 1964), and the companion volume, *Comparing Nations: The Use of Quantitative Data in Cross-National Research*, edited by Richard L. Merritt and Stein Rokkan (New Haven: Yale U. P., 1966).

7. Arthur S. Banks and Robert B. Textor, *A Cross-Polity Survey* (Cambridge: M.I.T. Press, 1963).

8. Gabriel A. Almond and Sidney Verba, *The Civic Culture* (Princeton: Princeton U. P., 1963).

9. Daniel Lerner, *The Passing of Traditional Societies: Modernizing the Middle East* (New York: Free Press, 1958).

10. See, for example, Frederick W. Frey, *The Turkish Political Elite* (Cambridge: M.I.T. Press, 1965). A sophisticated exploration of the problems involved in the use of quantitative data both to test hypotheses about political development, and also to suggest new ones, is presented by Raymond Tanter in "Toward a Theory of Political Development," Paper for the Midwest Political Science Convention, Chicago, Ill., April 29, 1966 (mimeo.) 36 pp.

quarters at the University of Michigan, was set up to facilitate research in American political behavior, with a focus on electoral statistics and legislative roll calls, but it subsequently expanded the range of its interests in domestic politics, and has begun to venture in tentative fashion into the field of cross-national studies. The International Data Library and Reference Service of the University of California (Berkeley) is collecting sample survey data from Asia and Latin America and encouraging their use by social science for comparative analysis, including political aspects. Other universities—such as U.C.L.A., Stanford, Michigan State, Pennsylvania, and Yale—are beginning to sponsor cross-national comparative studies of political and related phenomena, utilizing both survey and aggregative statistical data.

A Council of Social Science Data Archives, headquartered in New York, with William Glaser as executive director, has now been established to help strengthen the data archives of more than a dozen cooperating universities. Hopefully this activity will make quantitative data more readily available to political scientists interested in comparative politics and administration. Drawing on survey data revealing the characteristics and attitudes of individuals, students of comparative politics will tend to converge in their interests with the students of American political behavior.

Interesting as all these developments in the utilization of quantitative materials for the comparative study of political systems may be, the gap between the data available and valid theories of political development remains a wide one. As Brian Berry points out in a review of the Yale *Handbook*, attempts to draw inferences from cross-national comparative studies regarding stages of development are very questionable. He admits that the data do demonstrate differences in "levels," but he points out, "levels and stages are not the same thing. The former is a static, cross-sectional concept, and the latter is a dynamic, sequential, longitudinal concept."[11] Hopefully the use of longitudinal data, more of which seem to be available than one might initially think, will deepen the usefulness of statistical information and contribute more richly to the formulation and testing of developmental theory. Meanwhile the gap remains broad, and much more can be done from the other side to improve the theoretical speculations about political development which now prevail. Let us approach an examination of this dimension of our subject by taking a look at postwar tendencies in the study of comparative politics

---

11. Brian J. L. Berry, "By What Categories May a State Be Characterized?" *Economic Development and Cultural Change,* Vol. XV, No. 1 (October 1966), p. 93. The same point is made independently by Michael Haas who writes, ". . . do intercorrelations among cross-sectional slices of a large number of countries at one point in time constitute acceptable tests of development theory?" "Aggregate Analysis," *World Politics,* Vol. XIX, No. 1 (October 1966), p. 107.

which have used the conventional models of comparative government
as a point of departure.

Area Studies in Comparative Politics

The main stream of research and conceptualization in the study of
comparative politics since the war flows from, and constitutes also a
reaction against, the traditions of comparative government as they had
become established during the interwar years. Quite in contrast to the
narrowing of focus which characterizes the quantitative approach, the
prevailing framework for comparative government rested primarily on
case studies of individual polities. Insisting that governmental systems
could only be understood in the total context of their cultural and
historical settings, the new approach in comparative politics expanded
the analysis of political institutions and structures to include a wide
range of ecological forces, thereby converging with the contemporary
movement to establish "area studies" as an interdisciplinary framework
for understanding selected world regions.

Whereas the quantitative approach seeks to abstract from the rich
complexity of real life a few measures or indices which are relatively
amenable to quantification and therefore to comparison, the "area approach" directs attention to the unique variety of particular historic,
geographic, and cultural situations. The former approach is "nomothetic"
where the latter is "idiographic."

The area approach differs from the traditional one in comparative
government, therefore, insofar as it draws more heavily on related disciplines, notably on cultural anthropology, but also on human geography, ecology, and modern history. Two reasons may be given. As
political scientists turned their attention to Asia, Africa, and Latin
America, they found that scholars from these related disciplines had
already made a good start. The cultures of diverse African tribes had
been mapped by anthropologists and ethnographers, and the ancient
civilizations of Asia and the Middle East had been outlined by historians and Orientalists. Political scientists, building on the work already
done, were necessarily affected by the outlook and methodology prevalent in other social sciences.

But there was a more important reason also. It had been possible
to think about government in Western countries as a separate subject
of study because of the relatively high degree of structural differentiation which prevailed there. To a considerable degree one could de-
marcate in the United States, in England, France, Germany, and even
in the Soviet Union, a separate sphere of life identifiable as political
and administrative, a set of concrete social structures which could be

called governments. The methods and concepts of political science had, accordingly, been built around the study of these institutions. One found, for example, identifiable boundaries between state and local governments on the one hand, and central governments on the other. The organs of government—legislative, judicial, administrative—lent themselves to study as discrete fields of analysis. Gradually political parties, interest groups, and voting behavior secured recognition as parallel fields of specialization. In a world of sovereign states who regarded their mutual relationship as subject to regulation by international law, the field of international politics and law also came into existence.

In the new states of Asia, Africa, and to some degree even in Latin America, these formal distinctions made little sense. In the third edition of their text, Carter, Ranney, and Hertz assert that there are three main types of political system: the presidential, the parliamentary, and the Communist. Not only was it possible to classify Western polities in these terms, but the contemporary states of the rest of the world also seemed to fall into these three categories.[12]

As they described the characteristics of non-Western polities under these headings, however, the authors of this text encountered grave difficulties. They found that, although a state might have, on paper, a presidential or a parliamentary form of government, the actual behavior of legislatures, chief executives, courts, and political parties was quite different from the patterns familiar in Western societies. Should one call a polity "parliamentary" if the legislature did not, in fact, determine the choice of prime minister and cabinet, even though by charter it was supposed to have this prerogative?

In short, the established modes of analysis in comparative government tended to break down when confronted with the realities of non-Western politics. One apparent solution was simply to add a new noninstitutional category of "non-Western" system to the prevalent typologies. This could be done, however, only by admitting that formal structures were not definitive, and that governments were essentially reflections of an underlying dynamism or "political culture." An early protagonist of this view was Gabriel Almond, who suggested that all political systems might be classified under such sociological headings as Anglo-American, Continental European, totalitarian and "pre-industrial."[13]

Almond himself soon moved beyond this position as the many vari-

12. Gwendolen M. Carter, John H. Hertz, and John C. Ranney, *Major Foreign Powers*, 3rd ed., (New York: Harcourt, 1957) pp. 666 ff.

13. Gabriel Almond, "Comparative Political Systems," *Journal of Politics*, Vol. XVIII, No. 3 (August 1956), pp. 391–409. For an incisive critique of this scheme of classification see Arthur L. Kalleberg, "The Logic of Comparison," *World Politics*, Vol. XIX, No. 1 (October 1966), pp. 69–82.

ations among non-Western polities became evident. A broad spectrum was soon drawn between "traditional" "transitional," and "modern." In the absence of a more detailed classification scheme, one solution seemed to be to view every polity as unique, understandable only in terms of its own idiosyncratic identity. By combining the full range of data provided by history, geography, cultural anthropology, language study, and empirical observations of government at work one might hope to gain a particularistic insight into the operations of each one of these new and exotic polities.

This point of view informed the writings of a new outpouring of country studies, oriented toward the politics (and sometimes also the administration) of government, written by members of the Committee on Comparative Politics and others who were influenced by it.[14]

Each of these works had its own rationale, its own particular focus and methodology. Any characteristic of the society under investigation which seemed to the author relevant to the operation of its political system was eligible for inclusion in the analysis. To the extent that a general theoretical framework characterizes these works, it would be the "input-output" model of any political system presented by Gabriel Almond in the introductory chapter of *Politics of Developing Areas*.[15] Frequently they stressed the "input" functions, notably interest articulation and aggregation, with particular reference to the role of interest groups.

Yet it was precisely here that the area approach to a study of comparative politics began to show its inherent limitations. The input-output framework had been formulated as an attempt to specify the

14. Representative examples include:

David Apter, *Ghana in Transition* (rev. ed.) (New York: Atheneum, 1963); *The Political Kingdom of Uganda: A Study in Bureaucratic Nationalism* (Princeton: Princeton U. P., 1961);

Leonard Binder, *Iran: Political Development in a Changing Society* (Berkeley: U. of California Press, 1962); *Religion and Politics in Pakistan* (Berkeley: U. of California Press, 1961);

James S. Coleman, *Nigeria: Background to Nationalism* (Berkeley, U. of California Press, 1959);

Herbert Feith, *The Decline of Constitutional Democracy in Indonesia* (Ithaca: Cornell U. P., 1962);

Joseph LaPalombara, *Interest Groups in Italian Politics* (Princeton: Princeton U. P., 1964);

Lucian Pye, *Politics, Personality, and Nation Building: Burma's Search for Identity* (New Haven: Yale U. P., 1962);

Fred W. Riggs, *Thailand: The Modernization of a Bureaucrat Polity* (Honolulu: East-West Center Press, 1966);

Myron Weiner, *The Politics of Scarcity: Public Pressure and Political Response in India* (Chicago: U. of Chicago Press, 1962);

W. Howard Wriggins, *Ceylon: Dilemmas of a New Nation* (Princeton: Princeton U. P., 1960).

15. Cited, note 4 above.

universal functional requisites of any political system. Comparative politics at this point showed its great indebtedness to sociology, especially to the structural-functional models formulated by Talcott Parsons and his followers.

More than that, it tended to regard the governmental system as a dependent variable, an epiphenomenon based on social, psychological, cultural, and economic determinants, or at best as a mode of processing "inputs" generated by these forces and converting them into governmental "outputs." The capacity to see politics as itself an essential, indeed a formative, variable in processes of social change was almost lost. Irony lay in the fact that, of all kinds of social systems, the transitional societies of the "third world" are the ones in which governmental initiatives mean the most. Not so much is lost by regarding governments in traditional societies as mere reflections of social structures, and in modern societies as a way of institutionalizing parallelograms of social pressures. But in the "developing" countries, it is precisely the power-holding political elites that seek, through governmental action, to reshape society and drive it into a new world.[16]

By its stress on the input-output model, whether based on economics or general systems theory, the new studies in comparative politics revealed another weakness based on the use of models drawn from other social sciences. At the risk of some simplification, let us note that it is possible for a society to become institutionalized as a corporate entity, fulfilling the requirements of a formal organization. These requirements include a definite membership, plus the ability to formulate collective goals or norms and to implement them. At least ideally speaking, the modern nation-state meets these requirements. It takes all the permanent residents of a specified domain (including those temporarily abroad) as its members (citizens). It has procedures for adopting collective goals or norms—these include the "input" processes of interest articulation and aggregation and the "output" processes of rule-application and rule-adjudication. To link these functions together, it has processes of communication, on the output as well as the input side. To maintain the system, it has processes for recruiting members to its key governmental roles, and for conditioning citizens to accept and comply with their rights and responsibilities. These are the pattern maintenance functions of political and administrative socialization.

Modern Western polities can be analyzed quite well in terms of these categories. The model, indeed, is an equilibrium system which seems to fit the most developed polities. But ironically the scheme was devised primarily as a tool for the study of non-Western polities. Yet

16. Halpern, Manfred, "Toward Further Modernization of the Study of New Nations," *World Politics,* Vol. XVII (October 1964), pp. 157–181. See p. 165 for a parallel argument.

it was precisely here that the tool showed its limitations. To a greater or less degree not only all non-Western societies, but also all premodern and traditional Western societies, have not been institutionalized in the model of a formal organization. To a considerable extent they were unable to formulate collective goals and norms, and their subjects did not recognize as authoritative policies which they had no share in making.

A more relevant model could be found in the structure of international politics which exists in the world today. Although the United Nations may claim the right to make decisions that are authoritative for all states, in fact its ability to enforce its decisions is limited, and many states, including members as well as nonmembers, are prone to reject its official decisions when they do not like them. To a considerable extent, moreover, relations between the states are based on reciprocal influence patterns, not on collective goal-setting processes, and not all states, as we have mentioned, are members. Thus the pattern of international politics can be thought of as an arena in which struggles for power and influence continuously occur. Balance-of-power considerations, the desire to avoid war, the fear of small powers and the aggressiveness of great powers: these are the elements of decision-making in such an arena. At this point let us observe that comparative politics and international relations have a great affinity.[17]

It is perhaps unnecessary to labor the matter.[18] More to the point, even if the political system model could not apply directly, it did provide a good starting point. A different question now needed to be raised. Under what conditions and in what manner do "political systems" of the injut-output type come into existence? The question that arose, in other words, concerned the nature of "political development." Quite apart from the fascinating questions which arose concerning the politics of countries in the third world, a different order of problem had also made its appearance. Was it possible (and was it also desirable) for countries whose polities were not organized in the input-output fashion to transform themselves—with or without external intervention and help—so as to achieve a political system which could be thought of as more "developed"?

At this point another discipline, which has not yet been mentioned in this paper, made its influence felt: economics. In 1960 Rostow had

17. Parallels between the international system and politics in transitional societies were drawn in my essay, "International Relations as a Prismatic System," *World Politics*, Vol. XIV, No. 1 (October 1961), pp. 144–181. See also, in this context, Herbert J. Spiro, *World Politics: The Global System* (Homewood, Ill.: Dorsey, 1966), especially pp. 249–293.

18. I have already pointed to some of the difficulties involved in applying the Almondian "political system" model to developing countries in "The Theory of Developing Polities," *World Politics*, Vol. XVI, No. 1 (October 1963), pp. 147–171.

published his essay on stages of economic growth.[19] The possibility that there were corresponding or similar stages of political development became a fascinating subject of speculation. At the same time, Americans engaged in technical-assistance programs overseas became increasingly aware that unless the political systems of these countries were able to maintain stability and deal with critical problems of growth and change, American foreign policy goals would be negated. Yet they recognized that little could be done as a matter of deliberate U.S. policy to influence the course of political change without running extreme risks. But even if such policies had been practicable, it became clear that we still know very little about how social systems change and how modern political systems come into existence.

Political Development as a New Focus

It was against this background that a new emphasis began to appear among scholars interested in comparative politics, an interest in "political development." By raising a critical theoretical problem, the study of political development promises to accomplish several unintended by-products. It may well provide a bridge between the quantitative-behavioral and the area-studies approaches to comparative politics described above. Perhaps more importantly, by raising some key theoretical issues, it may well bring normative political philosophy and empirical political theory into closer relation to the central concerns of political science, for the study of political development raises again in urgent form some of the perennial issues which have perplexed political thinkers from Plato and Aristotle to Bentley and Lasswell.

Normative aspects of the subject were raised in the Spring of 1961 when the Brookings Institution sponsored a conference on the theme, "Research Needs for Development Assistance Programs." One of the papers for this conference, entitled "Foreign Assistance and Political Development," was prepared by Howard Wriggins, a political scientist then on the policy planning staff of the State Department.[20] Wriggins undertook to spell out some of the functions performed by government in the more developed polities. He suggested that to the extent that any state was unable to fulfill these functions, it was politically under-

19. W. W. Rostow, *The Stages of Economic Growth* (London: Cambridge U. P., 1960).

20. The conference papers were published as Robert E. Asher, et al., *Development of the Emerging Countries: An Agenda for Research* (Washington, D.C.: Brookings Institution, 1962).

developed. By contrast with the earlier Almond model, functionalism was used here to specify the functional requisites of a developed polity, rather than to describe the functions performed in any political system. Actually, both models referred to characteristics of polities which had been institutionalized as formal organizations, and neither specified the stages of development by which polities had in the past, or could in the future, reach this level of development.[21] Another early effort to make the concept of political development operational was published by Philips Cutright in 1963. He formulated a statistical index of levels of political development in terms of degrees of democratization as measured by parliamentary and election records, political stability, and other criteria.[22]

The Committee on Comparative Politics

It remained for the Committee on Comparative Politics, however, to make the theme of political development a major focus of theoretical attention and inquiry. In 1963 Gabriel Almond proposed a new theoretical framework designed to relate his political system concept to the problems of political change.[23] Two years later he wrote another essay explicitly advocating a developmental framework for the study of political systems.[24] That he has not abandoned this approach may be judged from the publication in 1966 of a new book devoted to the comparative analysis of political systems from a developmental viewpoint.[25]

Concurrently the Committee on Comparative Politics sponsored a series of conferences and institutes leading to the publication of a set of volumes exploring various aspects of political development.[26]

It would be interesting and instructive to trace the evolution of the

21. A more recent discussion of the definitional problem by von der Mehden lists thirteen criteria of a "developed" political system, but rejects this line of reasoning as a useful basis for the study of development politics. Fred R. von der Mehden, *Politics of the Developing Nations* (Englewood Cliffs, N.J.: Prentice-Hall, 1964), p. 6.

22. Philips Cutright, "National Political Development: Measurement and Analysis," *American Sociological Review,* Vol. XXVIII (April 1963), pp. 253–264. The essay by Deutsch suggesting measurable indices of political development cited in footnote 5 above, was published in 1961.

23. Gabriel A. Almond, "Political System and Political Change," *American Behavioral Scientist,* Vol. VI, No. 10 (June 1963), pp. 3–10.

24. Gabriel A. Almond, "A Developmental Approach to Political Systems," *World Politics,* Vol. XVII (January 1965), pp. 183–215.

25. Gabriel A. Almond and G. Bingham Powell, *Comparative Politics: A Developmental Approach* (Boston: Little, Brown, 1966).

26. Lucian Pye (ed.), *Communications and Political Development* (Princeton: Princeton U. P., 1963).

Joseph LaPalombara (ed.), *Bureaucracy and Political Development* (Princeton: Princeton U. P., 1963).

concept of political development reflected in these volumes. For example, in the communications volume, published in 1963, Pye writes in his introduction that political development can be thought of in terms of "cultural diffusion, and of adapting, fusing, and adjusting old patterns of life to new demands. From an historical perspective it is possible to conceive of the evolution of the nation-state system as a basic element supporting the gradual diffusion throughout all societies of what we might call a world culture."[27]

By 1965 Pye had come to share a view that was generally adopted by members of the Comparative Politics Committee. In the introduction to his political culture volume, he writes:

The key elements of political development involve, first, with respect to the population as a whole, a change from widespread subject status to an increasing number of contributing citizens, with an accompanying spread of mass participation, a greater sensitivity to the principles of *equality*, and a wider acceptance of universalistic laws. Second, with respect to governmental and general systemic performance, political development involves an increase in the *capacity* of the political system to manage public affairs, control controversy, and cope with popular demands. Finally, with respect to the organization of the polity, political development implies greater structural *differentiation*, greater functional specificity, and greater integration of all the participating institutions and organizations. (ital. added)[28]

Coleman adopts the same criteria in his introduction to the volume on education and political development. He states that the efforts of the committee to arrive at a "clearer working conception of the political development process have suggested the notion of a development syndrome" including the following three principles: differentiation, equality, capacity. He promises a fuller elaboration of these ideas in the final volume of the political development series.[29]

Meanwhile Pye himself has published further personal reflections on the concept of political development.[30] In this essay Pye points to

Robert E. Ward and Dankwart A. Rustow, *Political Modernization in Japan and Turkey* (Princeton: Princeton U. P., 1964).

James S. Coleman (ed.), *Education and Political Development* (Princeton: Princeton U. P., 1965).

Lucian W. Pye and Sidney Verba, *Political Culture and Political Development* (Princeton: Princeton U. P., 1965).

Joseph LaPalombara and Myron Weiner, *Political Parties and Political Development* (Princeton: Princeton U. P., 1966).

Leonard Binder, James S. Coleman, Joseph LaPalombara, Lucian W. Pye, and Myron Weiner, *Crises in Political Development* (Princeton: Princeton U. P., in press).

27. Pye, *Communications, op. cit.*, p. 19.

28. Pye, *Political Culture, op. cit.*, p. 13.

29. Coleman, *Education, op. cit.*, p. 15.

30. Lucian W. Pye, "The Concept of Political Development," *Annals of the American Academy of Political and Social Science*, Vol. 358 (Spring 1965), pp. 1–13. Subsequently reproduced as Chap. 4 in his book, *Aspects of Political Development* (Boston: Little, Brown, 1966), pp. 31–48.

the great variety of meanings attached to the term, "political development." He includes the following: political prerequisite of economic development; politics typical of industrial societies; political modernization; the operation of a nation-state; administrative and legal development; mass mobilization and participation; the building of democracy; stability and orderly change; mobilization and power; and one aspect of a multidimensional process of social change.[31]

After summarizing briefly the arguments for each of these positions, with useful citations to the relevant literature, Pye speaks again of the "development syndrome" and mentions the principles of equality, capacity, and differentiation as key ingredients on which "there does seem to be a more solid basis of agreement."[32]

It is striking that in all these discussions one finds continually references to criteria by which a *politically developed* system can be identified, but not, it seems to me, any serious consideration of the *stages* by which a primitive or traditional society, through whatever transitional stages, might have evolved in the past, or be expected to change in the future, in order to achieve the conditions prescribed as necessary for a developed polity. The voluminous writings in the Princeton University Press series on political development are full of fascinating and informative detail about conditions and problems in countries described as politically "underdeveloped," but they give few specifications of the stages or dynamics of change from less to more developed polities.

Ward and Rustow, it is true, direct attention to the need for such a "dynamic" analysis as contrasted with the normal type of "static" comparisons of political systems. "It would help enormously," they write,

if we had a larger measure of understanding of how societies which are, in a relative sense at least, considered "advanced" came to achieve their present levels of economic, social, and political "development." Are there regularities to be found among their several developmental experiences? Are there discernible stages or sequences of change through which all or some tend to pass? Or, at least, do they face similar problems or crises and do these occur in some regular sort of sequence?[33]

Without providing an answer to their own questions, the Ward and Rustow volume goes on to give a wealth of historical and interpretative information about selected aspects of the developmental history of Japan

---

31. *Aspects . . .* , *op. cit.*, pp. 33–44. Another classification of the divergent meanings or models used in the study of political development may be found in Robert A. Packenham, "Approaches to the Study of Political Development," *World Politics*, Vol. XVII, No. 1 (October 1964), pp. 108–120. Packenham uses the following classification of approaches: legal-formal, economic, administrative, social system, political culture (including personality theory), and mentions also "geographical" and "stages of modernization" approaches. The notes to Packenham's essay also provide an excellent selected bibliography of the literature.

32. *Ibid.*, p. 45–47.

33. Ward and Rustow, *op. cit.*, p. 11.

and Turkey. In the concluding chapter the two editors collaborate again in an essay which specifies some of the developmental crises that seem to be encountered by countries going through the processes of modernization. These, of course, are the crises to be discussed in greater detail by the final volume in the series—still unpublished at this writing. However, the essential characteristics of these crises are described by Pye under the following headings: identity, legitimacy, penetration, participation, integration, and distribution. He suggests that in England these crises occurred in the sequence of their listing above, but that in other countries they may occur in a different order. It is also apparent that these crises are easier to solve if they come one at a time, but become more difficult to cope with if several come close together.[34]

No doubt the analysis of the problems to be solved by political systems in the process of their own transformation constitutes an important contribution to the theory of political development, yet it still leaves unsettled, it seems to me, the critical question of whether there are key developmental stages which can be recognized and which, indeed, may determine whether or not a society can solve the crises with which it is confronted.

Critiques of Alternative Aproaches

The point can be illustrated by Kenneth Organski's recent book, entitled *Stages of Political Development*.[35] Despite the promise of its title, Organski fails to provide a real theory of stages in political development. He does, however, seem to come closer to this goal than anyone else. Basically, Organski is also concerned with a set of problems (crises) faced by developing polities. The problems that fascinate him, however, are primarily economic. Starting, indeed, with a theory of stages of economic growth, drawn from the work of Rostow, Organski asks what the political prerequisites are for the solution of the problems that occur at each of these stages. He reaches the conclusion that there are essentially four stages: political unification, industrialization, national welfare, and abundance. During the first stage, national governments gain effective political and administrative control over their populations. Without such control, Organski argues, all policies designed to encourage economic growth through industrialization are bound to fail. Premodern European states were able to achieve such unification, but contemporary non-Western societies, according to Organski, are still struggling with this stage of development. It appears that the first three crises listed by

34. *Aspects* . . . , *op. cit.*, pp. 62–67.
35. A. F. K. Organski, *The Stages of Political Development* (New York: Knopf, 1965).

Pye also involve this stage of political unification, namely the crises of identity, legitimacy, and penetration.

During the second stage of economic development, the industrial revolution, governments have to make possible the accumulation of capital which can only be done at great social cost. Here Organski is most interesting and relevant for our present purposes. He believes that, historically speaking, three different patterns of government have proven successful in solving the problems of industrialization: the bourgeois (i.e., Western democratic), the Stalinist (i.e., communist rule in the 1930's), and the "syncratic" (i.e., fascist politics, as in Italy, Spain, and Argentina). Organski's position is interesting for it suggests that quite different political systems may be able to solve a crucial economic crisis of development, and thus makes clear the difference between governmental patterns of development, and the various crises encountered by developing polities. It is interesting, also, that the Pye list does not seem to identify any crisis corresponding closely to the problems of the industrial revolution.

The remaining portions of the Organski volume are less relevant to our present concerns. The politics of national welfare, he believes, arise only after the industrial revolution, and involve problems in the wider distribution both of power and of consumer goods and services. Here, again, he discerns three patterns, as exhibited by the Western democracies, the Nazi state, and Russian communism since Stalin. The corresponding crises in Pye's list might be those of participation, integration, and distribution. On Organski's showing, they would be characteristic of contemporary developed, but not of the less developed, polities.

(Organski's final stage arises in response to the crises precipitated by the technological revolution of automation and may be disregarded in this context.)

Several other theories have postulated stages of political development formulated primarily in terms of the class or social characteristics of the elite. One of the most influential was Edward Shils who proposed a fivefold classification for the analysis of transitional political systems. His categories were: political democracy, tutelary democracy, modernizing oligarchy, totalitarian oligarchy, and traditional oligarchy.[36]

This typology has been modified in various ways by its author and by other writers who have adopted the scheme. A rather different framework, perhaps more immediately relevant for our present purposes because it embraces the characteristics of both traditional and modern polities, was formulated by John H. Kautsky. He also suggested that we might analyze political development in terms of five categories: traditional aristocratic authoritarianism, a transitional stage of domina-

36. Edward Shils, *Political Development in the New States* (The Hague: Mouton, 1962).

tion by nationalist intellectuals, totalitarianism of the aristocracy, totalitarianism of the intellectuals, and democracy. He says of this scheme that it should not be mistaken for an adequate description of any or all existing political systems. "There are," he adds, "an infinite number of variations, subtypes, and mixed and transitional forms that make it impossible to find any of the five types in pure form." He argues that, by formulating these "five types in pure form," it is possible to facilitate comparisons and thereby formulate generalizations and advance our understanding of political processes.[37]

Kautsky's thesis bears comparison with Organski's. Both are concerned with the role of major classes in the stages of transition or industrialization. Both identify the aristocracy and peasantry as key classes in traditional polities, and capitalists (or managers) and industrial workers as critical in industrial societies. Organski stresses the "bourgeoisie" as a crucial class in the development pattern of the Western democracies, and Kautsky distinguishes between the "old middle class" of traditional orders and the "new middle class" of industrialized societies. Organski's concept of "syncratic" polities can be compared to Kautsky's "totalitarianism of the aristocracy," based on fascistic models; and Organski's "stalinist" model should be compared to Kautsky's "totalitarianism of the intellectuals" which he finds particularly relevant to the politics of development.[38] Kautsky concludes on the hopeful note that the rule of nationalist intellectuals in developing countries may be transformed into democratic polities instead of into a totalitarianism of the intellectuals. Organski finds the present phase of the industrialized polities merely transitional to a future automated society with still indeterminate political characteristics.

A complex but intriguing theory of stages and alternate paths of political development is presented by David Apter in the larger framework of modernization. He pays serious attention to the characteristics of traditional societies as the starting points of change, using a two-dimensional classification scheme based on three authority types (hierarchical, pyramidal, and segmental) and two value types (instrumental and consummatory). Depending on the character of the traditional base, and subject to the contradictory and varied influences of the West, Apter discerns two main developmental sequences: a secular-libertarian model approaching democracy through reconciliation systems, and a sacred-collectivity model approaching totalitarianism through mobilization systems. Alternative sequences arise from processes of ritualization and "retraditionalization" leading toward neomercantilism. There is room in Apter's scheme also for the analysis of modernizing autocracies, mili-

37. John H. Kautsky, *Political Change in Underdeveloped Countries: Nationalism and Communism* (New York: Wiley, 1962), p. 4.
38. *Ibid.*, pp. 6, 90–119.

tary oligarchies, and other complex patterns of political modernization.[39]

A serious criticism of these stage theorists is made by Samuel Huntington in a recent essay attacking approaches to political development which use modernity and industrialization as basic reference points, and neglect to consider seriously the possibility of political decay.[40] He argues that one should have a concept of development that might be applied, historically, to any political system of the past as well as of the present. In this sense, the Chinese, Greek, Roman, or Egyptian polities might, in their prime, have been regarded as highly developed political systems. He then goes on to object that while the concept of political development is unnecessarily restricted by being linked to modernity, it is confusingly broadened by being linked with every kind of modernization process—economic, social, cultural—which can conceivably have any relation to politics.

Thirdly, "political development," Huntington says, is inconsistently thought of as referring both to ideal types of development wherever and whenever they might occur, and also to all the actual processes of change which are going on in the non-Western world today. It is one thing to ask how much political development is occurring in the third world, and quite another to assume that whatever is happening there must be political development. A fourth objection by Huntington links to his third. Political development seems to be thought of as always an irreversible process, whereas we can readily identify many examples of political decay. If we assume that the processes of change in the third world are necessarily developmental, then we lose the capacity to identify what is going on in places where processes of decay are dominant.

Huntington's criticisms seem to be well stated and cogent but his proposed solution is not helpful. He suggests that political development should be identified with institutionalization. He argues that a well-institutionalized polity would be marked by high levels of adaptability, complexity, autonomy, and coherence, and that these qualities are to be found in ancient as well as in modern societies. He also argues that what is going on today in the third world should frequently be characterized as a process of decay rather than of development (institutionalization).

For reasons that will become apparent below, I agree that a political

---

39. David E. Apter, *The Politics of Modernization* (Chicago: U. of Chicago Press, 1965). Many of Apter's key concepts are drawn from Marion J. Levy, Jr., whose recent two volume work, *Modernization and the Structure of Societies* (Princeton: Princeton U. P., 1966) includes an extended discussion of political modernization in the context of a comprehensive structural-functional analysis of social transformations.

40. Samuel P. Huntington, "Political Development and Political Decay," *World Politics*, Vol. XVII, No. 3 (April 1965), pp. 386–430.

system cannot be considered developed just because it is modern in the sense of being up-to-date or contemporary. There are, however, qualities of a modern political system which cannot be found in even the most well-institutionalized examples of ancient polities. Specifically, in none of the traditional societies was the state structured as a formal organization capable of adopting and enforcing collective goals, based on a general conception of universal citizenship (membership). One does not have to argue that such a system is desirable or even that it is the most effective or stable kind of political system to be able to impute to it a quality of being "developed."

Huntington's essay is also disappointing because it does not go further in the analysis of political decay or breakdown. He might well have identified new types of political system or "stages" to be found in some countries of the third world if he had introduced several categories of stagnated, abortive, or collapsed polities. An effort to move in this direction, however, has been made by S. N. Eisenstadt.[41]

Eisenstadt argues, essentially, that the early stages of industrialization, modernization, or structural differentiation create a range of political problems which may or may not be successfully solved by government in the societies concerned. When acute failures of coordination and control occur, a condition of stagnation may arise which blocks the forward movement of political development, precipitating conditions which also differ significantly from those prevailing in the traditional societies out of which they originally emerged. Following Eisenstadt's lead, one would want a theory of political development to include provision for stages of decay and stagnation as well as growth and equilibrium.[42]

A rather different kind of critique of the concept of political development is made by Roland Pennock in a recent essay.[43] Unlike Huntington, Pennock does not challenge the characteristics which have been imputed to political development, but rather seeks to add to them. He starts by pointing out that political development cannot be regarded as an unilinear phenomenon. Instead it includes, he says, political culture, informal political institutions, governmental and constitutional

41. See S. N. Eisenstadt, "Breakdowns of Modernization," *Economic Development and Cultural Change*, Vol. XII (1964), pp. 345–367; and also his "Continuity of Modernization and Development of Administration," *CAG Occasional Papers* (Bloomington, Ind.: A.S.P.A., CAG, 1965.)

42. Elsewhere I have described as "prismatic" a condition of substantial structural differentiation marked by inability to sustain the integrative processes required for effective coordination of different functionally specific social structures. See my *Administration in Developing Countries: The Theory of Prismatic Society* (Boston: Houghton, 1964), Part Two, especially pp. 206–240.

43. J. Roland Pennock, "Political Development, Political Systems, and Political Goods," *World Politics*, Vol. XVIII, No. 3 (April 1965), pp. 413–434.

arrangements, and "the operation of the whole, including the mutual relations of the various elements."[44]

In addition to all these variables, Pennock declares, the study of political development should also include an analysis of the extent to which a polity is able not only to satisfy its own survival needs but also to satisfy the requirements of human beings, of the populations subject to its rule. These human needs Pennock calls "political goods." Among them he includes such matters as security, welfare, justice, and liberty. Although he admits that there may sometimes be an element of conflict between these political goods, he argues that they can be reconciled or at least balanced against each other. He thinks there is a widespread consensus on the value of these political goods, across cultural boundaries, and that the extent to which they are realized can be determined with at least as much precision as the other major variables normally attributable to the concept of political development.

Pennock recognizes that, due to circumstances completely outside its own control, two polities of equal capacity might provide quite different degrees of a political good. Thus the level of security may be influenced by external attack or protection as much as by domestic politics. Pennock seeks to deal with this by an "other things being equal" proviso. However, I think we must probably go beyond this in order to deal more effectively with the quite legitimate point Pennock raises, namely that the degree of political development achieved by any polity ought to be measured as much by the consequences which flow from development as by the intrinsic character of the developing system.

In a paper entitled "The Ecology of Development" I sought a few years ago to deal with the same problem.[45] I distinguished between the ability of a social system to shape or reshape its environment, and the degree to which it was determined in its characteristics by the environment. In general, I argued, one test of the level of development attained by a system was the ratio between these two variables: the more developed a system, the greater the ranges of choice open to it, not only within the constraints set by its environment, but even more to reshape its environment so as to enhance its freedom of choice. Such a range of choice might, I think, be interpreted to include its ability to select and to meet the goals suggested by Pennock's concept of "political goods." Thus development might involve not the production of any particular political goods, but the ability to choose among them.

In this connection, Pennock calls attention also to a statement by Karl Deutsch asserting that political development should include a system's capacity to absorb and utilize more information taken from

44. *Ibid.*, p. 416.
45. Fred W. Riggs, "The Ecology of Development" Comparative Administration Group Occasional Paper (Bloomington, Ind.: CAG, 1964).

its environment, to respond to this information, to change its environment more effectively to satisfy its needs, and to enhance the range and diversity of the goals that can be satisfied.[46]

It is worth mentioning in this connection that the concept of "administrative development" raises problems quite similar in character to those covered by the term "political development." In 1963 I wrote an essay on "Administrative Development"[47] which included a mathematical model designed to illustrate some possible stages of development in quantitative terms. The model included three main dependent variables—performance level, level of differentiation, and degree of "integration"—and three independent variables: challenges posed by the environment, efforts to make the existing system work better, and efforts to change the existing system. A set of operations was devised to govern changes among the dependent variables in response to inputs generated by the independent variables. The system tended to stabilize at different levels of development with relatively more or less equilibrium, including possible conditions of acute malintegration or stagnation, and illustrated, I believe, some of the necessary conditions for attaining higher levels of development. One of its features was that the higher the level of differentiation of the system, the easier it became for it to bring about basic system changes.[48]

Toward a Dialectical Theory

It is remarkable that the new and still vague concept of "political development" should be thought ripe for presentation in the form of a "theory." We lack accepted theories for the standard fields of political science despite the vast amount of research and the many publications devoted to them. Can one point, for example, to a "theory of American government," or a theory of "local government"? There are, to be sure, narrow-range theories and hypotheses which explain and even predict certain phenomena of political parties and voting behavior. One can also find many statements about how particular institutions operate, but these are largely descriptive propositions, rarely explanatory theories.

46. Karl W. Deutsch, *The Nerves of Government: Models of Political Communication and Control* (New York: Free Press, 1963), pp. 139–140.

47. "Administrative Development: Notes on an Elusive Concept and the KEF-PRI Model." Comparative Administration Group Occasional Paper (Bloomington, Ind.: CAG, 1963).

48. The KEF-PRI model, for reasons of space, was dropped from the text of this essay as it now stands in the volume edited by John D. Montgomery and William J. Siffin, *Approaches to Development: Politics, Administration and Change* (New York: McGraw-Hill, 1966).

Yet the expectation has been aroused that in regard to political development there ought to be a "theory." What's more, it is thought (perhaps because of the grammatical form of the phrase) that "political development" ought to refer to a single, operationally defined variable. By contrast, other topics in political science normally refer to a congeries of interrelated behaviors, phenomena, and institutions, but not to a single variable. Are these expectations realistic? In my opinion "political development" should be thought of as a good label, like "voting" or "politics," under which to consider a wide variety of phenomena. As to the matter of a theory, there has already been produced a surprisingly rich harvest of propositions and models relating to various aspects of these phenomena, but there is not yet, in my opinion, anything that deserves to be called "the theory" or even "a theory" of political development.

Despite this negative finding, or perhaps because of it, I feel impelled to suggest some ideas, hopefully new ones, about the characteristics and stages of development relevant for political science. This approach will combine the three criteria of political development suggested by Lucian Pye and his associates—differentiation, capacity and equality —with a typology of developmental stages that I have proposed elsewhere on the basis of key governmental technologies.[49]

It is strange that the key technologies of government are often looked upon as cultural traits, not subject to cross-cultural transmission except at the risk of imperialism and intervention. Non-Western societies, it is argued, ought to be free to develop their own forms of government, drawing freely on their own cultural heritage and history, evolving patterns of governance best suited to their own needs. Presumably they may not need political parties, legislatures, courts, or bureaucracies— they should find their own functional equivalents.

All one needs to do to see the matter in a different light is to look on governmental institutions and practices as matters of "technology" rather than of "culture." We do not, for example, feel put upon by the Chinese because we learned from them how to print, to grow silk, or to make Chinaware. The organizational technology necessary for establishing and running political parties has already spread all over the world. It is used by communist as well as by democratic parties, in the least developed as well as in the most developed societies. To the Indians the Congress Party is just as indigenous as the Communist Party is to Russia, the Labor Party to England, and the Democratic Party to America. However long a history each of these parties may have, each also had a definite beginning and pattern of growth, and was first invented somewhere. At one time the political party was not indigenous, not a

49. "The Comparison of Whole Political Systems," paper given at the seminar on Comparative Methods, University of Minnesota (mimeo.), April, 1966.

part of the established culture. And neither was printing European before it was "invented" or introduced into Europe.

My point is that we must examine the impact of new political technologies on any country without worrying about where they came from. This is not just a matter of adopting an attitude but goes to the heart of the problem of understanding the stages of political development.

In downgrading the importance of political technologies we have not only been victimized by our reluctance to appear to be foisting Western cultural practices on people with a different cultural and historical background. We have also been carried away by our enthusiasm for functionalism to such an extent that we have discarded all serious interest in structural analysis. Yet if we are to make meaningful statements about relations between structure and function, we must have strictly structural criteria for defining and describing institutions or political technologies. Only after we have understood these institutional matters can we proceed meaningfully to functional theory.

Technological change is subject to sudden qualitative jumps, determined simply by the presence or absence of a given pattern or method. By contrast, functional categories are normally subject to scaling and quantitative measurement. The interaction between these qualitative technological changes and quantitative functional changes gives a dialectical character to development, generating stages. Let me illustrate this point in the field of communication. Functionally, one can describe growth in the communications function in terms of the increasing size of audiences that can be reached by a single speaker. Technologically, the qualitative jumps represented by the introduction first of writing, then of printing, and much later, of telecommunications, are key factors in the expansion of audience size. One can meaningfully, therefore, speak of communications in the stages of preliterary, preprinting, pretelecommunications, and posttelecommunications. Audience size depends, of course, on other variables also, but these qualitative jumps are basic.

Applied to the problems of government, major leaps forward in technology have typically involved an increase in structural differentiation, in the specialization of roles relating to the various functions of the political system. Such increases in differentiation, however, while solving some problems also create new difficulties in coordination or integration. Thus the mere introduction of a new governmental technology by no means guarantees the solution of political problems. The major technological inventions in government seem to be the techniques of bureaucratic organization, of representative assemblies or legislatures, and of political parties. Other related technologies include the use of examinations as a test for recruitment, the procedures of voting as a means of polyarchic decision-making, judicial procedures for the settlement of disputes, and the creation of private associations and corporations as continuing legal entities.

A theory of stages based on the introduction of political technologies can be related to the tests of political development formulated by the Committee on Comparative Politics: *equality, capacity,* and *differentiation.* Let me suggest that technological advances in government characteristically involve a sudden increase in levels of structural differentiation, and hence a series of stages. By contrast, the principles of equality and capacity have to do with what Pennock calls "political goods." They refer in other words to "outcomes." Capacity measures the ability of a political and administrative system to adopt collectively authorized goals and to implement them. Equality reflects the extent to which members of the polity have a chance to participate in the shaping of its policies and to share in the benefits secured by their implementation.

The less differentiated a polity, the less relevant are these two goals. In a truly primitive folk society, behavior is governed by custom, by traditionally determined norms, so that the need for "governmental" services is minimal, if not totally absent. Correspondingly, the question of equality does not arise in relation to nonexistent governmental processes. By contrast, in a highly differentiated society, marked by "abundance," it may be possible to sustain political processes that have a high level of capacity and at the same time to permit substantial equality of participation in both the inputs and outputs of government.

Conflicts between these goals are most acute in transitional stages. From this point of view, even the most "developed" polities are still in transitional phases of development. Let us assume, for the moment, that at an intermediate stage of structural differentiation (let us call it "semidifferentiated"), it is not possible to provide either equality or capacity to any substantial degree, but it is possible to provide either more than the other. In other words, an inverse relationship, within limits, prevails such that an increase in equality means a decline in capacity, and an increase in capacity can be secured only by a drop in equality.

Let us assume, however, that an increase in the level of differentiation makes it possible to achieve higher levels both of equality and capacity, but that such an increase can be generated endogenously only when a balance between the two principles of equality and capacity prevails. We can then imagine a set of developmental traps in which the proximate goals of development are seen as either an increase in equality or an increase in capacity. Normally the elite are likely to demand increase in the level of inequality as a means to raise the capacity level; whereas popular movements of the subelites press for an increase in the level of equality, even if the price is a drop in the capacity level of the system. Roughly the former kind of demand can be labeled "Rightist," and the latter type "Leftist."

So long as politics takes the form of a struggle between the Rightists and the Leftists, each will view its specific demands—for increased capacity or for more equality—as the epitome of political development. Both will be likely to miss the point that only by establishing a balance between the two principles will it be possible to heighten the level of structural differentiation, and thereby to enable both of the goals of equality and capacity to be realized to a greater degree.

A Provisional Paradigm

Figure 16.1 is a simple diagram that can be used to illustrate this

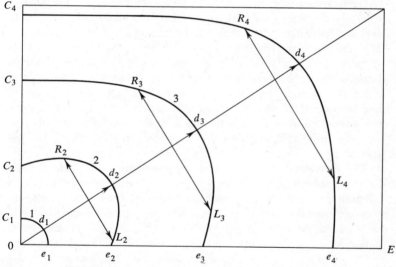

FIGURE 16.1—Paradigm for Political Development

principle. In this figure let the horizontal axis represent degree of equality of participation of members of a population in the making of governmental decisions and in the sharing of the benefits generated by governmental activities. Note that this is not social equality as measured by social standing or equivalence of income, but relates only to the relation of a population to governmental inputs and outputs. Let the vertical axis represent the capacity of a government to solve the problems confronting it. Each of the curves 1, 2, 3, and 4, suggests possible combinations of the two values of equality and capacity at a given level of differentiation. Each curve suggests an inverse correlation such that an increase in one value entails a decline in the other, except for parts of curve 4.

A movement toward $R3$, for example, designates an increase in capacity accompanied by a decline in equality; a movement toward $L3$ the reverse. By contrast a movement of the curve from $d3$ toward $d4$ makes it possible for both capacity and equality to increase as structural differentiation rises.

The RL lines suggest the normal politics of Rightists versus Leftists, each insisting on its rival developmental goals of more capacity or more equality. It may be that the level of differentiation can be increased only by achieving a balance between these two goals, as at $d2$ or $d3$. From these curves one can see how, logically speaking, an increase in differentiation could give the Leftists more equality and the Rightists more capacity than either could have achieved at a lower level of differentiation. However, it is also possible to visualize a dilemma in which the Rightists would secure a higher level of capacity at a lower level of differentiation than they could obtain at a higher level, provided they could be sure of overcoming the Leftists at the lower level. Thus $p1$ marks such a relatively advantageous position for Rightists as contrasted with $p2$. Similarly, if the Leftists are victorious at a lower level of differentiation, they might be able to secure a higher level of equality than they could be sure of getting at a higher level of differentiation. The assumption made here is that an increase in differentiation is possible only from mid-points on the curve, i.e., from $d3$ to $p2$, but not from $p1$ to $p3$.

The theoretical framework just presented can be thought of as a dialectical scheme in which the R and L counterpressures are the thesis and antithesis, and the movement from d_1 to d_2, from d_2 to d_3, etc. are syntheses. In other words, the perennial struggles between Right and Left, not only in contemporary Western polities, but also at other levels of development, shape the repetitive cycles of political history. The movement to higher levels of differentiation marks the long-term secular trend of political development. To illustrate the thesis-antithesis cycles met with at different levels of differentiation, one need only think of the changes between monarchic and democratic polities depicted by Aristotle, the alternations between feudal and bureaucratic regimes which occur in traditional civilizations,[50] and the swings between rule by political parties and by military juntas in contemporary non-Western societies.

An elaboration of the framework suggested above would require that a clear distinction be made between the original invention of a new political technology, and its subsequent adoption through emula-

---

50. For an examination of the feudal-bureaucratic antinomy, see my paper, "The Ambivalence of Feudalism and Bureaucracy in Traditional Societies," (Bloomington, Ind.: CAG, 1966).

tion by others. Whereas a very special configuration of circumstances may be a necessary prerequisite for the stage of invention, it might not be essential for the subsequent stages of borrowing and adaptation. This distinction between endogenous and exogenous processes of development may be one of the most crucial differences between the patterns of change in premodern European societies and those taking place today in the third world.[51]

The simple dialectical model of development suggested by the figure above is intended to characterize processes of endogenous differentiation. A third dimension would probably be needed to represent exogenous change patterns. In general, I think, the more exogenous the dynamics of change, the more feasible it would be for a political system dominated either by Rightists or Leftists to utilize a borrowed political technology to serve, hopefully, their special interests in greater capacity or equality, respectively. We can see in the third world today, for example, how organizational techniques and political party structures have been utilized by nationalist leaders to advance the cause of equality, and by modernizing oligarchies to promote governmental capacities.

At an earlier period, in premodern Europe, the new technology of elected legislatures was used by Leftists, as in the first French republic, for equalitarian objectives, and also by "enlightened despots" to consolidate the administrative capacity of absolutists. Even earlier parallels can be found if we examine the way in which new bureaucratic techniques were adopted by emperors and kings seeking to consolidate their power by means of more efficacious governmental structures. The Leftist equivalents in traditional societies were local officials and tribal leaders who borrowed bureaucratic forms from adjacent or defeated bureaucratic empires, but by transforming public offices into ascriptive titles of feudal nobility, served the equalitarian objectives of the officeholders.

Much more study of this subject is needed before we can safely formulate hypotheses about the subsequent fate of such exogenous transformations, but I hazard the guess that in many if not most cases the resultant system of governance proved unstable and quickly generated acute crises leading typically to alternations, in a new manner, between Rightist- and Leftist-dominated phases of government at the same level of differentiation.

Relationships and Integrations

The framework for a dialectical analysis of political development offered here may prove helpful in relating the approaches and con-

---

51. The distinction between endogenous and exogenous change models is discussed in my book, *Administration in Developing Countries: The Theory of Prismatic Society* (Boston: Houghton, 1964), pp. 38–42.

cepts of several writers in this field to each other. Consider, for example, the ideas advanced by Karl von Vorys in a recent essay.[52] He argues that the new states face acute crises of disorganization as previously small-scale, largely traditional polities confronted a tremendous range of new economic, political, and social problems. Whereas in the older European nation-states new social structures formed over long periods the capacity to solve many of these new problems, thereby reducing the burden on government, in the new states the formal machinery of government has suddenly found itself virtually the only major instrumentality with full responsibility for dealing with these difficulties. As these governments struggle to their feet, they find themselves lacking the capacity to control their own populations, whether by coercion and the use of violence, or by means of voluntary persuasion.

Thus von Vorys stresses the problem of capacity, showing how it is related to the developmental phenomenon of increasing differentiation. He might have gone on to show how the principle of equality is organically related to the principle of "capacity to persuade," for the essence of democratic freedoms is not that the government propagandizes a subject population into accepting its will, but rather that a government responsive to a mobilized and equalitarian citizen-body carries out policies for which there already exists widespread support. Thus the legitimacy of government is determined in large part by the extent to which a consensus exists among the governed population on the desirability of state policies, as well as the obligation to obey legally constituted authorities. Clearly many countries in the third world are caught in a double bind by the impetus to increase governmental capacities through coercion which, in turn, undermines confidence in the rulers, thereby strengthening revolutionary tendencies toward equalitarianism, and intensifying the need for more coercion. The victory of revolutionary impulses tends, by contrast, to bring to the front regimes which are unable to govern effectively, also leading to reliance on coercion.

When a polity gets caught in a developmental trap by moving very far in the direction either of the Right or the Left, it tends to fall into the conditions of political decay or breakdown discussed by Eisenstadt and Huntington. However, I believe that such conditions are not peculiar to any particular "stage of development" or level of structural differentiation, but can occur at any level. It should perhaps be added that the danger of such breakdowns is probably greater at intermediate levels of differentiation than at either low or high levels. In other words, this

---

52. "Toward a Concept of Political Development," *Annals of the American Academy of Political and Social Science*, Vol. 358 (March 1965), pp. 14–28. Von Vorys' ideas are tested and illustrated in his book, *Political Development in Pakistan* (Princeton: Princeton U. P., 1965).

is a peculiarly great risk for transitional societies by contrast with both traditional and modern. Formulated in my own terms, the "prismatic" condition tends to become most pronounced and most frequent in the intermediate stages of development.

Another treatment of the idea of breakdowns in the fundamental transformations of the third world is provided by Halpern who defines the word "transitional" to refer to political systems "in which the structural changes and demands set loose by the uncontrolled forces of transformation exceed the will or capacity of political authority to cope with them." By contrast, Halpern defines "modernizing" as a characteristic of political systems which achieve "the will and capacity to deal with social change."[53] In terms of the dialectical framework, Halpern's "transitional" polities would be those which, under the domination either of Rightist or Leftist forces, have become caught in a developmental trap, whereas his "modernizing" polities might be those in which a creative balance had been generated between these dialectically opposed forces, thereby making possible a successful advance to a higher level of structural differentiation.

Huntington's idea of institutionalization as developed can also be seen in a different perspective by using this dialectical model. Actually, some of the highly institutionalized polities of traditional societies might better be characterized as having become lodged in a developmental trap. The Chinese bureaucratic empire is a leading example of a system which was dominated for long periods by a Rightist political elite entrenched in a vast bureaucracy. I believe that the characteristic of Chinese society which made this continuity possible was a relatively high degree of "universalism," institutionalized in an examination system which opened the door to imperial office for the most able and ambitious young men to be found in Chinese society. This highly successful institution, then, not only facilitated equilibrium but also blocked further development.

A contrasting type of highly institutionalized system was that of India in which the extreme "particularism" of the caste system made possible a paradoxical type of equalitarianism in its political institutions, as reflected in the substantial autonomy of castes and communities. The apparent paradox of relatively universalistic bureaucratic China and relatively particularistic nonbureaucratic India actually helps to explain the persistence of these two contrasting types of institutions. The more participative a polity, the stronger the equalitarian tendencies which

---

53. Halpern, cited in note 15 above, p. 177. A more detailed typology of "transitional" and "modernizing" political systems is given by Manfred Halpern in "Notes on the Revolution of Modernization in National and International Society," *NOMOS VIII, Revolution: Yearbook of the American Society for Political and Legal Philosophy* (New York: Atherton Press, 1966) pp. 188–193.

undermine its capacities, thereby raising structural tensions and precipitating institutional changes. Conversely, the more hierarchic a polity, the greater the elitist particularisms which undermine universalistic recruitment, thus throwing it into crisis. Consequently an extremely hierarchic traditional polity (China) can survive only if there are powerful countervailing forces of a universalistic character (examinations), and an extremely participative traditional polity (India) can last only if highly particularistic social pressures (caste) are pitted against it.

European history, by contrast, is marked by rapid institutional transformations, and frequent swings between the Rightists and the Leftists. Indeed, the ideas of class struggle and of a political "Right" and "Left" emerge from European history, not from the experience of China or India. Clearly the reason for this difference is related to the precarious balance between the juxtaposed principles of capacity and equality in the West, and the dialectical tensions thereby created which led to the emergence of new political technologies and more structurally differentiated polities. The history of political development, therefore, is causally related to the relative failure of institutionalization in Europe by contrast with the high degree of institutionalization in China and India.

An interesting test of this framework is provided by the research of Martin Needler on Latin American political development.[54] Needler attempted to relate measures of economic development to criteria of political development. He discovered, to his surprise, and quite empirically, from an examination of quantitative measures, that economic development was related to two different measures of political change —stability and participation—provided they were averaged. But he found an inverse relation between these two political variables. In his own words, "a country developing economically develops politically, but this heightened level of political development can appear either as a greater fidelity to constitutional norms or as a higher degree of participation in political processes."[55]

This apparently strange finding becomes explicable in terms of the dialectical framework offered above. Needler found that a relatively high degree of both "stability" and "participation" could be secured in the most advanced countries, but in the transitional societies they seemed to be in conflict. In our terms, the principle of stability is the same as capacity, and represents Rightist domination, whereas the principle of participation is the same as equality and represents Leftist domination. The lower the level of economic development (or of differentiation) the lower the level of both equality and capacity as shown in figure 16.1. But at intermediate levels of differentiation the choice

---

54. Martin C. Needler, *Political Development in Latin America: Instability and Evolutionary Change* (in manuscript).
55. Chap. 5, p. 15 of the manuscript.

between the Right and Left becomes more critical, and countries opting for one must be correspondingly low in the other.

From a somewhat different point of view Ann Ruth Willner has argued that the present state of political development theory is "underdeveloped," in part because it fails to throw a clear light on the nature of traditional polities from which transitional systems emerge, and in part because it fails to relate its theories of politics in the third world to the established traditions of scholarship in comparative government and the study of Western polities.[56] What has already been said above about China and India should illustrate some of the possibilities of relating a dialectical theory of political development to the antinomies and change processes of traditional polities, and also establishing links of continuity and comparability between transitional and modern polities.

One could perhaps go even further. In the discussion of exogenous change processes, it was pointed out that new political technologies can be appropriated by either Rightists or Leftists to enhance their own demands, respectively, for greater capacity or equality in government. The same kinds of statement may be made about the role of traditional values and institutions in modernizing countries. New political technologies can be utilized not only to preserve but even to enhance traditional practices and ideas. The phenomena of neotraditionalism, to be found I believe in every country of the third world, are to be understood not merely as survivals. More frequently than not they are involved in a dynamism of circular causation whereby neotraditionalism helps to shape the processes of modernization, considered as a response to the challenge of the West in the contemporary world, and at the same time the borrowed technologies of the West are used to strengthen and consolidate selected traditions. We find, for example, strong signs of Sanscritization in India and vigorous neo-Confucianism in Nationalist China. This ambivalence of developmental change, a salient characteristic of the "prismatic" model, can hopefully be further elucidated by a dialectical theory of political development.

The dialectical approach also enables us to relate the various conceptions of political development discussed by Lucian Pye and Robert Packenham to each other and to a unified theoretical framework. When Pye speaks of the "political prerequisites of economic development" and the "politics typical of industrial societies," we can translate these phrases into the statement that high levels of structural differentiation are linked by circular causation to economic growth, i.e., both as preconditions and as consequences. "Political modernization" refers to the

56. "The Underdeveloped Study of Political Development," *World Politics*, Vol. XVI, No. 3 (April 1964), pp. 468–482.

emulative effects of exogenous change, whereby countries desiring the advantages apparently secured by the governmental technologies of Western, relatively differentiated, societies have borrowed them and seek, often with limited success, to utilize them for similar ends. "Administrative and legal development" refers to the Rightist demand for greater capacities, frequently mistaken for development; "mass mobilization and participation," and "the building of democracy" refer to the Leftist demand for greater equality, also frequently mistaken for development.

The categories of "stability and orderly change," and "multidimensional processes of social change" refer, I should think, to the difficulties involved in seeking to achieve a balance between the principles of capacity and equality and thereby to generate conditions favorable to increases in structural differentiation, while recognizing that such transformations invariably bring in their train new and continuously acute problems. The themes of "mobilization and power" and the "operation of a nation-state" refer to problems of international development at a different level, primarily in the interstate rather than the state system. If we look at international relations as itself a political system, then we can see the rise of new states as a demand for "equality" within this system, whereas the older pressure of the superpowers for dominance and influence is a demand for enhancing the "capacity" of this world political system. World political development, presumably, will not be secured either by a Rightist demand for world conformity or a Leftist demand for unfettered state sovereignty, but rather by some balanced structure of power making possible a breakthrough to a more integrated and structurally differentiated but yet pluralistic world order.

The various types of political system and stages of development described by Shils, Organski, Kautsky, Cutright, and others can also, I believe, be related to the schema for dialectical analysis of political development presented above. However, limitations of time and space make it impracticable to try to work out the relationships here. Perhaps higher priority in any event ought to be given to efforts to operationalize the approach to a theory of political development presented in this paper. Hopefully such an effort would not only shed light on the political problems confronted by the non-Western states undergoing modernization today but also, and certainly just as importantly, illume thereby a wide range of problems confronted by contemporary political science in the study of American and other Western polities.

Hopefully also such an exercise will build new bridges between the various subfields of political science which have arisen as reflections of the distinctive patterns of structural differentiation in Western polities. Not only will comparative government be transformed, but influential linkages to political behavior, quantitative methods, state and local government, public administration, political parties and legislatures, international relations, and political theory will also be established. Perhaps new ways of defining the discipline and dividing it into subspecialties for analytic purposes will be generated. If so, this inquiry into the "theory of political development" will have been more than justified.

17

Use and Misuse of Development Theory

KARL VON VORYS

THE POLITICS OF CHANGE is not exactly a novel focus of interest. Few great religions of the ages ignored the stresses and strains of human transition. Few significant philosophers of all times neglected the dynamics of the authoritative allocation of values. Still—and here lies a clue to the inertia of human knowledge—only recently did the study of political development emerge as a systematic approach to political analysis. In fact, even now the theoretical framework is only rudimentary; the data are scarce and the concepts (including the concept of "political development") remain imprecise. Clearly, it is too early for a comprehensive evaluation. Nevertheless the direction and the general outlines of this new approach are apparent. A preliminary estimate therefore may suggest actual and potential contributions. It may also reveal false starts and warn against future pitfalls.

I.

Perhaps the most salient feature of the study of political development is its relevance. It is relevant, first of all, to the evolution of our discipline. Political science for long has suffered from a certain ethnocentricity. As a systematic study it is rooted solidly in Western civilization. European and American cultures inspired most of its theory; European and American states provided most of its data. Political science, moreover, used to be a rather formalistic study. It concentrated with almost meticulous care upon legal and institutional characteristics. Research in depth often meant analysis at the lowest institutional level or examination of the minutest legal nicety.

This is no longer so. The last decades saw a revolution in meth-

350

odology. To the delight of some and the consternation of others, the research techniques of the physical sciences and sister social sciences proved facile enough to be adapted to the study of politics. Computers and other mechanical aids radically accelerated data processing. Finally, the emergence of a large number of newly independent states offered potential laboratories where controlled experiments could be conducted.

The resurgent vitality of the discipline exploded the traditional bounds of analysis. More and more scholars crossed the forbidding limits of our civilization and ventured into area specialties of Asia and Africa. More and more scholars refused to be exhausted by institutions or legal systems and proceeded to explore political behavior and, more particularly, the interrelationship of the political system and its (intra-societal and extrasocietal) environment. Some at the end of the last decade even sought to unite these two new directions. In pursuit of a more general understanding of political processes they embarked upon a comparative study of politics on a global scale.

Comparative politics proved to be a fertile endeavor. It promptly confirmed that governmental organization in newly independent states was, in general, patterned after Western European models. More important, it soon exposed these similarities as superficial and trivial. In the essential processes of the assignment of roles and the determination of rules the differences are decisive. Concepts such as "politics," "political system," even "government" lose most of their meaning in such cross-cultural transfer. It is not merely that newly independent states present a wide variety of configurations, although they certainly do that. What is crucial is the apparent absence of patterns of legitimacy with any expectation of persistence. In the West, political science has generally relied on equilibrium models in which order was predominant and change was controlled. Asia, Africa (perhaps Latin America) offer for study chronic conditions of disequilibrium and challenge our discipline to develop new theoretical instruments which can cope with constant disoriented change.

Beyond its academic (and the scientific) significance, the study of political development is also relevant to a crucial problem of our time: the instability of political systems. During the last few decades demands on governments accelerated rapidly. Even in the few wealthy countries with well-established institutions, rising pressures for economic rewards and social change present major tests to the political system. In other countries, deviational challenges routinely cross the system's boundary of viability.[1] Recent history is littered with discarded constitutions; political violence, coups, and revolutions have become chronic.

---

1. At last count only three Latin American republics were still operating under the same constitution which was in force in 1945. Eleven have experienced three or more coups or revolutions in the same period. In Asia twenty-four states were in

The viability of political institutions is no doubt a major concern of indigenous decision-makers. Their own hegemony as well as their country's destiny is at stake. That is not all. It is also of consequence to people throughout the world. The prospects for international order may lie in the balance.

There have always been smaller political entities; some have been frail indeed. Still their impact upon international order, individually or collectively, has remained modest, even negligible. The major powers have always defined legitimacy and determined the particular pattern of territorial settlement. Through empires they exercised authority over most of the earth's surface and the majority of its people. Through technical and military superiority they were able to shift their resources of control to distant places and thus deterred or subdued occasional challenges.

International order, of course, was never a particularly sturdy arrangement. The major powers were rarely disinclined to offer contradictory formulas of legitimacy or to advance conflicting territorial claims. Moreover, they were at times subject to severe internal strain which generated predatory behavior. These problems are still with us, but now they are significantly aggravated by the emergence of a mass of newly independent states.

The emancipation of colonial territories in Asia and Africa has substantially raised the individual and collective saliency of lesser powers and thus radically fragmented the international environment. Consensus on issues including the basic principles of international order now demands the agreement of some 120 "sovereign" states. What makes matters worse is that a substantial majority of these "sovereign states" are sustained more by international definition than by internal cohesion. They emerged, after all, from artificial political entities contrived to preserve mercantile privileges or to serve administrative conveniences. Their borders often enclose a collection of most diverse ethnic and cultural groups while separating arbitrarily segments of the same tribal group. A national focus of orientation becomes operative only fleetingly (if at all), and then only in the face of major cataclysms or massive external aggression. Mostly, they represent only fragile combinations of small-scale economic units with rudimentary specialization and tenuous conglomerations of traditional societies in various stages of disruption. These "sovereign states" occupy vast territories; they claim authority over hundreds of millions of people but they are not endowed with viable political systems. These have yet to be developed. Until they

---

existence in 1951; only eleven have escaped the violent overthrow of their governments. The record in Africa, especially in sub-Sahara Africa is much shorter, but no more encouraging.

are, political instability in these countries, coupled with a new-found saliency, further imperils the already tenuous prospects of international order.

II.

The conjunction of the requirements of policy and the course of political inquiry undoubtedly accounts for another major feature of the study of political development: its prescriptive character. To be sure, we have not yet seen a spectacular collaboration of decision-maker and political scientist. On the contrary, public officials exhibit a distinct reluctance for such an affiliation. Perhaps they are too insecure to encourage independent analyses of policy and a scholarly design of political programs. Probably they doubt the benefit of such a course. There are after all relatively few indigenous political scientists, and these have usually been trained in the more traditional skills. In any case, their academic environment is not especially favorable to scholarly activity. There are few universities, and these are heavily dependent upon public funds. A young lecturer must know that official displeasure may be fatal to his ambitions. Yet he must also realize that his students routinely provide the vanguard for political agitation. Above all, this young lecturer must recognize that his students are in dire need of minimal political education. Thus even if he is fully expert in quantitative methods he may still sacrifice the adventure of original research for the safety of teaching of conventional wisdom.

Foreign political scientists may be more available, may be more independent, and some may be better trained. These advantages, however, are more than offset by the fact that they are, after all, aliens. The struggle for and the achievement of independence evoked a pride which refuses to admit anything that would even remotely jeopardize the tenet of sovereign equality. Economists and engineers from abroad are welcomed; sociologists and anthropologists may freely roam the countryside; but political advisors are viewed with alarm as a return to colonialism.

The lack of direct access to central decision-making denies the political scientist control over political planning. It does not vitiate, however, the prescriptive thrust of the study of political development. The problems to be faced remain too dramatic and too persistent, while strategies which ignore or neglect the exigencies of political realities are bound to fail.

They have certainly failed so far. It was indeed not so long ago, that in a burst of optimism, many felt assured that independence and a constitution (often one bequeathed by the colonial power) completed the construction of the political system. Further changes would occur within this framework and could be handled through minor adjustments. Long-term persistence would rest on a substantial improvement in the standard of living and, in some instances, through a build-up of the armed forces—just in case. In short order, governments assumed the economic initiative. Five year plans were busily drawn up; investment priorities were proclaimed; new revenue structures and increased tax rates were announced; foreign loans and grants were negotiated. Meanwhile, the armed forces were trained, equipped, and well paid.

The results should really be evident by now. The military proved a very uncertain ally. It demonstrated far greater efficiency in arranging and manipulating *coups* than in implementing public policies. The yields of economic planning are not much more encouraging. Statistics suggest rather modest gains. Industrial indices may rise, but agricultural output shows little improvement. Indirect taxes generate some additional revenue, but direct taxes yield (per capita) less than ever. Evasion and tax delinquency remain rampant. National income inches up hesitantly; the marginal rate of saving (except for annual fluctuation) is minimal. To be sure, some individuals have made gains; a few have made dramatic gains.[2] The preponderant majority, the rural masses, however, are not noticeably better off.

The political decision-maker can hardly blame his disappointment on the generals. They are by and large quite competent officers. Their skills, however, are the skills of command, skills based upon the use of force and skills which for the purposes of the political system's viability are of limited relevance. It is an easy panacea to turn to the men on horseback. The fact is, however, that the resources of coercion in Asia, Africa, and Latin America are in short supply. They are too scarce to be effectively dispersed throughout the countryside. They are too scarce to be easily extended into the villages where most of the population resides. Besides, coercion is primarily a negative instrument. Apart from combating external predatory initiatives it is peculiarly suitable for the prevention and suppression of deviant behavior. Force is much less useful and may even be dysfunctional as an incentive for positive, constructive activity. As it happens it is exactly the positive incentives which are crucial to viable political systems. They are the product of political leadership; they are the skills of persuasion, skills for which the generals in fairness cannot be expected to have any special qualifications.

2. One of the interesting results of economic development programs is an increased skewness of the income pattern.

Nor can the political decision-maker blame his disappointment on the economic planners. Technically by economic criteria the designs were usually sound. Unfortunately they relied for implementation upon illusory political capacities, capacities which economists have no special competence to evaluate. In any case, the lesson is unmistakable. Economic development will remain an illusion and hence cannot support the political system unless it is converted into reality through a substantial political capacity to control. Until such a substantial margin is, in fact, developed, the priorities are, or at least should be, clear.

The study of political development, moreover, is not merely prescriptive in substance, it is prescriptive in analysis as well. In the study of chronic disequilibrium or in an effort to construct a strategy which would reequilibrate such a disequilibrium, the traditional instruments of political science are not terribly helpful. Essential concepts must be refined, methodology must be modified, and new techniques must be developed. Most of this is still in the future. The prospects are promising, but progress so far has been a bit unsteady.

The concept of political development itself could stand a more uniform and more specific definition. Clearly it applied to change, but surely only to a very special kind of political change. There is a consensus that it denotes structural change, not merely a shift in personnel or variation of policy, incidental to the succession of the tribal leader by his oldest son or the replacement of a senior bureaucrat by a subordinate. There is also some agreement that the structural change must be autonomous to the political system rather than be compelled by foreign invasion or domestic revolution. Views differ, however, on the questions whether political development denotes progress toward a specific objective, and if so what this specific objective may be.

Then there is the concept of viability. Generally, it suggests long-term persistence, and this connotation is justified in the sense that no political system can be characterized as viable which is overthrown in a single generation. At the same time, it is apparent that survival, over time, is by itself insufficient evidence. A system which has lasted many centuries, even millenia, may at the same time be on the threshold of collapse. Evidence of long-term persistence, moreover, is peculiarly suitable to ex post facto analysis. It is especially relevant for a scholar who is interested in the past or one who has a sufficiently passive disposition to stand by while events occur and order themselves. Political scientists who seek to predict, and especially those who dare hope to effect the course of the future, need a more immediate and more delicate tool.

One possibility is to consider viability as a quantitative relationship between the political system's capacity to control and the demand on control which confronts it.

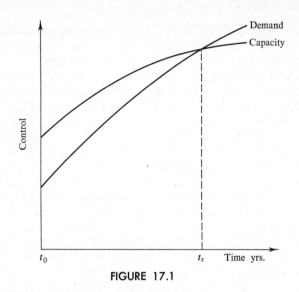

FIGURE 17.1

We can write equations for each curve. Logarithmic ones probably would be most suitable.

$$y_1 = a_1 + b_1 \log t$$
$$y_2 = a_2 + b_2 \log t$$

where a is the value of C and D at time t_0 and b indicates the shape of the curve.

Intersection of the two curves depends not only upon the gap between the capacity to control and the demand on control at time t_0 but also upon the comparable rate of acceleration of the capacity to control and the demand on control at the same time. Accordingly a nonviable system is indicated when the gap is narrow and/or the curves converge at so rapid a rate that intersection occurs at $t_x < 30$. Such a pattern would indicate a high probability that the political system will be overthrown within a generation. Naturally the curves themselves could change during the interim between t_0 and t_x, thus advancing the projected intersections; but the odds at t_0 would be considered unfavorable. In contrast, absolute viability may be defined as the absence of an intersection, i.e., no value for t_x. Again the curves could change but the probabilities would be favorable that in case of an unexpected acceleration in the demand on control enough time would be available for the generation of comparable marginal rates for the system's capacity to control. Instances where $t_x > 30$ could be defined as relative viability with the measure of $V = t_x - 30$.

Such a definition of viability, of course, requires further elaboration before it can serve as a basis for analysis. Here it is possible to identify only a few main components of the capacity to control and the demand on control. A political system's capacity to control may be perceived as a weighted aggregate of its capacity to coerce and its capacity to persuade, each of which is composed of further ingredients. In the case of capacity to coerce these could include the resources of the personnel of coercion and those of the instruments of coercion which then are represented by values of quantity modified by coefficients of quality. Similarly, demand on control can be viewed as a weighted aggregate of deviational challenges which in turn are functions of the deviational base (the share of the environment involved), deviational distance (the extent of incongruence between the emerging new set of norms in the environment and those implicit in the political system), and the deviational velocity (the rate at which new norms are emerging).

If it is in fact possible to develop satisfactory indices[3]—and surely the prescriptive thrust of the study of political development moves us along in this direction—we may then determine the values of capacity to control and demand for control at time t_0. This will tell us the existing margin. It does not help us much with the slopes of the curves. These may be estimated most satisfactorily by plotting prior values of C_c and C_d and then fitting a curve through some such statistical method as that of least squares. Needless to say, the larger the series of t_{-1}, t_{-2}, t_{-3}, ... t_{-n}, the higher the probability of the extension of the curves past t_0.

Unfortunately for most newly independent states this series is likely to be very short. These are states where essential data for indicators and indices are sparse and reach back only a few years. An alternative approach which is not dependent upon past data is indicated. It may be feasible to infer the future convergence (or divergence) of the curves from a model interrelating the level of aspirations (S), the level of expectation (E), and the level of attainment (T) at time t_0.[4]

A more accurate definition and calculation of viability would probably spur further progress in political analysis. It is expected that when such mathematical instruments are applied to most countries in Africa, Asia, and Latin America, the result would indicate a precariously narrow positive margin of capacity to control over the demand on control. Worse still, they are apt to reveal the prospect of further deterioration due to more rapid acceleration of the demand on control than the current growth rate of the capacity to control. Given the growing intensity of the international demonstration effect and the rather rumpled

3. For an attempt to accomplish just this, see my forthcoming study, *A General Theory of Political Development*.
4. For a detailed presentation of the *S-E-T* model, see my monograph "Political Multiplier Effects of Foreign Aid," Foreign Policy Research Institute, University of Pennsylvania, 1966.

state of charisma, it is doubtful that short of a rigorous policy of total isolation the demands on control will decelerate. Any significant increment in the political system's viability, therefore, will rest upon the successful strategy to maximize the rate of increase in the capacity to control. It may be possible to import some control resources—foreign troops can add to the coercive ingredient of control, international prestige to the persuasive ingredient—but in the final analysis such a successful strategy will depend upon the most careful investment of extremely scarce internal resources of control. The margins are so slim that any waste, any miscalculation, may be fatal. Whether the political processes in Asia, Africa, and Latin America will be characterized as development rather than chronic chaos may, therefore, depend upon the ability of the political scientist to construct new and reliable models of political marginal analysis.

III.

The relevance and the prescriptive thrust all promise extraordinary horizons for the study of political development. They also may be responsible for notable lapses. These include an apparent commitment to the integrity of all existing newly independent states. Presumably this appeals to the indigenous decision-makers. It might seem to support international order. Actually it legitimizes the balkanization of Africa and accepts for the basis of analysis an international status quo frozen into an artificial mold. At a time when the challenges to legitimacy are mounting, scholarship is not served by so arbitrary a restraint on the range of inquiry.

Then there is the singular tendency of political development theory to rise rapidly to the highest levels of generality. In some instances it seems almost to have soared well above any practical application. It exhibits a lush abundance of paradigms and an almost Thomist dedication to morphology. Such a course, if permitted to gain ascendance, would be altogether regrettable. Classifications such as "consumatory and instrumental value types" or "hierarchical, pyramidal and segmental authority types" are not essentially more helpful than the category of "parliamentary government" which includes both Britain and India and "federal system" which describes both the United States and Nigeria. They rudely simplify into an artificial unity a wide range of fundamental diversity due to cultural (and other) multiplicity. Worse still, such classifications offer definitions in lieu of data; then they proceed with synthesis, thus preempting analysis.

Most unfortunate, however, is the entanglement of development theory with modernization. There may be a few benefits from such a liaison (although it is difficult to imagine what they are), but consider the harm already done: we are saddled with the spurious traditional-modern dichotomy.

In the early stages of development theory the point of departure was assumed to be traditional societies in low-level equilibrium. This was a fundamental, time-consuming error. Societies in Asia, Africa, and Latin America at one time may have been "traditional"; they can hardly be so characterized now. All but a few obscure ones have modern social and economic components, and even if the masses of people are committed to traditional norms, the loyalty of most has become extremely precarious. The conceptual confusion was not alleviated by a more recent characterization of these societies as "transitional." The new term accepts departure from the norms of the past but also implies a position on the course toward a new order. It suggests the progress of re-equilibration. In fact, the disruption of the traditional patterns in these countries has been accompanied by neither an effective definition of a new direction nor by the generation of a sturdy reintegrating force. Instead there is a confusion of norms and an acceleration of anomie. Indeed the most significant feature of these societies and hence a crucial point of departure for development theory is a chronic condition of disequilibrium.

The liaison of modernization and political development caused difficulties on the other end of the process as well. Modernity, insofar as it has any practical meaning at all, is a rather ethnocentric concept. It denotes a combination of high values of those indicators which Western countries consider most salient. A modern society is depicted as healthy, educated, industrial, and affluent. It is variously defined in terms of available inanimate power and mechanical tools or by the extent of competitive allocation of roles and rewards. A modern political system is generally perceived as democratic. It is defined in terms of equality and participation.

Such indicators of modernity may well describe the accomplishments of Western civilization. They cause mischief as objectives of the political development process. To begin with, even in the West the specific criteria for these indicators are somewhat equivocal. An educated society has a different meaning in Europe and in America. The concept "industrial economy" is apparently not the same in Italy and Germany. Equality until recently was compatible with segregation in the United States, and participation meant universal male suffrage in Switzerland. The confusion is compounded by the ease with which modernity tolerates low values in its supposedly essential indicators. In a number of modern countries of Western Europe industry, especially large-scale industry, is still a relatively minor sector. In some others inanimate power resources do not significantly exceed those in "underprivileged" countries. Nazi Germany was not denied modernity though the very idea of equality made Der Führer laugh.

The ambiguities of modernity need not be overstressed. Far more unfortunate is its ethnocentric implication that the goal of political development must be some facsimile of the system which is currently predominant in the West. Such a conclusion is analytically unsound. Granting the proposition that the demands on the political system in our times are of a magnitude that up to this point of history only the Western pattern could satisfy and control, it still does not logically follow that no alternative pattern can possibly be devised. Furthermore, there is no assurance that our systems will prevail even in the West. They may collapse, of course, but more probably they may develop further to a new level of equilibrium. Such a new equilibrium may have components and indicators which we cannot predict at this point. As long as this possibility exists it is also conceivable that political systems can reach this new equilibrium while bypassing the currently predominant formula of modernity.

The conclusion that the goal of political development must be some facsimile of Western systems is moreover substantively pernicious. Current formulas of modernity may have meant viable political systems in the West exactly because they were indigenous and were peculiarly suitable to Western environment. They may be unsuitable, worse still they may be unattainable, in the native environments of newly independent states.

Perhaps it would be possible to improve substantially the level of public health in Asia and Africa, though this would require breaking the rigorous hold of superstition in rural areas, increasing to a remarkable degree the number of physicians and nurses, and constructing many, many hospitals in the countryside as well as in the towns. (Incidentally such a concerted effort would as a by-product aggravate the already formidable population pressure.) The chances of a significant rise in the level of general education in the foreseeable future are somewhat less promising. These are states where functional literacy rarely exceeds 10 per cent. These are cultures which, with a few exceptions, are endowed only with rudimentary alphabets, sparse vocabularies, and primitive literatures. In any case, the sustained program necessary would cost more time and money than most modernizers are willing to concede and most newly independent states have available.

The prospects of industrialization are dim indeed. Few of these agricultural countries possess a minimum quantity and an essential variety of mineral deposits. Fewer still can claim a rate of investment required for sustained capital formation.[5] Yet surely the most fantastic goal is affluence. The distance to be traversed is overwhelming. Almost all of the newly independent states must start at per capita income levels which were exceeded by the United States, Great Britain, and even Tzarist Russia during the eighteenth century.[6] Moreover, progress so far has been wholly inadequate. Some of these states have actually experienced a decline in per capita income. Even in those with positive increments the marginal rates are very modest indeed, well below those preceding take-off into self-sustained growth in North America and Europe.[7] Indeed it takes only a simple calculation to discover that if any massive improvement in the standard of living will occur at all, this will require not generations, but centuries.

This then should be clear: these indicators of modernity when set as overt objectives of political development impose tests upon the political system which at least in the initial generations will inevitably stamp it a failure. This is not all; we must not forget the political criteria of modernity. To be sure, once universal suffrage, representative assemblies and parliamentary responsibility are included in the objectives of the political development process, they may be accomplished without prolonged delay. Participation and equality may even serve as popular rewards, although it is quite possible that as far as the political system's capacity to persuade is concerned, a *pretense* of participation and a *pretense* of equality would do just as well. These political objectives, however, have rather unfortunate by-products as well. They improve the efficiency of the formulation and the presentation of already radically inflated demands and simultaneously intensify the effectiveness of the penalties imposed for failure to satisfy these demands. To the frail political systems of Asia and Africa this means disaster.

IV.

Some of the difficulties and diversions encountered by development theory are undoubtedly initial by-products of growth. A certain ethnocentric tendency is natural to men, even to scholars. Rapid expansion

5. Walter W. Rostow suggests that take-off occurs when productive investment rises over 10 per cent of national income. (*The Stages of Economic Growth*, London: Cambridge U. P., 1961), p. 39.

6. See: Simon Kuznets, *National Product since 1869* (New York: National Bureau of Economic Research, 1949), p. 120, and *Six Lectures on Economic Growth* (New York: Free Press, 1959), p. 27.

7. Average annual per capita income growth rates at constant prices in selected countries: Ghana, 1957–1964: − 1.5%; Korea, 1953–1964: 2.6%; Lebanon, 1953–1964: − 2.3%; Morocco, 1953–1964: − 1.6%; Pakistan, 1953–1964: 1.6%; Sudan,

in scope and the introduction of new methodologies are frequently accompanied by conceptual ambiguities. Flights into abstraction are usual when problems are fundamental and tough but the pressure for solutions is impatient and intense.

The pressure for solutions is indeed intense. Periodic military and social distractions notwithstanding, "wealthy" countries continue to accumulate and their *average* citizens continue to enjoy regular and substantial increments in their standards of living. Meanwhile, the international demonstration effect already potent and disruptive in the urban societies of Asia and Africa is gradually but relentlessly infecting the rural masses. Not unnaturally as they become aware of Western consumption patterns, they too would like to share in them. Not unnaturally as they witness their communities crumble into irrelevance, they seek escape from fear and loneliness. They need a new order; they search for a new community. There are still restraints: the remnants of traditional norms, the mistrust of the unknown, and perhaps others. These are daily impaired by men who turn to employment in the towns, by women who enjoy equal vote to their husbands' or by children who are better educated than their parents. We are approaching the threshold of a revolution of rising frustrations.

No decisive solutions have as yet emerged; but the prospects are encouraging. Some of the most able political scientists including most who pioneered in comparative politics are attracted to development theory. They are supported by a steadily growing number of scholars from the other social sciences. Case studies of particular Asian and African countries and their political programs are accumulating. Cross-cultural instruments of analysis are being perfected.

Success, however, has its own perils. If and when, after intense and detailed effort, useful models of political marginal analysis are constructed, these may well document the suspicion that a number of existing political systems are not only not viable, but they are not likely ever to generate political development. It may even happen that scientific analysis will demonstrate that some of the newly independent states themselves cannot be expected to survive in their present configuration, but will in the absence of continued and substantial foreign support decompose or become absorbed into larger political entities. What will then be the prescription of development theory in the face of the rather natural resistance of indigenous decision-makers: revolution, foreign conquest?

There is, however, an even more perplexing prospect. It may be possible to design a successful political strategy for many, hopefully

---

1953–1964: 1.5%; Syria, 1953–1964: 2.3%; Thailand, 1953–1964: 1.0%; Tunisia, 1955–1964: 2.6%; Turkey, 1953–1964: 1.6%; United Arab Republic, 1953–1964: 1.6%; Viet Nam (South), 1955–1964; 0.1%.

most, states in Asia, Africa and Latin America. Such strategies, however, would probably require the most efficient utilization of political resources toward the maximization of their system's capacity to control. Efficiency in turn may well depend upon a comprehensive design which extends over the full range of human behavior. Political criteria may emerge not only paramount but unlimited in relevance. In short, the successful strategy may become a prescription for a totalitarian state.

It would be unfortunate indeed if advance in political science would hand the decision-maker the most effective strategy of total mastery. It would be outright tragic if the fruits of development theory would present the Asian and African masses with a choice between continued frustration and chaos on one hand and total submission on the other.

Index

Index